THE RISE OF THE GREAT POWERS
1648–1815

The rise of
the great powers
1648–1815

Derek McKay and H. M. Scott

Longman
London and New York

Longman Group Limited
Longman House, Burnt Mill, Harlow
Essex CM20 2JE, England
Associated companies throughout the world

*Published in the United States of America
by Longman Inc., New York*

First published 1983
Second impression 1984

British Library Cataloguing in Publication Data

McKay, Derek
   The risk of the great powers 1648-1815.
   1. Europe—Politics and government—1648-1789
   2. Europe—Politics and government—1789-1815
   I. Title   II. Scott, H. M.
   940.2'5   DA273

   ISBN 0-582-48553-3
   ISBN 0-582-48554-1 Pbk

Library of Congress Cataloging in Publication Data

McKay, Derek.
   The rise of the great powers, 1648-1815.

   Bibliography: p. 345
   Includes index.
   1. Europe—History—1648-1789. 2. Europe—
History—1789-1815. 3. Great powers—History—17th
century. 4. Great powers—History—18th century.
5. Great powers—History—19th century. I. Scott,
H. M. (Hamish M.), 1946-   II. Title.
D273.5.M36 .   940   82-159
ISBN 0-582-48553-3   AACR2
ISBN 0-582-48554-1 (pbk.)

Printed in Singapore by
The Print House (Pte) Ltd

For Ragnhild Hatton

Contents

List of maps   x
Preface   xi

1   The rise of France, 1648–88   1
    The peace of Westphalia, 1648   1
    The last stage of the Franco-Spanish War, 1648–1659   6
    Swedish supremacy in the north, 1648–1660   10
    Louis XIV's assumption of power and the War of Devolution,
        1661–1668   14
    Louis XIV's preparations to attack the Dutch Republic,
        1668–1672   23
    The Dutch War, 1672–1679   28
    The peace of Nymegen, 1678–1679   34
    'The Arbiter of Europe', 1679–1688   36

2   The rise of Britain, 1688–1714   43
    The Nine Years War, 1688–1697   43
    The peace of Ryswick, 1697   50
    The War of the Spanish Succession: from diplomacy to war,
        1697–1702   54
    The War of the Spanish Succession, 1702–1713/1714   58
    The peace of Utrecht–Rastadt, 1713–1714   63

3   The emergence of Austria and Russia, 1660–1721   67
    The creation of the Austrian empire and the defeat of the Turks,
        1660–1699   67
    The Great Northern War, 1700–1721   77
        The formation of the anti-Swedish coalition, 1697–1700   77
        Charles XII defeats the northern allies, 1700–8   81
        The collapse of the Swedish empire, 1708–16   83
        The collapse of the northern coalition and the conclusion of
            peace with Sweden, 1716–21   88

4   British diplomatic ascendancy and the entente, 1714–1731   94
    The European system after the peace of Utrecht–Rastadt   94

Contents

Austro-Spanish rivalry and the beginnings of the Anglo-French
    entente, 1714–1716   101
The Quadruple Alliance, 1717–1720   111
The collapse of the Quadruple Alliance system, 1720–1724   118
Uneasy peace in the north, 1721–1725   124
Cold War in Europe, 1724–1728   126
The decline of the Anglo-French *entente*, 1728–1731   134

5   *The recovery of France, 1731–1739*   138
The European states system after the Second Treaty of
    Vienna   138
The great powers and the Polish election of 1733   141
The War of the Polish Succession, 1733–1738   145
The Austro-Russian War against the Ottoman Empire,
    1735–1739   154

6   *A new pattern, 1739–1763*   159
The War of Jenkins' Ear   159
The War of the Austrian Succession, 1740–1748   162
The peace of Aix-la-Chapelle, 1748   171
The unofficial Anglo-French War in America, 1748–1755   177
The Diplomatic Revolution   181
The Seven Years War in Europe, 1756–1763   192
The Seven Years War overseas   197

7   *Diplomacy and the European states system*   201

8   *Partition diplomacy in eastern Europe, 1763–1795*   215
The European system after the Seven Years War   215
The first partition of Poland, 1763–1772   222
Habsburg attempts to acquire Bavaria, 1777–1785   229
Russian expansion in the Balkans, 1772–1792   234
The destruction of Poland, 1772–1795   242

9   *Anglo-Bourbon relations in Europe and overseas, 1763–1790*   253
Anglo-French relations after the Seven Years War,
    1763–1774   253
Britain, the Bourbon powers and American independence,
    1775–1783   257
British recovery and Bourbon eclipse, 1783–1790   265

10   *Europe and the French Revolution, 1789–1802*   272
The outbreak of the Revolution   272
The origins of the War of 1792   275
The War of the First Coalition, 1793–1797   280
The War of the Second Coalition, 1798–1802   290

11   *Napoleon and Europe, 1802–1815*   303
Napoleon and the European states system   303
The renewal of the Anglo-French War and the formation of the
    Third Coalition, 1802–1805   305
The destruction of the Third Coalition, 1805–1807   311

Contents

Tilsit and the Franco-Russian *rapprochement*   317
The Grand Empire   320
The challenge to the Napoleonic Empire, 1808–1812   325
The defeat of Napoleon, 1812–1815   333

12   *The great powers in 1815*   339

   Bibliography   345
   Maps   360
   Index   370

List of Maps

1 The Baltic 1648–1721   360
2 Western Europe 1648–97   362
3 Europe in 1714   363
4 Italy 1713–48   364
5 Russian expansion in the Balkans 1774–1812   365
6 The partitions of Poland 1772–95   366
7 The expansion of revolutionary France 1789–99   367
8 Europe under Napoleon 1810   368

Preface

This volume is chronologically the first of three which survey the development of the European states system from 1648 to 1945. The second of these, by F. R. Bridge and Roger Bullen, appeared in 1980 and dealt with the mature states system of the nineteenth century. The preceding period, from the end of the Thirty Years War to the congress of Vienna, saw the emergence of the great powers who were to dominate Europe after 1815, and this is the theme of the present volume. But whereas the full flowering of the European system in the nineteenth century took place in conditions of almost permanent peace, its birth was accompanied by repeated, and often almost continuous, warfare. We have provided short accounts of these wars, but in general we have concentrated on the diplomacy which accompanied the rise of the great powers. Domestic history has only been discussed where this is essential for an understanding of foreign policy.

Diplomatic history has been rather out of fashion in recent years, rather surprisingly since foreign policy was the principal concern of rulers and statesmen in the late seventeenth and eighteenth centuries, and the wars which resulted were important influences on the evolution of government and the development of society. This survey is intended to introduce students of this period to the relations of the great powers. No adequate account of this exists in English. The best introduction is a series in German, which was published before the First World War, while valuable series in French date from no later than the 1950s.

We are very grateful to the staff of Longman for their advice and encouragement, and for so patiently waiting for us to finish the book. For typing our manuscript we have to thank Mrs Irene Perkin and Mrs E. L. Scott. Roy Bridge and Roger Bullen read the whole text and made many helpful suggestions for improving it and Jeremy Black helped us check the proofs. Over many years Professor Ragnhild Hatton has been a source of inspiration and practical advice to us both: we should like to acknowledge what we, together with all students of the seventeenth and eighteenth centuries, owe to her enthusiasm and scholarship. Our wives have helped us most of all.

Derek McKay and H. M. Scott,
London and St Andrews
December 1981

CHAPTER ONE
The rise of France, 1648–1688

In the mid seventeenth century the German jurist Samuel von Pufendorf defined a states system as 'several states that are so connected as to seem to constitute one body but whose members retain sovereignty'. Such a system existed in the eighteenth century and achieved its classic form between 1815 and 1914. It had been unknown to observers in the sixteenth and first half of the seventeenth centuries, since European politics consisted then of the seemingly unending struggle of minor states against the dominance of the House of Habsburg. But in the decades after 1648 the states system defined by Pufendorf gradually evolved, and by the early eighteenth century had become established in its modern form, one in which several leading powers were almost equally matched. The great powers of the eighteenth and nineteenth centuries were Britain, France, Austria, Russia and Prussia. Three of these had clearly emerged by the 1710s, and Russia and Prussia were generally recognised as major states by the middle years of the century. The first modern great power was France, and she achieved this position in the generation after the peace of Westphalia.

THE PEACE OF WESTPHALIA, 1648

The treaties of Münster and Osnabrück, collectively known as the peace of Westphalia, brought the Thirty Years War to an end in 1648. In the century and a half before this peace, relations between the European powers had been dominated by the apparent attempt of the House of Habsburg to achieve hegemony and even, at times, universal monarchy. This had become possible because of a fortuitous series of marriages and deaths which had made the Habsburg Charles V ruler of a vast empire. As king of Spain (1516–56) his monarchy had

1

included not only Spain and immense territories in the Americas and Indies but also the Balearic Islands, Sardinia and Sicily in the Mediterranean, and Naples and Milan in Italy. As duke of Burgundy (1506–55) Charles had ruled a chain of provinces which encircled France: the so-called Burgundian Circle of the Netherlands, Luxemburg and Franche-Comté. As archduke of Austria (1519–55) his possessions had been roughly the same as modern Austria, together with parts of Alsace in western Germany. Finally, he had also been elected emperor of the German Holy Roman Empire (1519–55). Using the wealth of his European and overseas lands and the muscle of his unrivalled Spanish and German infantry, Charles had fought to keep this Habsburg monarchy intact against the challenge of France and also to defend Christendom against the menace of the Muslim Turks in the Balkans and Mediterranean and the Protestants in Germany. The task had been too much for one man, and Charles had accepted this by abdicating in 1555 and dividing his dynastic empire.

The Emperor's brother, Ferdinand I, who had already acquired the elective monarchies of Bohemia and Hungary (although only a sliver of Hungary was free from Turkish control), succeeded him in Austria and was elected Holy Roman Emperor. Charles's son Philip II (1556–98) took Spain with its overseas empire and the Italian and Burgundian lands. Spain, which had now become the dominant partner in the Habsburg family alliance, was to lead the struggle against militant Protestant Calvinism in western Europe and against the continuing naval threat from the Turks in the Mediterranean. Although Philip increased his possessions by annexing Portugal and her overseas empire in 1581, he failed to suppress a revolt in the Netherlands and prevent the establishment of the Dutch Republic there. He also could not stop the emergence of a hostile Catholic Bourbon monarchy in France after the French Religious Wars, but Spain under him and his son Philip III (1598–1621) was clearly the dominant European power. In the meantime Philip II's Habsburg cousins, as German emperors and rulers in central Europe, managed to stem the Turkish advance in Hungary but could not fully maintain their authority or check the growth of Protestantism in Germany or their own lands.

The Spanish and Austrian Habsburgs intermarried and were the chief bulwarks of the Catholic faith, but during the late sixteenth century they failed to pursue a common family policy. This changed, however, when Ferdinand II became ruler of the Austrian, Bohemian and Hungarian lands between 1617 and 1619 and was then elected to the Imperial throne. His ambitions produced the Thirty Years War (1618–48), during which the two branches of the Habsburgs followed what amounted to a joint dynastic policy. They aimed to further the Catholic Counter-Reformation, to strangle the infant Dutch Republic and to assert real control within the Holy Roman Empire by the Emperor Ferdinand II (1619–37) and his son Ferdinand III (1637–57).

This final bid for Habsburg hegemony was effectively destroyed, largely because of the opposition of France. For most of the sixteenth century French rulers had tried to limit Habsburg power and to preserve their own independence: the Habsburgs not only appeared capable of reducing all European states to satellites, but the Spanish branch, with its Italian and Burgundian lands, seemed directly to throttle France. The French therefore conjured up successive coalitions with a wide range of anti-Habsburg forces, a policy which culminated in the Thirty Years War. Here Catholic France, at first diplomatically and then, after 1635, militarily, co-operated with her traditional allies, the Protestant Dutch Republic, Denmark, Sweden and some German states, against Spain and Austria with their Catholic German allies. Although the war, which was largely fought in Germany, did have its religious side, it was essentially one for and against the power of the Spanish Habsburgs in western Europe and that of their Austrian cousins in the German Empire and their family lands in central Europe.

The Thirty Years War in its final stages proved a massive defeat for the Habsburgs. The senior partner, Spain, had been decisively beaten by the French and the Dutch: with her Catalan, Portuguese and Neapolitan provinces in revolt she appeared on the point of collapse. In the east the Emperor Ferdinand III was threatened by the conquest of his own family lands by the French, Swedes and their German allies. In 1648 peace was signed in Westphalia by all the combatants except France and Spain who continued fighting till 1659. Cardinal Mazarin, who was effective ruler of France during the minority of Louis XIV (1643–1715), refused to make peace with Spain, which he believed was France's main enemy and which he was determined to destroy.

The territorial changes effected by Westphalia were surprisingly few and were limited to the German Empire. Yet the peace was one of the most important in European history and it has often been seen as opening the modern era of international relations. Westphalia signalled the end of the long period of Habsburg family ascendancy, particularly of the Spanish branch, and the beginning of that of Bourbon France. It also established the Dutch Republic, Sweden and Austria as major powers in their own right. By 1648 Spain under Philip IV (1621–65) had been defeated and appeared to be disintegrating. She had also become separated from Philip's Austrian cousin: Ferdinand III made peace with Mazarin as well as with the other combatants and left Spain to fight on alone against France. However, Spain did conclude peace with the Dutch Republic in 1648. This brought their eighty-year struggle to a close with Madrid's formal recognition of Dutch independence. Spain's former rebel subjects were now a major state with a powerful navy and the strongest economy in Europe. The Southern Netherlands remained in Spanish hands, but Madrid had formally to accept the closure of the River Scheldt and the port of Antwerp. The Dutch had no territorial designs on the province and were becoming aware that it might serve one day as a buffer against their own French ally. They did, however, intend to turn it into an economic satellite and were largely to succeed. The Dutch, especially the merchant oligarchs who mainly directed the government of the Republic, above all wanted neutrality and the peaceful development of trade. They had become a major power because of their mercantile supremacy in European and world markets and the strength of their financial institutions. However, this commercial dominance was to be challenged soon after the peace with Spain by the new English Republic which resented Dutch success and had a navy of its own capable of disputing it. London wanted to protect its colonies and its trade from Dutch encroachments and tried to do so by issuing the Navigation Ordinance of 1651. This led to the short and inconclusive First Anglo-Dutch War of 1652–54, which was fought almost completely at sea. Although the Dutch had to accept the ordinance, and a naval balance emerged, their commercial supremacy continued; English naval power was to prove ephemeral and declined with the restoration of the monarchy in 1660.

France's triumph at Westphalia lay less in the extent of her immediate annexations than in destroying Habsburg predominance and laying the foundations for her own future expansion. Her territorial gains were all taken from Austria and the Holy Roman Empire, not from Spain. They were strategic points on France's vulnerable eastern border, ones which would allow her to interfere in Germany and weaken the so-far intact Spanish Burgundian Circle. In the peace France's sovereignty was finally acknowledged over the three bishoprics of Metz, Toul and Verdun in Lorraine – these had actually been in French hands since 1552. (In 1661 Lorraine effectively became a French satellite when its duke allowed France military access.) Austria ceded to France her rights to ten towns in Alsace (the *décapole*), although they remained within the Holy Roman Empire and the city of Strasbourg kept its independence. The terms of this transfer were deliberately left vague by both sides: the French intended to exploit them so as to absorb more of Alsace in the future and to interfere in the Empire, while the Austrians hoped eventually to regain their losses. The fortress of Breisach, at the southern tip of Alsace and on the right bank of the Rhine, was also ceded to France. Although these gains were to open two centuries of disputes between France and the German powers, they were of more immediate importance, especially Breisach, in disrupting Spain's famous 'Spanish Road', the military line of communications between Italy and the Southern Netherlands. The latter and Franche-Comté were now effectively isolated and ripe for seizure by France. She also seemed capable of further expansion in Germany, especially as France (and her Swedish ally) had guaranteed the Westphalian settlement there and Germany as a whole was weak after the devastating years of war.

The territorial changes within the German Empire itself were small but important. The cession of territory round the Baltic to Sweden (see p. 10) seemed to promise to make her a permanent factor in German politics, particularly as Sweden, unlike France, was given a seat in the Imperial Diet (Reichstag). The gains by Saxony of Lusatia, by Bavaria of the Upper Palatinate and by Brandenburg-Prussia of Halberstadt, Minden and Magdeburg, together with East Pomerania, helped the trend towards increasing the power of the larger German princes. Their growing strength, expressed by their standing armies and their political absolutism, and their freedom from Imperial control, were the most important feature of the Westphalian settlement in Germany. Not only were the princes allowed to impose their own religion on their subjects, but they could now legally conduct an independent foreign policy and conclude treaties, subject to the meaningless restriction that these should not be directed against the Emperor or Empire. The Emperor himself lost the right to declare war, make peace or levy taxation in the name of the Empire, without the consent of the Imperial Diet. These changes, which all confirmed the power of the princes and limited that of the Emperor, were to be the basis of the Imperial constitution till the dissolution of the Holy Roman Empire in 1806.

The terms of the settlement, in one sense, merely reflected the long decline in Imperial power, but they were also significant because the Emperor Ferdinand II and his son Ferdinand III had tried, and nearly succeeded, to reverse the trend. Their attempt, which the Spanish Habsburgs had supported, had been defeated militarily, and this defeat was confirmed by the peace. The idea that the Empire itself was an actual state, capable of pursuing its own policies, was finally dead. This did not mean, however, that the Emperor was now powerless within the Holy Roman Empire or that the Imperial title had no value. Emperors continued after 1648 to interfere within Germany and to have a great deal of influence there, particularly among the smaller states. The Habsburg emperors themselves, moreover, were by far the strongest of the German princes because of the size of their own hereditary lands. The Emperor was also still recognised as the defender of Christendom against the Turks, and prestige reaped from victories in the Turkish Wars of the late seventeenth century (see pp. 74ff.) was to enhance his authority in the Empire. The Imperial title could also bring its bearer tangible material support, if the princes and the Emperor agreed on a common purpose, as in the later wars against Louis XIV of France.

After 1648 a distinction has to be made between the emperors as rulers of the Holy Roman Empire and as rulers of Austria. They partly compensated for their failure in Germany by their success in their own hereditary lands. Unlike their Spanish cousins the Austrian Habsburgs were more powerful than in 1618. Absolutism had increased and religious uniformity been imposed in Austria and Bohemia, while the Bohemian elective monarchy had been made hereditary in 1627. The Austrian Habsburgs' family lands were now a power in their own right, one which was soon to expand dramatically.

The peace of Westphalia was important in establishing a territorial base-line which was continually referred to in treaties down to 1789. It also established certain general principles which influenced international relations throughout the same period. The practice was begun of calling a general congress to conclude wars. At Westphalia all the European powers were present except England, which was involved in civil war, and the more remote Poles, Russians and Turks: future congresses usually included representatives of most European powers. The procedures employed in these congresses, as well as questions of precedence, were tentatively developed at Westphalia. Where there did seem a great difference, however, between the Westphalian congress and the later ones was that Westphalia was in fact two congresses. Religion was important enough at the end of the Thirty Years War for the Protestant opponents of the Emperor to negotiate at Osnabrück and the Catholics at Münster. But the peace concluded the last war which could in any sense be called religious, and it inaugurated a period of almost complete secularisation in European politics. The principle was now accepted that each state could have its own religion (although the same rule was not applied between a ruler and his own subjects). At the same time, while states were still to strive for hegemony, there was also a general acceptance that all states were independent and theoretically equal, at least if they were monarchies. The concept of a united Christendom with a secular and a religious head (the Emperor and the Pope), which Charles V had briefly tried to revive, had been dying for centuries and suffered a death-blow with the Reformation and the fragmentation of Christianity. It was now finally buried after Westphalia and was only to re-emerge in a rather different form with Napoleon and his 'new order'.

THE LAST STAGE OF THE FRANCO-SPANISH WAR, 1648–1659

Surprisingly, France's victory in the Thirty Years War did not lead to large conquests from Spain or even to the assertion of French ascendancy in Europe. Cardinal Mazarin, the chief minister of Italian origin during the regency for Louis XIV, had deliberately rejected the idea of peace with Spain in 1648: he believed that, once free of the war in Germany, France could defeat Spain so decisively that she would have to surrender not only the Burgundian Circle (the Southern Netherlands, Luxemburg and Franche-Comté) but even her Italian possessions and Catalonia. These aims went far beyond extending France to her 'natural frontiers' of the Rhine, the Alps and the Pyrenees*: it amounted to an intention to absorb Spain's European empire, a far cry from the fear of Spain which had forced France under Cardinal Richelieu to intervene in the Thirty Years War. However, Mazarin had miscalculated badly because of the outbreak of the *Frondes* (1648–53). These domestic revolts paralysed the French government and allowed the Spaniards to recover and to invade France. The successful French general, Condé, who had destroyed the Spanish infantry at Rocroi (1643) and Lens (1648), deserted to the enemy and even allowed Spanish officers into Paris.

Once the *Frondes* were over in 1653 and Mazarin regained control, the pattern of French victories and Spanish defeats was repeated, showing the complete supremacy of French arms. However, although the Portuguese were to recover their independence from Spain (finally recognised in 1668), Philip IV managed to suppress the revolts in Catalonia and Naples. He also reasserted Spanish control over Italy and the western Mediterranean, where France was handicapped by her inferior naval power. French military efforts were concentrated on the Southern Netherlands. Although there was now no support from the neutral Dutch, Mazarin could eventually supplement his own troops with English ones. Cromwell's Protectorate, with its disciplined army and expanding navy, had made war on Spain in the West Indies in 1655, and in 1657 it agreed to a French alliance. Consequently, in June 1658 English Ironsides and French troops defeated Spain at the battle of the Dunes and captured Dunkirk. English intervention made Spain anxious for peace, and this was signed in November 1659, the peace of the Pyrenees. This peace set the seal on the conclusion of Spain's long reign as the dominant European power: from now on Spain was to be a power on the defensive, engaged in a lengthy struggle to prevent the partition of her European and overseas empires by the other powers.

Mazarin had been equally keen on peace by 1659. The financial strain of the war was beginning to tell and it was clear that further campaigns would be needed to force Spain to make major concessions, such as the cession of the Southern Netherlands. He seems to have felt he had not much longer to live and wanted to pass on a

*The 'natural frontiers' did not become an objective of French policy till the French Revolution. Although seventeenth and eighteenth-century governments often thought in terms of defensible frontiers, their ambitions were never limited by France's natural geographical boundaries and often went beyond them.

France at peace to the young Louis XIV. Moreover, the Cardinal also saw the chance for a dynastic marriage between the King and Spain. Mazarin was prepared to settle for fairly minor territorial gains in return for a marriage. Accordingly, in the peace of the Pyrenees France's gains were limited in the north to Artois and small parts of Flanders, together with Roussillon and Cerdagne in the South. Dunkirk was ceded to England – it was later sold to France by the restored Charles II in 1662. France's southern border had therefore reached the Pyrenees: Mazarin agreed to this, not so much because it was a 'natural frontier', but because it was all he could get in the circumstances. France had failed to absorb the Burgundian Circle, but the acquisitions in the north, together with those made at Westphalia, had broken and weakened Spanish encirclement. In Italy Spain was still the predominant power, although the Duke of Savoy was effectively a French satellite and his Alpine fortress of Pinerolo was in French hands.

The peace treaty included an agreement for the marriage of Louis XIV to the Spanish Infanta, Maria Theresa, and this took place in 1660. Louis's mother, Anne, had wanted the marriage for sentimental reasons, as she was Philip IV's sister, but the real purpose was to secure a claim to the Spanish succession. Maria Theresa was Philip IV's daughter by his first marriage, and his second marriage had so far only produced another daughter, Margaret Theresa, and a run of sickly, short-lived boys – the last of whom, the later Charles II, was not born till 1661. Although Maria Theresa had to renounce the succession on her marriage, this was in return for a dowry. The French knew full well the Spaniards would be unable to pay this and intended to exploit the clause in the future if the succession to Spain was in doubt. Even if the dowry had been paid, it was questionable in Spanish and French law if a princess could renounce both her own and her unborn children's God-given rights. Moreover, as long ago as 1646, when Mazarin had been considering a possible marriage, he had written, 'once the Infanta marries his majesty, we can hope for the succession to the Spanish thrones, whatever renunciations she has to make'. The ambiguities in the peace of the Pyrenees were eventually to be exploited by France in the same way as those in Westphalia.

During this final, and ultimately successful, decade of the struggle against Spain France had had to fight on her own, except for the English intervention at the very end. The French army, which at times numbered 150,000 men and which had been reorganised by Le Tellier to ensure direct royal control, had proved far superior to that of Spain. The Spanish court had also fought the war alone: it had been diplomatically isolated largely through Mazarin's negotiating skill. The Cardinal had managed to construct a diplomatic system which provided France with security and gave her more confidence in facing

Spain. He had been determined to keep the Maritime Powers* away from Madrid, to maintain good relations with both, despite their war of 1652–54, and, if possible, to persuade them to join France. Although he failed to get further military help from the Dutch, they remained essentially pro-French, while the English had entered the struggle on the French side in 1657. He also worked hard to stay on good terms with both Protestant and Catholic princes in Germany and to extend the range of relationships France had enjoyed during the Thirty Years War: this would protect France's gains at Westphalia, increase her own influence in the Empire and counter that of Austria. The immediate intention was to prevent a renewal of the connection between the Austrian and Spanish Habsburgs and block the dispatch of Austrian help to Spain during the Franco-Spanish War. Mazarin succeeded fully in the latter, and only a few Austrian regiments assisted the Spaniards in the 1650s. However, he had mixed success in opposing Austrian influence in Germany. He failed to stop the Emperor Ferdinand III's having his son Ferdinand elected king of the Romans in 1653: this meant the son would succeed the father as emperor without a further election. But, when first the young Ferdinand died in 1654 and then the Emperor himself in 1657, the Cardinal was presented with a chance to interfere. He immediately began to work underhand to have Louis XIV, or at least a non-Habsburg, elected emperor. Habsburg influence was still too strong, however, and Ferdinand's eighteen-year-old son, Leopold, was elected emperor in 1658. None the less, the new Emperor Leopold I was forced by the princes to accept a 'capitulation', clearly partly inspired by French diplomacy, which bound him not to send military help to Spain.

Mazarin's diplomatic offensive in the Empire culminated, after the Imperial election, with France's joining an association of states known as the League of the Rhine. This league had originally been the creation of the Catholic Archbishop-Elector of Mainz, John Philip von Schönborn, who had been largely responsible for forcing the 'capitulation' on Leopold I. Schönborn had managed to fuse together a league of Catholic Rhenish and Protestant north-German states: the intention was to keep their independence from the Emperor and to prevent the extension of the Franco-Spanish War into north-west Germany. In 1658 this was converted into the League of the Rhine, with France now joining Mainz, Cologne, Hesse-Cassel, Brunswick-Lüneburg, Neuburg and Sweden (as ruler of the Swedish lands in Germany). Over the next four years the league was joined by Hesse-Darmstadt, Württemberg, Münster and Trier, and finally in 1665 by Brandenburg-Prussia. The league's declared aim was to defend the territorial settlement of Westphalia and princely liberties, and this

*'Maritime Powers' was the contemporary shorthand for the Dutch and English.

essentially meant against the Emperor. France provided subsidies to hire mercenaries, and there was a permanent secretariat at Frankfurt. The league's success and strength owed most to the good personal relations between Mazarin and Schönborn. Although Mazarin gradually turned the league into an instrument of French policy, he could not push it too far: Schönborn and his associates were primarily intent on preserving neutrality and maintaining peace in Germany after the devastations of the Thirty Years War. They did not want to become mere satellites of France, and Mazarin on the whole respected this. For the moment, at least, the German princes and France still recognised that they had much in common in opposition to Austrian Habsburg power and a possible revival of the Austro-Spanish family connection. However, over the next generation the princes were to become aware that France posed as great a threat to their independence as the Habsburgs.

SWEDISH SUPREMACY IN THE NORTH, 1648–1660

By the peace of Westphalia Sweden had become a European as well as the leading Baltic power. Her gains in Germany – Bremen and Verden, Wismar and western Pomerania with Stralsund and Stettin (Szeczin) – gave her direct control of the mouths of the three rivers, the Weser, Elbe and Oder. These new possessions, together with seats in the Imperial Diet and her guarantee of the peace settlement, also allowed her to interfere continually in Germany and seemed to make her a permanent factor in Imperial politics. This, of course, was welcome to the French, who had used Sweden during the Thirty Years War as a counter to the Austrian Habsburgs and intended to continue this policy. But Germany had always been of secondary importance to the Swedes. Even during the Thirty Years War they had intervened in the Empire principally to defend their position in the eastern Baltic.

Sweden's Baltic empire had been created entirely by military conquest over the previous century through wars against Denmark, Poland and Russia. In 1648 Westphalia had added German conquests to an existing large trans-Baltic empire: the traditional dependency of Finland, the whole eastern Baltic coast and much of the interior from Viborg (Viipuri) to Riga, and the Baltic islands of Gotland and Ösel. Yet on the Scandinavian peninsula itself Sweden had not yet reached her modern boundaries. She had recently annexed the western provinces of Jemteland and Herjedalen from Denmark, but the Danes still ruled much of modern southern Sweden as well as Norway itself. This meant that the Danes held both sides of the entrance to the Baltic, the Sound, although the Swedes had won exemption from

Sound dues. This was important because Sweden's empire ensured she had almost complete control of the trade in metals, grain and 'naval stores' (timber, hemp and flax), which were produced in the Baltic hinterland and were vital to western Europe. Only some Prussian and Polish ports were free from her grip.

Sweden's population was small: only half the empire's 2.5 million was Swedish. But her sound administration, near monopoly of European copper production, a successful arms industry and a splendid army practising revolutionary methods and led by rulers and generals of genius, had made her the dominant northern power. Her rivals lacked her advantages and military strength. The weakest was Russia whose monarchy had disintegrated during the 'Time of Troubles', and who had also to cope with periodic invasions from the Poles in the west and the Turks' Tartar vassals in the south. Russian power only recovered slowly during the the first half of the seventeenth century. The elective monarchy in Poland, which by contrast had proved far more effective than Russian tsardom in the first decades of the century, was to decline relentlessly, and Polish armies had consistently been beaten by the Swedes. Denmark had proved the strongest and most tenacious of Sweden's enemies, but she had suffered an unremitting series of defeats and annexations.

Sweden valued the gains made in Germany at Westphalia mainly because of the leverage provided against Denmark from the south. Her main concern after 1648 was not to be the systematic development of her German position but a continuation of the struggle for supremacy around the Baltic. Until the end of the century the struggle was still essentially one between Sweden and Denmark. In 1648 the Danes wanted revenge for past losses, while the Swedes were looking for an opportunity to expel them from the southern provinces, especially Scania (Skåne). The Swedes also inevitably wished to complete their control of the Baltic coastline by seizing the Polish and possibly the East Prussian ports. (East Prussia was ruled by the Elector of Brandenburg with the title of duke of Prussia.) Although Poland was less of a historic enemy than Denmark, she had proved almost as serious a foe since the beginning of the seventeenth century: as the standard-bearer of the Catholic Counter-Reformation in northern Europe Poland had posed a religious threat to Protestant Sweden, but more importantly Poland's Vasa rulers claimed the Swedish throne and wanted to regain Livonia (Latvia). Poland's Russian neighbours had a long-standing grievance against Sweden because all their outlets to the Baltic were in her hands. Moreover, the Westphalian peace had created new rivals for Sweden. The Elector of Brandenburg wanted to add Swedish Pomerania, with its important ports, to the poorer eastern part he had received in 1648, and the rulers of Brunswick-Lüneburg (the later electorate of Hanover) were soon to hope for Bremen and Verden. Not only, therefore, was Sweden's Baltic empire incomplete in her own eyes: she was herself surrounded by several irreconcilable enemies.

For the moment Sweden had clear military superiority over her enemies, but her naval supremacy was less certain. A navy was essential to hold the empire together, and Sweden's was stronger than those of the other Baltic powers. However, the western Maritime Powers, the Dutch and the English, were heavily dependent on the Baltic trade. They could send their own superior fleets almost at will into the Baltic. Their main aim was to maintain an equilibrium there. In the Swedo–Danish War of 1643–45 the Dutch fleet had helped the Swedes, but they were soon to shift their support when they felt the balance had been tipped too much in favour of Sweden.

Sweden's natural resources were poor, and her rulers had been determined that the empire and the campaigns to win it should pay for themselves. However, the whole imperial enterprise produced huge financial and political problems and was really too much for Sweden. One of the most serious crises occurred after the Thirty Years War during the 1650s under Queen Christina. When she abdicated in 1654, her successor was her cousin, Charles X (1654–60). He was a soldier of genius, whose solution to the domestic crisis was to try to bind the country together by an even more expansionist policy which aimed to establish total Swedish domination of the Baltic. First of all he looked towards Poland, hoping to annex her ports and complete Swedish control of the eastern and southern Baltic coast. The Polish King, John Casimir (1648–68), had given him reason enough by reviving the Polish Vasa claim to the Swedish monarchy at Christina's abdication. However, the real reason Charles attacked Poland at this time was the increasingly unstable internal situation there – the election of the weak John Casimir to the Polish throne had led to a further erosion of the declining power of the crown and had strengthened the position of the greater nobles. More immediately, the Swedish attack coincided with a massive Cossack revolt in the Polish Ukraine, on the south-eastern borders with Russia and the Ottoman Empire. In 1654 the Russian Tsar Alexis (1645–76) answered appeals from the Cossacks and intervened to seize the Polish Ukraine. The huge Polish state seemed about to disintegrate, and there were inevitable fears in Stockholm that Russia would annex large areas and then go on to attack Sweden's Baltic lands. Charles X was determined that if anyone took parts of Poland it should be Sweden. He now seemed to have been offered the opportunity to gain the Polish and possibly the Prussian ports.

The War of the North (1655–60) began with Swedish armies scoring spectacular victories in Poland between 1655 and 1657. However, the size of the country and the fragmentation of central authority made it difficult for Charles to get the Poles to admit defeat and to cede any territory. Moreover, his military victories frightened both

Poland's neighbours and her enemies: Austria sent troops to help John Casimir in 1656, and the Russians decided to change sides, unsuccessfully attacking Livonia and Riga in 1656–58.

More importantly, in June 1657 Frederick III of Denmark declared war, encouraged by Austrian diplomacy and by that of the Dutch who now feared total Swedish control of the Baltic. No proper alliance was concluded between Sweden's enemies, however, and the coalition proved to be a far less formidable one than in the Great Northern War after 1700. But Charles X now needed to disengage from what had in any case become an impossible situation in Poland and to turn his attention to tackling the Danes who were a greater and more immediate danger to Sweden proper.

War against Denmark offered Charles the chance to pursue a more dramatic imperialist policy. He intended not only to seize the Sound, which would give Sweden control of all Baltic trade, but also to destroy Denmark's monarchy, aristocracy and national independence. In January and February 1658 Charles led his army on a series of impressive marches across the frozen sea to the gates of Copenhagen itself. The helpless Danes had to sign a peace at Roskilde, ceding all present-day southern Sweden and the island of Bornholm. The Swedish King clearly only meant this as a preliminary and in the spring attacked Copenhagen, intending to raze the city. A confused period then followed as the Dutch and Austrians, the two former enemies, tried to bring naval and military aid to Frederick III. (This was a clear sign that the antagonisms of the Thirty Years War could be forgotten in the face of what appeared a greater danger.) Denmark's independence was saved only by the dispatch of a Ducth fleet to the Baltic in 1659. But the death, the following year, of Charles X, and the succession of a minor, Charles XI, finally brought the Swedish adventure to an end.

It was largely French diplomatic intervention which managed to impose a northern settlement acceptable to the regency for the young Charles XI in 1660. France interfered because she wanted to retain Sweden as an ally against Austria in Germany and eastern Europe. The French hoped to transform Sweden into a loyal dependant rather than the imperialist power she had become under Charles X. They also felt it important to preserve Poland and to use her, together with Sweden and the Turks, despite their hostility towards one another, to form an eastern barrier against the Austrian Habsburgs.

In the Danish–Swedish peace of Copenhagen, negotiated by France, Sweden gained the southern provinces of Scania, Blekinge, Bohuslan and Halland (Halland was already held on a long lease), but she had to return Bornholm. She also had to accept her failure to achieve the complete command of the Sound and of the Baltic which Charles X had wanted. At the complementary Swedish–Polish peace of Oliva, Stockholm's gains were limited to Casimir's renunciation of the Swedish throne and recognition of Sweden's sovereignty in Livonia. As important, the treaty recognised the ruler of Brandenburg-Prussia, Frederick William (the 'Great Elector', 1640–88), as full sovereign duke of Prussia instead of his holding it as a fief of Poland. The Elector had swung to and fro between the Swedes and Poles in the past war to try to achieve this. Finally, in 1661, Sweden and Russia made peace at Kardis, where Swedish control of the Baltic provinces was accepted by Tsar Alexis. The Tsar had in fact halted his campaigns against Riga in 1658 and renewed his war against Poland once the Swedes had turned on Denmark. His war with Poland continued till the peace of Andrusovo in 1667, when Russia gained parts of the Ukraine with Kiev and Smolensk.

With the 1660–61 settlements Sweden's empire reached its greatest extent. However, she had proved incapable of the imperialist role Charles X had striven for. French diplomacy had been needed to rescue her at his death; yet although the Swedish empire itself was never to gell into a political and economic unity, there was no serious danger of disintegration from within. The real threat to its future survival came from its external enemies, Denmark, Poland, Russia and, increasingly, Brandenburg-Prussia. The oldest enemy, Denmark, was to remain the most dangerous for the rest of the century, because she was the closest and the most determined on revenge. Moreover, the Danes' recent humiliation led to a strengthening of the Danish monarchy which was declared absolute in 1660. On the other hand, the monarchy in Poland was continuing to lose ground to the nobility. Poland was now becoming a minor power, lacking an effective national army, and an object for subjection and partition by her neighbours. Although Russia was to take the first share at Andrusovo, the Russian state itself had proved incapable, as yet, of breaking into the Swedish Baltic provinces. It was inevitable, however, that it would try again in the years ahead. For the immediate future both Poland and Russia would soon be preoccupied with a renewal of Turkish expansion in the south (see pp. 71ff.). This would give Sweden a breathing-space in the eastern Baltic. But on the southern shores of the sea Brandenburg-Prussia's army and ambitions were growing fast, and over the next generation would be directed against Sweden.

LOUIS XIV'S ASSUMPTION OF POWER AND THE WAR OF DEVOLUTION, 1661–68

When Cardinal Mazarin died in March 1661 Louis XIV was twenty-two. He almost immediately assumed absolute power, ruling as his own first minister. For more than half a century the King and France – it was impossible to separate the two – were to dominate European politics. This French ascendancy, which only a union of almost all Europe could eventually destroy, was built on a mixture of France's inherent strength and Louis's own personality. France's abundant resources had always made her a great power, potentially the leading one. But it was only in the 1660s and 1670s, when these resources were fully mobilised and the system of absolutism reached its height, strengthening the monarchy at home and abroad, that France quickly became the undoubted dominant European power.

The French population of 18 to 19 million was larger than that of any European state, including Russia. Louis XIV had three times as many subjects as the Spanish or English kings. France's rich agriculture and resilient peasantry made the country almost self-sufficient. Under Louis's controller-general of finances, Colbert, industrial and commercial enterprises were also expanded rapidly and soon threatened to outstrip those of England and the Dutch. France's tax system had glaring faults, but it gave the ruler far great revenues than in any other state. This was because of the strength of royal government within France. Although it has now become fashionable to question the extent of Louis's absolute power, at the time it was the envy of most European monarchs. They copied his bureaucracy, his tax system, his army, his palaces and his style of ruling. Yet none could match, at least in the seventeenth century, his ability to raise revenue and soldiers and to use them largely as he wished.

Louis personally controlled his army and foreign policy. The two were closely bound together, for foreign policy depended on military might. Under Le Tellier and his son Louvois a standing army was developed which was tightly controlled by the crown through a bureaucracy which supervised recruiting, supplying and officering. With Louis's encouragement the army rapidly increased in size. At Louis's accession its peacetime strength was 72,000 and this rose at times to 200,000, while in wartime it trebled and even reached nearly half a million in his last great war. Its generals, especially Condé and Turenne at the beginning, and the master fortress builder and siege expert, Vauban, largely established the pattern of warfare followed by Europe as a whole till the French Revolution. In addition, Colbert, at the beginning of Louis's personal rule, was building a navy which seemed capable of overtaking those of the Dutch and English.

The French diplomatic service was to set the pace just as much as the army. Louis had the finest diplomatic corps in Europe. It covered most of the Continent, and its function was not only to negotiate but also to bring as many rulers and ministers as possible under French influence through the distribution of presents and pensions. Ample funds, especially in the early years, brought English kings, German princes, Swedish ministers and Polish and Hungarian nobles on to the payroll. The direction of France's diplomacy as well as of her military campaigns was firmly in the King's hands. Although he had only average abilities, he slaved over state papers throughout his life, so much so that a modern historian has called him 'the bureaucratic king'. His ministers were always mere servants, although some, such as his first and last foreign secretaries, Lionne and Torcy, and his war minister, Louvois, could influence the style he adopted.

Generations of historians have tried to reduce all Louis XIV's foreign policy to a system, to find one unifying theme. Not surprisingly, they have largely failed. Both Europe and the King changed considerably over the half-century of his personal rule, and it is now clear that Louis adopted a far more pragmatic approach to problems than used to be thought. Yet some underlying constants in his policies can be detected. He was determined thoughout his reign to give France borders which would make her entirely safe from invasion, to make her a strong house which could not be broken into. It was also inevitable, given his close personal control over foreign and military affairs, that his own personality affected France's relations with Europe. Like most rulers and nobles of the time he was, as Lionne told Queen Christina of Sweden in 1662, 'sensitive to the last degree in anything which affects his honour'. In his eyes the defence of the honour or reputation (*gloire*) of France was inseparable from his own. It must be protected above all else, especially as he was convinced that France was the leading state in Europe and that he was the leading sovereign and his house the leading dynasty. Although Louis's stress on his own person seems abnormal to modern eyes, to justify policies on the basis of a state's national honour, reputation and prestige is still very much the norm, even in the second half of the twentieth century. In an age when rulers looked on their states as their personal family property, it was inevitable that they should stress their personal honour, reputation and prestige. This also explains why most international disputes tended to be over dynastic claims. Dynasticism was a dominant theme in international relations throughout the seventeenth and eighteenth centuries.

When all is said and done about Louis XIV's power and pretensions and about his preference for war and diplomacy before everything else, in practice his territorial demands for France were not that large. One can hardly compare them with those of Napoleon or even Frederick the Great. He certainly never strove for European hegemony on a Napoleonic scale, and unlike Frederick the Great who came to power at a similar age, entertaining similar wide ambitions, Louis took six years before engaging in his first war. He also, despite the occasional triumphal entry into a captured city and accompanying his armies at the opening of campaigns, had the sense to realise his limitations as a general and left actual fighting to others. Despite his pretensions, he usually sought limited objectives. He had a natural moderation and refused to push matters to extremes. He said himself, '...the more one loves *la gloire*, the more one ought to be sure to achieve it safely'. Consequently, he always counselled his generals against taking risks and seems almost to have preferred to gain his objectives without battle. There were surprisingly few major battles won by France in the period of undoubted French ascendancy. He preferred to exhaust his enemies rather than crush them in the field. Warfare in his reign therefore tended to become one of superior defences and of attrition.

Mazarin left Louis with a France at peace and with a network of alliances and relationships to protect her from a possible revival of Spanish and Austrian Habsburg power. Given Louis's own ambitions and the pressures of a court which accepted war as the normal way for young nobles to prove themselves, it was inevitable that he would use French power aggressively before long. Almost immediately French foreign policy began to show a new aggressive spirit and concern with honour and reputation in a series of ostensibly petty quarrels about questions of precedence. There were disputes with Spain in 1661 and the Papacy in 1662 over violent affrays involving ambassadors and their servants. In both cases Louis asserted himself belligerently and forced Madrid and Rome into humiliating surrenders. Yet, despite these displays of French power, Louis was slow to go to actual war. This was probably because of the influence of the cautious ministers he had inherited from Mazarin, especially Lionne and Le Tellier, his foreign and war ministers. There were also serious domestic difficulties at the beginning of Louis's personal rule, and Colbert was undertaking a financial reconstruction which was to double royal revenues between 1661 and 1667.

Although, in retrospect, the growing weakness of Spanish power is a central theme of the late seventeenth century, this was not so apparent in 1661. There was always the danger of a recovery, as had happened during the *Frondes*. The main enemy was therefore still seen as Spain, particularly as her territories remained largely intact around France's northern and eastern as well as southern borders. For the time being it was clear that the Austrian Habsburgs, whose relations with Madrid were uneasy after the accession of Leopold I in 1657, were fully occupied with problems in Hungary and with the Turks on their eastern borders (see pp. 71ff.). Initially it seemed imperative in Paris to consolidate the gains made from both Habsburg powers in 1648 and 1659 and to assert effective control over the vulnerable points on France's borders, the so-called 'gates'. These points, the long northern frontier, Lorraine, Alsace, Burgundy, the Savoyard Alps and the Pyrenees, could all be used as invasion routes into France. The 'gates' in the Pyrenean frontier had been largely closed in 1659, but this was the only safe frontier. There were, therefore, attempts in the early 1660s to enforce royal bureaucratic rule in the parts of Alsace won in 1648, and in 1662 to bribe the Duke of Lorraine to allow his duchy to be absorbed by France. Although the Duke refused, Lorraine was effectively under French military control, as was the Italian Alpine duchy of Savoy. The most vulnerable area, however, remained the north, where the Spaniards had made repeated and dangerous attacks throughout the last war. The gains in 1659 had gone some way to solve the problem, and in 1662 Louis bought the port of Dunkirk from the impecunious Charles II who had been restored to the English throne in 1660. But it was clear that Paris was far too vulnerable, and this meant that the French King would try to push his frontiers further away from the capital at the next opportunity.

Almost the first ten years of Louis's personal rule were to be spent in attempting to grab what he could of the Spanish Netherlands to the north and Spanish Franche-Comté to the east. This policy was part of a wider one: to isolate Spain and force her, and the other powers, to accept French Bourbon claims to at least a share in the Spanish succession in spite of the renunciations made by Louis's wife, Maria Theresa, at her marriage. It seemed essential to settle this problem because her father, Philip IV, was not expected to live much longer. He now had a male heir by his second wife. But this child, Charles, born in 1661, was known to be a particularly ailing infant. Besides Maria Theresa, the daughter of his first wife, Philip had a daughter from his second marriage, Margaret Theresa, who was betrothed to the Emperor Leopold.

It proved easy enough to isolate Spain by maintaining Mazarin's diplomatic system and by dispensing generous foreign subsidies. The League of the Rhine was continued and extended, being renewed in 1661 and 1663. This effectively neutralised the strategically important territory of north-west Germany, separated Austria from Spain and paralysed the Emperor Leopold in Germany. Although Louis's actions in Alsace and Lorraine had aroused some apprehension among the German states, the King had no aggressive ambitions towards Germany at this stage and Lionne managed to reassure them. Intermittent French help was given to the Portuguese rebels who eventually recovered their independence in 1668. Just as important were measures to maintain friendship with both Maritime Powers and to keep them away from Spain. The restored Stuart, Charles II of England, was anxious to be Louis XIV's friend and pensioner, while the Dutch were even more eager for French goodwill.

John de Witt, the Dutch Grand Pensionary and the most important member of the oligarchical regime in the Republic, believed that Dutch security depended on friendship with both England and France and on the pursuit of a largely neutralist foreign policy. Above all, he was intent on friendship with the French. This was partly from historical reasons and also from a growing awareness of the extent of French power. But there was also the uncomfortable knowledge that Charles II of England wanted the restoration of the power of the House of Orange in the Republic in favour of his nephew the young

William of Orange. The Dutch therefore concluded a defensive alliance with France in 1662. However, there were already signs of future problems between the Dutch and Louis XIV. Throughout the early 1660s Louis tried to interest the Dutch in various projects to partition the Spanish Netherlands. But the Dutch were understandably nervous and increasingly alive to the advantage of leaving things as they were – with a weak Spanish administration in Brussels. The French could be depended on to limit any revival in Spanish power which might threaten the Republic. On the other hand, it was hardly an inviting prospect to have the absolute French monarchy and its large army as an immediate neighbour. Even suggestions of Dutch territorial gain were not attractive: the Dutch burghers had no wish to absorb the Southern Netherlands cities, particularly Antwerp, and to allow them a share in their own commercial prosperity. Yet the Dutch were afraid to reject Louis's proposals outright, and there was no question of their taking open military action against France.

Louis XIV's policy of friendship with both Maritime Powers was severely tested after 1664 with the outbreak of colonial conflict then open war between them. Commercial and colonial rivalries had not been solved by the First Anglo-Dutch War (1652–54) and were increased by Charles II's accession. The English were mainly responsible for a steady deterioration in relations with the Republic. Charles II had his own Navigation Act passed: this was intended to harm the Dutch and to encourage English commercial and colonial enterprises in North America and West Africa. In 1664 an English squadron seized the Dutch settlement of New Amsterdam (New York); Dutch factories on the Guinea coast were also raided. War followed in 1665. In this Second Anglo-Dutch War (1665–67) the Dutch, who managed to finance their navy easily enough, soon gained the upper hand, whereas Charles II was chronically short of money and the English navy had deteriorated markedly since his restoration. The war culminated in the spectacular Dutch raid up the Medway and the burning of ships and the docks at Chatham. Peace was signed at Breda in July 1667 and was largely achieved through the moderation of the Dutch Grand Pensionary, de Witt. He allowed the English to have the right to a naval salute in the Channel and to keep New Amsterdam. The Dutch gained Surinam, retained their exclusive position in Indonesia and won important relaxations of the Navigation Act in north-western Europe. However, as one English diplomat remarked, this was a 'snarling peace'. The commercial jealousies were still there and were to erupt in a further war within five years.

Louis XIV had been somewhat embarrassed by appeals from both sides for his help. Although he eventually declared war on Charles II (January 1666), as he was obliged to do under the terms of his alliance with the Dutch, he managed not to take any real part in the struggle or to offend either side. His main concern was to keep the two powers away from Spain. Their war itself gave him a good opportunity to attack Spain while they were occupied with their own quarrel. He was also able to use the preparations for helping the Dutch as a convenient cover for a Spanish war. Such a war had become inevitable after 1665 when Philip IV died.

Louis took his wife's claims to the Spanish succession very seriously, particularly as they offered the chance to annex strategically important areas. During the early 1660s he had tried unsuccessfully to persuade Madrid to nullify Maria Theresa's renunciation. At his death Philip IV left the throne to his young son, who became King Charles II; in the event of whose death it was to go to his daughter by his second marriage, Margaret Theresa, who was still engaged to the Emperor. Undeterred by this, Louis hit upon the idea of using a local inheritance law, which applied in Brabant, in the Spanish Netherlands, the law of devolution. This gave preference to daughters of a first marriage over sons of a second one. French lawyers also dredged up similar laws in other parts of the Netherlands, Luxemburg and Franche-Comté, where first daughters enjoyed partial rights of inheritance. Using these completely bogus claims – the laws had never applied to dynastic inheritance – Louis demanded the cession of large chunks of the Southern Netherlands and smaller pieces of Luxemburg and Franche-Comté. The devolution claims had given him a plausible excuse for annexing Spanish territory, while the undoubted rightful ruler, Charles II, was still alive. But, not unnaturally, the Spanish regency of the child-King's Austrian mother, Maria Anna (she was Leopold's sister), rejected Louis's claims. It also showed its anti-French sentiments by allowing Charles's sister, Margaret Theresa, to marry her uncle, Leopold I, in 1666. (Margaret Theresa's father and mother had also been uncle and niece.)

In May 1667 Louis XIV's armies invaded the Southern Netherlands, beginning his first and shortest war, the War of Devolution (1667–68). For the first time Europe was made aware of the extent of French military reorganisation under Louis: the outclassed Spanish troops were forced to retreat before the French advance with scarcely a struggle. It was clear that any serious resistance to the French would have to come from elsewhere. France's allies in the League of the Rhine, whose main concern was to prevent their own states becoming a battlefield, ensured that Austria could not help. Initially the Maritime Powers were too occupied with their own naval war. However, French successes, or rather France's military parade, immediately alarmed England and the Republic into making their peace at Breda (July 1667). Both powers were aghast at the situation in the Netherlands. The Dutch were not only concerned with the military threat which French annexations would bring: just as dangerous as this were the ominous signs that Colbert wanted to take Antwerp for France and open the River Scheldt to shipping. However, the Dutch leaders, particularly de Witt, were convinced that they could not fight France. De Witt explained their dilemma: 'To abandon Spain would amount to presenting the Netherlands to France; to help her on our own, would be madness.' His policy, therefore, was to try to retain French friendship while finding some way of limiting her territorial gains without running the risk of direct conflict with France. In England, however, both Charles's new ministry, the Cabal, and his parliament were more openly anti-French because of Louis's Catholicism and absolutism. This seems to have influenced their actions as much as the strategic danger to England from the Netherlands.

Discussions between the Maritime Powers, after the conclusion of their own peace, eventually led to a remarkable diplomatic turnabout, when the two states signed an alliance in January 1668. Swedish accession to the treaty (largely to show their diplomatic independence from France) converted it into the Triple Alliance. This association of the three Protestant powers, all of which had been friendly to France, was intended to mediate in the Franco-Spanish War and to exert diplomatic pressure on both sides: it was not intended as an anti-French coalition. Although it suggested peace on the basis of terms which Louis had already offered Spain, the alliance contained a secret clause threatening military intervention to reimpose the frontiers of 1659 on France if agreement were not reached. De Witt had not wanted to go as far as this and probably had no intention of carrying out this clause. The Dutch states-general, annoyed at new French commercial tariffs (see p. 24), and the English had pressed him to it. None the less the alliance seemed a slap in the face to Louis, and it certainly shocked him, especially as he immediately discovered the secret clause. Although he occupied Franche-Comté early in 1668 so as to destroy the fortresses there and to strengthen his hand, he agreed to treat. Peace was signed on 2 May 1668 at Aix-la-Chapelle (Aachen) after a short congress held between the two combatants and the Maritime Powers. Twelve places in the Southern Netherlands, including Lille and Tournai, were ceded to France. Louis had offered Spain the option of ceding these or Franche-Comte. The Spaniards had decided on the former, largely because they knew it would make France's future relations with the Maritime Powers more strained. The territory gained by Louis was not very important, and instead of contributing to a more rational and defensible frontier for northern France it formed an enclave in the Spanish Netherlands.

Louis would hardly have been satisfied with these gains at Aix-la-Chapelle, but he intended them as a mere preliminary to much greater future ones in the Netherlands. In the event he was never to make these and, with hindsight, he might have been wiser to have continued the war and risked the consequences. His generals had argued against making peace. But Louis had listened to his own natural caution and to the men raised by Mazarin – his foreign and war ministers, Lionne and Le Tellier. They argued that France should not continue fighting while she was isolated diplomatically: they wanted to disperse the Triple Alliance before proceeding to annex the defenceless Spanish Netherlands and Franche-Comté. But there was also a further reason for making peace and for not humiliating the Spaniards at this time. In January 1668, as the Triple Alliance was being signed, Louis had made a secret partition treaty with the Emperor Leopold over the Spanish succession.

This partition treaty had developed out of the French foreign minister Lionne's earlier successful negotiations to keep the German princes neutral during the Franco-Spanish War. It had seemed sensible to the French court to try to reach agreement with the other main claimants to the Spanish succession, the Austrian Habsburgs. This was all the more necessary because of the continual reports coming from Madrid about the condition of the Spanish King Charles II. He was four when he succeeded his father in 1665. Generations of inbreeding had made him a physical weakling and a near-imbecile. It was widely expected that a childhood illness would kill him before his tenth birthday. In the event he was to survive, and the succession issue was not to be so acute again till the 1690s. However, during the late 1660s his death seemed imminent. This was likely to lead to an immediate European struggle for control of the whole Spanish empire between the French Bourbons and Austrian Habsburgs. While Louis XIV claimed the succession for his wife and their children, Leopold I had a string of claims in his own right as well as from his recent marriage to Margaret Theresa. The Spanish and Austrian Habsburgs had also concluded a family compact in 1617 which provided for reciprocal successions if one line failed. Although both Louis XIV and Leopold firmly believed in the justice of their claims, the legal niceties were less important than who had the strength to get his way and whom the Spaniards themselves would accept. Moreover the inheritance was so vast, in Europe as well as outside, that its transference would dramatically increase French or Austrian power. The Spanish succession was therefore always of fundamental concern to the rest of Europe because of its implied threat of European hegemony.

The French approached Vienna over a possible partition in 1667 and were encouraged when there was no immediate rejection. The Viennese court had found itself in a dilemma over the Franco-Spanish War of Devolution: how could they fulfil their acknowledged obligations to their Spanish relatives, given the pro-French attitudes of the German princes and their own military weakness? They were also hampered by continuous problems with their Hungarian subjects and the Turks (see pp. 71ff.). On the other hand they were determined not to let the Spanish succession slip from their grasp. French diplomacy managed skilfully to exploit these Austrian doubts and desire for peace in the west, and Paris was fortunate that Leopold's leading minister,

Lobkowitz, wanted agreement. In effect the French offered the Emperor peace and a share in the succession in return for acknowledging that France also had a right to the inheritance. Recognition of the latter would be a significant gain for France and would drive a wedge into the family solidarity of the two Habsburg branches. The Austrians none the less accepted the French offer: Lobkowitz preferred to align with France rather than come to terms with the Triple Alliance powers and create an anti-French bloc. A secret partition treaty was quickly negotiated and agreed on in mid-January 1668 in Vienna. The treaty provided that, if Charles II of Spain died, the Spanish throne with the American empire, Milan and ports on the Tuscan coast, should go to Leopold or his children. The French Bourbons were to inherit Spanish Navarre, the Southern Netherlands, Franche-Comté, Naples and Sicily, and the Philippines.

It was as much because of this partition treaty and the need to get the agreement of the Spanish regency, as because of pressure from the Triple Alliance, that Louis XIV made peace with Spain on such easy terms at Aix-la-Chapelle. There seemed little need to be greedy when there was the prospect of these huge gains. The Spaniards themselves were tacitly to accept the partition treaty, although it was never even formally signed between Leopold and Louis XIV. By doing so Madrid in effect accepted the principle of the Bourbons' having a stake in the succession, in return for being spared immediate major annexations. However, the Franco-Austrian partition treaty was soon to be a dead letter, as was France's attempt to solve the succession problem by agreement with both Vienna and Madrid. Charles II of Spain's painful struggle and survival through childhood made the succession issue of far less immediate importance than problems raised by Louis XIV's further ambitions.

LOUIS XIV'S PREPARATIONS TO ATTACK THE DUTCH REPUBLIC, 1668–1672

Four years after making peace with Spain at Aix-la-Chapelle Louis XIV attacked the Dutch Republic. In doing so he finally abandoned the alliance system constructed by Richelieu and Mazarin and designed to protect France from Spain. The war against the Dutch was to lead to the first determined attempts to resist Louis's progress by force and to the beginning of an anti-French system in Europe. With hindsight his decision to attack the Dutch must be seen as a mistake: its consequences were to dog him for the rest of his reign. But at the time no one at the French court opposed this policy, for it fitted in with the views of all groups.

The French King had been furious about the Triple Alliance of 1668 and put all the blame for it on the Dutch. He accused them of trying 'to impose their law' on him and of telling him what he should do. He railed against their 'insupportable vanity' and 'bad faith' and was angry at their 'ingratitude' towards France, since he believed his country had saved them in the past from conquest by Spain. All his royal and religious prejudices came to the surface against a republic of Calvinist 'cheese and herring merchants', who were claiming the right to act as a great power because of their commercial success. He came almost to believe it was his moral duty to destroy their state and to subject them to some form of monarchical authority, either his own or that of the native House of Orange. There were, however, other political and economic motives, which have often seemed more important to historians.

The annexation of more or all of the Spanish Netherlands and Franche-Comté remained a fixed objective of Louis's foreign policy. The refusal of Spain's child-King, Charles II, to die meant that the Franco-Austrian partition treaty of 1668 could not be imposed and that, for the immediate future, any further gains from Spain would have to be taken by force. Although Spain herself was now incapable of preventing this, the Dutch seemed determined to resist it by diplomatic means and possibly by force. The French therefore concluded, as Louis's minister Louvois put it, that 'the only way to conquer the Spanish Netherlands successfully is to humble the Dutch and, if possible, to destroy them'.

Modern historians have tended to stress the economic causes of the war, drawing comparisons with the undoubted economic basis for the contemporary Anglo-Dutch wars. And there certainly was fierce commercial rivalry between France and Holland. Louis's controller-general of finances, Colbert, had been setting up state-funded industries and overseas companies, as well as creating a navy almost from scratch. But his commercial enterprises had had only limited success, because French traders had found it difficult to establish themselves in European and world markets which were already dominated by the Dutch. Colbert's mercantilist views, which held that the volume of world trade was static, led him to conclude that France could only gain a share of this by taking it from the Dutch. Almost from the beginning of Louis's personal rule, therefore, he had been waging a tariff war against Dutch trade (much as the English were doing with their navigation laws) to try to get French imports and exports carried in French instead of Dutch ships and to try to break the Dutch monopoly of such commodities as sugar. Preliminary tariffs in 1664 were followed by far more rigorous ones in 1667 and 1670–71. Although the Republic retaliated and in 1672 banned all French imports for a year, it could not use the tariff weapon effectively because Dutch commercial success depended on free trade. However,

Colbert decided that tariffs were only a partial answer and that France's economic success could only be assured by the military destruction of the Dutch and the forcible seizure of their commerce. He consequently became as determined on war as the many young militarists at the French court. He declared: 'As we have destroyed Spain on land, we must destroy Holland at sea. The Dutch have no right to seize all trade.'

Louis welcomed and encouraged Colbert's view of the Dutch, as it coincided with his own wish to ruin them. But trade was not his main reason for going to war. The King was not very interested in economic matters, and to fight a war simply for commercial gain would be to reduce himself to the level of the Dutch herring merchants he despised. He attacked the Dutch to humble and even to annihilate an ignoble and heretical so-called friend who had insulted him. The war itself would also provide a further opportunity for Louis to prove his virility to his court by defending his honour and winning military glory. These were motives enough for war in the seventeenth century.

As soon as he had concluded peace at Aix-la-Chapelle in May 1668 Louis XIV deliberately began to plan to attack the Dutch. The war was to take four years to organise. Originally he had intended to begin it in three, but diplomatic problems with the German princes caused Louis to defer it till 1672. This delay once again illustrates the King's caution. Instead of rushing into war he was determined to wait until he had strengthened his army and navy, isolated the Dutch diplomatically and constructed a new system around France which would replace the traditional and now defunct relationship with the Republic. The size and efficiency of the army were increased by Le Tellier and his son Louvois, who, despite his youth, played an equal part and was proving an administrator of great talent. At the same time Colbert was able to spend lavishly on building an Atlantic and Mediterranean fleet, which was quickly catching up on both the Dutch and the English.

Before these military forces could be unleashed Lionne was put to work to destroy the Triple Alliance and gather a group of client states round France. This proved a fairly easy, if rather lengthy, undertaking and was largely a question of cash. France's main effort was concentrated at first on England, whose navy was needed to supplement Colbert's. She proved willing enough to abandon the Triple Alliance and to join in an attack on the Dutch. The commercial differences between the Maritime Powers remained after the last war, and the opportunity was now being offered of an alliance with the huge strength of France to revenge the humiliation of the attack on Chatham. Charles II believed a new war would be popular, and he welcomed Louis's approach for personal and domestic reasons. He had probably considered his recent alliance with the Dutch as a way of increasing his own worth in Louis XIV's eyes. Throughout the sinuous foreign policies of his reign Charles remained basically pro-French and an admirer of Louis and his government. He now saw a successful liaison with the French King as a means to acquire subsidies which would reduce his dependence on parliament and let him implement absolutist and Catholic policies at home. However, he failed to realise that the war would cost him more than the French subsidies and force him either into a growing client relationship with Louis or into an even more vulnerable position *vis-à-vis* parliament. Charles's military and financial weakness meant that England was always a secondary power throughout the Restoration period. That Louis recognised this is shown by the comparatively trivial sums he was ready to spend in subsidies to her.

In June 1670, through the mediation of his favourite sister, 'Minette', who was married to Louis's brother, Charles II signed the secret treaty of Dover. This treaty was essentially a personal understanding between the two kings: only two of Charles's ministers were informed, since wider publicity would have been too risky in the English political climate. Charles agreed to attack the Dutch coast with his own troops and ships at the same time as Louis launched his own assault. In return France was to provide subsidies of £225,000 a year and England was to make territorial gains around the Scheldt estuary, which would allow her to develop a commercial base there. Significantly, Louis left unsaid what he intended to take for himself. In the second part of the treaty Charles declared his intention to announce his conversion to Catholicism at a time of his own choosing, and Louis promised additional subsidies and even troops in case of opposition in England. Charles himself was the instigator of this conversion clause, and he seems to have intended it to prove his good faith and to extract more money from France. When Charles had to involve more ministers in the signature of a second treaty in December 1670, he deliberately hid this clause from them, knowing the uproar it would provoke. This second treaty fixed the date for the joint attack as spring 1672.

The English defection effectively dissolved the Triple Alliance. In 1671 Sweden abandoned it as well and agreed terms for an alliance with France, which was eventually signed in April 1672. Subsidies and individual pensions were paid to the Swedish regency: the Swedes welcomed an attack on the Republic which might weaken Dutch power in the Baltic. France extracted from the Swedes not only their desertion from the Triple Alliance but also a promise to intervene militarily in Germany in case the German princes helped the Dutch. In the event the Swedes were to prove of little value to the French (see p. 31): as Louis's ministers in Stockholm had warned him, the Swedish army and administration had seriously deteriorated.

With the collapse of the Triple Alliance Louis's only remaining worry was the attitude of the German powers. Spain was now so militarily weak and divided by factional quarrels at court that she could be safely ignored and dealt with once the war had begun. However, the German princes were far more important, because the French had decided to attack the Dutch along their eastern border rather than crossing the Spanish Netherlands and trying to force their way over the rivers and past the fortresses which guarded the Republic from the south. As a preliminary to this eastern invasion plan French troops occupied all Lorraine in 1670. Its duke, Charles IV, who had shown too much independence for Louis's taste and was leaning towards the Dutch, had to flee. The occupation, which showed every sign of being permanent, had its long-term value in closing one more of the 'gates' of France and in finally separating the Spanish Netherlands from Franche-Comté, but its immediate importance was to clear the way for the march of French troops northwards to the Dutch border.

The occupation of Lorraine, which was part of the German Empire, aroused protests from some of the German princes and from the Emperor Leopold. It produced much suspicion about France's ultimate intentions in Germany. None the less, despite this and the fact that the League of the Rhine had collapsed in the mid-1660s, Louis's foreign minister, Lionne, managed before his death in 1671 to wage a successful diplomatic campaign in the Empire and to deny the Dutch any support there. Between 1670 and 1672 several bilateral treaties, usually involving the payment of French subsidies, were negotiated with the Rhenish archbishop-electors, Saxony, the Palatinate, the Brunswick duchies, Bavaria and others. The alliance with Bavaria seemed of particular value because the electorate could block possible Austrian moves across southern Germany. However, Brandenburg-Prussia, which was of equal importance because of its large army and possessions on the lower Rhine, proved elusive. The Great Elector was to vacillate between the French and the Dutch throughout the early 1670s. Subsidies and the fear of Louis's army inclined him towards France, but an appetite for the Pomeranian lands of Sweden, France's ally, disposed him towards his fellow Calvinists in the Republic. Although Brandenburg-Prussia was equivocal, Louis could count on allies of even more strategic value: the Archbishop-Elector of Cologne and the Bishop of Münster agreed to allow Louis to use their territories as a way into the Republic and to join in the attack. The French diplomatic offensive was rounded off a few months before the outbreak of war by a treaty with Emperor Leopold. Although Franco-Austrian relations had not become warm after the partition treaty of 1668, and Austria bitterly resented the occupation of Lorraine in 1670, she had wanted to avoid direct conflict with France so as to concentrate on the subjection of her Hungarian lands. Consequently, in November 1671 the two powers signed a neutrality agreement:

Leopold promised not to interfere in the Dutch War provided it did not spill over into the Empire.

Throughout the winter of 1671–72 France stockpiled supplies in Cologne. Her army had never been in finer trim, her revenues were in surplus, and her English, Münster and Cologne allies remained determined to enter the war. But what had the Dutch been doing to save themselves? They had been warned as long ago as summer 1668 by their envoy in Paris that Louis intended 'to take revenge without fail'. France's hostility was shown clearly enough by the tariff policy and subsequent diplomatic moves. Yet the Dutch oligarchs and the Grand Pensionary, de Witt, did little to defend themselves. In part this came from a refusal to believe that France would actually attack them. De Witt himself showed a surprising lack of diplomatic initiative and seemed incapable of envisaging a system different from the one he had always depended on, that is, one based on French friendship. In February 1672 the Republic did sign a defensive treaty with Spain and this brought some help from the Governor of the Southern Netherlands during the year. But this had little effect on the outcome of the initial French attack because of the complete collapse of the Republic's own army. This was in a disastrous state at the beginning of the war. Supplies were short at a time when Dutch citizens were selling munitions to the French. Although the Dutch navy was in better shape than ever, efforts were only made to prepare the army for war at the start of 1672. As leader of the large city merchants, de Witt had found it difficult to advocate rebuilding the army in case it strengthened the interests of their domestic political rivals, the supporters of the young Prince William of Orange. The Orange family had always been associated with the army, and they had used it to increase their own power in the past. The Dutch oligarchs did not intend to allow a revival of Orangist power which seemed to have been finally crushed in 1650 on the death of William's father.

THE DUTCH WAR, 1672–1679

War was declared first by the English in March 1672. A month later Louis left Paris to direct the French campaign in person. He was to accompany his armies throughout the war and took an active part in deciding the strategy followed, although he did not command directly in the field. The march from France was organised by Louvois with clockwork precision, and in the second week of June the French army crossed the Rhine and invaded the Dutch Republic from the east. Over 100,000 strong and with Turenne, Condé and Luxembourg for generals, the invasion force advanced rapidly across Dutch soil, taking some fortresses and avoiding others, as the enemy army, a quarter of its size, retreated in disarray. By the end of June the French controlled the provinces of Guelderland and Utrecht, and their German allies had taken Overijssel, Drente and half of Groningen. The Republic was prostrate, but the French possibly advanced too cautiously, worried about outrunning their supplies. The Dutch therefore seized the chance to open the dykes and flooded the area south of the Zuider Zee. This saved Amsterdam and the province of Holland, which could now only be reached by sea. Further French advance, at least for the rest of the year, was now clearly impossible, while Anglo-French naval action against the Republic had failed.

The French had not expected to be halted in this way, and the opening of the dykes gave the Dutch enough time for a European coalition to be created which would ultimately save them. But at the time this setback seemed irrelevant, a minor delay to the French advance which would be overcome when the floods cleared. In the meantime Louis's troops occupied all the landward provinces. Consequently, when de Witt's desperate government asked for peace at the end of June, offering huge cessions of Dutch territory, their terms were contemptuously rejected. In the flush of victory, and encouraged by Louvois, whose influence had increased since Lionne's death, Louis was now aiming at the destruction of Dutch independence, while Colbert was planning to take over their commerce. The French King had little interest in helping the English and was merely demanding for his allies the useless northern port of Delfzijl.

France's understandably vast ambitions were not to be realised because of changes in the Republic itself. The disasters of the summer had totally discredited de Witt's regime. He resigned in July and, together with his brother, was hacked to pieces in the streets of The Hague by an Orangist mob on 20 August. The twenty-two-year-old William, Prince of Orange, had already been named stadtholder of Holland and Zeeland by the desperate estates. His supporters now seized all positions of authority, and although his power rapidly diminished as the war progressed, for the moment he had total control. There was no question now of accepting Louis's terms or even of trying for peace. William, who had been considered by both his uncle, Charles II of England, and Louis as a docile ruler of a Dutch rump state, was determined to fight to the finish. Although in continual poor health and unsuccessful as a general, William probably did more than anyone else to curb Louis's ambitions. He became obsessed with what he saw as the danger of French hegemony in western Europe, which he felt threatened the Dutch state most of all. He soon grasped that only a coalition of the other European states could destroy French power. His first steps, therefore, were to reorganise Holland's military defences, to revitalise Dutch diplomacy and to appeal for outside help.

By autumn 1672 France's attack on the Republic had caused alarm in several parts of Europe. Louis's careful diplomacy before the war had been undermined by the dramatic success of his armies and the extent of his demands. It was one thing to punish the Dutch but quite another to destroy them. The alarm was greatest in Germany, where a large number of pamphlets appeared warning that France would soon try to subject the Empire as well. Louis's successful aggression, his military occupation of part of the Empire around Cologne and Cleves, as well as of Lorraine beforehand, led to increasing hostility in Vienna. Both the Emperor and the Elector of Brandenburg were sufficiently worried to move troops westwards at the close of 1672 to try to exert pressure on Louis's Cologne and Münster allies. The Spaniards had been just as alarmed, rightly fearing that once in control of the Dutch Republic Louis would simply annex the Southern Netherlands. Consequently, when Louis returned in triumph to Paris for the winter of 1672–73, with his army occupying the Republic's eastern provinces, an anti-French coalition was already in the making. It was formally concluded on 30 August 1673 at The Hague between the Dutch, Spain and Austria and the exiled Duke of Lorraine, and was to be heavily subsidised by the Dutch.

In 1673 the Dutch War was fast becoming a European one. Austrian forces, with the help of some German princes, attacked French lines of communication and French-held territory from the lower Rhine to Alsace, while the Spaniards in the Netherlands, encouraged by William of Orange, opened hostilities on France's northern borders. The French army in the Dutch Republic was now dangerously exposed, and it was impossible to protect its supply routes while defending France's own frontiers. Gradually, during 1673, Louis had to accept that permanent gains from the Dutch were impossible and that a new purpose had to be found for the war. The original aim of chastising the Dutch had in any case been achieved. By the end of 1673, therefore, French troops had evacuated all but a few garrisons in the Republic and the war settled down until 1678 into one along France's own borders – the territorial gains France might now make would, in the traditions of French policy, be from Spain or the German states. However, unlike under Richelieu and Mazarin, France was now to be faced by a coalition of the other powers, which was to be the pattern for the rest of Louis's reign. The King's attack on the Dutch Republic had produced a complete reversal of the earlier power alignments. The Dutch had come to terms with the two Habsburg powers, while the German princes were beginning to feel that France rather than the Emperor was the greater threat to their independence. It was not to be long before Louis's English allies were to move in the same direction. As Louis himself said, 'My allies were becoming my enemies'. Above all he had destroyed a century of Franco-Dutch friendship and created bitter Dutch hostility which was to be as fundamental for the next half-century as that between the House of Bourbon and the Habsburgs.

By spring 1674 Louis was becoming increasingly isolated in Germany; by the end of the year, despite promises of more French money, only Bavaria maintained a benevolent neutrality towards France. In April and May 1674 Cologne and Münster made peace with the Dutch, and on 28 May the German Imperial Diet declared war on France, summoning all the princes to assist the Emperor Leopold. Their contributions of men and cash were not to be very great, but in July 1674 Frederick William of Brandenburg-Prussia joined the coalition. This came after much soul-searching since he had been forced out of the war the previous year following defeats by France. Louis's response to the situation in Germany was to try to terrorise the population in the campaigning areas along the Rhine: the Palatinate was devastated in 1674 for the first time. Lionne's subtle diplomacy had now been abandoned in favour of Louvois's strategy of intimidation, and this inevitably created profound distrust and tended to knit the anti-French coalition together. Louis's other ploy of calling on his Swedish ally to intervene against Brandenburg-Prussia had the same effect upon his enemies. The Swedes in any case proved incapable of mounting a serious incursion and they were decisively beaten by Frederick William at Fehrbellin (27 June 1675). A Danish invasion of Scania soon made Sweden withdraw from war in Germany to concentrate on her own defence.

The other partner in the Triple Alliance, won over before the Dutch War, England, proved as little help to the French as the Swedes. Charles II's hopes of naval victories against the Dutch were disappointed during 1672 and 1673. Even with French naval help, England failed to defeat the Dutch fleet, destroy her commerce, blockade the Dutch coast or make landings there. This failure, and the gradual discovery by Charles's Protestant ministers and by parliament of the absolutist and Catholic implications of his association with France, led to a domestic crisis in 1673. Charles was denied funds by parliament and forced to make peace with the Dutch (treaty of Westminster, February 1674) on the basis of the status quo. Over the next four years there were to be increasing pressures, encouraged by William of Orange's skilful use of propaganda, for England to join the anti-French coalition.

Although observers were slow to recognise it at the time, Anglo-French relations were undergoing a fundamental change in the 1660s and 1670s. Previously Spain's role as the leading proponent of the Counter-Reformation in western Europe during the sixteenth century and the rivalry between her and England overseas had made the English traditionally hostile to Spain. This had been seen as late as the 1650s, when Cromwell's Protectorate was at war with her. It was therefore natural, in a Europe where France and her allies were struggling against the dominance of the Habsburgs, that England would usually align herself on the French side. Lack of commercial rivalry, unlike that with the Dutch, had meant that Anglo-French relations had been consistently good. Until 1688, and in some measure beyond, English foreign policy was largely concerned with the north-western peripheries of Europe, particularly the area of modern Belgium and the Netherlands. It was an axiom of English policy that a strong military power should not dominate this area or gain supremacy in the Channel. Previously the threat here had come from Spain. But the growth of French military power and the ambitions of Louis XIV meant that France was now coming to be seen by many Englishmen as posing the same threat. Moreover, Colbert's commercial and tariff policies and the massive increase in the size of the French navy, with its newer and better designed ships, were a direct danger to England. Colbert's tariffs damaged English trade more seriously than they had the Dutch, and the construction of Atlantic as well as Mediterranean bases for the new French fleet seemed an ominous portent for English control of the 'Narrow Seas'.

All the factors, except the wider colonial issues, which made Anglo-French rivalry so intense and so continuous in the period between 1688 and 1815, were already in existence in the 1670s. But in the reign of Charles II the rise of French power failed to produce an immediate reorientation in English policies. Partly this was because of the King's own Francophile attitudes, but also because English politicians were slow to realise the naval, military and commercial threat from France. Many in fact only really became aware of it through their opposition to Charles's domestic policies: they came to see that these were based on the absolutist Catholic monarchy of Louis XIV and that the French King himself ultimately posed a threat to England. However, for the rest of Charles II's reign and that of his brother James II, England on the whole was to remain insular and tied up with her own political conflicts and to take no action against French power. Not even the sustained efforts of William of Orange could drag England into continental affairs, although there were several false signs that she might intervene. It was only after William himself became king of England that she began to interfere in Europe on the anti-French side. Louis XIV appreciated England's limited importance and, after the events of 1670–74, he neither valued her as an ally nor feared her as a foe. He merely felt it necessary to distribute money to Charles and to the King's opponents to neutralise her.

The withdrawal of England from the Dutch War in 1674 was not therefore a serious blow to Louis, but his position had become difficult because of the way the formation of the coalition around the Dutch had extended the scale of the war. He was also for the first time having to experience the problems of expenses outrunning his income, while the work of economic reconstruction carried out by Colbert was now in ruins. Moreover, in 1674 and 1675 he had to face serious peasant revolts. None the less, despite these problems, Louis was still finding less difficulty than his enemies in fielding troops, and his armies were proving almost as successful as before. However, what is remarkable in the warfare of this time, given the superiority of French arms, was Louis's lack of tangible territorial success. In part this came from a failure to concentrate on one front in campaigns which had spread to Catalonia and Sicily as well as the Southern Netherlands and Rhineland. But it also came from the rather cautious warfare Louis's armies were waging. Under the increasing influence of the young Louvois, but probably just as much from his own inclinations, Louis was beginning to depend more on a sluggish strategy based on manoeuvres and sieges. It was through Louvois's influence and that of his protégé Vauban that Louis began see the value of territorial gains which could be fortified and turned into impregnable frontiers of iron and stone. Attacks by the Emperor's forces in Alsace in the mid-1670s brought home to Louis that his eastern borders were as vulnerable to enemies as the northern ones.

France's inherent military and economic strength was beginning to tell in the war by 1677. Her enemies had shown themselves far less capable of bearing the strains of a long struggle and their coalition was also beginning to break up. Spain, who had optimistically hoped to push France back to the borders of 1659, had made a negligible military contribution. The Emperor Leopold had made a serious effort to pursue what became known as his 'German mission', to revise the peace of Westphalia in the Empire's favour over Alsace and Lorraine. But Austria's finances were in disarray and Leopold had to fight while continually looking over his shoulder at the situation in Hungary and on his borders with the Turks (see pp. 70–73). Although the German states had shared the Emperor's aims, they soon lost their enthusiasm for the war, especially those princes in the Rhineland who had to bear the brunt of the fighting. In the Dutch Republic, as early as 1674, the merchant oligarchs, including those who had supported William of Orange, had become alarmed at the cost of the war and at the inroads neutrals, such as England, were making at their expense in European markets. Once the immediate threat from France's army had gone, they lost their interest in the war and had none in the objectives of their allies. Especially in the province of Holland and in the main city of Amsterdam there were increasing demands for the end of the war, the restoration of good relations with France and the reconstruction of Dutch trade. It was largely through the personal efforts of William of Orange, who recognised the danger France posed to all the allies, that the unstable anti-French coalition was kept together for so long.

THE PEACE OF NYMEGEN, 1678–1679

There had been spasmodic negotiations for peace since the second year of the war. This pattern of almost continuous negotiating during hostilities was to be the usual one in the seventeenth and eighteenth centuries: such talks were not often meant seriously, but gave the combatants the chance to gain information and divide their enemies. By 1676, however, both sides were exhausted enough to be willing to consider a negotiated settlement. Peace talks opened under English mediation at Nymegen (Nijmegen) in the Dutch Republic in September 1676. The congress included all the belligerents, and, although procedural difficulties delayed proper discussions till the following spring, it was now taken for granted that Protestant and Catholic powers should negotiate in the same place. Louis XIV had significant advantages. His armies had been increasingly successful in the final years of the war and he had total control of his own policy-making, whereas his opponents had grown more and more dissatisfied with one another's contributions to the war. The French King's tactics at the congress were to exploit his enemies' differences and to win the Dutch over to a separate peace, which would benefit them at the expense of the Austrian and Spanish Habsburgs. William of Orange did his best to counter Louis and to keep the allies together. His hand was strengthened by his marriage in November 1677 to Mary, the daughter of James, Duke of York, the brother and heir of Charles II of England, and by signs early in 1678 that England might re-enter the war, this time against France. But this was not enough to halt the growing pressure in the Republic for peace. Consequently, the long negotiations eventually produced a separate Franco-Dutch peace, signed on 10 August 1678. The resulting withdrawal of Dutch subsidies and the threat of the full weight of France's armies falling on them in 1679 made it impossible for Spain and the Emperor to continue fighting. They were forced to make peace on 17 September 1678 and 5 February 1679 respectively. The three separate treaties are known collectively as the peace of Nymegen.

The Dutch and French made peace on the basis of the territorial status quo, but Louis also greatly relaxed French commercial tariffs, thus abandoning Colbert's plans to ruin Dutch trade and his own less specific ones to destroy the Republic itself. The peace was therefore a considerable victory for the Dutch. From now on, however, the Dutch would inevitably be as concerned with their own security as with their trade. Although Louis seems to have harboured no more plans to annihilate them and many in the Republic wanted to repair their relations with him, the shock of 1672 was in the event to prove too traumatic. The French King could hardly be trusted not to do the same again and the Dutch Stadtholder, William of Orange, was convinced that Louis was a permanent menace to the Republic's independence. The most immediate problem seemed to be containing future French expansion from the south, and this had not been solved at Nymegen. William's answer was to try to promote a permanent coalition of those powers threatened by France and to build a physical barrier in the Spanish Netherlands of fortresses manned by troops under Dutch control. But such a barrier was not a part of Nymegen and the European coalition had disintegrated under the impact of the separate Dutch peace. None the less the Dutch were to be the potential leaders of any future coalition.

The real victim at Nymegen was Spain. Besides surrendering Haiti in the Caribbean, she finally had to cede Franche-Comté to France. This cession broke up the Burgundian Circle around France, gave Louis XIV possession of yet another of the 'gates' to his kingdom, and reinforced his control of Alsace. Louis's gains in the Spanish Netherlands were more modest, largely because of the resistance of the Dutch in the peace negotiations. Here France mainly exchanged fortresses with Spain to produce a more defensible frontier. Under Vauban's influence Louis was accepting the idea of a barrier of his own along his northern borders with the Southern Netherlands, one which would make further territorial advance northwards less important. He also seems to have accepted that further gains there, at least for the moment, were impossible because of Dutch resistance.

Louis's interest in further territorial gain was in fact shifting away from the north towards his eastern borders: the Dutch War had brought home to him how vulnerable these were. At Nymegen he firmly resisted Leopold I's attempts to reverse the Westphalian settlement and maintained his grip on the French parts of Alsace. He was also only willing to return Lorraine on terms which would have robbed the Duke of his capital and fortresses. The new Duke, Charles V, preferred to stay in exile, and Lorraine therefore remained in French hands. Although Louis added to this by keeping control of Freiburg, which gave him access to the Danube valley, the settlement in the Rhineland was not very satisfactory to him: he was determined to redraw his borders there in the near future.

Louis and his contemporaries considered Nymegen a French triumph, a peace which he had been able to dictate to his enemies. Although his territorial gains had not been large, he had made the choice himself to show moderation to achieve an agreement which effectively broke up the enemy coalition. There seemed little likelihood that the coalition would be renewed, at least in the immediate future, and by the end of the war France had demonstrated her clear military superiority. Louis had proved capable of taking on all the European powers and forcing them to peace. France's ascendancy was never more apparent, and it was immediately affirmed in 1679 when France imposed a diplomatic settlement on northern Europe. At the treaties of St Germain and Fontainebleau, Brandenburg-Prussia and

Denmark were forced to return the territories they had seized from France's Swedish ally in the recent war. The Swedish–Brandenburg settlement, which ceded an insignificant part of Swedish Pomerania to the Great Elector, was imposed under the threat of an occupation of his Rhineland territories by France. He was willing enough not only to avoid this but also to accept a French pension, in effect becoming a French satellite. Sweden herself appeared just as much a satellite because she was not even consulted over the peace settlement. A few weeks after signing the treaty of St Germain in June 1679, the Great Elector summed up the general view of the diplomatic situation, when he wrote that 'France has already become the arbiter of Europe..., henceforth no prince will find security or profit except with the friendship and alliance of the King of France'.

'THE ARBITER OF EUROPE', 1679–1688

In the years after the peace of Nymegen Louis XIV was no longer willing to pursue an adventurist, open-ended war policy as in 1672. Instead he relied on France's clear military superiority and her predominance in the European states system to achieve specific strategic objectives around France's borders. The arrogance and insistence on powers' accepting French supremacy still remained, becoming in many ways more intense with the establishment of Louis's court at Versailles from 1682 and the growing cult of the 'Sun King'. But Louis now used threats rather than open war. These threats were combined with short terroristic campaigns to intimidate his neighbours into submission. This policy fitted in well with the views of Louis's ministers, the bullying Louvois, who effectively acted as war minister, and the prickly and overbearing Colbert de Croissy, the brother of Colbert and foreign minister from 1679. The tactics were to succeed in the 1680s and could even have achieved more than they did, because of the military weakness of the other powers, their failure to combine and the involvement of the Emperor and the German princes in a struggle with the Turks (see pp. 71ff.).

Louis's military superiority was even more apparent after the Dutch War. He was to keep 200,000 troops under arms for most of the following decade, beginning the practice adopted by most European powers throughout the eighteenth century of maintaining standing armies in peacetime. At the same time the fortifications expert Vauban worked on his construction of an impregnable linear fortress system round France. This consisted of two lines of fortresses, positioned like armies on the battlefield, and was designed to keep France's enemies out, while allowing her access to their lands. Vauban was already well advanced in building this 'iron barrier' in the north, but the last war had shown the vulnerability of France's eastern border. Here the Germans were now considered her 'true enemies' rather than the Spaniards to the north. To construct a proper fortress system along the eastern frontiers France needed to acquire more land from her neighbours. Because of its defensive nature this approach of Louis meant that further territorial expansion would be limited, but it also meant that he would be very determined to have the territory judged necessary for this impregnable barrier.

During 1679 and 1680 Colbert de Croissy and Louvois began adopting very dubious legal methods to acquire the land wanted. Special courts, called chambers of reunion, were set up to judge what were the dependencies of the territories ceded to France since 1648 and to 'reunite' them. The bewildering confusion of feudal rights and relationships in these areas allowed Louis, through judgments in these courts, to claim more of the Spanish Netherlands, almost all Spanish Luxemburg, more of Lorraine, parts of the Saar valley, the duchy of Zweibrücken (which belonged to Charles XI of Sweden) and the rest of Alsace, but not Strasbourg. French troops seized most of these lands, and then, in September 1681, the Imperial free city of Strasbourg, which had not been claimed under the reunions' policy, was forced to accept Louis's sovereignty. It surrendered without a fight, when Louvois massed troops outside the city and threatened 'all would be burnt and put to the sword'. Strasbourg was vital to France because it controlled the bridge across the Rhine, which the Emperor's army had used to invade Alsace three times during the Dutch War.

The same day as Strasbourg fell (30 September 1681) Louis's troops entered Casale in northern Italy, which he had bought from the Duke of Mantua. This, together with the fortress of Pinerolo, which Louis already held, allowed France to pin down the duchy of Savoy, whose duke was effectively a French vassal, and to threaten the Spanish duchy of Milan. Two months later (November 1681) French troops began a siege of Luxemburg, the intention being to add it to what had already been seized in the Moselle valley, an important access route to and from north-eastern France.

All the lands taken under the reunion claims were important strategic points of entry and exit between France and her neighbours. All were immediately fortified by Vauban and incorporated into his fortress system. In taking them the French met with no resistance: the Spaniards and minor German states involved were all cowed by Louis's standing army and could only appeal to the Dutch and the Emperor Leopold for help. The Dutch Stadtholder, William of Orange, had been working since Nymegen to build a further coalition against Louis, and on the same day as the French entered Strasbourg and Casale he had signed a Dutch alliance with Charles XI of Sweden, who was angry over Zweibrücken. Further Dutch alliances followed with the Emperor (February 1682) and with Spain (May 1682), aimed at resisting France. But active opposition to Louis was out of the question. The Dutch burghers, especially in Amsterdam, wanted no further conflict with France and were fully aware of the weakness of both Spain and the Emperor.

Leopold and the Austrian court wanted to act: the fall of Strasbourg, which they considered the main 'door' into Germany, came as a profound shock. But effective resistance to France required the support of the major German princes, and this was not forthcoming. Six out of the eight electors – Mainz, Trier, Cologne, Saxony, Bavaria and Brandenburg-Prussia – were allied in some way to France, who had used a mixture of subsidies and military intimidation with telling effect. Louis's most loyal ally among these seemed to be the Elector of Brandenburg-Prussia, who was receiving a large subsidy and hoped to usurp Sweden's role as France's main ally in the north. The position of the French King was now so strong in Germany that he was beginning to believe he had enough support to ensure the election of a French candidate, possibly even himself, as emperor if Leopold died. Louis's aim at this time was to undermine and destroy the Emperor's power in Germany. Leopold's intervention in the last war had badly frightened Louis, and he looked on him as his most dangerous enemy.

Louis had little real need to fear Leopold, and there was also no immediate threat of a European coalition against France. Not only was the Emperor weak in Germany, but he was in grave danger himself along his Hungarian borders where a Turkish attack was imminent (see pp. 70–73) in 1681–82. The French King was doing his best to encourage the Turks and trying to persuade the pro-French King of Poland, John Sobieski, not to help Leopold. Although he was eventually unsuccessful with Sobieski, in spring 1683, as the Turkish army began its march on Vienna, Louis assured the Sultan that he had nothing to fear from France. It seems that Louis hoped to see Leopold totally destroyed by the Turks, so that France could lead the German princes in a crusade against the Ottoman Empire. This would have made the French King complete master of Germany and inevitably have led to his becoming emperor.

When the Turks besieged Vienna in summer 1683, Louis did nothing to help the Emperor. The city had to be saved by a Polish and German army under Sobieski and Duke Charles of Lorraine. Louis used the opportunity to renew the siege of Spanish Luxemburg (abandoned in 1682 when it had seemed that the Dutch might aid it) and to seize places claimed by the reunion judgments in the Southern Netherlands. The decisive defeat of the Turks before Vienna in September 1683 was therefore one for Louis himself. There was some consolation for him, however, in that Leopold could not immediately withdraw from this struggle in the east. In the coming months Louis's power reached new heights.

Encouraged by the relief of Vienna and believing the Emperor and the Dutch would now help them, the Spaniards foolishly declared war on France in autumn 1683 to try to save Luxemburg. Louis replied with a short, devastating campaign, which lasted till spring 1684. Towns in the Southern Netherlands were bombarded and Catalonia was invaded. By June 1684 Luxemburg had fallen to Vauban and the terrified Spaniards had collapsed. Although William of Orange had declared he 'would rather die than allow Luxemburg to be taken', the frightened Dutch burghers refused to help the Spaniards and urged them to make peace. There was by now a strong neutralist party in the Republic which wanted to renew the old friendship with France. The Spaniards had also received no aid from the Emperor: he had taken the momentous decision to pursue the war against the Turks and to compromise in the west for the time being. Charles II of Spain therefore had to ask Leopold to mediate for peace with Louis at Regensburg (Ratisbon) in August 1684.

The negotiations at Regensburg led to peace between France and Spain and to a temporary settlement in the German Empire, which let Leopold and the princes concentrate on the Balkans. If he had wanted to, Louis could easily have ruined the negotiations and begun a general war for extensive gains against Spain and in the Empire. But he no longer had the appetite for this kind of warfare and was satisfied to achieve limited objectives. He also intended to prevent the formation of a coalition against him, which the indefatigable William of Orange was still trying to build. Consequently, France agreed to a twenty-year truce with Spain and the Emperor, which allowed her to keep all her reunion gains as well as Strasbourg and Luxemburg. Louis, who was now at the peak of his power, hoped to make these acquisitions permanent by a definitive peace in the near future. But, for their part, the Emperor, Spain and William of Orange planned eventually to retake what had been won by Louis's military intimidation.

Louis had sound reasons to be satisfied with the truce of Regensburg: Vauban could now complete the eastern and northern defences of France undisturbed. Austria and the German princes, with Papal encouragement, were fully occupied in Hungary, where the struggle during 1684 and 1685 seemed as indecisive as in previous Turkish wars. In 1685 the Catholic James II came to the English throne (1685–88) and was expected to align himself with France. His son-in-law, William of Orange, was isolated and powerless, particularly because of the pro-French mood in Amsterdam. Yet, over the next few years, events were to move decisively in William's favour. In part this was Louis's own fault.

In October 1685, after years of increasing persecution, Louis revoked the edict of Nantes of 1598 and ended toleration for Protestants in France. About 200,000 French Protestants, or Huguenots, fled the country. The direct effect on France herself of the loss of so many merchants, industrialists, artisans, soldiers and sailors is still a matter for debate, but has possibly been exaggerated by historians: she was compensated somewhat by a similar, but smaller, influx of Scots and Irish Jacobites in the 1690s, when, for example, at least 12,000 Irish troops entered French service. Probably more important were the effects on France's relations with Europe and the economic advantages other states gained. The Catholic states, including the anti-French Pope Innocent XI, whom Louis had hoped to impress by his religious zeal, felt he could have displayed it more appropriately by helping Leopold against the Turks. The protestant powers were enraged, and an element of religious conflict now coloured their relations with France. The Huguenot refugees fled largely to England, the Dutch Republic and Brandenburg-Prussia, where their economic and military skills were welcomed and proved valuable. The Dutch alone are said to have acquired 9,000 sailors and 12,600 soldiers. The Huguenots also acted as skilled propagandists, especially in Holland, the centre of European printing, where they castigated Louis as a tyrant and the 'anti-Christ' and pursued a paper war against him for the rest of his reign. The flight of the Huguenots finally destroyed the pro-French group in the Dutch Republic, mainly because of religious sympathy for them but also because Huguenot merchants had often acted as Dutch commercial agents in France. William of Orange's popularity rose to the level it had been a decade before. His hostility to France was accepted as the right course, and he was allowed to build up the army and navy. In England, although James II had permitted the Huguenots to settle, there was increased suspicion of Catholicism and of James's own intentions. In Brandenburg-Prussia the horrified Calvinist Elector Frederick William resisted the attraction of Louis's subsidies and allied with the Dutch in 1685. The Great Elector's son, Frederick, who succeeded in 1688, was to prove William of Orange's most loyal ally against France. Brandenburg's Baltic rival, Sweden, was similarly shocked by the French action, and for most of the 1680s and 1690s the Swedes were usually to be found in the anti-French camp.

The persecution of the Huguenots, although it helped create widespread hostility to Louis among Protestant states, did not in itself, however, lead to the coalition against France that William wanted. To be effective a coalition would have to have the support of both the Emperor and the majority of the German states. William's aim was to unite the economic and naval strength of the Dutch with the manpower of Austria and Germany, and he continually hoped, without any success, that the Emperor would end his war in Hungary and turn to the west. However, in July 1686 the states of southern and western Germany, including Bavaria and the Palatinate, together with the Emperor, Spain and Sweden (in their capacity as princes with territory in the Empire) formed the League of Augsburg to defend the treaties of 1648, 1659, 1678/79 *and* 1684. At this stage they were not so much concerned to reverse Regensburg as to prevent Louis from extending his control further into the Rhineland. In 1685 a Neuburg prince, the father-in-law of Leopold himself, had succeeded to the Palatinate. Louis claimed part of the electorate for his sister-in-law, as she was a Palatine princess, although he did not intend at this stage to put her claims into effect. The League of Augsburg itself would hardly have deterred him, as it was a miserable affair without any real military strength. The German states and Leopold were fully occupied in Hungary.

The European situation was only to change decisively during 1686 and 1687, when Leopold's troops followed up the capture of Buda with a crushing victory over the Turks near Mohács. After this victory in 1687 the Turkish army revolted and Sultan Mehmed IV was deposed. For a year the Ottoman Empire was paralysed, and Leopold's forces were poised to take Belgrade and to penetrate deep into the Balkans. These remarkable, and unexpected, victories had a direct impact throughout Europe. The whole German Empire had contributed as much to the victories, as had Leopold as Austrian ruler, and they were looked on as a triumph for Germany itself. The Emperor's stock rose dramatically, and both Protestant and Catholic princes considered him a champion of Christendom, unlike Louis who had refused to help. Leopold's own past persecution of Hungarian Protestants was forgotten by their co-religionists in Germany, who only remembered Louis's recent attacks on the Huguenots. Almost overnight the French King's support in Germany disintegrated, and he was branded as the 'Christian Turk'. Saxony and Bavaria were now firmly in Leopold's camp, and the Bavarian Elector, Max Emmanuel, had married the Emperor's daughter in 1685 and was to act as his commander-in-chief in the siege of Belgrade (1688). Brandenburg-Prussia had deserted France over the Huguenot question. Even the Rhine electors were wavering, and the last straw for Louis appeared to be the mortal illness of the pro-French Elector of Cologne and Bishop of Liège, Maximilian Henry, early in 1688. At the French court it seemed it would be only a matter of time, possibly even months, before the Emperor turned from the Balkans to lead a comparatively united German Empire against France on the Rhine to try to reverse the Regensburg settlement.

While these developments were all too obvious to Louis XIV, there were other hidden, and potentially more dangerous, changes taking place. France was losing her overwhelming military supremacy: the Dutch and German states had all begun to copy the French model. Almost all the German princes were building their own professional armies, and through their experience in the Turkish War were to adopt innovations such as replacing the pike by the bayonet and using light cavalry, the hussars. Louvois was to resist the introduction of bayonets and he was also slow to begin the replacement of matchlock muskets by the more rapid-firing flintlock ones. None the less, the French military machine was to retain the edge until the end of the century. This was despite Louis's increasing financial problems. The days of surplus revenues were over long before Colbert died in 1683. Lavish spending on Versailles in the 1680s and heavy military expenditure, together with foreign subsidies, meant that Louis would have to fight wars on a hand-to-mouth basis.

By summer 1688 it was clear to the French King and his chief advisers, Louvois and Colbert de Croissy, that they had to act before they lost control of the situation completely in Germany and before a European coalition, built round the Emperor and the Dutch, struck first. The Turks had to be encouraged to continue fighting in the Balkans, so that Leopold could not attack along the Rhine and more time could be won for Vauban to finish his impregnable eastern border. The testing point seemed to be the question of Elector Maximilian Henry's successor in Cologne and Liège. His territories were of vital strategic importance, since they provided links for the Dutch with the Empire and with the Spanish Netherlands. When the Elector died in June 1688, Louis pressed for the French pensioner and Bishop of Strasbourg, William Egon von Fürstenberg, to succeed him. But an inconclusive election followed between him and the younger brother of Max Emmanuel of Bavaria, Joseph Clement, who was supported by the Emperor. An appeal to the Papacy led to Innocent XI's deciding for the Bavarian prince. His decision came at the end of August, a week before Max Emmanuel led Leopold's troops to the conquest of Belgrade. These two events put the seal on a decision which the French had already taken. On 24 September 1688 Louis XIV's troops poured into Cologne and crossed the Rhine to besiege Philippsburg, which was believed to be the key to both French Alsace and the electorate of the Palatinate. By these actions the French King was embarking on a struggle which would involve him in war with all western Europe. The three decades of French ascendancy were now to be challenged and the first effective checks put on Louis's expansion.

CHAPTER TWO

The rise of Britain, 1688–1714

THE NINE YEARS WAR, 1688–1697

Louis XIV's attack across the Rhine in autumn 1688 began the longest of his wars to date, the Nine Years War. But it also opened a quarter-century of almost continuous warfare in which the new power of France was at stake. This struggle was to become complicated in the later 1690s by the emergence of the Spanish succession as an urgent issue. In the event France survived these wars with her territory almost intact and even managed to place a Bourbon on the Spanish throne, but her European predominance was at an end. France's defeat was the work of a European coalition of the Maritime and German Powers. This coalition was to be increasingly led by Britain, and it is the rise of Britain as a great power which is the key development in these years.

Louis had never intended to begin a general war in September 1688. He had wanted a short campaign similar to that against the Spaniards in 1683–84, which would encourage the Turks to continue their war and frighten the Emperor and the German states into confirming the peace of Regensburg. The King also hoped to resolve the Cologne election and the Palatinate question in favour of Fürstenberg and of his German sister-in-law. Unlike in 1672, no major war had been planned, and Louvois had only prepared for a few months' campaigning. But Louis had seriously miscalculated. Although the attack certainly kept the Turks at war in the Balkans, its impact on Leopold and the Germans was the opposite of what had been intended. According to the English minister at Regensburg, the French campaign and the attempt at further intimidation and at making a defensive waste in front of Alsace by burning the Palatinate at the turn of 1688–89, 'so enraged the Germans...that the several states were never so united and animated to revenge them'. Already in October 1688, just after the initial attack, Brandenburg-Prussia, Saxony, Hanover and Hesse-Cassel had agreed to fight Louis, and Max Emmanuel of

Bavaria was ready to lead an army formed by the Emperor and the princes on the Rhine. Compromise was now impossible.

Although the Nine Years War was provoked by Louis's ambitions in the Rhineland, it became a much wider conflict because of the actions of the Dutch Stadtholder. Over the previous few years William of Orange had worked continuously to build an anti-French coalition, and in the process Dutch diplomacy had become almost a match for that of France. Yet his success had been limited, and it was Louis's own actions which eventually allowed William to form his coalition in 1689. William himself was to be a member of this as king of Great Britain because of his successful invasion of England in November 1688, an invasion which led to the deposition of James II and the Glorious Revolution of 1688–89.

William's decision to gamble on this invasion was probably only taken in summer 1688. His wife Mary was the elder daughter of the Catholic James II by his first wife, and she was his Protestant heir. William and Mary's court had inevitably become the refuge for opponents of James II's increasingly Catholicising and absolutist policies. Relations between England and the Dutch were hostile, but William had refused to act against James in case it damaged his wife's succession prospects. However, the pregnancy of James's second and Catholic wife and the birth of a male Catholic heir in June 1688 spurred William to action to secure Mary's succession and to prevent a close Anglo-French alliance, which both William and the Dutch oligarchs were convinced would soon be concluded. The Stadtholder was therefore given an almost free hand to use Dutch troops to invade England. He wanted to force England's growing naval and commercial power into the scales against France. In planning the invasion William not only had the support of Brandenburg-Prussia but the tacit approval of the Emperor and even the anti-French Pope Innocent XI in return for assurances that Catholics would be tolerated in Britain.

The invasion was a gamble because of what might happen once William reached England and because of Louis's attitude. France could probably have prevented it by landing her own troops and using her larger navy. In the event Louis did nothing to stop the invasion. He had offered James help, but the offer was rejected, for the English King had always tried not to be Louis XIV's dependant. Louis, however, expected James would be able to resist on his own and that this would lead to a civil war which would neutralise England and William himself. Moreover, in autumn 1688 Louis felt it was more important to act in the Rhineland against the German powers whom he considered his most dangerous enemies, especially as it seemed too late in the year for the Dutch to mount an invasion. By moving into the Rhineland in September 1688 Louis dispelled fears in the Republic of a possible attack, and William was able to use the Dutch fleet unhindered to land his forces at Torbay in November. James II's immediate humiliating collapse meant that William was in control of England by the year's end and that James was a refugee in France by the new year. In February 1689 William and his wife Mary became joint sovereigns in England and two months later in Scotland.* Their accession was accompanied by the triumph of parliamentary government.

William's success in Britain led rapidly to the formation of the durable European coalition he had wanted for so long. On 12 May 1689 the Dutch and Emperor Leopold signed the Grand Alliance which aimed at forcing France back to her borders of 1648/59. Leopold's signature was a decision to intervene in the west while continuing to fight in the Balkans, where the Turkish War was to last till 1699. He had committed himself to his 'German mission' in the Rhineland which would benefit the Empire as a whole, but he also insisted that the other allies should promise to support his claims to the Spanish succession if the childless Charles II died during the war. William and the new Grand Pensionary in Holland, Heinsius, brought the Dutch easily enough into the alliance. In Britain the new King effectively controlled foreign policy and he formally signed the Grand Alliance as William III in December 1689. Both Spain, which had been at war with France since April 1689, and Savoy joined the coalition in June 1690. The major German princes and Sweden were also to associate themselves with the Grand Alliance.

France was to fight the Nine Years War on her own, isolated except for the loose relationship with the Turks. She faced a fairly solid coalition of states who had all been bullied by Louis over the last two decades and who were to manage to stick together through this war and that of the Spanish Succession until the ascendancy of France was destroyed. The Nine Years War itself was to provide the first clear signs of a change in the European states system. Until the 1680s France was the only great power, but this war was to see the emergence of Britain, Austria and even the Dutch Republic as apparent great powers. As yet, however, they were hardly on a par individually with France. During this war they were to imitate Louis by adapting their economies to the demands of standing armies and prolonged warfare. Their success made the Nine Years War one of attrition, decided as much by the exhaustion of resources as by victory on the battlefield.

The Nine Years War not only saw the emergence of Britain as a great power but it also proved to be the first of that long series of Anglo-French wars which lasted till 1815 and have been called the 'Second Hundred Years War'. Economic as well as strategic factors were to assume an increasing role in this prolonged conflict. But in the 1690s the main issue was the survival of the Revolution settlement,

---

*The English and Scottish realms were not formally united till 1707, and the Irish realm was only united with them in 1800.

with its provisions for a Protestant succession to a constitutional monarchy, one which was dependent on a parliament controlled by the landed and commercial classes. Louis's protection of James after his flight to France meant that a French victory would probably have led to the imposition of a Catholic absolutist monarchy, which would inevitably have been a vassal of France. The war was therefore a struggle for Britain's constitution, religion and independence. During this struggle Britain built her navy to a level which assured her permanent naval predominance, as well as establishing a powerful army; she also underwent a revolution in her financial structure. The creation of the National Debt (1693) and the Bank of England (1694) gave her a modern financial system, the basis of her commercial and industrial supremacy in the next century. This new system was backed by parliament. During the Nine Years War the commercial and landed classes represented there managed to double the country's revenues by effectively taxing their own wealth for the first time. In the short term this allowed Britain to play a part in the struggle in her own right and to join the Dutch in subsidising their alliance partners. In the long-term these measures were to prove that the parliamentary system was far more capable of raising funds than the absolute monarchy in France. The reliable credit system which financed this and subsequent wars was supported by investors in government loans. These men were confident that they would be repaid and had an incentive to support the new order in Britain because a restored Stuart monarchy would be likely to refuse to honour these debts.

The Glorious Revolution also transformed Britain's foreign policy. The British now abandoned their old hostility to the Dutch (although suspicions remained) and accepted William's view of the threat of French hegemony. Britain was brought decisively on to the continental stage as a military power as well as a diplomatic and naval one. Until 1714, however, Britain's new role in Europe could not be separated from her link with the Republic, which was equally committed to maintaining the Revolution of 1688–89. This resulted partly from William III's dual role as British king and Dutch stadtholder, but the close relationship was to survive his death. During the 1690s the two Maritime Powers were to co-operate closely to try to destroy French naval and commercial power and to defend the Spanish Netherlands against France. Their commercial differences now seemed of far less importance: despite what the mercantilists thought, there was really enough trade in Europe and the world for both powers, and they also began to concentrate on different areas, the British dominating the North American and Caribbean trade, while in the Far East concentrating on India and leaving Indonesia to the Dutch.

Contemporaries, including William and Louis, hardly grasped the long-term importance of the Anglo-French struggle or even realised that Britain would emerge as a European power. Although British troops (almost as many as fielded by the Dutch) and money were used extensively on the Continent, British politicians and generals played little part in the actual direction of the Nine Years War. Only at sea was command given to English rather than Dutch admirals. William III kept tight personal control and leaned heavily on Dutch and Huguenot advisers and generals. The King had come to Britain essentially to use her power in the continental struggle against French expansion. What had begun as a determination to protect Dutch independence and was largely inspired by personal hatred of Louis became almost a crusade to protect Europe as a whole from what he saw as the danger of French hegemony. The King and his advisers spoke of defending the 'liberty of all Europe' and of the 'European commonweal', but his most immediate aims during the war remained the defence of Dutch security and his new position in Britain. He did not share the belief held by some in both countries that the war was one of constitutionalism against absolutism. Although he had more sympathy with the corresponding view that it was a religious struggle against Louis, this could hardly be said openly when William was allied with Catholic Spain and Austria.

William had great difficulty in persuading his alliance partners to see the overall significance of the struggle. It was not easy to keep the coalition itself together or to agree on a general strategy. There was initial agreement that Louis XIV should be forced back to the territory France held in 1659. This meant for the Emperor Leopold and the German princes the reconquest of Lorraine, Strasbourg, parts of Alsace and some fortresses on the Rhine. Leopold was taking his role as emperor very seriously and his power in the Empire had increased dramatically since his election because of the prestige won during the Turkish War and because of Louis XIV's mistakes. The princes, most of whom now had standing armies of their own, showed an unusual willingness to co-operate in the war against Louis and to accept Leopold's leadership. But they had no intention of sacrificing their independence. Their co-operation would last only as long as they felt the danger from France was more important than their private interests. The most self-sacrificing of the princes was Frederick of Brandenburg-Prussia (1688–1713) who provided substantial military help and shelved his demands for Swedish Pomerania since the Swedes were members of the alliance. The Emperor's own private interest in the Spanish succession had not as yet assumed primary importance. For the present the Rhineland seemed far more important. Here Leopold was acting for the whole Empire rather than just for his own dynasty or Austrian hereditary lands, and in doing so he could count on the support of the Empire. However, he was determined that if Charles II of Spain should die he would assert his rights to the succession.

The fighting in the Nine Years War was so widespread that it has been called, without much justification, the 'first world war'. This was because of minor colonial conflict between British and French settlers in North America and the occasional scrap in the Caribbean and along the coasts of India. The war was essentially fought out in western Europe around the borders of France. The continuing struggle between Leopold, with Polish, Russian and Venetian allies and the Turks (see pp. 74–76) can be considered to some extent linked to it because of French encouragement of the Porte.★

The one area where a decisive result was reached was in the British Isles, where the new regime had inevitably been weak. By the end of 1689 William was in complete control of England and Scotland, but Ireland was in revolt and James II was able to land there in March 1690 with French troops. James's decisive defeat at the Boyne (July) and his subsequent flight led to the pacification of Ireland and the restoration of the Protestant ascendancy. Nevertheless, there was always to be the threat of a Jacobite rising in England or Scotland till the mid eighteenth century, and this was to be a lever available to both Louis XIV and his successor. The real danger to the new order in Britain, however, had come not so much from supporters of the Stuarts at home as from the threat of a direct French invasion. At the beginning of the war the French navy, built by Colbert and his son, Seignelay, was larger than that of either Britain or the Dutch. In June 1690 the French fleet defeated an Anglo-Dutch one off Beachy Head and won temporary command of the Channel. But Louis had not initially prepared for an invasion, largely because he had considered the struggle with Britain less important than that on the Continent. Two years later, when an invasion force was ready, the French fleet was defeated by an Anglo-Dutch one at La Hogue (May 1692) and no crossing could be made.

La Hogue not only spelt the end of serious invasion attempts but also of France's Atlantic navy. The French fleet was now starved of funds, especially as there was no one after Seignelay's death in 1690 to press its claims. French naval power in the western Mediterranean was also checked by the Anglo-Dutch fleets sent in 1693–94 to help the allied war effort in Italy and Spain. Britain's feverish naval building completed this destruction of French naval power. With her fleets largely confined to port, France now switched to a privateering war against Anglo-Dutch shipping. This caused serious damage to the commerce of both powers, but especially to the British who lost 4,000 ships. The Anglo-Dutch response was a blockade of French ports, though this was not very effective. It also proved impossible for the British to use their navy in an offensive way in Europe or even against French possessions overseas. Louis XIV could only be defeated on the Continent, as William III and later Marlborough realised, and this needed a British commitment of men and money.

★The 'Porte' or 'Sublime Porte' was the contemporary term for the Turkish court.

The most important fighting of the Nine Years War took place round France's borders and was to prove a largely indecisive conflict of sieges and manoeuvres. Unlike in Louis's previous wars he was now on the defensive: he had not prepared for an expansionist war himself and was already holding the territory in dispute. The allies largely failed to destroy the French fortifications barrier in Flanders, the Rhineland and the Alps. The greater part of the forces involved on both sides was engaged along the Spanish Netherlands and French Flanders border. Here the Dutch, with considerable British and a little Spanish help, concentrated their war effort and made it a far more dangerous area for Louis than it had been in the 1670s. The French King none the less had the better of the battles there, at Fleurus (1690) Steenkerk (1692) and Neerwinden (1693) but failed to follow them up. Louis had no more success than William in breaking through the enemy fortresses or overcoming the defensive military tactics employed by both sides. Along the Rhine, where the German princes provided the bulk of the troops under the Emperor's command, the campaigns proved no more decisive. The one area where the allies had great hopes, as the British envoy put it, of forcing a 'door…into France, big enough…for us to get in at, and enter the strong man's house', was Italy. In 1690 the Duke of Savoy, Victor Amadeus II, joined the Grand Alliance in an attempt to emancipate himself from a long period of French military occupation. He was, however, a very untrustworthy ally. Throughout his long reign (1675–1730) he was to shift from one alliance to another to extend his territory and to preserve his independence not only from the French but also the Spaniards, and later the Austrians, in Milan. The war in northern Italy, where Austrian and Spanish troops helped Savoy, in the event was also to be indecisive, but it renewed European interest in the peninsula and this was to last till 1748. The only decisive campaigns of the Nine Years War took place in northern Spain. Here French troops had invaded Catalonia at the beginning of the war and by 1697 had captured Barcelona. There were tangible military victories and territorial gains here because of the inability of the Spaniards to offer more than token resistance and the failure of the allies to provide enough help.

The war was indecisive because the two sides were almost equally balanced and because Louis XIV was determined to fight a defensive war, turning France into a fortress where internal lines of communication allowed him to move troops as needed. Now in his fifties, Louis had grown even more cautious with age. His military thinking, which in the 1660s and 1670s had been prepared to countenance the more fluid campaigning of Turenne and Condé, was now fixed on the linear frontier concept of Vauban. After the death of Louvois in 1691 the King took over the direction of the war and after 1693 no longer accompanied the armies on campaign. Instead he tried to keep a tight rein over his forces from Versailles and was very reluctant for his commanders to fight a battle unless victory was certain. He was to become even more cautious from 1694, because he realised that the allied armies were numerically nearly the equal of France – both sides were fielding more than a quarter of a million men. Louis was becoming concerned that French armies no longer enjoyed supremacy and this was particularly clear in the Southern Netherlands where William III, despite his poor generalship, had shown himself to be a very good organiser and disciplinarian, producing a Dutch infantry which was the best in Europe. What the allies lacked, however, were generals with sufficient imagination to break free of Louis's static defensive warfare. Louis also had to take account of the terrible harvest of 1693 which produced wide-scale famine and deaths. The country was far less capable of bearing the ever-increasing burden of taxation and recruitment.

THE PEACE OF RYSWICK, 1697

By 1693 Louis XIV realised that the allies' military effort was not going to collapse, and William had also concluded that a total victory was impossible. Both rulers wanted peace, but as yet both were determined to hold out for their own terms. France was engaged in peace negotiations, usually held in secret, with one or more of the allies every year from 1692, in an attempt to try to break up the coalition. There was no shortage of tension between the allies, and this increased as the war went on. The Maritime Powers, in particular, resented Leopold's refusal to end his Turkish War, and they felt they were bearing a disproportionate burden of the war in the west. They certainly had grounds for complaint with Leopold, who showed a good deal of personal inertia and incompetence in pursuing the war.

Louis had failed in these initial negotiations to break up the coalition because he was not prepared to disgorge his earlier gains, at least those made in the 1680s. The negotiations with the Maritime Powers were also continually bedevilled by Louis's loyalty to James II and to the principle of the divine right of kings. He consistently refused to recognise William III as British king. William himself was intensely suspicious of Louis and his supposed designs for universal monarchy. Consequently, it was not till 1696 that Louis achieved his first breakthrough, when, after lengthy secret talks, Victor Amadeus II of Savoy made peace (treaty of Turin). Louis had to agree to substantial concessions, surrendering Nice and the fortress of Pinerolo to Savoy and undertaking to abandon the fortress of Casale. This confirmed the Duke's escape from French control and began Savoy's territorial expansion. The peace immediately undermined the position of the troops of Victor Amadeus's Austrian and Spanish allies and opened Spanish Milan to French invasion. The two powers therefore made an armistice with Louis which only applied to northern Italy. This allowed France to transfer 30,000 men to help her hard-pressed forces in Flanders and the Spanish Netherlands.

William III, with some justification, was upset by what he called a 'villainous' step by his allies: he felt he had to end the war with France before his own position in the Spanish Netherlands collapsed. There was, in any case, considerable pressure from politicians in Britain and the Republic for peace. Rather surprisingly, the Dutch cities, including Amsterdam, had felt the threat from Louis XIV was serious enough for them to put up with the heavy indirect taxation necessary to support a Dutch army of 90,000 men. But the continual disruption of trade was now undermining their earlier resolve. English commercial interests were probably suffering more from the war than the Dutch, although those in both countries involved in finance and in supplying the armies had benefited. It was also difficult for the public and politicians in the Republic and Britain to share William's broader concept of the French danger once the immediate threat to their security was over. There had been bitter complaints in the English parliament from the Tory squires, who paid the land tax, against William's expensive and apparently unsuccessful continental strategy of coalitions and large-scale warfare round France's borders.

At the end of the 1696 campaigning season William III was determined on peace whatever his allies said. Louis himself was equally willing. The economic and financial exhaustion experienced by the Maritime Powers was also being felt by France. By 1697 Louis was ready at last to swallow his pride about recognising William III. This was one aspect of an increasingly moderate tone in the French King's diplomacy in the last years of the war. The threatening attitude of the first years was abandoned. This probably was partly caused by the deaths of Louvois in 1691 and Colbert de Croissy in 1696 and the growing influence of Pomponne, who became foreign secretary in 1696.★ Above all Louis believed that more could be gained from peace than from continuing the war. He was becoming convinced that the chronic invalid Charles II of Spain was near to death and he felt it essential to break up the coalition before this happened. France would have far less chance of gaining from the Spanish succession if she were still at war with Spain and if Austria's allies were still committed, as they were during the war, to support Leopold's claims. Peace was essential to concentrate on the dynastic and diplomatic battle ahead.

A peace congress opened in May 1697 at William's palace at Ryswick (Rijswijk) near The Hague, with the Swedes as the official

---

★He had been foreign secretary during the Dutch War and had been sacked afterwards, possibly because of Louis's dissatisfaction with the peace negotiations.

mediators. They in fact played little part in it and the real talks took place between William's adviser, Portland, and Louis's general, Boufflers, who found it easier to come to a settlement privately than in a large conference. This was especially the case because Leopold's representatives were determined to prevent peace so that his allies would remain committed to support his own claims to the Spanish succession. William III himself had no intention of continuing the war, or pressing in the negotiations, for Leopold's wishes in the Rhineland or over the Spanish succession. William had no way of knowing at this stage that a Bourbon candidate would eventually be given the whole succession, and it seemed more important for Dutch and British security in 1697 to obtain Louis's recognition of the 1688 Revolution than to continue the war to further Leopold's claims.

Once William and Louis's representatives had hammered out a settlement, William's Spanish and Austrian allies had to accept its terms. Leopold, despite much huffing and bluffing, could not face the prospect of fighting France on his own, especially as he was still at war with the Turks and the German princes were clamouring for peace. The peace of Ryswick was therefore signed by the Maritime Powers and Spain with France on 20 September 1697 and by the Emperor Leopold a month later.

By the peace terms Louis recognised William III as British king, although he refused to expel James II from France. He retained the whole of Alsace and Strasbourg, but he returned other areas seized under the reunion claims as well as places captured during the war on the Rhine. Lorraine was returned to its duke, though France retained enough of it to ensure effective military control. Finally Louis gave way over the Palatinate and Cologne issues. Where Louis had made the most important concessions over the reunion claims was in returning places in the Southern Netherlands and Luxemburg to Spain. As he also evacuated Catalonia, despite the military disasters Spain had suffered, culminating in the capture of Barcelona, it was clear that Louis wanted to curry favour in Madrid because of the Spanish succession question.

The peace itself was very unpopular in France, where it was difficult to understand why territory had been returned when France had not suffered military defeat. The peace was certainly a defeat in comparison with the high point of French power before the war. The recent surrender of Casale and Pinerolo seemed to indicate a withdrawal from forward positons in Italy, while French influence in Germany was still at a low point. During the war Louis had also seen the collapse of France's traditional association with the northern and eastern powers: Sweden had sided with the allies, the Turks had been defeated in the Balkans and the equivocal Polish King John Sobieski had died in 1696 to be followed by the election of the Austrian and Russian candidate, Augustus of Saxony. On the other hand Louis had retained the essential gains on his eastern frontier, while the need for peace to concentrate on the higher stakes in the offing over the Spanish succession counted for most with him.

On the allied side the Emperor Leopold was disgruntled with the settlement, although Austria's own direct contribution to the war had been small compared with that of the German princes. Neither Leopold nor the princes had achieved their aim of forcing France back to the Westphalian borders, and Louis had managed to keep Strasbourg. Yet the King's more extensive ambitions in the Rhineland had been thwarted, and Austria herself was to gain dramatically in the east at the peace with the Turks in 1699 (see p. 76). These gains would greatly strengthen her overall position in the future. Leopold's increased influence in the German Empire had also been maintained.

The real allied victor was William III, although he was depressed about what the future held. Through the war and his coalition he had set definite limits to French power. Although, as William realised, Louis had not been defeated in battle and the ultimate threat of French ascendancy remained, it is already possible to see the development of a division of power in Europe rather than the preponderance of one state. Above all William had managed to keep his new throne and maintain the Revolution settlement in Britain. Although Louis's continuing to shelter James II was ominous, he had to swallow the bitter pill of accepting publicly Protestantism and constitutional monarchy. The war had also allowed the new order in London to destroy militant Jacobitism and also to bring Scotland and Ireland under more direct control. French naval power had been crushed and the English navy, with the Dutch now trailing behind, had effectively asserted its supremacy. Britain herself had now emerged as a power in her own right on the European stage. As to the Dutch Republic, William had continued to put the protection of its security as his main military priority in the campaigns in the Spanish Netherlands and had managed to persuade some British politicians, especially the Whigs of its importance. However, it was clear during the war that a way had to be found to turn the Spanish Netherlands into a permanent buffer. Therefore in 1698 the Republic and the Spaniards were to agree to the Dutch garrisoning some fortresses there in peacetime as well as war. From then on the main focus of Dutch foreign policy was to become the desire to maintain and extend these barrier fortresses.

There was little chance that Ryswick would become a permanent settlement, despite the exhaustion of the combatants. The peace had not resolved the vital issue of the Spanish succession, while neither the French nor the Grand Alliance partners considered the agreements over the areas around France's borders as more than interim ones. It says much for the resilience of the economies of the European states that within four years of the peace they could embark on an even fiercer and longer war.

THE WAR OF THE SPANISH SUCCESSION: FROM DIPLOMACY TO WAR, 1697–1702

In the late 1690s Charles II of Spain's declining health brought to a head the problem of his succession which had vexed Europe since his accession in 1665 (see p. 22). A physical and mental cripple, Charles had no children of his own and was the last male Spanish Habsburg. Who succeeded him was of importance to Europe as a whole because of the size of his empire, which was still vast despite the cessions to France over the previous forty years and the final loss of Portugal in 1668. The Spanish empire stretched round the globe from the Philippines in the east to Caribbean islands and Central and South America in the west. In Europe the Balearic Islands, Sardinia and Sicily were stepping-stones across the Mediterranean to Naples and Milan in Italy, while in the north-west of the Continent the Southern Netherlands and Luxemburg were still Spanish possessions. Under Charles II Spain had continued her fall from the major power of the early seventeenth century to a second-class power and the principal victim of French aggression. Important towns in the Southern Netherlands and all Franche-Comté had been lost to Louis XIV, and it was only through the military support of her allies in the Nine Years War that more of the Southern Netherlands and Luxemburg had not been seized. The agreement in 1698 allowing the Dutch to garrison fortresses in the Southern Netherlands had been the final recognition of Spain's military helplessness. A similar decline was visible overseas: Spanish trade with the New World and imports of bullion had fallen substantially, and both English and Dutch merchants were making increasing and illicit inroads into Spanish America.

Despite the obvious and steady collapse of Spanish power, the ruling officials and grandees in Madrid were determined to hold their empire together and to prevent a final partition. Unfortunately, it was not merely a question of replacing one king by another. Throughout Charles II's reign the nearest claimants were already rulers of the leading European states of France and Austria. Louis XIV was the son and husband of Spanish infantas, while Leopold was the son and husband of their younger sisters. Louis claimed the Spanish throne for his children rather than for himself, whereas Leopold claimed it for himself in the first instance. Which of them had the better legal claim is not really important: both men were convinced of their rights and were determined to accomplish them by force, while the Spaniards themselves were less concerned about legality than which candidate could preserve Spain intact.

In the two years after Ryswick serious efforts were made by Louis XIV and William III to solve the Spanish succession problem by negotiation. Neither ruler wanted another war, and Louis recognised that William had to be involved. The size of the Spanish empire, and the interest of the Maritime Powers in it, meant that Louis could not treat the problem as a mere dynastic issue, and he saw the need to make substantial concessions to achieve a peaceful settlement. William was prepared for a diplomatic settlement because his own position was weak: both in the Republic and in London political criticism of the heavy expenditure during the Nine Years War had forced him to reduce his armed forces considerably. Consequently, Louis and William tried to agree on a partition which they could then present to Madrid and Vienna for their acceptance.

William was anxious to prevent Spain's passing directly to France or even to Austria: this would create a monstrous accumulation of power under one ruler. He was also determined to exclude France or a Bourbon prince from the strategically vital Southern Netherlands and from Spain herself: French traders could be expected to gain advantages in Old and New Spain at the expense of those of the Maritime Powers. But the initial attempt at a settlement, the First Partition treaty of 1698, was ruined when the compromise candidate, the young Electoral Prince of Bavaria, Joseph Ferdinand,* died in February 1699. William and Louis therefore drew up the Second Partition treaty in June 1699. By this the Emperor Leopold's younger son, the Archduke Charles, who was not the direct heir to Austria, was to have Spain, the overseas empire and the Southern Netherlands, while Louis's immediate heir, the Dauphin Louis, was to have the Italian lands. With William's approval, Louis XIV began negotiations with the dukes of Lorraine and Savoy to exchange Milan and Naples for their duchies. These would be added to France and be of immediate benefit in strengthening her frontiers.

This partition treaty stood no chance of acceptance in Austria or Spain. Although Leopold I always insisted that he was claiming the Spanish succession for himself and that it was up to him what he did with it, he seems to have realised that it was pointless trying to re-create the vast empire which had existed under Charles V in the early sixteenth century. His intention was that his elder son, Joseph, should have Austria and become emperor, while his younger son, christened Charles appropriately enough, should have the Spanish lands. But if this did not prove possible, Leopold was determined that one of his sons, preferably the elder, should have the Spanish possessions in Italy. Expansion in Italy had been a constant aim of the Viennese court in the 1690s and they had tried to insist that several of the Italian states,

*Joseph Ferdinand, the 'Bavarian Baby', was the son of Elector Max Emmanuel of Bavaria and Maria Antonia, the daughter of Leopold I. Maria Antonia was Leopold's only daughter by his Spanish first wife. Leopold's two sons, Joseph and Charles, were by his German third wife. Their claims to the Spanish throne, therefore, came through Leopold himself.

including Milan, were Imperial fiefs. However, Leopold I did not have the energy nor his ministers the diplomatic expertise to bring about an acceptable negotiated solution. The Emperor left the initiative to others, complaining all the time that no one consulted him but showing no signs of wanting to compromise. His massive gains from the Turks by the peace of Karlowitz in 1699 (see pp. 76–7) made him more confident and obstinate, and he was also convinced that his Spanish relative would designate the Austrian Habsburgs the sole heir. Consequently, he refused to consider the Second Partition treaty. Moreover, the terms were unacceptable. This was not only because Leopold's direct heir, Joseph, was to get nothing unlike Louis's heir, but also because the lands assigned to the Archduke Charles were not what Vienna wanted. For, as one of Leopold's ministers declared in August 1699, what they wanted was 'Milan, Naples and Sicily; the rest can be taken by whoever wants it'. With no navy and few commercial interests, Spain and its world empire held fewer attractions for the Austrians than Italy.

The Second Partition treaty produced an equally hostile reaction in Madrid, where the Spanish court was determined to prevent partition. Just before Charles II died (November 1700), therefore, he was persuaded to make a will, leaving the whole monarchy to Philip of Anjou, the younger grandson of Louis XIV. If he rejected his inheritance, it was then to be offered to the Archduke Charles. By insisting that Anjou should also renounce his claims to the French throne, the Spaniards intended to keep Spain separate from France but hoped to use the power of France, the strongest European state, to effect the plan. Louis XIV quickly accepted the will for his grandson, although France herself would gain no territory. Philip's succession would advance the interests of the Bourbon family and France herself would benefit from a French prince south of the Pyrenees: the Spanish Netherlands and Spanish Italy would provide a friendly buffer zone around France, which could also expect commercial privileges in Spain and overseas. But Louis had no real choice, since the Spaniards had trapped him by the way they had framed the will: refusal would mean that the whole inheritance passed to the Austrian archduke. Standing by the Second Partition treaty was impracticable, because Louis knew that William III would not support him in a war to impose partition on both Spain and Austria.

The Viennese reaction to the will and the succession of Anjou to the Spanish throne as Philip V (1700–46) was predictable enough: Leopold rejected both, and in 1701 sent an expedition to seize the Spanish lands in Italy. Although he could not match French might, he counted on the Maritime Powers joining the war to support him against France, and his hopes were not to be disappointed. William III had concluded from the start that Philip V would be nothing but a French puppet and he had wanted to form a new coalition between the Maritime Powers and Austria to enforce a partition of Spain. The domestic politicians in both England and the Dutch Republic had disagreed at first and were prepared to trust Philip, believing he would become a good Spaniard. If Louis had persuaded Spain to buy off the Maritime Powers by territorial or commercial concessions, he could have maintained their goodwill and desire for peace. But to do so would have weakened Philip's position in Madrid at the beginning of his reign, and in fact Louis made a series of blunders which seemed to confirm William's predictions. French troops and advisers accompanied Philip to Madrid, French troops took possession of the Southern Netherlands for him, and the Dutch were forced to evacuate their barrier fortresses there. Almost immediately Philip granted concessions to French traders in Spain and gave a French company the *Asiento* contract to transport slaves from Africa to the New World. This raised fears in the Maritime Powers that France would supplant them in their legitimate trade with Spain and their sizeable illicit trade with Spanish America. Louis also made the serious mistake of maintaining Anjou's rights to the French throne. Although he probably intended that if Philip eventually succeeded to France one of Anjou's relatives should have Spain, Louis did not explain this and merely revived the spectre of a union of the two crowns. Louis's final error, which completed the disillusionment of both Maritime Powers and broke his promise at Ryswick, was to recognise James II's son, the 'Old Pretender', as King James III at the death of the exiled Stuart in September 1701. Sympathy for the young Prince and belief in the divine right of succession played a part in this decision, but it was also intended to please the Papacy, whose help was needed against the Austrians in the war in Italy during 1701.

Within a year of Philip V's accession Louis had made general war inevitable. The windfall of Charles II's will seemed to have put France on the road to hegemony and universal monarchy. The danger from France to the other powers was now much more serious than before, when Louis had been striving for fairly limited territorial gains round France's borders. It was therefore in a mood of desperation that William III brought the Maritime Powers and Austria together in the Grand Alliance of The Hague on 7 September 1701. This was an agreement for war to force a partition of Spain. While Philip V was to be allowed to keep Spain and its colonies, the Spanish and French thrones were to be kept separate. Leopold was to be satisfied with the Italian lands and, on the insistence of his allies, with the Southern Netherlands, which were to form a barrier to protect the Dutch Republic from France. There was a tacit understanding that Leopold should hand over his share to his younger son Charles. The Maritime Powers were also permitted to seize any of Spain's colonies they could and to extract commercial concessions from her, and a few months later the signatories agreed to guarantee the Protestant succession in

Britain. In fact the British throne passed to William's Protestant sister-in-law, Queen Anne, when he died in April 1702.

Although William died despondent about the chances of defeating France, the alliance he had created before his death was to achieve his life's ambition of reducing French power. He had continually worked to persuade the European powers to form coalitions as the only way of containing France. By his own initiative in invading Britain in 1688 he had not only contributed to her internal revolution but also firmly knit Britain and the Dutch Republic together against Louis XIV. Although his death ended the personal unity he had provided, the Maritime Powers remained determined to co-operate closely. The lead was taken in the Republic by the Grand Pensionary, Heinsius – no new stadtholder was appointed after William – and in Britain by Godolphin at the Treasury and by Marlborough as commander of the army. These three men were to be the executors of William III's foreign policy.

THE WAR OF THE SPANISH SUCCESSION, 1702–1713/1714

Louis's aims in this new war were straightforward enough: to preserve as much of Spain as possible for his grandson and to maintain the advantages this possession gave to France. He seemed in a much stronger position than in the Nine Years War when he had faced a similar coalition. He now had Spain as an ally and a large buffer zone in the Netherlands and in northern Italy around his kingdom. He had strengthened himself in Italy by an alliance with Savoy, while, unlike in the last war, he had direct influence in Germany through alliances with Bavaria and Cologne. Max Emmanuel of Bavaria had deserted the Emperor because he had been made governor of the Southern Netherlands at the end of Charles II's reign. He hoped to persuade Philip V to cede the province to him. Max Emmanuel's brother, the Elector of Cologne, followed his lead.

The aims of the Grand Alliance changed as the war developed and as they gained further allies. Immediate recruits were the north-German electorates of Hanover and Brandenburg-Prussia. The Hanoverian family was next in line for the British Protestant succession, since Queen Anne (1702–14) had no living children, while Frederick of Brandenburg joined the coalition as payment for being allowed by the Emperor to call himself king *in* Prussia.* Prussian troops as well

---

*Brandenburg-Prussia will now usually be referred to as Prussia. Frederick was called king *in* Prussia to try to maintain the fiction that he was only king in his Prussian lands and not those within the Empire. The powers soon began to call him king *of* Prussia.

as forces from other German states, usually subsidised by the Maritime Powers, were to play a crucial, and probably decisive, part against France. In 1703 Savoy was to change sides and join the allies; in the same year the Portuguese acceded to the Grand Alliance.

The overall aims of the Grand Alliance were decided by the Maritime Powers who provided the naval forces and most of the troops and heavily subsidised Austria and the other allies with loans and the direct payment for soldiers in their armies. On the whole the British and Dutch continued to co-operate closely. Republican and anti-Orangist elements were in control in The Hague after the death of the Stadtholder, William III, in 1702, and these had usually favoured a pacific policy, but now they were largely guided by fear of French domination of the Southern Netherlands. There was therefore no disagreement between the Maritime Powers on the need to create a 'barrier' in the Southern Netherlands and to install the Archduke Charles in Brussels. There was similar agreement on the need to defend the Protestant succession in Britain. As the war progressed, the Dutch, who were paying for an army of 150,000 men (double that of Britain), were to take a decreasing part in naval operations, and began to concentrate almost exclusively on this 'barrier'. Garrison towns there would also be a way of exploiting the province economically, and this was to be begun as soon as the area was occupied and administered by Anglo-Dutch armies in 1706. By this time the Dutch would have been prepared for a compromise peace, but on the whole faithfully followed the more ambitious aims of the British, increasingly the senior partners in their association. None the less, the British had to make substantial concessions in 1709 in the Anglo-Dutch Barrier treaty: this included a Dutch guarantee of the Protestant successssion, agreement to the Dutch having several garrison towns in the Southern Netherlands and trading concessions there from the future ruler of Spain and the Netherlands at the peace.

British domination of the Anglo-Dutch partnership, which had not been so apparent under William, was now clear to all in the Succession War: the British captain-general, Marlborough, always commanded Anglo-Dutch forces when they acted together. This dominance reflected the relative strength of the two states. Britain had a population three or four times that of the Republic and her economy was expanding much faster. The war damaged British trade much less than that of the Dutch, and Britain also managed to finance her war effort better than the Republic whose taxes and credit could hardly keep pace with the mounting demands of the war. By 1707 Britain was bearing the major share and, unlike the Dutch with their obsession with the Netherlands, was taking part in all areas of the expanding war and doing so with enthusiasm.

The chief influence on British war policy was William III's political and military heir, the Duke of Marlborough. His strategy was a bold one, of expelling the Bourbons and their allies from the German Empire, Italy and the Netherlands, turning the Mediterranean into a British lake and finally smashing French power for good. It was clear that only a continental war and a massive British commitment in men and subsidies would achieve these objectives. Consequently, the purely naval strategy, so popular with the Tory squires in parliament, was hardly practical, at least in the early stages of the war. Once Marlborough began to win his great victories, it became increasingly difficult to criticise his continental strategy because it was so obviously successful. For the first time in her modern history, therefore, Britain acted as both a leading land and naval power.

From 1704 onwards the allied coalition won a remarkable series of victories against France. Louis XIV himself, despite his advancing age, continued to direct the French war effort personally, and the bulk of his forces came from France herself: by 1710 he was fielding forces nearly half a million strong. Allied victories owed a good deal to the greater financial resources of the Maritime Powers and their ability to tap the manpower of Germany. But equally important was the energy of the allied leaders, Marlborough and the Austrian Prince Eugene, and the support they received from Godolphin and Heinsius in London and The Hague. In Vienna the Emperor Joseph I (1705–11) proved a far more effective ruler than his father Leopold had been. But if one man deserves credit for allied success, it was Marlborough, who had not commanded in a major battle before this war. He grasped that it was essential for the allies not to become enmeshed in the kind of war of manoeuvre and sieges which had bedevilled William III in the Nine Years War, a war of attrition which Louis XIV could win yet again. Both Marlborough and Eugene believed in dynamic, fluid warfare: they used the terrible fire-power of the infantry with its flintlock bayonet muskets for decisive battles in the field, and this produced startling results. In 1704 Anglo-Dutch forces under Marlborough co-operated with Prince Eugene's Austro-German forces to rout the French and Bavarians at Blenheim and free the Empire from the French threat – this was the first major military defeat of Louis XIV's reign. In 1706 Marlborough won another major victory at Ramillies, which led to the conquest of most of the Southern Netherlands, and in the same year Eugene's army, heavily dependent on British financial help, defeated the French at Turin and conquered all the Spanish lands in Italy. A French attempt to regain the Southern Netherlands was repulsed by Marlborough and Eugene at Oudenarde in 1708. The allies were now poised to invade France herself as they had broken through the outer bulwark provided by the ring of Spanish territories. Louis XIV himself had to act very much on the defensive, depending on the protection of the formidable 'iron barrier' of fortresses built by Vauban.

By the end of 1708 the coalition powers had achieved the main objectives of the Grand Alliance of 1701–2. Unfortunately, their aims had expanded dramatically since then, largely because in 1703 the British brought Portugal into the coalition since they wanted her naval facilities for operations against Spain and in the Mediterranean. The Portuguese King was in no position to argue against the navies of the Maritime Powers, but he did insist that the allies should commit themselves to expelling the Bourbons from Spain. The British agreed, seing the chance to gain extensive commercial concessions from the imposition of the Archduke Charles in Madrid. At the same time they concluded an Anglo-Portuguese commercial treaty (the Methuen treaty) which was to form the basis for Britain's monopoly of Portuguese trade in the eighteenth century.

The Tory ministers in Queen Anne's government had been particularly keen on this new Iberian dimension, even though it meant considerably extending the war aims to include an attempt to seize the whole Spanish monarchy. But the court in Vienna was far less enthusiastic, since their main objective was the Spanish lands in Italy. However, pressure from his British and Dutch allies, who stood to gain more than the uncommercial Austrians, brought Leopold's agreement and the dispatch of Archduke Charles with an Anglo-Dutch expedition to the Iberian peninsula in 1704. Before leaving Vienna the Archduke had to assign his rights to Spanish Milan to his elder brother, Joseph, an attempt to ensure that Austria herself would still benefit directly from the Spanish succession. Despite the proclamation of Archduke Charles as King Charles III of Spain and public commitment to his cause as one of her war aims, Austria contributed next to nothing to the allied war effort in Spain. Her armies were used instead to win Milan and Naples and then, after 1708, in helping rather grudgingly the frontal attack on France from the Netherlands, the one arena where decisive allied victories could force Louis XIV to accept complete defeat. In fact, for most of the War of the Spanish Succession the bulk of Austrian forces, and the expenditure of much British financial help, was concentrated in Hungary. Here a rebellion had been in progress with French encouragement since 1703 and was not finally suppressed till 1711.

Although Vienna was keen to push back the frontier between France and the German Empire to that settled at the peace of Westphalia, she expected the German states to shoulder the main burden of war along the Rhine. On the whole the Germans were willing to do so, and the Emperor's power within the Empire now probably reached its highest point since the Thirty Years War. This was a development which many of Joseph I's ministers welcomed, but Wratislaw, certainly his fattest and possibly his most intelligent minister, thought it more important to pursue the idea of strengthening the central core of the Austrian state itself. He wanted direct gains in northern Italy and also the annexation of Bavaria from Louis XIV's ally, Max Emmanuel, whose electorate was occupied from 1704 onwards.

The war in Spain was essentially a British affair. Following their decision to intervene, both Tory and Whig ministers were equally determined on a policy of 'no peace without Spain'. The Whig ministry which achieved supreme power in London in 1708, believed the conquest of Spain was feasible, largely because of the extent of allied victories elsewhere. In this it was to be misled, but involvement in the peninsula seemed to provide Britain with immediate tangible benefits: in 1704 British forces took Gibraltar and then in 1708 the Balearic island of Minorca which gave her navy control of the western Mediterranean. However, the attempt to foist 'Charles III' on the Spanish people proved as great a fiasco and drain on resources as Napoleon's intervention in the peninsula a century later. Philip V could depend on native support as well as on help from France, and the struggle became in effect a civil war. The Castilian heart of Spain remained loyal to Philip, while Catalonia, Aragon and Valencia supported Charles in what amounted to a revolt against the centre. But Charles's position was always the weaker and he could not have survived without British help; he was in effect a British puppet.

By 1708 the war had really become two – one against Louis XIV for the hegemony of western Europe and the other against Philip for Spain itself. The coalition appeared to have won the first, but the second was really beyond its resources and would not have been pursued so sanguinely but for success elsewhere. Even the triumph of the allies at sea could not ensure their victory in Spain. The Bourbon fleets, which were only half the size of the Anglo-Dutch ones, were completely outclassed and driven from the seas. The French thereafter depended heavily on privateers which did inflict heavy damage on British, and especially on Dutch, commerce. Unlike in the later wars of the eighteenth century, the British restricted their own naval operations almost exclusively to European wars, essentially assisting the campaigns in western Europe. They were probably sensible in not fighting a full-scale colonial war: the abortive expedition launched against French Quebec in 1711 by the Tory government indicated that such a war was beyond British resources at that time.

The great victories of the Grand Alliance in the Netherlands and Italy should have led to peace in 1709. Louis XIV had wanted a settlement since 1705–6, as had the Dutch. By 1709 with his country bankrupt and devastated by a savage winter, Louis was desperate for peace. He was willing to give way completely: to cede the whole Spanish empire to 'Charles III' and even to restore all he had taken in Alsace since 1648, including Strasbourg, as well as towns such as Lille in Flanders. However, Philip V now had enough support of his own in Spain itself for it to be impossible for Louis just to order him to leave. Unfortunately, the allies never really understood this, and were intransigent about Spain. In peace talks at The Hague in spring 1709 the allies demanded not only that Louis should contribute militarily to the expulsion of his grandson from Spain, but also that France should hand over 'cautionary towns' to ensure that the peace terms were carried out. Fearing that the latter would allow the allies to dismember France and unwilling to help against his grandson, Louis rejected the peace terms and decided on a last desperate struggle. Largely through the ruthlessness of his best general, Villars, and the resilience of the French peasant economy, France mustered enough troops to survive. Following the blood-bath of Malplaquet (September 1709), won by neither side, the war along France's northern frontiers developed into one of stalemate as the allies tried to batter down what was left of Vauban's 'iron barrier'. Further attempts at peace at Geertruidenberg early in 1710 failed again due to the obstinacy of the allies, even though Louis was desperate enough to offer to cede all Alsace and to pay subsidies to help expel Philip from Spain. The basic problem was the inability of the allies to win the war in Spain and eject Philip themselves, and their refusal at the same time to recognise this fact.

THE PEACE OF UTRECHT–RASTADT, 1713–1714

Although the Dutch would have liked peace once the Southern Netherlands had been freed from the Bourbons, allied unity showed no signs of cracking till 1710. Then, in the summer, the Tories came to power in Britain. They were determined to destroy Marlborough, ditch what they believed was his ruinously expensive continental war, and to abandon the policy of 'no peace without Spain'. The two men who dominated the new ministry, Robert Harley (later Earl of Oxford) and Henry St John (later Viscount Bolingbroke), were determined on peace, whatever the cost to their allies. However, although they represented the Tory squires (whose land taxes had helped finance the war and who hated the Whig monied men), they ensured that the peace benefited Britain, particularly her commerce.

The Tories began secret negotiations with the French in summer 1710 and by the following spring were close to agreement. During 1711 they were to do their best to limit Marlborough's campaign in Flanders and in the December they dismissed him. Although they were very keen on peace, a fact which helped to save Louis from further military defeats, an actual settlement took a long time because of the difficulties involved in persuading Britain's allies to accept the terms she and France wanted. The Tory desire for peace was certainly motivated by party considerations, but it was also a sensible policy, given that the full aims of the allies were unattainable. This became even more apparent in April 1711 when the Emperor Joseph I died without leaving a son. He was succeeded by his brother, the Archduke Charles. To insist that the new Emperor Charles VI was also 'Charles III' of Spain would clearly lead to a mammoth Habsburg empire. The danger of a French universal monarchy was now replaced by that of an Austrian one, and the Tories were therefore strengthened in their belief that any settlement must be based on the original aim of the Grand Alliance of The Hague, that is, partition of the Spanish Empire. However, their attempt to achieve a settlement through separate, secret and unilateral negotiations with the French led to bitter quarrels with their 'allies'. In the negotiations, which eventually led to the peace of Utrecht, it became clear that the Tory ministers preferred their French enemies to the Dutch and Austrians, the friends of their domestic opponents, the Whigs. They convinced themselves that the war had been fought for Whig financiers, a Dutch 'barrier' and Habsburg claims to Spain. They viewed the Dutch as trade rivals, and the cause, with the Austrians, of Britain's needless involvement in continental warfare. The secretary of state, Bolingbroke, who was chiefly in charge of the conduct of the peace negotiations and who established a particularly close relationship with the French foreign minister, Torcy, was especially hostile to Vienna, declaring in November 1711 that 'the house of Austria has been the evil genius of Britain'.

In January 1712 negotiations between all the powers involved in the war finally began at a peace congress in the Dutch city of Utrecht. These lasted more than a year. During this time the British took no further part in the war, although the Austrians tried unsuccessfully to pursue it in the Netherlands with reluctant Dutch help and in Catalonia by themselves. The calling of a general congress was a recognition that congresses were the accepted way of concluding wars, but the real terms were worked out between Britain and France alone. Even before the congress met the two powers had tacitly agreed that Philip V should keep Spain itself and the overseas empire and that Britain's own demands should be conceded. Although the Dutch, Austrians and German princes tried to hold out for the terms they wanted during the congress, they could achieve little, given Britain's financial and military contribution to the coalition. Dutch hopes of sharing commercial concessions in the Spanish empire with Britain were to be dashed, and even their demands in the Southern Netherlands were to be curtailed. However, Austria was to be the most disappointed power, and this was probably inevitable because of the extent of her ambitions and her own lack of effective military muscle. The accession of Charles VI (1711–40) meant that the Habsburgs pursued their claims to the whole Spanish inheritance seriously for the first time. The new Emperor had only returned reluctantly from Spain to Vienna and felt personally committed to his supporters there.

However, as the negotiations progressed his more realistic ministers like Prince Eugene and Wratislaw recognised that Austria could not fight both Louis XIV and Philip V without British help. Under Wratislaw's guidance, Austrian policy gradually moved towards accepting that they could not expect all Charles II's inheritance and would even have to renounce Spain itself. Wratislaw, who died in December 1712, hoped to create a more territorially compact Austrian state built round the hereditary lands and Italy. (It was for this reason that he also tried unsuccessfully to exchange the Southern Netherlands for Austria's neighbour, Bavaria.) Even after Wratislaw's death, Charles VI would have been willing to sign the unpalatable final terms of Utrecht but for last-minute French demands – the cession of Luxemburg to Bavaria, the withdrawal of Austrian troops from the Italian fortress of Mantua, which they had occupied for most of the war and intended to hang on to, and the immediate formal recognition of Philip V as king of Spain. In the event, when the Austrians made peace with France a year later at Rastadt they were to do so on terms substantially the same as those of Utrecht.

The peace of Utrecht was signed by Britain, France, the Dutch Republic, Savoy, Philip V of Spain and Prussia in April 1713. The actual peace terms, which were largely the work of Bolingbroke, effected a partition of the Spanish monarchy. Philip V was to keep Spain and the overseas empire and to cede Gibraltar and Minorca to Britain. The Emperor Charles VI was to have Milan, Naples, Spanish enclaves on the coast of Tuscany and the Southern Netherlands. Fortresses in the latter were to be garrisoned by the Dutch, who were to work out the precise terms in a new Barrier treaty with the Emperor and Britain. Sardinia was to go to Max Emmanuel of Bavaria, while Victor Amadeus of Savoy received Sicily with a royal crown. France herself was to cede a few towns in Flanders – Furnes, Ypres, Menin and Tournai – to the Southern Netherlands but was to keep Lille. Dunkirk, the main base for French privateers, was to lose its fortifications. In North America Louis XIV returned Hudson Bay to Britain and ceded Acadia (Nova Scotia) and Newfoundland, as well as the West Indian island of St Kitts. He also had to return to the Holy Roman Empire all places on the right bank of the Rhine, but kept those he held on the left, including Alsace and Strasbourg. The French were forced to surrender the commercial concessions they had extracted at the beginning of Philip V's reign. Instead the Spanish King had to grant the slave contract, the *Asiento*, to Britain, as well as the right to send an annual ship of 500 tons to the fair at Portobello in Central America. The British had also insisted on clauses to protect their own succession and to try to prevent future wars of succession: the notion that a country's succession was a matter of international concern and needed to be subject to international guarantees was central to the whole treaty and was a forerunner of similar attempts later.

Consequently, the Protestant succession in Britain was guaranteed and the French agreed to expel the Old Pretender ('James III') from France, where he had been living. Philip V had to renounce the French throne, which was to remain separate from that of Spain. In 1711 Louis's son, the Dauphin, had died and the next year the Dauphin's elder son and elder grandson also died. This only left Louis's great-grandson, the future Louis XV, who was born in 1710, as his successor. It was therefore stipulated in the peace that if this child died, the succession should not pass to the nearest blood relative, Philip V, but to the descendants of Louis XIV's late brother, the Duke of Orleans.

The terms of the peace of Utrecht were only slightly modified when Charles VI and the remaining German princes, including Hanover, made peace with France at Rastadt (March 1714) after a year of fruitless fighting along the Rhine. Charles VI himself received Sardinia, and France gained Landau on the right bank of the Rhine. To satisfy the Emperor's pride he was not called on to recognise the Italian settlement or Philip V as king of Spain, and no actual peace was signed between him and Philip V.

CHAPTER THREE

The emergence of Austria and Russia, 1660–1721

THE CREATION OF THE AUSTRIAN EMPIRE AND THE DEFEAT OF THE TURKS, 1660–1699

During the reign of the Emperor Leopold I, ruler of the Austrian lands (1657–1705) and Holy Roman Emperor (from 1658) Austria assumed the role she was to play over the next two centuries. She developed into the great balancing power between east and west in central Europe, with interests in the Balkans as well as in Germany and Italy. In the mid-seventeenth century Austria was a dynastic union of separate provinces with little else in common except the ruler. She consisted of the Austrian duchies, the kingdom of Bohemia and that narrow strip of Hungary not under direct or indirect rule by the Ottoman Turks. Since the division of the Habsburg lands into the Spanish and Austrian branches in 1555 (see p. 2), the junior branch in Austria had struggled to defend Europe against further Turkish attacks from the south-east. It also tried to increase its powers as elective emperor in Germany and occasionally joined the senior branch in Madrid in the pursuit of a common dynastic policy in Europe.

As far as their relations with the Turks were concerned, for most of the late sixteenth and early seventeenth centuries the Austrian Habsburgs had usually been content to stand on the defensive and had done their best to ignore the Turkish problem. They were able to do this quite successfully because the dynamism seemed to have gone out of Turkish expansion after its rapid and frightening advance in the second quarter of the sixteenth century. This advance had led to the destruction of the kingdom of Hungary by Sultan Suleiman I (1520–66) after his total victory at Mohács in 1526. Hungary had served as a buffer state between Christian central Europe and Islam; and three years after its collapse Vienna was besieged for the first time. By the 1540s Hungary had been divided into three. The Habsburgs clung on to the northern and western fringes. Transylvania in the east was under nominal Turkish suzerainty, but in practice was an independent principality. The rest was ruled from Constantinople (Istanbul) as a Turkish province, although the Sultans allowed their Hungarian subjects considerable freedom. This position in Hungary lasted for a century, because from the mid-1560s Turkish pressure in central Europe largely ceased. This was mainly because the Ottoman Empire, like its Habsburg adversary, was involved at many points on the map: against Poland and Russia in the lands bordering the Black Sea, against Persia (Iran) in the east, and in the Indian Ocean as well as in Arabia and North Africa. All these provided more pressing problems for the Porte in the century after Suleiman's death than further confrontation in Hungary, though this has not always been appreciated by European historians who see only the western face of the Ottoman Empire. With the exception of an indecisive war from 1593 to 1606, there was no formal campaigning between the Habsburgs and Turks between 1566 and the early 1660s, although unofficial hostilities continued: the frontier was fluid and unstable and fighting had become a way of life for the populations on both sides, who continuously raided each other's territory. Both governments welcomed the end of open warfare: in the case of the Turks the immense commitments of their empire were proving an increasing strain on the administrative and military machine. For their part the Austrian Habsburgs were preoccupied with their own internal problems and with Germany during the Thirty Years War (1618–48) and were content to accept the *de facto* armistice on their south-eastern border. But they could never ignore the Turks, who were only 80 miles from Vienna. The situation remained volatile, and this became all too apparent at the beginning of Leopold's reign.

The Thirty Years War itself significantly affected Austria's future development. It ensured that the Emperor could not impose political unity on Germany and make the princes his vassals. Instead the independence of the German princes was confirmed. But at the same time Austria became both a state in her own right and by far the strongest of the states within the Empire. This came about because of the creation of a standing army during the war and the retention of part of it afterwards, which allowed the Emperor to assert effective control over his own Bohemian and Austrian lands. It has often been said that Austrian power declined sharply at this time in Germany, and that because of this she was pushed towards the Balkans. This is nonsense. Vienna did not withdraw from Germany till the Bismarckian period. Until then she kept her eyes resolutely westwards, towards Germany and, at times, towards Italy. It was only in the very last decades of the monarchy itself that she willingly concentrated on the east.

Although the Thirty Years War shattered the close dynastic relations between the Spanish and Austrian Habsburgs and Spain was left to fight on alone against France (see pp. 3ff.), Austria remained committed to a foreign policy completely orientated towards the west. Leopold took his position as Holy Roman Emperor seriously and hoped to regain the Empire's lands which had been ceded to France in 1648, to prevent further French expansion and rid it of French influence. At the same time he was determined that if the Spanish Habsburgs died out, as seemed increasingly likely in Philip IV's last years and with the accession of Charles II (1665), as much as possible of the Spanish empire should be united with his own Austrian lands. Leopold was to try to pursue these dynastic ambitions, as well as his 'German mission' to contain France and to win back the western parts of the Empire lost to her, throughout his life. This meant a policy of almost consistent hostility towards Louis XIV of France.

In challenging the power of France, which increased rapidly during Louis XIV's personal rule, Leopold struggled with serious disadvantages. He was to be continually harassed by problems with the Hungarians and the Turks (see pp. 71ff.). He found it difficult to turn the German princes against France, because at least for most of the 1660s the majority was more suspicious of him than of Louis (see pp. 9f., 18). Neither the weak Spaniards nor the increasingly neutralist Dutch could be depended on as allies in any confrontation with France. Above all he had serious domestic weaknesses when compared with the French state under Louis. Although, as has been seen, Austria was far stronger than before the Thirty Years War, this did not make her a match for France. The great nobles and clerics in Bohemia and Austria had lost their independent political power, but Leopold's ability to extract taxation and recruit troops was severely limited by his lack of effective central institutions and administrators. The provinces and their wealth were almost completely in the hands of the great aristocratic and ecclesiastical landlords. At the end of Leopold's reign his revenues were reckoned as less than a fifth of those of France, while after Nymegen when Louis's army was over 200,000 strong Leopold could only raise 30,000 men from his own lands. This meant that throughout the period 1660 to 1714 the Austrian crown was dangerously dependent on both subsidies and auxiliary troops from other powers for the conduct of her foreign policy and wars.

The Emperor Leopold, whose reign lasted almost as long as the personal rule of his French cousin, was a completely different character from Louis. Timid, plagued by self-doubt and stomach cramps, he lacked Louis's natural capacity for ruling and application to business. He had an intense religious faith and a resigned fatalism which made even a Papal nuncio exclaim he wished 'the Emperor's trust in God were a bit less'. It was this trust, however, which got him through the greatest crisis of his reign in 1683 and made him so obstinate about his dynastic claims to the Spanish succession. He was also in the event to add far more territory to his dominions than Louis did for France.

During the 1660s Leopold dared not stand up to France. Not only was he at war with the Turks from 1663 to 1664, but the League of the Rhine (see pp. 9ff.) and Louis's other relationships with the German princes had led to a further reduction in Imperial power in Germany. Under the influence of his pro-French minister, Lobkowitz, who felt Austria on her own was too weak to challenge France in the Empire or over the Spanish succession issue, Leopold agreed to a temporary accommodation with Paris. In 1668 Leopold acquiesced in a treaty with Louis (see pp. 22f.) for the future partition of Spain, and he was to do little to resist the French before Louis's attack on the Dutch in 1672. This attack and Louis's pressure on the Rhineland before and during the war, especially the annexation of Lorraine, changed the situation (see p. 30). Almost overnight Louis's actions had made it possible for an embryonic coalition of the Dutch, Spain, some German states and the Emperor to be formed. This was intended to try to deny France further gains and even to reverse the Westphalian settlement as it affected the Rhineland. The Emperor's commander-in-chief, Montecuccoli, was able to lead an Austrian and German force on the Rhine. Although Louis had few difficulties in destroying the weak coalition against him, it frightened him enough, especially the Emperor's intervention and the support he received from the Empire, to believe that his border with Germany was his most vulnerable one. Because of this he embarked on his reunion policy (see pp. 36ff.).

After the peace of Nymegen (1678–79) Leopold's foreign policy was largely formulated to try to limit French expansion along the Rhine. For the while he could afford to be less concerned with the Spanish succession because Charles II of Spain, despite his mental and physical disabilities, had survived the dangerous illnesses of childhood, and it was not yet clear whether he could have any children of his own. Leopold himself had by now grown very hostile to Louis personally. He had a great hatred of anything French, including French fashions and language, both of which were becoming very popular in other German courts. He had also inherited the Habsburg family rivalry with the Bourbons. There was a strong group at his court, especially around the exiled Duke Charles V of Lorraine, who shared and encouraged this hostility to France. They feared Louis wanted the Imperial throne for himself as well as to break up the Empire, and they were determined to seize any chance to reduce French power. Austrian Habsburg diplomats were almost as busy as those of William of Orange in the years immediately after Nymegen in a futile attempt to build a coalition, especially one based on the German princes, to oppose Louis. The Austrian court was convinced, as late as 1681 and even into 1682, that France was its main enemy, and this made Vienna blind to the dangers building up in the Balkans.

Austria was forced to turn to the east because of the direct threat of Turkish invasion. Since the last thing that Leopold's court wanted was to challenge Turkish power, it had been determined to make any military commitment in the east as limited as possible. There was nothing to encourage expansion there. The crusading enthusiasm of Austrian Catholicism was satisfied expending itself on the Emperor's Protestants. Only the Papacy wanted a crusade against Islam. None the less, despite herself, Austria was to become embroiled in a massive struggle against the Turks in the 1680s and 1690s, a struggle which was to lead to vast conquests in the Balkans and to a consequential growth in the Emperor's prestige and power in Europe as a whole. She became involved for two reasons: the attempt by Leopold I to impose Catholicism and closer political control on the strip of Hungary he ruled directly, and a further bout of Turkish expansionism.

During the Thirty Years War the Habsburgs had managed to end the elective monarchy in Bohemia and to strengthen their hold on all their possessions outside Hungary. This was done by the systematic expulsion of Protestants and of any nobles sympathetic towards dissent, as well as by reducing the political power of the Diets. Between 1660 and 1680 Leopold and his ministers tried to put his Hungarian subjects 'into Bohemian trousers': to destroy Protestantism, the elective character of the Hungarian crown and the powers of the Hungarian Diet. (The latter had been described by a shocked French ambassador in 1667, as 'believing itself equal, if not superior, to its master'.) The intention was to end Hungary's existence as a separate state from Austria. This led to determined resistance by the Hungarian nobility, especially the gentry, and to twenty years of intermittent guerrilla warfare. The struggle was almost intractable because the Hungarian rebels to escape pursuit decamped across the borders into Turkish Hungary or into the Sultan's vassal state, Transylvania, which had a Hungarian prince and Hungarian Protestant nobility. Habsburg Hungary was reduced to chaos and could only be controlled through permanent garrisons of troops, usually German, loyal to the crown. Inevitably this conflict weakened Leopold in facing the ambitions of Louis XIV during the 1660s and 1670s, and the French King was willing enough to encourage Leopold's Hungarian rebels.

It was probably unavoidable that some of the Hungarians would eventually invite the Turks in to help, or that the Sultan would take advantage of the disturbed state of Habsburg Hungary to plan an attack on Vienna itself. Both these things happened in 1681–82, when the rebel leader Thököly appealed to the Turks and they seized the opportunity offered. Their decision, however, was essentially part of a significant, although ultimately transitory, revival in Turkish power which had occurred since the 1650s. The first years of the century had seen internal stagnation and disintegration and a lack of central control in the Ottoman Empire. In many ways this had allowed the Habsburgs the luxury of engaging in the Thirty Years War. But from 1656 direction of the Ottoman Empire was in the hands of successive members of the Köprülü family as grand viziers, or chief ministers, for Sultan Mehmed IV (1648–87). The Köprülüs carried out a ruthless and bloody purge of the domestic administration, achieved more control over the provinces and launched a series of aggressive wars.

In the eastern Mediterranean, where the Turks had been involved since 1646 in a naval war and desultory campaigns with Venice over Crete and parts of the Dalmatian coast, the war was pursued more vigorously and eventually led to the fall of Crete in 1669. Between 1658 and 1661 the Turks attacked their vassal principality of Transylvania and ended its autonomy. This alarmed Vienna, which looked on Transylvanian independence as part of their defences against the Porte, and the Habsburgs sent some help to the Hungarian nobility there. Anger at this caused Constantinople to tighten its control in Transylvania and declare war on the Emperor in April 1663. The Turks seem to have intended to attack Vienna itself. As usual, Leopold had serious problems raising soldiers to face this emergency, but by the time the Ottoman offensive began in the following year an army had been assembled, thanks partly to the efforts of Papal diplomacy. Several German states sent help, as did the League of the Rhine. These included a few thousand troops contributed by Louis XIV as a member of the league. On 1 August 1664 the Emperor's forces won an unexpected and spectacular victory under Montecuccoli against a Turkish army four times its size at St Gotthard (Szentgotthárd) 90 miles from Vienna. The French contingent only played a minor part, and this was the first indication of the superiority of German infantry and field artillery to the Ottomans. Leopold seemed to throw away the victory by immediately making peace at Vasvár. This agreement, which was essentially a twenty-year armistice, not only left the Turks in complete control of Transylvania but obliged the Emperor to pay a 'tribute' of 200,000 florins to the Sultan.

Leopold concluded this surprising peace because he had no wish for further involvement with the Turks and knew his forces were in no condition to invade Turkish Hungary. His priorities were to establish control within his own Hungarian lands and to face the French in the west. St Gotthard did at least make the Turks look elsewhere, and in 1671 they took advantage of a Cossack revolt in south-east Poland to attack her. The Turks were at first highly successful against the Poles and their inept King Michael Wisnowiecki and reached as far as Lvov. In this war, as in those against Austria, the local population suffered badly from raids by parties of Tartar horsemen who operated well in advance of the main Ottoman army. They lived off the countryside, burning and looting and taking prisoners for slaves. In 1674 the Poles staged a recovery when John Sobieski (1674–96) became king, and at the peace of Żuravno (1676) Turkish gains were limited to Podolia. Sobieski had been backed for the elective Polish throne by Louis XIV, who had hoped he would pursue an anti-Habsburg policy. Although he did give some help to the Hungarian rebels in the late 1670s, Sobieski's ambition by 1680 was set on expelling the Turks from Podolia and other parts of the Ukraine and extending his own power south into the Sultan's Danubian principalities of Moldavia and Wallachia. The Turks meanwhile, having been thwarted by the Poles and forced to make peace, turned, under a new grand vizier, Kara Mustafa (1676–83), to try to expand against the Russians in 1677. But in 1681 they had to conclude the treaty of Radzin with them, which amounted to a recognition of the status quo in the Ukraine. Kara Mustafa, who was a fruit-pedlar's son who had married into the Köprülü family, desperately needed some foreign success and loot to secure his own position.

The grand vizier determined on an attack on Vienna, the 'Golden Apple', a project which offered him the prospects of vast wealth and prestige, neither of which could be won in the poor Ukrainian steppes. He was well aware of the pressure being exerted by Louis XIV in western Europe, pressure which culminated in the seizure of Strasbourg and the siege of Luxemburg (see p. 37). He therefore welcomed the approaches of Thököly, and during 1682 he began to prepare to attack Austria. In 1681 Leopold had been willing to compromise with his Hungarian rebels, hoping to concentrate on the French threat along the Rhine. He and his court failed to appreciate the ultimate threat from Constantinople. They deluded themselves that Ottoman power had waned and that Ottoman interests had shifted permanently to the Ukraine after the Christian victory of St Gotthard. Leopold did not take the threat seriously till autumn 1682. Only once a huge Turkish force was already moving along the military road from Adrianople to Belgrade in spring 1683 were active defensive measures taken. In March 1683, largely through the diplomatic and financial support of the last great crusading Pope, Innocent XI, a military alliance was signed between Austria and Poland. This was despite the attempts of French diplomats to prevent it and desperate appeals for help from the Spaniards in western Europe. Some German states, including Saxony and Bavaria, promised the allies help, but their military contingents came too late to prevent Kara Mustafa from devastating Lower Austria and laying siege to Vienna. The speed of the Turkish advance proved decisive in this campaign of 1683, as the Habsburgs, unlike in 1664, had no time to organise a force to block its path, and both Leopold and his court were forced to flee the capital.

Kara Mustafa's army of possibly 90,000 men began the siege of Vienna on 16 July and remained there during two hot summer months. The Turks met brave resistance and they launched their assaults in a leisurely and haphazard way. Kara Mustafa lacked siege artillery and he put off serious attempts to storm the city in the hope that it would surrender voluntarily and its vast wealth fall into his hands intact. He not only disregarded the advance of relieving Austrian, German and Polish forces under the Duke of Lorraine, Max Emmanuel of Bavaria and King John Sobieski but even failed to take elementary precautions to protect his besieging army from attack. On 12 September 1683 the Christian army defeated him in a full day's battle outside the city. The Turks were outgunned and outmanoeuvred and fled back into Hungary in disarray. Kara Mustafa paid the inevitable price for failure and on Mehmed IV's orders was ceremonially strangled at Belgrade.

The relief of Vienna was accompanied by the simultaneous Spanish declaration of war on France (see p. 39). This produced a dilemma for Leopold: whether he should fight the Turks or join in resisting Louis XIV, the great 'Christian Turk'. The whole weight of the clerical groups in Vienna and particularly that of Leopold's confidant, Marco d'Aviano, favoured a crusade against the Ottomans. The military leaders, especially Max Emmanuel of Bavaria and Charles of Lorraine, agreed with them. It was probably Charles's influence which was decisive. He was Leopold's brother-in-law and would have had most to gain by a war on the Rhine where Louis still occupied his duchy. In any case a war of some kind would have had to be fought because the Turks were still in control of parts of Habsburg Hungary and the Sultan showed no signs of wanting peace.

Austria could not undertake the war alone, and so Leopold, with considerable Papal help, began a diplomatic offensive to find support for a crusade. The victory against the Turks produced waves of enthusiasm throughout Catholic, and even Protestant, Europe. In March 1684 the original Austro-Polish alliance was widened into the Holy League with the addition of Venice. (Russia was to join two years later, although she did not begin serious campaigning till 1695 – see p. 76). Innocent XI contributed large sums to the war effort and ordered the clergy throughout southern Europe to do so as well. For the first time since 1529 Habsburg policy now seriously envisaged destroying Turkish rule in Hungary. This would have the important by-product of weakening the semi-independence of Leopold's Hungarian subjects.

A corollary of this policy was Leopold's having to come to terms with Louis in the west and agreeing to the peace of Regensburg in summer 1684 (see p. 39). This allowed the German states to contribute substantially to the Turkish War. A military alliance was concluded with Brandenburg-Prussia (April 1686) and with other German states. Although the war took on the character of a new European crusade, with aristocrats from all over the Continent joining in, the bulk of the non-Austrian troops came from the Empire, where the princes wanted to hire out their standing armies at someone else's expense. By 1685 the Emperor was fielding 100,000 men in Hungary; of these 60,000 were Austrian and 38,000 from the Empire. In the event the war was to be as much a German as an Austrian achievement.

The Holy League occupied the Turks on three main fronts with varying success. Sobieski tried to drive south into the Danubian principalities, but he made little permanent headway because Poland's domestic problems prevented him from deploying adequate armies. The Venetians, however, managed to land troops – again mainly German ones from Hanover and Saxony – in southern Greece. By 1690 they had taken the Morea and Athens. The most spectacular victories took place in Hungary. After problems of supply were overcome in 1684 and 1685, the Emperor's armies took Buda (1686) and totally destroyed Turkish control of Hungary and Transylvania after the battle of Nagyharsány near Mohács in August 1687. This victory opened the way into Serbia and destroyed Turkish power in the Hungarian plain for good. It was followed in 1688 by the capture of Belgrade. Although this proved only a temporary gain – the Turks retook it in 1690 – permanent ones were the annexation of Transylvania and the Ottoman parts of Hungary, and the forcing of the Hungarian Diet to agree at Bratislava (September 1687) to make the crown hereditary in the Habsburg family. The Hungarian problem was to be by no means over for the Habsburgs, as there was to be a fierce rebellion during the Spanish Succession War. But the expulsion of the Turks was to make this a far less dangerous problem.

The early 1690s were to see an end of Habsburg conquests in the Balkans and a partial Ottoman recovery after the total military collapse and then the deposition of Sultan Mehmed IV in 1687. The reason of course was the outbreak of the Nine Years War in the west (see pp. 42ff.). This not only encouraged Constantinople to continue its war but led to the withdrawal of many German troops to fight on the Rhine. Turkish military power itself recovered somewhat under the forceful Mustafa II, but his troops were no match for any substantial Austrian force they had to face. This was proved by the bloody Christian victory at Zálankemén (August 1691). The Turks were by now militarily obsolete: their huge but poorly armed forces were no match for the murderous fire-power of German and Austrian infantry and field guns. Their supply system was also incapable of waging a long war in the sand-dunes, swamps and empty plains of the Hungarian battlefields. Yet throughout the 1690s the war in the Balkans was in a state of stalemate because the Austrians were unable to assemble enough troops to deliver the final blow and force the Sultan to make peace. It was not till September 1697, with troops freed after the armistice with Louis XIV in northern Italy (see p. 51), that Prince Eugene of Savoy won the decisive victory against an army led by Sultan Mustafa himself at Zenta. This massive Turkish defeat finally destroyed Turkish resistance and brought the war to an end.

The Austrian court was anxious for peace, so that it could concentrate on the Spanish succession problem in the west, and it had no further territorial objectives in the Balkans. There were few arguments against peace from Austria's Polish and Venetian allies, but Russia under the energetic leadership of Peter the Great had only just begun to campaign seriously around the Black Sea and the Tsar wanted to continue the war. Vienna refused to listen to him, and he soon found a fresh field for his ambitions in the north (see pp. 80f.). Peace talks were therefore conducted with the Porte under Anglo-Dutch mediation in 1698, eventually leading to the treaty of Karlowitz (January 1699). By signing the treaty the Ottoman Empire acknowledged the formal existence of non-Muslim states for the first time. Previously the Turks had only made truces, since they believed they were engaged in permanent war with the 'unbelievers'. In the peace itself they had to cede vast tracts of territory. All Hungary and Transylvania, except for the Banat of Temesvár (Timişoara) were kept by the Emperor. Russia, who made her own peace later, received Azov, while Poland regained Podolia, and even the Venetians kept their conquests on the Dalmatian coast and in the Morea.

The peace marked the formal beginning of the long retreat of Ottoman power in Europe. Although there were to be occasional and significant periods of recovery, the pattern was now clear: Europe, which had been on the defensive for more than two centuries, was forcing the Turks back. The simultaneous and steady collapse of the Sultan's authority and the resulting vacuum in the Balkans were to form the basis of the 'Eastern Question' of the nineteenth century. On the whole it was not to be Austria but Russia which ultimately benefited most from Ottoman decline, even in the eighteenth century. However, Austria did make further territorial gains in the Austro-Turkish War of 1716–18, when spectacular victories led to the cession of northern Serbia with Belgrade as well as the Banat of Temesvár. The war was largely a personal venture of the chief Austrian general and minister, Prince Eugene, and was deliberately planned as a war of conquest (see p. 103). In the event most of these gains were lost in the 1730s (see pp. 155ff.), and Karlowitz marked the effective limits of Austrian expansion in the Balkans till the occupation of Bosnia in 1878.

The gains in Hungary were largely worthless as an economic asset. Not only were the lands poor but the monarchy could never adequately solve the problem of how to tax its old and new Hungarian subjects or to bring them under strict control. However, the undoubted success of the Habsburgs against the Turks in the 1680s and 1690s, and the creation of a huge Danubian empire ruled from Vienna, raised Austria to the ranks of the great powers who dominated Europe till the First World War. She was coming to be generally accepted as a major power, an essential part of the emerging European states system. The western states were to see her as a vital factor in the coalitions against France, while the Russians were soon to consider her an equally valuable ally against the Turks. Yet it was Austria's territorial position and commitments, rather than her resources, which made her a great power, and these commitments were already too extensive to uphold on her own. She could usually cope with the Turks by herself, when she had no other commitments, as in 1697 and 1716–18, and her greatest gains were made during a few years in the 1680s when the bulk of Austria's resources were concentrated in the east. Yet even then the German states and the Papacy had given extensive help. Austria's most difficult times occurred when she was at war in both the east and the west. However, it was never possible for Austria, even without distractions in the Balkans, to face France successfully unless she had outside help. During the confrontations with Louis XIV and his successor Vienna's weak financial and administrative structure meant the emperors had to lean heavily on one or both of the Maritime Powers. Austria's position as a great power was always to be a precarious one.

Shortly after Austria's great victories against the Turks had been confirmed by the peace of Karlowitz, a new power was to emerge on the European political scene, one which was to dominate northern and eastern Europe in the eighteenth century and eventually to compete with Austria for control of the Balkans. This was Russia. Although her expansion, like that of Austria, was to take place to a great part at the expense of the Turks, Russia's position was first established through the defeat of Sweden.

THE GREAT NORTHERN WAR, 1700–21

The formation of the anti-Swedish coalition, 1697–1700

Sweden's career as a major European power was a comparatively brief one, and her actual strength in the seventeenth century has often been exaggerated. Her empire was scattered and fragile, frozen into its separate and vulnerable parts during the winter months, enjoying no natural frontiers and with little in common except perhaps Lutheranism. Territorial expansion had reached its peak under Charles X and had died with him in 1660. Only for brief periods during the Thirty Years War and the struggle against Poland in the 1650s had Swedish armies strayed far from the shores of the Baltic. Her resources were hardly enough to maintain the momentum of expansion, and, even with the tolls from the Baltic ports, Sweden's revenues had proved too low to wage war on the European mainland without foreign subsidies. This meant that in the seventeenth century she was in many ways a dependant of France and, together with Sweden's own enemy, Poland, and the Ottoman Empire, a part of the Bourbon eastern barrier against the Austrian Habsburgs.

The dangers of this role became fully apparent during the regency which governed Sweden for the child-King, Charles XI (1660–97). Dependence on foreign subsidies brought the humiliating intervention in Louis XIV's Dutch War (see p. 31). Defeated in Germany by Brandenburg-Prussia in 1675, Sweden was then attacked by Denmark and came close to collapse. The support of her French ally at the peace settlements of 1679 allowed her to escape without serious loss, but her weakness and vulnerability were now clear. It was to get away from this position, and because he believed Sweden had expanded enough, that Charles XI himself consciously adopted a neutralist stance and used diplomacy to play a balancing role in the 1680s and 1690s. He realised that any war made Sweden liable to attack on three sides, in southern Sweden, in Germany and in the Baltic provinces. He therefore tried to avoid conflict with Denmark and with Brandenburg-Prussia. During his personal rule Sweden was usually to be found in the various anti-French groupings in western Europe, although the aid she gave to the coalition in the Nine Years War was insignificant. After 1685 Sweden's German rival, Brandenburg-Prussia, was also a member of the same camp, and for nearly two decades the rulers of Brandenburg were to be more concerned with containing Louis XIV in the west than with expelling the Swedes from Germany. Fairly amicable relations with both the Danes and the Brandenburgers, and Charles XI's refusal to be dragged directly into the Nine Years War, meant that during most of his reign the north was largely free of conflict. In 1691 the King even managed to conclude an armed neutrality treaty with Denmark to prevent the Nine Years War spreading to the Baltic and to protect Scandinavian commerce.

Charles XI devoted most of his energies to the work of internal consolidation and reform. He successfully raised the crown's political and economic power at the expense of the nobility, and he began a thorough reorganisation of the bureaucracy, army and navy. By his death the army was 90,000 strong and a national force no longer dependent on mercenaries or foreign subsidies. His fifteen-year-old son, Charles XII (1697–1718), inherited a monarchy that was more absolute and stronger than at any time during the century.

Sweden's supremacy in the Baltic had rested heavily on the weakness and divisions of her neighbours, and there were few signs at Charles XII's accession in 1697 that any change was in the offing. Sweden's most persistent and dangerous enemy had always been her nearest neighbour, Denmark. While the Danes still retained Norway, they had lost absolute control of the Sound and appeared to have been effectively contained and permanently weakened. They were also being squeezed from the south by Sweden's German possessions and by the dukes of Holstein-Gottorp whose lands in Schleswig and Holstein were mixed in typical feudal confusion with those of the Danish crown. The dukes had acted as Swedish satellites, a role reaffirmed in 1698 when the reigning Duke, Frederick, married Charles XII's eldest sister Hedvig Sophia.

The two north-German states of Hanover and Brandenburg-Prussia posed no immediate threat to Sweden's possessions in Germany. The Elector of Hanover, George Lewis, preferred the Swedes to his closer Danish neighbours and was in any case more interested in the struggle against France. Frederick, the Elector of Brandenburg, shared Hanoverian concern about countering the French menace in the Empire and was chiefly occupied with persuading the Emperor Leopold to accept his use of the title of king *in* Prussia, which he was to manage in 1701. Berlin's ambitions against Swedish Pomerania – so evident in the 1670s – had been temporarily shelved.

Poland had been Sweden's main enemy in the eastern Baltic for most of the seventeenth century, but since the 1670s she had been absorbed in an indecisive struggle in the south with the Turks. She also seemed to be sinking irretrievably into anarchy: the magnates were asserting their own particularist power and seizing the remaining political and military powers of their elective king. On the other hand Russia, or Muscovy as she was still more generally known, had recovered from the chaos of the early-seventeenth-century 'Time of Troubles'. Yet she appeared incapable and even uninterested in trying to regain her former territories along the Baltic. In the 1660s she had successfully recovered parts of the Ukraine from Poland and then from the 1680s had engaged in intermittent war with the Turks. War with the Ottoman Empire had kept both Poles and Russians far too occupied to risk challenging the Swedes throughout Charles XI's later years.

The absolutism created by Charles XI survived his death, and royal power was not challenged from within during his son's lifetime. Unfortunately, Charles XII's youth was too good an opportunity for Sweden's enemies to let slip. Above all the Danish King, Christian V, and then his more ambitious son, Frederick IV, who succeeded in 1699, were determined to use their substantial navy and army to annex the Holstein-Gottorp lands and even to regain southern Sweden. During 1698 and 1699 the Danes negotiated relentlessly to build a coalition against Sweden and to force her young ruler into a war on several fronts. They found a willing ally in the new ruler of Poland. This was the young German Elector Frederick Augustus of Saxony who had been elected Polish king, as Augustus II, in 1697. Ambitious and vigorous, he came to be called Augustus the Strong because of the number of children he fathered: they were said to be as many as the days of the year. He intended to use his Saxon army and revenues to revitalise Poland by making the monarchy hereditary. His first step was to try to increase his prestige there by regaining Livonia and its great port of Riga from Sweden.

In 1699 the Russian Tsar Peter (1682–1725) was brought into the coalition. He was regarded as the junior partner and was very much an unknown quantity. But eventually his dynamic personality was to dominate the coming war as much as that of Charles XII of Sweden. During the summer of 1698, on his way back from his famous tour of Europe, Peter had met Augustus in Poland. The two young rulers had taken to each other: they were equally ambitious, physically tough and fond of heavy drinking. The Tsar had helped Augustus's election in 1697 by moving troops up to the frontier, beginning the process which made Poland a Russian satellite. He now welcomed the new coalition as a chance to regain those lands in Ingria and around the Neva which he believed were rightly Russia's and which Sweden had seized in 1617. He rushed into the venture without adequate preparation or assessing the consequences, but he was not rash enough to hope for Estonia, let alone Livonia which his senior partner Augustus wanted. However, when Peter and Augustus signed an alliance against Charles XII in October 1699, they believed the youth would prove an easy victim. Both misjudged his father's reorganisation of Sweden and overestimated their own power. Peter, in particular, deluded himself over the effectiveness of the military reforms he had introduced since the beginning of his personal rule in 1695.

In joining the anti-Swedish coalition Peter took the decisive step which eventually made Russia part of the European states system. Until his reign she had been largely isolated. There were no regular diplomatic representatives abroad and the Europeans considered her only slightly less barbarous than the Turks. During the sixteenth and seventeenth centuries Poland and Sweden, by conscious design as well as by geography, had prevented her contacts with the west and denied her all but the most perfunctory technological, economic and cultural relations. Similarly, the Turks and their Tartar vassals had blocked her way to the Black Sea. Her one port was Archangel, far to the north on the White Sea and open only briefly in summer. Yet the products of Russia's forests and plains were in continuous demand in western Europe.

Peter's policy in seeking to attack Sweden and gain some of the Baltic coastline followed earlier sixteenth-century traditions of Russian policy, but to do so as part of a broad coalition with Denmark and Poland was a new development. He was also abandoning the policy of the past generation or so of trying to conquer territory from Poland and the Ottoman Empire. In 1667 Poland had been forced to cede parts of the Ukraine and Kiev to Russia. This and the decay of Poland itself ended the menace of Polish aggression and closed a long period of Russo-Polish hostility. The Turks and the Crimean Tartars, who controlled the southern steppe land and the northern shores of the Black Sea, were subsequently judged the greater danger, especially because of a resurgence of Ottoman power in the 1670s (see p. 72). In 1686 Russia had achieved fleeting membership of the European states system by joining the Holy League with Austria, Poland and Venice (see p. 74). Following this, desultory and fruitless campaigns were conducted in the south. Peter, however, breathed new life into the struggle and, by energetically building a river fleet on the Don, captured Azov in 1696. He hoped to seize land further south and put a fleet on the Black Sea, but Russia's revived interest was not shared by her allies who wanted to end their conflict in the Balkans. Peter's grand tour of Europe in 1697–98 was undertaken mainly to persuade them to change their minds. But Russia was too remote and under-valued to influence them.

This tour and his meeting with Augustus II completely changed Peter's policies. The Tsar became more aware of the realities of European politics and the opportunity of expansion against Sweden. This would compensate for having to give up the Turkish War, which Russia was too weak to pursue alone. Moreover, if his country were to develop as the Tsar wanted, that is, with direct contact with the western naval powers and with radical domestic reform programmes, it was essential to expel the Swedes from part of the Baltic coastline: Russia would control her own economic outlets instead of having to use Archangel or Swedish middlemen, and the Baltic Germans would provide her with their administrative and commercial expertise. By seizing at least Ingria and the mouth of the Neva, Peter would have his 'window towards the west', where he could build a real sea-going navy instead of the river galleys he had constructed on the Don. The war against Sweden was not so much for prestige or revenge but for Russia's economic and cultural future: Peter's ultimate aim was the massive economic development of Russia, making her a commercial bridge between Asia and Europe. He therefore ended his war with the Turks by the peace of Constantinople in summer 1700, some months after the other Holy League allies had concluded the peace of Karlowitz. His only gain was Azov, which did not bring direct access to the Black Sea. But he was now free to concentrate on fighting the Swedes.

Charles XII defeats the northern allies, 1700–8

Denmark, Poland and Russia completed their coalition in autumn 1699 and counted on defeating Sweden in a short war. However, the war was to lead instead to remarkable Swedish victories and the collapse of the coalition. The Swedes themselves had expected a Danish attack but were taken unawares by a war on two fronts, though this had always been likely because of the nature of the empire. In February 1700 Frederick IV attacked the Holstein-Gottorp lands and Augustus's troops poured into Livonia. During the summer Peter also attacked Ingria and Estonia. Only Sweden's lands in Germany were unmolested. Unfortunately for the allies, their young, inexperienced victim turned out to be a military genius with a far superior army. Charles XII, who was now eighteen, was also given immediate naval help by Britain and the Dutch, who wanted a balance in the north and to prevent total Danish control of the Sound. Moreover they believed that a rapid Swedish victory would allow them to hire troops from both sides for a possible struggle with Louis XIV over the Spanish succession (see pp. 54ff.). An Anglo-Dutch fleet landed Charles's army on Zealand, which allowed him to threaten Copenhagen, the capital of the power he feared most, Denmark. Frederick IV quickly made the peace of Travendal in August 1700, recognising the possessions of the Duke of Holstein-Gottorp. Charles then shipped his army himself to Ingria taking Peter completely by surprise. It needed only 8,000 Swedes to rout 23,000 Russians at Narva during a snowstorm in November 1700, making Peter evacuate Ingria. The Tsar could probably have been forced to make peace after this humiliation. But the Russians' poor showing led Charles contemptuously to refuse to bother pursuing them. In any case he dared not leave Augustus of Poland's strong Saxon army in his rear in Livonia.

A general peace would have been possible in 1701. The coalition was in disarray and posed no real threat to Sweden's Baltic empire. Although Augustus II was undefeated, his Saxons had failed to take Riga and he wanted peace. However, Charles had acquired a taste for war and wished to punish the Elector-King whom he blamed for forming the coalition against him. In summer 1701, therefore, he invaded Poland: he aimed to defeat Augustus, end the dangerous dynastic union between Poland and Saxony and turn Poland with its important grain port of Danzig into a dependant. For the next few years he became bogged down not only in campaigns against the Saxons but also in what amounted to a civil war in Poland, where the native nobility was divided into Saxon and Swedish factions: Poland's century of outside interference and aristocratic conflict had begun. By 1704 Charles XII managed to get Augustus deposed and to have Stanislas Leszczyński elected as Swedish puppet king. A year later the Saxon troops had all been expelled, and in 1706 Charles invaded Saxony. He had not attacked the electorate before because of promises to the Maritime Powers not to enter the Empire and thus disturb their German allies in the war against Louis XIV. He now quickly forced Augustus to make peace and recognise the loss of his Polish crown at Altranstädt in September 1706.

By 1706–7, Charles appeared to be the arbiter of Europe, capable of intervening decisively in the War of the Spanish Succession. For the first and only time this war and the Great Northern War appeared about to converge. Both sides hoped Charles would help them and looked anxiously towards his camp in Saxony where he stayed for a year. But Charles had no intention of intervening, as he saw no advantage for Sweden. How his troops would have fared against western armies is problematic.

The year 1707 was decisive in the Great Northern War because once again Charles XII could have rested on his laurels and concluded a general and advantageous peace. However, his sole aim was to turn against Russia, and he had used his year in Saxony to raise contributions there to finance a campaign as well as to plan it. He was determined to deal with Peter because from 1702 Russian troops had reappeared in the Baltic provinces. The next year Peter began to build a new capital, St Petersburg, on the Neva in Ingria, which showed his intention to stay there. Then in 1705–6 he overran Courland and devastated wide areas of Estonia and Livonia. While Charles XII was in Saxony, he had also been sending troops and money to build up a military and political position in Poland. Russo-Swedish rivalry had now extended from the Baltic provinces to include Poland as well. In fact Charles had seriously miscalculated after 1700 by concentrating on Poland and Saxony instead of strengthening his position in the Baltic provinces, which were far more important for the Swedish empire.

Peter had learned from the humiliation of Narva and in the following years worked feverishly with the help of foreign experts to reform his army, and later his administration, on Swedish lines: his reforms were chiefly shaped to military needs. Despite Charles's contempt for these reforms, the Tsar's energy did succeed in releasing Russia's vast reserves, and this made the eventual defeat of Sweden inevitable. Russia, moreover, unlike Sweden, had the economic and demographic resources necessary to maintain a great-power position. However, at this stage Peter's new army was untried and, for the first time, Russia had to face Charles on her own. The Tsar would have been willing to make peace, provided he could have kept St Petersburg. But Charles only wanted a military solution, threatening to 'depose' Peter. He was over-confident and expected Russian military power would easily be 'broken and destroyed'. He was furious at Peter's recent ravaging of the Baltic provinces and interference in Poland. He intended to expel the Russians from both and to help Stanislas Leszczyński regain the areas of Poland lost to Russia in 1667. These ambitions required total victory and the imposition of a dictated peace. By playing for the highest stakes, and losing, Charles was to increase the pace of both Sweden's decline and Russia's rise as the leading Baltic power.

The collapse of the Swedish empire, 1708–16

On invading Russia with 40,000 men in 1708, Charles intended to march directly on Moscow by way of Smolensk. Unfortunately, reinforcements and essential supplies from the Baltic provinces failed to reach him in time, and Peter, refusing to commit his army to battle, turned the country into a desert through scorched-earth tactics. Short of food and continually harried by attacks on stragglers, Charles decided to follow a more southerly invasion route through the Ukraine, which had been left comparatively untouched. Here the Cossack leader, Mazepa, who wanted freedom from Russian control, had offered Charles military help. The wild steppe borderland of the Ukraine was in a fluid political state between Russia, Poland and the Ottoman Empire, and Cossack rebellions such as this one had occurred often before. But Mazepa was in fact taken by surprise when Charles moved south, as he had hoped to play him and Peter off against each other. In the event he brought the Swedish King only a few bands of irregular cavalry, and his rebellion proved of little consequence to the Tsar.

Charles XII and his Swedes had to live through the dreadful winter of 1709 in the open steppe, when even birds were frozen to death in mid-flight. Survival rather than conquest became uppermost in their minds. On 8 July 1709 the Swedish force of 20,000 was totally destroyed by Peter's army of 50,000 at Poltava far to the south near the River Dnieper. Charles himself managed to escape with a few cavalry across the Turkish frontier, where he stayed for the next five years. This catastrophe had real as well as symbolic importance and proved a turning-point in the history of the north. Poltava not only halted the dynamic career of Charles XII but also proved an irreversible defeat: it destroyed Sweden's great-power position and paved the way for Russian ascendancy. The future of the whole Swedish empire, built and maintained by military might, was put in doubt. Sweden's past successes had been won by lightning campaigns fought at the expense of other countries. Now she was enmeshed in a war of attrition which her resources were too poor to sustain. Defeat was inevitable, but it was not immediate. A steady erosion of Swedish power took place over the next decade, as the Swedes were gradually forced to accept that a defensive policy around the Baltic was all that was possible: the role which Charles XI had envisaged in the 1680s and 1690s.

Peter's victory at Poltava reflected the success of his internal reforms, and the destruction of Mazepa and Cossack power allowed the monarchy more direct control of the Ukraine. The victory also made Europe take Russia seriously, and it opened the door to immense territorial expansion. Almost immediately after Poltava Peter's troops occupied all the Baltic provinces, including Livonia, which Augustus had wanted for Poland. The Tsar's forces also restored Augustus to the Polish throne, effectively making him a puppet. Poltava therefore led to Russian domination of Poland, which was almost as much a victim of the Great Northern War as Sweden. It was inevitable that these successes should lead to a revival of the original northern coalition of 1698–1700. But its aims now expanded: Russia wanted all the Baltic provinces and even to extend her influence into northern Germany; the Danes were looking beyond Holstein-Gottorp to Sweden's German possessions; and Augustus of Saxony–Poland was also looking to the latter to compensate for Livonia.

After Poltava Charles had fled into Turkish territory and was allowed to stay at Bender in Moldavia. He hoped to extend the whole scope of the Russo-Swedish War by persuading the Turks and the Crimean Tartars to help against Peter. This attempt initially made sense: he had found the Turks and their Tartar vassals in 1709–10 highly alarmed at the expansion of Russian power in the south-east, and he quickly persuaded the Sultan and the Crimean Tartar Khan to declare war on Russia in November 1710. Peter had not wanted this diversion but tried to make the best of it. Beginning the Tsarist tradition of posing as defender and liberator of the Sultan's Balkan Christians, he tried to encourage them to revolt. Although the subject peoples were attracted to the idea of Russia as their natural protector and Peter had great hopes of assistance, they refused to show their hand until he proved his military worth.

In June 1711 Peter confidently led an invading army into the Danubian principalities of Moldavia and Wallachia. However, he met considerable problems because of lack of naval bases on the Black Sea coast and communication difficulties in his rear across the sparsely populated Ukraine. As he advanced southwards he received little local support and his supply troubles became insuperable. Soon he was surrounded by a Turkish army five times the size of his own on the River Pruth and he faced almost certain destruction. He was very lucky that the Turks agreed to sign peace (the Pruth treaty, 22 July 1711). The skill of the minister he sent to Constantinople, Shafirov, and disunity among the Ottoman leaders, led the Porte to spare his army and grant lenient terms. The Turks' main concern was to re-establish the status quo around the Black Sea. Peter had to surrender his only gain from the last war, Azov (see p. 81), and the fortresses built along the Dnieper, disband the navy he had kept on the Don since 1695 and promise not to interfere in Polish politics. Although the Tsar soon ignored this last promise, his attempts at expansion to the south, which had absorbed so much of his energy and resources in the 1690s, had ended in complete failure. The Turks, however, did not cause him serious trouble for the rest of his reign. Although Charles XII was to persuade them to declare war again in 1712–13, no actual military intervention followed, as the Turks did not want all-out war against Russia. Charles's protests eventually led to his semi-imprisonment by the

Sultan, who took no further part in the northern struggle. The Otto-man Empire, whose administration had been dominated up to now by Rumanian–Slav elements (who were suspected of having sym-pathised with the Tsar), was to come more under the influence of Greek administrators. These pressed for expansion against Venice in the Morea and then against Austria in Hungary to recover the losses suffered at Karlowitz (see pp. 76, 103).

Charles XII stayed in the Ottoman Empire till November 1714, evidently still attracted by the concept of a vast Swedo-Russo-Turkish conflict, although there was no longer any possibility of this. He sent repeated orders to Stockholm forbidding peace and demanding the raising of fresh armies. In fact the options had narrowed disastrously for Sweden, which was now engaged in a losing battle to hold on to her Baltic empire. The Baltic provinces had been lost to Russia, which also managed to defeat the Swedish fleet at Hangö in July 1714 (Rus-sia's Baltic fleet grew from nothing in 1703 to seventeen ships of the line in 1714 and to thirty-two by 1724). Then between 1712 and 1715 Sweden's German possessions fell to a combination of old and new enemies. In 1710 the Danes had invaded Scania only to be repulsed, but from 1711 Russian and Saxon troops joined them in operations against Sweden's lands in Germany and against Holstein-Gottorp. The security afforded from Sweden by the growing number of Rus-sian troops in north Germany led Hanover and Prussia, who were now becoming free of the Spanish Succession War, to join in the Northern War and pick up the remaining scraps of Swedish territory. But the two powers only entered the war gradually. In 1712, as the Danes seized Bremen, the Elector of Hanover, who had previously sympathised with Sweden because of shared hostility to Denmark, occupied Verden. He claimed to be 'safeguarding' this Swedish pos-session for Charles XII, but the Elector, who became King George I of Great Britain in 1714, intended to have Verden, and Bremen as well, for himself. He was biding his time before actually declaring war. However, in May 1715, he signed a treaty as elector with Den-mark, by which he bought Bremen for 30,000 thalers, received a Danish guarantee of this and of Verden for himself and guaranteed in return Danish possession of the Duke of Holstein-Gottorp's lands in Schleswig. He also promised to declare war on Sweden, which he did after making a treaty with Russia in the October. Hanover's close neighbour, the new King of Prussia, Frederick William I (1713–40), who had occupied Swedish Stettin in 1713, had also declared war on Charles XII in May 1715.

In November 1714 Charles XII appeared at the fortress of Stralsund in Pomerania. He had ridden 900 miles across Europe in a fortnight. But instead of sailing straight to Sweden to take personal control of his country which had now endured fifteen years of war, he wasted another year in a fruitless defence of Stralsund, and only at its fall did he return to Sweden. By early 1716, when Wismar fell as well, Sweden had lost all its trans-Baltic possessions and the Russians had made great inroads into Finland. Faced now by an alliance of Russia, Denmark, Saxony–Poland, Prussia and Hanover, Sweden had no hope of regaining her empire, but Charles's return and his retention of absolute power meant the allies could only achieve peace by dictating it in Stockholm itself. It was above all Charles himself who refused to make peace. Rash and obstinate he certainly was, but it was not madness which made him cling on despite the bankruptcy of his country and the heavy toll on its manpower. He was determined to retain some of his empire and not to make peace till he had received 'satisfaction' for the assaults on his honour. To agree to any other terms would mean abandoning Sweden's great-power position, and this he refused to accept.

The Great Northern War had been fought so far largely in isolation from the rest of Europe, which had been preoccupied with the War of the Spanish Succession. However, this gradually changed as the war in the west came to an end in 1713/14 (see pp. 63ff.); from 1715 to 1716 the northern and western diplomatic systems tended to merge. At his accession to the British throne in 1714 George I was firmly committed to Russia and wanted to bring his new kingdom as well as Hanover into the war quickly. British power allowed him to play a much greater part than his possession of Hanover would have done. George and his chief Hanoverian minister, Bernstorff, intended, with British naval and diplomatic help, to make Hanover the leading north-German power. Possession of Bremen and Verden brought access to the Baltic and the North Sea, but they also wanted to turn the neighbouring duchy of Mecklenburg into a dependency. Eventually these ambitions were to cause rifts with Russia, Prussia and Austria as well as Sweden. George I's British kingdom also had grounds for intervention in the Baltic. Since 1710, when Peter had occupied the Baltic provinces, the Swedes had blockaded the coastline and interfered with the vital trade in naval stores. Swedish privateers had also attacked British and Dutch shipping. Consequently, George I found little difficulty in persuading his English ministers and the Dutch to send a joint fleet to the Baltic in 1715 to convoy merchant ships. Although the Dutch insisted on strict neutrality, George managed to use the British ships to assist in the allied capture of Rügen and Stralsund. Its presence there the next year as well greatly helped the incipient Russian navy to safeguard Peter's conquests in the eastern Baltic. The British position was regularised in 1717 when war was declared on Charles XII after the discovery of Swedish dealings with the Jacobites. The latter ensured parliamentary support for the continued dispatch of annual fleets to the Baltic.

The collapse of the northern coalition and the conclusion of peace with Sweden, 1716–21

The final expulsion of the Swedes from Germany was quickly followed in 1716 by the collapse of the anti-Swedish coalition. In this final stage of the war quarrels among the allies were as important as the attempts to force a peace settlement on Sweden. The allies split into Russia and Prussia on the one side and Hanover and Denmark on the other. Augustus II of Saxony–Poland would have preferred to support Hanover, but he sat on the fence, largely because of his dependent position in Poland. The coalition broke up principally over the clash of Hanoverian and Russian ambitions in north Germany. Russian troops had been there since 1711, and in 1716 substantial Russian contingents were moved into Denmark as well, in preparation for an abortive allied attack on Scania. Moreover, in April 1716 Peter married his niece to the Duke of Mecklenburg, at the same time as he intervened in a quarrel between the Duke and his nobility and helped him suppress the noble-dominated estates. The Tsar intended to turn the duchy into a satellite and to keep Wismar for himself as a naval base. With his wide-ranging plans for Russia's commercial expansion, he envisaged an early version of the Kiel Canal to link Wismar and Hamburg, which would allow Russia to trade directly with the west without passing through the Sound and paying its tolls. The Russian occupation of Mecklenburg, which showed every sign of becoming permanent, led to a crisis which made Europe even more aware of Russia's new strength than Poltava. But it was above all George I and his Hanoverian ministers who grew desperately worried in summer 1716 at Russia's position in neighbouring Mecklenburg. Frederick William I of Prussia, on the other hand, sided with the Tsar. There was a good deal of personal and political jealousy between him and his father-in-law, George I. But the Prussian King also shared Russia's wish to keep Poland weak and was most anxious about the vulnerability of East Prussia to Russian arms if he quarrelled with the Tsar.

In summer 1716 it seemed that, if a confrontation occurred with Peter the Great, George would only be able to count on Denmark, which already had Russian troops on its soil. He therefore looked round for ways of exerting pressure on the Tsar, especially ones which would cost Hanover itself little in troops and cash. Besides British naval and financial strength, he could depend on tacit Austrian and French support. The Emperor Charles VI was willing to apply diplomatic pressure: he wanted British naval protection in the Mediterranean during his war with the Turks (see p. 103), and he also shared Hanoverian fears of Russian power in north Germany and of Prussia's growing standing army. The French, who had seen the final collapse of their former eastern barrier against the Habsburgs since the outbreak of the Northern War, had been uncertain which side to support in the Baltic. But the Regent Orleans's need for an alliance with Britain in summer 1716 (see p. 108) made him willing to abandon Sweden, guarantee Hanover and its possession of Bremen and Verden and support George I diplomatically. Consequently, attempts by Peter and Frederick William to conclude defensive alliances with France in 1716–17 were steered by the French into innocuous treaties of friendship. Having failed to break the diplomatic front George had built against him and being unwilling to challenge the major western powers, Peter eventually withdrew his troops from Germany in autumn 1717, leaving only 3,000 men in Mecklenburg to protect the Duke.

Although George I and Peter's confrontation over Mecklenburg began because of Hanoverian interests, it very soon developed into genuine British concern about Peter's control of the Baltic provinces and the all-important naval stores, and about Russian naval strength. In fact the rivalry which now emerged between Britain and Russia was to be one of the most important features of the Great Northern War in its final stages. Opposition to Russia, however, had not been unanimous in Britain and helped cause the split in George I's Whig ministry in 1716–17. With Charles Townshend and Robert Walpole's departure from the ministry early in 1717 George could depend on British naval strength against both Russia and Sweden, although no declaration of war was made against Russia.

The greatest success of George I's anti-Russian policy was achieved on 5 January 1719 when Hanover, Charles VI and Augustus II (who had listened to Austrian representations) concluded the alliance of Vienna aimed against both Russia and Prussia. This was signed after the conclusion of Austria's Turkish War (see p. 115, 117f.) and it looked as though Austrian troops would co-operate directly with forces raised by George I. Austria and Saxony-Poland also believed they would be able to depend on British naval help. George's diplomatic association with the Danes and French was to make his international position a strong one. Certainly Frederick William I was frightened enough to abandon Peter the Great, who was himself intimidated into withdrawing his troops from Poland. He also made no attempt to oppose the entry of Hanoverian troops into Mecklenburg where they expelled the Duke and restored the power of the noble estates. The Russian threat to north Germany had therefore been effectively removed, at least for the time being, but Russia's position on the Baltic and its eastern shores was as strong as ever.

This potentially very dangerous, although bloodless, confrontation between George I and Peter the Great took place while both rulers were still at war with Sweden. Their quarrel gave Charles XII, who was now confined to Sweden proper, more room for diplomatic manoeuvre in 1717–18. Under the guidance of his minister, Görtz, he resorted to an ingenious and desperate diplomacy, negotiating with both sides and hoping to salvage some of his Baltic empire. To strike at the British he also negotiated with the Jacobites and with Alberoni in Spain. Talks held with Peter the Great's diplomats in the Åland Islands in 1718 inspired fears in Britain that a Swedish–Russian–Spanish–Jacobite combination was in the offing. But the talks failed because of Charles's own reluctance to surrender the Baltic provinces, particularly the port of Reval. Peter was determined to hold out, counting on the total collapse of Sweden. At the same time Charles was striking out in a new direction, and with an army rebuilt during his couple of years in Sweden, he invaded Danish Norway in 1718. Its conquest would give Sweden direct access to the North Sea and provide some compensation for losses elsewhere. However, the expedition ended when Charles was killed at the siege of Frederik-sheld in December 1718.

The death of Charles XII, followed by the conclusion of the Vienna alliance four weeks later, rapidly changed the situation in the north. The Russians had withdrawn eastwards and a far more accommodating government assumed power in Stockholm. The new regime of Charles XII's younger sister, Ulrika Eleonora, and, after her abdication in 1720, of her husband Frederick of Hesse, was forced to abolish absolutism and accept aristocratic parliamentary control. Sweden now wanted peace desperately, and, with British mediation, Stockholm came to terms with all her enemies except Russia. As important as this conciliatory attitude in Sweden was that George I's policy in the north during 1719 came under the firm control of the British minister, Stanhope. He insisted that George's hostility to Prussia, which his chief Hanoverian minister, Bernstorff had done his best to encourage, be abandoned and that Frederick William be won over, as happened in August 1719. Britain's French allies were to play a crucial role in helping her achieve this settlement as well as the ones with Sweden. French diplomats had been active in all the northern courts on behalf of Britain and this seemed fully to justify the Anglo-French *entente*.

Sweden hoped that by being conciliatory she could expect British naval protection against the Tsar, who was now unleashing terror raids on the Swedish coast around Stockholm. By the treaty of Stockholm, 20 November 1719, Sweden and Hanover made peace: Hanover obtained the cession of Bremen and Verden and thus became the second largest north-German power. Peace was then made on 1 February 1720 by Sweden with Britain and Prussia. The Swedes, largely through French insistence, managed to retain Wismar and part of Pomerania (including Stralsund) but ceded the rest of West Pomerania and Stettin to Prussia giving her complete control of the River Oder. The Prussian King had now effectively abandoned the Russian camp, and, in agreements made in August 1719 with Hanover and Britain, he and George I had allied and guaranteed their territories, including their gains from Sweden. At last on 14 June 1720, through the treaty of Frederiksborg, Anglo-French diplomacy achieved the most difficult of the peace settlements, that between Sweden and Denmark. Here Denmark surrendered her claims on Wismar and Rügen, forced Sweden to renounce her exemption from Sound dues and received the Holstein-Gottorp lands in Schleswig. Sweden's new rulers were willing enough to agree because Duke Charles Frederick of Holstein-Gottorp was the son of Charles XII's elder sister and a claimant of the Swedish throne.

The Swedish monarchy had been encouraged to believe they could compensate for their losses in the western Baltic by receiving outside help to force Peter the Great to disgorge all his conquests except for Narva, St Petersburg and Kronstadt. This agreed with Stanhope's aims, for British diplomacy was now based on the conviction that British and Hanoverian security in the north depended on co-operation with France and Prussia. Stanhope wanted to build an impressive coalition of Britain–Hanover, France, Prussia, Austria, Saxony and Denmark to help Sweden against Russia and to recover Swedish losses in the Baltic provinces, thereby renewing a balance in the north. However, his attempts to form this coalition in 1719 to 1720 were stillborn. The South Sea Bubble crisis seriously weakened Britain in 1720 (see p. 118), while the British navy failed to prevent further Russian raids on the Swedish coast. Stanhope also could not raise the necessary military muscle to intimidate the Tsar, since the other powers were understandably reluctant to challenge him directly. In particular, France, though prepared to give diplomatic support, would not provide troops to establish what amounted to British supremacy in the Baltic. Frederick William feared a Russian attack on East Prussia, while the Emperor, who was expected to provide the bulk of the forces, was equally evasive. Vienna was not only less anxious about the Tsar now that his troops had left Germany and Poland but was also coming to see his possible value as an ally. The Emperor's ministers were highly alarmed at the new alignment of the north-German Protestant powers, Hanover and Prussia, with their connections with Britain, France and the two Scandinavian kingdoms. They feared this would undermine Charles VI's authority in Germany, and this fear seemed confirmed by a Prusso-Hanoverian front which emerged in response to a minor religious quarrel among the German states over persecution of Protestants in the Palatinate in 1719–20. There seemed a real danger that the Elector of Hanover might use his power as British king to challenge the Emperor in the Empire as Sweden had in the past. It was above all George's new and increasingly close connection with Prussia which was a major factor in the rapid breakdown of relations between London and Vienna in 1720–21 and in the consequent failure of the two north German powers to win Imperial consent to their conquests of Bremen, Verden and Stettin.

Seeing little prospect of real help against the Tsar and subject to repeated devastations of their coastline, Swedish resistance to Peter's demands collapsed. They therefore used French mediation to conclude the peace of Nystad with him in 1721. Sweden ceded Livonia, Estonia, Ingria, Kexholm and part of Karelia to Russia, which returned the rest of Finland. Sweden had now clearly become a second-class state, a Baltic rather than a European power. The loss of possessions on the European mainland (only Wismar and a stretch of West Pomerania were left) made direct intervention difficult. None the less, Sweden only slowly renounced her European pretensions and continued to mount occasional expeditions during the eighteenth century, two against Russia but also one against Prussia in the Seven Years War. Although, unlike Poland, Sweden did not dissolve into internal chaos and only suffered minor territorial losses until the Napoleonic Wars, she shared Poland's fate of continual foreign interference in her domestic politics.

The long-term effects of the Great Northern War were probably more important for Europe than the Spanish Succession War: this was because of the rise of Russia. Though Hanover and Prussia gained territories from their belated involvement in the Northern War, neither was yet a great power: Hanover's strength hinged on her dynastic connection with Britain, while Prussia's subsequent power followed from the conquest of Silesia in 1740, not from the gain of Stettin. Russian victories and expansion could no more have been predicted in 1700 than Sweden's collapse and territorial losses. Yet Russia's rise was probably inevitable. That it happened when it did, however, in the first decades of the eighteenth century was the direct result of her military defeat of Sweden. By 1721 Peter had conquered the Baltic provinces, bringing access to the sea, made Poland almost a satellite (the Tsar was the *de facto* guarantor of a constitutional settlement in 1716 between the Poles and Augustus II) and expanded Russian influence into north Germany. This influence was to be extended further in the coming years by Peter's protection of the Duke of Holstein-Gottorp against the Danes. Although the Tsar's new capital of St Petersburg was vulnerable to Swedish attack across the Finnish border and he had still not gained an ice-free port, he had clearly made Russia the dominant Baltic power. Over the next half-century she was to become probably the strongest European power as well. Like France and Britain, Russia had the strength to act independently as a great power without depending on outside support. Her geographical position on the periphery of Europe also gave her much freedom of manoeuvre.

Despite Russia's great influence in the later years of the century, after Nystad her role in the European states system was still rather ambivalent. Only the Austrians and Prussians were really willing to accept her as a member. The British and French were determined to shut her out. No major power would ally with her on terms of equality. Yet Russia was now a part of Europe and a permanent factor in the states system. Peter himself had visited the west again in 1717 and a body of permanent Russian ambassadors abroad had been established (see p. 204). Moreover, there seemed every reason to expect that Russian influence would continue to increase in Europe itself, since Peter clearly intended to maintain his vast standing army and to pursue further economic and administrative reforms necessary to support it. His navy also showed every sign of continuing its steady growth. It had proved superior to the Danish and Swedish fleets, and had so far been largely invulnerable to the British fleet acting so far from home. However, although future Russian rulers were to continue to expand the army, Peter's fleet was to be allowed to decline after his death. This was one factor in the eventual reconciliation between Britain and Russia.

CHAPTER FOUR

British diplomatic ascendancy and the entente, 1714–1731

THE EUROPEAN SYSTEM AFTER THE PEACE OF UTRECHT–RASTADT

The Utrecht-Rastadt peace settlement partitioned the Spanish monarchy and at the same time realised the ambitions of William III to humble France. It was followed by a sharp decline in French prestige and a corresponding rise in that of Britain. But Britain did not take the place of Louis XIV's France: the defeat of France ended the era of the predominance of one power and led to a more fluid European states system. This new system was one which came to embrace the whole of Europe except the south-east: problems which arose in any area outside the Balkans, and even at times those in their colonies, almost inevitably became the concern of all the European powers. In 1700 there had been no single system. The Continent was roughly divided into three: the north and east around the Baltic where Sweden, Denmark, Poland, Russia and the north-German states struggled for supremacy, the remote lands in the south-east stretching from the Balkans to the northern shores of the Black Sea where the Ottoman Empire faced the expanding Austria and Russia, and the rest of Europe to the west of the Oder and the Carpathian Mountains. Events in one area certainly affected the other two, especially as some states had overlapping interests, but essentially the three areas were separate from one other and the Spanish Succession War and the Great Northern War took place with hardly any contact between them. However, as the eighteenth century progressed, the barriers gradually broke down.

It was not immediately clear which powers would play the leading roles after 1714: there was no state which was obviously dominant in the way France had been. In 1700 observers could have pointed to France, the Maritime Powers – they were usually seen as acting together – Austria, and possibly Sweden in the north, as the great powers, but with France way ahead of the rest. By 1756 the great powers had become Britain, France, Austria, Russia and, in effect, Prussia, all apparently equally matched. Even at the close of the War of the Spanish Succession, such a change would have seemed highly unlikely. Then it appeared that Britain and the Dutch Republic – now clearly separate in policies as well as rulers – Austria and France would rule the roost. In the north, although Russia had decisively beaten Sweden (see pp. 84ff.), she had not yet established herself as a permanent feature in Europe. As to Prussia, her pretensions and strength only became apparent in the 1740s.

The Utrecht settlement had been largely Britain's handiwork and there could be no doubt now that she was a great power. But her small population, lack of a standing army and her important non-European interests meant that she could not dominate the Continent in the style of Louis XIV. Certainly Britain was to use her diplomatic, financial and naval power to exert more influence than any other state till the 1730s. None the less, she only managed to do so because France was passive and no other state was asserting itself effectively.

Britain's own gains at Utrecht were more apparent than real. Earlier hopes of seizing parts of Spanish America had been abandoned during the war, and the direct gains in the colonies were largely empty wastes in Canada which were of trivial importance. But the British in any case had been less intent on acquiring colonial territory than trading stations and commercial concessions: successive British ministries in the early eighteenth century were to be largely indifferent to extending colonial possessions. At Utrecht the Tory peacemakers had felt it more important to insist on trading privileges from Spain and to ensure that neither the Dutch nor France shared them. In the event the expectations of a Spanish-American commercial bonanza proved disappointing. Britain's trade with Spanish America was never the unqualified success of that with Portugal, where she came to monopolise trade with both Portugal and, indirectly, Portuguese Brazil.

The peace of Utrecht and the defeat of France could not by themselves ensure British commercial supremacy in the eighteenth century. In many ways the struggle for this had only just begun, and the French were still to prove the most dangerous rivals. Britain's eventual and complete success came not so much from treaties and trading concessions as from the ability of her merchants and manufacturers and of the royal navy to exclude and destroy competitors. Britain's navy had achieved total mastery in the Spanish Succession War, and this dominance was preserved at Utrecht. The fleets of Bourbon France and Spain had been swept from the seas, while the Dutch fleet had acted largely as a junior partner of Britain. The peace also contributed to Britain's increasing dominance of strategic coasts and islands, which allowed her to police the main European trading routes and to dispatch ships to all the waters round the Continent. The acquisition of Gibraltar and Minorca, the division of Spanish Italy between the non-naval powers of Austria and Savoy, together with the alliance with Portugal, all ensured British command of the routes to America and the East as well as of the western Mediterranean. Friendship with the Dutch and the Danes allowed access and contributed to eventual predominance in the Baltic. These relationships were to be more important to Britain in this respect than her rulers' possession of the German electorate of Hanover after 1714. Although Hanover demanded constant British intervention in the Baltic, it provided no naval facilities there.

British governments, with parliamentary encouragement, were to feel the same need to keep 'a fleet in being' as continental states felt for standing armies. This was not only to protect Britain's commerce but also to prevent foreign and Jacobite invasion. British naval supremacy itself was not to go unchallenged. Spain under Philip V tried repeatedly to rebuild her fleet, while Peter the Great created a sizeable Russian navy in the Baltic. Above all there was always the threat that France might attempt to re-establish herself as a naval power, as did happen in the 1730s.

In the half-century after the peace of Utrecht Britain continually used her naval supremacy and ability to pay subsidies in order to intervene in any European quarrel which might threaten the Protestant succession or her own commerce. But she was also usually willing to intervene in quarrels which disturbed the general peace and upset the balance which had been established at Utrecht. In British eyes the peace was based on the idea of an overall balance on the Continent which could be adjusted by an occasional intervention by Britain: neither of the two great continental powers, France and Austria, should be allowed to achieve hegemony. The Utrecht settlement had prevented the union of the Spanish monarchy with either France or Austria (Spain was to pass to Savoy if Philip V's line failed), and Spain's European empire had been partitioned in such a way as to guard against a preponderance of power. It was also intended to put limits on both France and Austria.

William III and the Dutch had worked to raise a military barrier in the Southern Netherlands against the French, and Austria and the German states had hoped for the same along the Rhine. However, the Utrecht settlement did not simply build physical barriers of strings of fortresses round France or a ring of strengthened countries round her borders in the manner of the 1815 settlement. It created barriers manned by more than one power, which could be used against Austria as well as France, and which depended on British support for their maintenance. In the Southern Netherlands sovereignty passed to the Emperor, but he had to share power with the Dutch who garrisoned the 'barrier' fortresses: both states checked each other and their mutual hostility meant British help would be necessary for the province to serve as a successful barrier against France. In Italy, where France and

Spain were excluded, French expansion was blocked by Austrian control of Milan and Naples and by a stronger duchy of Savoy. But the extension of Savoyard power, which depended heavily on British diplomatic and naval support, meant that Austria could not be master of the whole peninsula. The barriers created at Utrecht, largely under Bolingbroke's direction, were therefore areas of divided influence, which could be used against France and Austria, and which Britain herself could expect to dominate. It is very doubtful, however, if these barriers would have been strong enough to contain France if she had been determined to destroy them, as she was to demonstrate in the 1730s and 1740s. Essentially the barriers held because of France's weakness and refusal to test them in case by doing so she revived the victorious coalition of the Spanish Succession War.

In making the Utrecht settlement the Tory ministry could be accused of having weakened Britain's position in relation to France. They had destroyed Britain's alliances with the Dutch and the Emperor, alliances which might be needed to hold France to the settlement, given Britain's lack of a large military establishment. The Whig ministers after 1714 were to be very aware of this weakness of Britain. But Bolingbroke had hoped to overcome it, not by depending on the Grand Alliance powers, but by adopting a more flexible role in European politics. Britain would depend on her navy, the local anti-French and anti-Austrian balances and barriers created at the peace and at the same time be reconciled with France and Spain. Consequently, during the peace negotiations, and in the year after Utrecht, very close relations developed between the Tories and Louis XIV's ministers. On the whole Bolingbroke's Whig rivals, despite their traditional and sentimental attachment to the Grand Alliance, were to adopt very similar policies to his soon after they returned to power, and they were to maintain them till the 1730s.

Although attempts were to be made almost immediately to change the Utrecht settlement, and its survival depended essentially on the attitudes of the statesmen who came after it, the territorial and dynastic arrangements were not to be substantially altered before the 1730s and 1740s. The settlement did mark a comma, if not a full stop, in European history: it ended a long period of warfare in western Europe, embodied major changes of territories and dynasties, and inaugurated a new European states system after the defeat of France. The reduction in French power was clearly as important, at least in the short term, as the rise of Britain.

The change of ministry in London in 1710 had saved Louis XIV from what had seemed inevitable and complete disaster. The terms of the peace were a personal triumph for the King's own courage and obstinacy in holding on after his terrible defeats. Although his grandson had not kept all the Spanish empire, Philip V was king of Spain itself and the colonies. He could be expected to turn his kingdom into a permanent ally of France rather than her enemy as in the past. France had also managed to preserve her eastern frontier intact and to make only minor concessions in Flanders. Her frontiers in 1713–14 were more defensible than when Louis had begun his personal rule in 1661. They had hardly been breached during the last war and they were not to be breached again before the Revolution. However, after 1713 France faced stronger restraints in the Dutch and Austrian presence in the Southern Netherlands and the Austrian in Milan than had been provided by the former Spanish rulers there. Outside Europe, in Canada, or New France, the outer defences of the colony had been lost, but this was not considered very important, especially as France retained access to the fur trade and the Newfoundland fishing banks. More important was the destruction of France's war fleets and the reduction of her external trade to a trickle. The Spanish Succession War, which had followed on so quickly after the Nine Years War, had also left France bankrupt and with a massive burden of debt. However, the country itself was intrinsically as strong as ever. Whatever the faults of her absolute monarchy and financial system, France could marshal far more men, materials and cash from her large population and rich agriculture than any other continental power. Nevertheless, despite this inherent strength and the potential for recovering her former European position, there was no doubt about her defeat and weakness in 1714. Her armies, which had been larger and superior to all others in the late seventeenth century, had been shown to be inferior to those of the Maritime and German Powers. Except fleetingly under de Saxe in the 1740s, Europe was not to take its military standards from France again until the Revolution. French diplomatic supremacy and Louis XIV's alignments had all been shattered: it would take a generation to mend them. But France's greatest weakness after the war came not from her loss of prestige and military defeats: what worried the old King most was the uncertainty about his own succession and the survival of the absolute monarchy itself. The successor to his throne was a child, his great-grandson, the future Louis XV, born in 1710.

The Austrian court, particularly the new Emperor, Charles VI, was bitterly disappointed with the peace settlement. But despite this dissatisfaction Austria had certainly gained most in terms of territory. These gains were huge and came immediately after similar ones from the Turks. Austria had confirmed her position as one of the major European powers, and even more than ever the Emperor could be considered as ruling a state in its own right separate from the Holy Roman Empire. With the vital help of the Maritime Powers and the German princes, and the military genius of Prince Eugene of Savoy, Austria had managed to free herself from the twin dangers of France and the Turks: in the wars of 1688–1714 Louis XIV's ascendancy had been destroyed, and in those of 1683–99 and then of 1716–18 the

Turks were pushed back deep into the Balkans. Although the lands in Hungary and then in Serbia annexed at Karlowitz (1699) and later at Passarowitz (1718) (see pp. 117f.) were poor, their possession removed the Ottoman threat to Austria and central Europe for good. At Utrecht–Rastadt the Austrians received territory which France had coveted for over two centuries, the Southern Netherlands, Milan, Naples and Sardinia. Austria was now clearly dominant in Italy, where she was to remain till 1866 and even till 1918. Her dominance there was the price Louis XIV had to pay to see Philip in Spain. However, in the Empire Austria had failed to effect Leopold I's 'German mission' over Alsace and Lorraine or to erect a barrier strong enough to prevent further French expansion or military adventures along the Rhine. Within Germany itself the Emperor's power had now reached its limit. It had steadily risen from the 1680s as the princes looked to Imperial leadership against France. But his dominant position there was not to last after 1714. Once the war against France was over and Austrian troops were withdrawn from the Empire, Vienna's influence began to decline. This was not because of a revival of French influence but the continued growth of the military and political power of the German states. In particular Hanover, Saxony and Prussia were reinforced by their territorial connections outside Germany, and the fact that all three now had royal titles made them believe themselves equal to the Emperor.

Austria's failure to sustain her influence within Germany was compensated for in some ways by increasing central control of the Austria–Bohemian hereditary lands, the pacification of Hungary after the suppression of the Rákóczy revolt (1703–11) and the direct gains from the French and Turkish Wars. However, the actual value of these gains was questionable, especially the former Spanish lands which were separated physically from the core of the monarchy, were difficult to administer and provided a temptation to others to attack. The wealth which was expected to come from Italy never materialised, and the Southern Netherlands were to prove a heavy financial and military burden.

Ostensibly Austria's military victories against the Turks and French and her large acquisitions had made her the greatest European power, at least in size. Some European statesmen were to consider her the preponderant state and to fear her hegemony. However, her continuing financial and administrative weaknesses made such a position impossible. She had only survived the Turkish War of 1683–99 with Papal and German help and the Spanish Succession War with that from the Maritime Powers. Although she emerged from the last war with a comparatively light burden of debts, this was because her credit-worthiness was so poor that few would lend money to the Emperor. Any risk of military conflict with a European power immediately made Austria dependent on others.

Europe possessed a remarkable number of secondary states in the early-eighteenth century, the German and Italian princes, Portugal, Denmark and Poland. Their number was to grow by Sweden, the Ottoman Empire, Spain and the Dutch joining them. While the Dutch were to accept their new role, the Swedes, Spaniards and Turks made periodic attempts to escape theirs. In Italy Victor Amadeus of Savoy had unlimited ambitions for territorial expansion in the north and centre. At Utrecht British patronage had brought him the crown of Sicily, but relations with the new Hanoverian dynasty were difficult at first because of his family connections with the exiled Stuarts. Over the next half-century Victor Amadeus and his successor were to switch the allegiance of their second-class, but strategically important, state to take advantage of quarrels among the powers.

If Savoy's time was yet to come, that of the Dutch Republic was almost over, for the peace of Utrecht marked a turning-point in its European position. The long struggle with France had really ruined the Dutch, who had been forced to spend vast sums on an army as well as on their navy. Their debts rose fivefold from 1688 to 1713, and this called for the heaviest taxation in Europe. Although it has often been said that their commercial position was deteriorating, there was in fact no actual decline in the volume of trade after 1713. They managed to convert the Southern Netherlands into an economic satellite, and they continued to dominate the European carrying trade till the 1730s – in the years from 1721 to 1730 42 per cent of ships entering the Baltic were still Dutch and only 20 per cent were British. None the less, the Dutch economy failed to expand with the British and French, who moved ahead. This was probably inevitable, once the Republic's Anglo-French competitors began to develop: it is surprising that Dutch success lasted as long as it did. The oligarchs who controlled Dutch policy were obsessed by their debts and by what they believed to be their declining share of world trade. They therefore refused to pay for a great-power policy or even to keep 'a fleet in being'. They were convinced that the only way of holding on to their trading position was to pursue a defensive and even a neutralist policy, one which put peace before everything else. Although it took contemporaries a while to grasp the collapse of the Dutch as a force in European politics, by the mid-century this was clear enough, and the Dutch were often dismissed, not quite accurately, as merely a British satellite.

Spain should have ultimately benefited from the Utrecht settlement, and in many ways she was stronger than before: her far-flung, haphazard European empire, which was impossible to defend or administer, had been lost, and this should have encouraged the court of Madrid to concentrate on internal reform and on more effective control and exploitation of the Indies. Philip V was to undertake domestic reforms, using French models, and his defeat of the Archduke Charles's provincial supporters allowed him to extend central-isation and royal authority throughout the peninsula. However, the new Bourbon monarchy failed to see the advantages of the surgery of Utrecht, and it was to embark on a continuous pursuit of its lost Mediterranean lands.

The two decades after the treaties of Utrecht–Rastadt were ones of peace among the great powers in western Europe – Britain, France and Austria. They acted conservatively and, on the whole, tried sincerely to settle differences by negotiation rather than by war. The equilibrium among the powers following the defeat of France may have inhibited their policies. But the main reason disposing the courts to peace seems to have been a general feeling of insecurity at home. There was heavy indebtedness after the last war and a desire for domestic recovery. Above all, however, there was a fear, common to Britain, France and Austria, about the future of the succession to their thrones. This was especially the case in France: the weakness and insecurity felt in what was potentially the strongest and most dangerous of the powers prevented general war. Once France recovered her confidence, war was to follow. Although the majority of the statesmen directing the policies of the powers till the 1740s were convinced of the advantages of peace, there was no general revulsion against war itself. The nobility as an estate, especially on the Continent, still considered war their particular vocation. European statesmen were to give the famous projects for perpetual peace of the Abbé de St Pierre a sceptical, if not totally amused, reception.

AUSTRO-SPANISH RIVALRY AND THE BEGINNINGS OF THE ANGLO-FRENCH *ENTENTE*, 1714–1716

The peace of Utrecht–Rastadt left unsettled many of the problems of the Spanish Succession War: those in Italy were the most intractable and were not finally solved till 1748. At the same time the British and French succession issues, which seemed to have been settled by the peace, were revived almost immediately by the deaths of Anne (1714) and Louis XIV (1715). Although peace had been restored in western Europe, the Great Northern War (see pp. 86ff.) was still in progress, and a new war began in the eastern Mediterranean in 1714 when the Turks attacked Venice's possessions there.

The two rivals for the Spanish crown, Philip V and Charles VI, had refused to make peace with each other or to recognise their respective titles and possessions, and both seemed determined to pursue their claims by war when the occasion arose. Philip V's successes in 1714–15 in capturing Barcelona from Charles VI's Catalan supporters and then in expelling an Austrian garrison from Majorca encouraged the King to try to regain what Spain had lost in the Mediterranean. This policy received considerable support in Spain, where the loss of the Italian lands and Mediterranean islands was felt very keenly. His first aims were to seize Charles VI's gains of Sardinia, Naples, the Tuscan ports and Milan, but ultimately Philip intended to win back Sicily from Savoy and to expel the British from Gibraltar and Minorca. Because of this revisionist policy, Philip began to reorganise his army and rebuild a Mediterranean fleet, as soon as conflict was over in Spain itself.

Philip's expansionist ambitions were encouraged by his second marriage (1714) to Elizabeth Farnese, niece of the Duke of Parma. Strong-willed and ambitious, the new Queen was soon to rule her husband. Philip himself, as he grew older, was to become increasingly mentally deranged and to suffer from bouts of hypochondria and religious mania. Almost from the beginning of their marriage Elizabeth was obsessed by the knowledge that her future children would not inherit Spain, since Philip already had heirs by his first wife. She therefore wanted to find territories for her offspring to inherit and a haven for herself if she were widowed. Naturally she thought of Parma and Tuscany, as she had dynastic claims to both. Her ambitions were to influence Spanish policy strongly in the 1710s and 1720s, but her husband Philip's desire to recover Spain's former Mediterranean empire was of equal, and often greater, importance. Another factor, which was of some significance in the fifteen or so years after Utrecht, was Philip V's claim to the French throne. He believed – and probably French law and sentiment would have supported him – his renunciations at the peace were invalid and he was the rightful heir to France if his nephew, the later Louis XV, should die. Initially the main instrument used by Philip and Elizabeth to carry out their plans was the Italian Alberoni. He began his career in Madrid as envoy of the Duke of Parma but soon rose, through Elizabeth's patronage, to become Philip's unofficial adviser and then, in 1716, chief minister. A cheerful and long-suffering cleric, Alberoni was loyal to the personal interests of both the King and Queen, but he also believed Italy itself would benefit from the restoration of Spanish influence. Although he was later to be accused of encouraging and inflating the ambitions of the royal couple, in fact he often seems to have acted as a restraint.

Charles VI had only spent six years in Spain during the last war, but he remained emotionally attached to the country for the rest of his life. This attachment was fostered by the Spanish exiles who accompanied him to Vienna and whom he formed into a council of Spain to administer his Italian lands. Until the late 1720s these Spanish advisers often influenced him as much as his German ministers. Although it is doubtful if the Emperor seriously believed he would regain the Spanish throne after 1714, he refused to recognise Philip and insisted on styling himself 'Catholic King'. Personal pride played a part in this, but he also believed the title helped legitimise his position in the Southern Netherlands and Italy. Like his rival Philip, Charles VI was also unhappy about the Utrecht Italian settlement. He had managed to acquire Sardinia at Rastadt, and was determined to complete Habsburg control of the peninsula by forcing Savoy to surrender Sicily: the island had historically been part of Naples (the kingdom of Two Sicilies), and it also served as a granary for the huge city of Naples. Moreover, the Austrians, already in control of Milan and the Tuscan ports, would have liked an excuse to annex Parma and Tuscany, which they claimed were fiefs of the Holy Roman Empire. Outside Italy the Emperor's further grievance with the 1713/14 settlement was the position of the Southern Netherlands. Here Charles's authority was limited by Dutch garrisons and by Anglo–Dutch insistence on keeping the River Scheldt closed to shipping.

In the first years of his reign the young Emperor Charles VI himself was interested in developing the industrial and commercial potential of his Italian and Netherlands territories, as well as wanting to adopt a forward policy in the Mediterranean. But the predominant influence at Vienna was Prince Eugene, whose past military victories had given him great prestige and authority. He did not share the Emperor's economic or Mediterranean interests and wanted further war in the Balkans. This was because the Turks had followed up their success against Peter the Great on the Pruth (see p. 85) by what appeared a determined push to undo the whole Karlowitz settlement (see p. 76). In 1714 Sultan Ahmed III attacked the Venetians to try to regain what had been lost to them in Dalmatia and Greece. By 1716 he had succeeded in doing this. Prince Eugene feared the Turks would attempt to repeat their success by invading Hungary, and he also welcomed the chance to win further victories against the Porte. But he put off intervening till 1716 in order to make the necessary military preparations. For the moment his wishes carried most weight at the Austrian court, so that a largely defensive policy had to be followed elsewhere. And this was also to be true in relation to the disputes in the western Mediterranean, despite the personal ambitions of Charles VI himself.

Austrian and Spanish quarrels were the principal cause of tension in the years immediately after the peace of Utrecht–Rastadt, but they did not lead to a general war. This was because of developments in Britain and France, which made both powers determined to prevent one breaking out. Within two years of the settlement both Queen Anne and Louis XIV were dead. The Queen's Tory ministers just before her death had negotiated secretly with James Stuart, the Old Pretender, to try to prevent a Hanoverian succession and the Whig ascendancy which they knew would follow. But the Pretender's refusal to renounce his Catholic faith wrecked this attempt, and the Elector of Hanover succeeded to the British throne peacefully as George I (1714–27) in August 1714.

George immediately dismissed the Tories and appointed Whig ministers, and his accession finally assured the survival of the parliamentary monarchy. This had proved highly successful in waging the last war. It had paid for it with less strain than the other combatants, and Britain herself had emerged as the clear victor. There were, however, some features of the parliamentary system which weakened Britain in her relations with other powers. Ministries were heavily dependent on the approval of parliament and even of public opinion, both of which were taking an increasing interest in foreign affairs. Continental rulers were therefore often suspicious of promises made by ministers who might fall and have their policies reversed. Yet this problem, and the related one of the parliamentary opposition, never produced the paralysis found in the limited monarchies of Poland and Sweden.

Although most parliaments in the eighteenth century, whether dominated by Whigs or Tories, wanted to avoid involvement on the Continent, the new Hanoverian monarchs, especially George I, were to try to commit Britain to promote Hanoverian interests. The Hanoverian connection itself was to mean that Britain would have great difficulty in ignoring the Continent in the future even if she wished to. But at the beginning of George I's reign the most immediate problem was the stability of the new dynasty. Although the Tories lost the election after being driven from office by the King, some of their leaders renewed their contacts with the Pretender. Bolingbroke, the architect of the Utrecht peace, fled to James's court in Lorraine, where plans were already under way for a revolt to depose George I. The Whig ministry, with Charles Townshend and James Stanhope as the secretaries of state,* therefore made their priorities the safeguarding of the Protestant succession and Britain's commercial position, both of which appeared to have been confirmed by the recent peace. The succession was the more important and was to remain so over the next generation. Because of its success and longevity, it is all too easy to forget the weakness of the Whig regime in its first years. The Jacobite revolt of 1715–16 was eventually to destroy both the Tories and the English Jacobites and to consolidate the Whig ascendancy, but this was not immediately obvious. There was no certainty that the party strife and instability of the past would now end. The Jacobites also provided foreign states with a lever against Britain: the real threat, of course, came from France, as was to be shown during the 1745

---

*Until 1782 British foreign policy was conducted by two secretaries of state who divided responsibility for relations with the powers on a geographical basis. One secretary usually tended to be dominant.

revolt. Consequently, every British government from 1689 to 1750 had to be alive to threats of foreign help for the Stuarts, especially as Britain did not have a large standing army.

The foreign policy, which the Whig ministers of George I were gradually to adopt to defend the succession and commercial interests, was to be more akin to their Tory enemies' ideas of depending on the navy, diplomacy and friendship with France instead of the traditional Whig recipe of close alliances with the Dutch and Austria (the 'Old System') and military intervention on the Continent. It was only in the 1740s that this was revived (see pp. 166ff.). But it took the Whig ministers some time to move in this direction, and there was always the competing pull of the Hanoverian ruler and his German advisers who wanted more direct intervention on the Continent.

Immediately after George I's accession in 1714, his Whig ministers tried to rebuild the Grand Alliance of the last war with the Dutch Republic and the Emperor, in order to defend themselves in case Louis XIV should help the Jacobites. But they failed, because of Austro-Dutch quarrels over the Barrier settlement in the Southern Netherlands and because the Emperor himself tried to extract a British promise of naval support for an aggressive policy in the Mediterranean. For their part, although the Whigs adopted a tough and hostile policy towards the French King, they did not want a new war, and they were soon trying to establish friendly relations with Spain so as to confirm and extend Britain's commercial privileges.

Whig hostility was to cause Louis XIV considerable alarm. In the two years between the peace of Utrecht and his death in September 1715 the King and his foreign minister, Torcy, wanted peace and to restore French prestige through diplomatic means. Above all they were anxious to prevent a renewal of the Grand Alliance which had led to their recent humiliation. Louis was now in his mid-seventies and was painfully aware of the precarious position his infant successor would inherit. He believed the main external danger came from Britain, and he saw the Whigs as the heirs of William III. He was therefore careful not to provoke the British unduly: although he allowed the Jacobites to plot in France, he refused to give them any direct help. Above all he felt it was vital to try to neutralise Britain's former continental allies, Austria and the Dutch. Consequently, early in 1715 France made tentative approaches to Vienna, emphasising their common Catholicism. At the same time Louis tried to mediate between Philip V and Charles VI, both to help his grandson in Spain and to ease international tension. The Austrians, faced by an imminent war with the Turks in the Balkans, did not reject these overtures outright. But they had not replied positively before Louis's death, and this brought to an end all serious efforts for a Franco-Austrian *rapprochement* for another twenty years.

Far more significant and successful were the simultaneous

approaches which Louis XIV made in The Hague. The Dutch had always feared France above all because of the Southern Netherlands, and France herself had sound reasons now to feel equally vulnerable in the same quarter because of Marlborough's recent victories there and the cession of the province to Austria at Utrecht. Louis therefore offered the Dutch a treaty to neutralise the Southern (or Austrian) Netherlands, and it was received with great interest. Although no treaty was signed in Louis's lifetime, future French governments were to pursue the same idea with some success: once the Dutch had security to the south, there would be little incentive to enter anti-French coalitions or even to be over-concerned about European affairs.

When Louis XIV died in September 1715 the Grand Alliance had not been revived, but the situation facing France with his five-year-old great-grandson, Louis XV (1715–74), as ruler, seemed very unstable. High childhood mortality meant the young King's survival to manhood was questionable: the succession issue would inevitably be a permanent one over the next decade. Although Utrecht had laid down that the Orleans family should succeed the new King, most Frenchmen regarded the child's nearest blood relative, Philip V of Spain, as his true heir. None the less, Philip, Duke of Orleans, who was the late King's nephew, managed to have himself declared sole regent of France immediately on the accession of Louis XV. The new Regent was inevitably weak: he was threatened from without by his main rival for the succession, Philip V, and from within by supporters of the Spanish King, who included most of Louis XIV's former ministers. Consequently, Orleans's chief aims, and those of France, had to be very personal ones, to survive as regent and to preserve the rights of his own family to the throne. This above all needed a policy of peace.

Initial French fears that the old King's death would be followed by attacks from a revived Grand Alliance of the Maritime Powers and Austria were to prove groundless. George I's government was in fact highly relieved to see the last of Louis XIV and welcomed Orleans's becoming *de facto* ruler. They had been negotiating with him secretly before Louis's death for a treaty to confirm the Hanoverian and Orleanist successions. However, just as Orleans became regent a Jacobite revolt, the 'Fifteen, was breaking out. The Regent, because of his weak position in France, was forced to act equivocally towards the Pretender. He did so because James Stuart was popular at the French court and also because there seemed some chance that the Jacobites might overthrow the new and vulnerable Hanoverian monarchy. The British government was naturally disappointed and infuriated by Orleans's attitude, but the Whig ministers took swift military action to suppress the revolt, which was largely confined to Scotland. To guard against direct French intervention, London also negotiated anxiously with the Dutch and Austrians for a triple alliance throughout autumn 1715. These negotiations eventually failed, because neither of their former allies felt the same fear of France and also because they were at loggerheads themselves over completing a treaty for the barrier in the Southern Netherlands. The Emperor eventually signed the Barrier treaty in November 1715 largely in response to desperate appeals from George I. Early Jacobite success in Scotland had led the Hanoverian King to ask for Dutch military support, but the Republic refused to send troops till the Barrier treaty had been concluded to their satisfaction. Dutch forces were then sent and an Anglo-Dutch alliance was signed in February 1716, which included a guarantee of the Protestant succession.

In the event the Jacobite revolt proved easy to put down and was over by spring 1716. The British none the less continued to feel they needed an alliance with Austria as well as the Republic. Although they refused to satisfy Charles VI's personal ambitions in the Mediterranean, where he still wanted to seize Sicily from Savoy, the Emperor finally agreed to conclude an alliance because of the impending Austro-Turkish War, which his leading minister Prince Eugene was determined to fight. Vienna was anxious for British naval protection against a possible Spanish attack in Italy during the war in the Balkans. In June 1716, therefore, George I and Charles VI signed the treaty of Westminster, a defensive alliance which promised both help against attack. In the Austrian case it was Spain which was feared, while the British needed the protection against France.

Britain's alliances with Vienna and The Hague gave her a high degree of security, although continuing bickering between her allies over the Southern Netherlands prevented the conclusion of a new three-power Grand Alliance. Unfortunately, the British had given their commitment to protect the Emperor without being clear of the situation in the Mediterranean, particularly in Spain. It had appeared to London that the real danger of disruption came from the Emperor's personal ambitions and this is why the British ministers had continually refused to countenance them, whether against Savoy or against Spain. They had largely misjudged the ambitions of Spain, where, under the growing influence of Alberoni, Philip V had shown himself very conciliatory towards Britain. In December 1715 and July 1716 commercial treaties were signed between Britain and Spain, which put into effect, and expanded, the concessions given at Utrecht and restored Britain's favourable seventeenth-century trading privileges in Spain herself (in 'Old Spain'). The Spaniards intended these concessions to win Britain's support, or at least neutrality, in the Mediterranean, where she had naval predominance. Philip V and Alberoni wanted British goodwill because they were well advanced with preparing a fleet to reconquer Spain's lost islands and southern Italy. As their intentions were unknown in London, George I's government interpreted Spanish concessions as a sign that they wanted friendship, at a time when Franco-Spanish relations were evidently poor. Mistakenly believing that Philip had no immediate ambitions in the Mediterranean, the British were even hoping eventually to associate Spain loosely with their own Dutch and Austrian grouping.

By summer 1716 George I's position in both Britain and Europe had markedly improved. The Jacobites had been crushed, the Whigs had a large majority in parliament, alliances had been concluded with the Dutch and the Emperor, while the Spaniards were eager for the King's friendship. In the north (see p. 87) peace seemed likely, as the Swedes had finally been expelled from Germany. France was now effectively isolated: the British, Austrian and Spanish courts all appeared hostile to the Regent. Orleans's only success had been at The Hague, where assurances during winter 1715–16 that he wanted to pursue Louis XIV's suggestion of neutralising the Southern Netherlands had placated the Dutch. At home the Regent's position was obviously far weaker than that of an absolute monarch, especially as France was experiencing a period of aristocratic revival. Support for Philip V's claims to the succession and for direct influence on the regency itself was almost universal at the French court and included men like Torcy and the new foreign minister, d'Huxelles. In addition, the economic problems of France after the last war were all too apparent, and Orleans wanted to begin financial, and administrative reform. A modest and peaceful foreign policy was therefore vital. Although he was undoubtedly thinking of his own interests, it is difficult to argue that he sacrificed France for them. The main need of the country, besides peace to recover from the last war, was to safeguard the stability of the Bourbon dynasty.

The Regent Orleans always had to tread warily in his foreign policy so as not to antagonise the powerful groups in France, who hankered after Louis XIV's traditional anti-British and anti-Austrian policies and who wanted a close alliance with Spain to further Philip's territorial ambitions. However, from spring 1716 Orleans and his close adviser and former tutor, the Abbé Dubois, had concluded that all his problems could be solved by a *rapprochement* with Britain and a mutual defensive alliance. This would remove the danger of a revival of the Grand Alliance and help secure the Orleanist succession. The collapse and final defeat of the Jacobite rebellion in Britain clarified the issues for Orleans. He no longer had to conciliate the Stuarts and in this way poison his relations with George I. He could now approach London more decisively. Although he had rejected an attempt by the harassed British government for an alliance in December 1715 in the middle of the rebellion, in March 1716 he instructed Dubois to revive the idea. It was now the British who were uninterested, and over the following months George's ministers displayed traditional Whig hostility to France. They demanded the destruction of naval facilities at Mardyck, which had been built to replace those at Dunkirk, and the expulsion of the Pretender from the Papal enclave of Avignon, before an alliance could be signed. But Orleans felt too vulnerable to give up, especially when the British went on to conclude their alliance with Austria (June) and a commercial treaty with Spain (July).

In July 1716 Dubois was dispatched to The Hague, ostensibly on a book-buying expedition. But the real purpose was to waylay in secret the British secretary of state, James Stanhope, who was accompanying George I on a summer visit to Hanover. The two men had known each other since 1698 and could talk openly as friends. Dubois, who was now in his sixties, proved an intelligent and patient diplomat. He was devoted to Orleans's interests and hoped success would bring a cardinal's hat for himself. Stanhope, some twenty years younger, although having a reputation as a fiery Whig, was just the man to grasp the opportunity being offered, especially when he realised its potential advantages. Their talks, which were continued in similar secrecy at Hanover during the summer, were surprisingly successful. This was despite the hostility of the former ministers of Louis XIV in Paris and of the majority of the Whig ministers in London. The negotiation progressed largely because of the personal desire of George I for agreement, a desire which soon matched that of the Regent himself. Stanhope, as well as the other English ministers, had to take the King's own wishes seriously because of his undoubted constitutional rights to conduct foreign policy. Moreover, outright opposition to his wishes could lead to dismissal and the appointment of new ministers. They similarly had to pay attention to George's Hanoverian advisers, particularly to the chief one, Bernstorff.

During the summer of 1716 George and Bernstorff became convinced of the advantages that would come from agreement with France. The Elector-King himself realised that an alliance would effectively undercut the Jacobites and protect his dynasty against further rebellions. But George also felt an alliance would be useful to him as elector of Hanover. It would finally remove any danger that the French might interfere in the north, as they had done in 1679, to prevent the collapse and partition of the Swedish empire. More important, however, was the prospect that France could exert pressure for George's benefit on the Russian Tsar. Throughout the early summer (see p. 88) the troops of George's 'ally', Peter the Great, had been occupying Hanover's neighbour, Mecklenburg, much to the alarm of both George and Bernstorff. Prussia was on close terms with Peter, while George's Austrian allies were fully committed in the Balkans, where war with the Turks finally broke out in the July. Peter the Great was also known to be angling for French support. It seemed essential, therefore, to ensure that if France intervened in the north, she should do so on George's behalf and on no one else's.

George's English minister, Stanhope, certainly understood the precarious position of Hanover in summer 1716. Consequently, agreement between him and Dubois was reached quickly, and an Anglo-French alliance was signed on 28 November 1716. The chief obstacles to agreement had come from the Whig ministers in London, that is, from the other secretary of state, Townshend, and his brother-in-law, Robert Walpole. They did not share Stanhope and the Hanoverians' anxiety over the Russians in Mecklenburg, and they preferred Britain to stay exclusively within an Austro-Dutch alliance system. They therefore pressed hard over the question of Mardyck and for the expulsion of the Pretender from Avignon, believing the Regent would not give way. To their surprise Orleans did, and in the treaty France agreed to destroy the harbour at Mardyck and to force James Stuart to leave. At the same time Britain and France promised to guarantee and defend each other's possessions (including Hanover and George's gains from Sweden of Bremen and Verden) and to uphold the Utrecht settlement of the Anglo-French successions. A little over a month later (4 January 1717) the Dutch acceded to the treaty, and it became known as the Triple Alliance. But essentially it was, and remained, an alliance between Britain and France.

This Anglo-French *entente*, which lasted for fifteen years, was as revolutionary as the later Austro-French Diplomatic Revolution of the 1750s, and was completely foreign to the normal pattern of Anglo-French relations from 1689 to 1815. The *entente* was always very precarious: it was never popular in either state, and the two nations continued to dislike each other as fiercely as ever. Many French ministers, diplomats and soldiers, particularly those who had served Louis XIV, felt it betrayed France's true interests and only benefited Orleans and Britain. The ordinary Whigs in Britain shared this suspicion of the relationship, although once in government all Whigs tended to recognise its value.

The alliance was of course of great personal value both to George I and to Orleans. It was probably the most important diplomatic factor in stabilising the Hanoverian dynasty: it removed the most dangerous source of potential foreign support for the Jacobites, at a time when neither they nor the Tories were a completely spent force. George gained as elector of Hanover because he received French diplomatic backing in the north (see p. 89). In a wider sense the alliance helped push Britain into the leading diplomatic role in Europe. Almost immediately Stanhope was to use French support to mediate in the Mediterranean and then in the Baltic.

There is no doubt that Dubois's negotiations, which were conducted outside the official channels of French diplomacy and shared many of the features of the later *secret du roi* (see pp. 181f.), were intended mainly to serve the Regent's interests. The alliance led to some extent to a French diplomatic dependence on Britain. Both Orleans and Dubois were largely to follow the British lead in Europe and to support them in the Mediterranean and Baltic. On occasions they were even to help preserve and restore Britain's trading privileges with Spain. In the long run this was probably damaging to France's economic development, but their alliance with Britain brought benefits which compensated for this. France gained security abroad and was allowed, during the critical period of Louis XV's minority, to recuperate in peace after the damaging last war. Moreover, Orleans and Dubois were to go much further in their European diplomacy than meeting the narrow requirements of the Orleanist succession. In conjunction with Stanhope they were to try to develop the Anglo-French alliance into a complete system for European collective security. This was to be based on the maintenance of the Utrecht settlement, which neither France nor Britain wanted to undo and were determined to uphold in its essentials.

THE QUADRUPLE ALLIANCE, 1717–1720

Before the close of 1716 Stanhope and Dubois had begun to work together to extend the Anglo-French alliance (or Triple Alliance as it became in January 1717) into an agreement which would embrace the other western powers. In particular, they aimed to reconcile Spain and Austria, whose antagonism and refusal to make peace with each other was a threat to European peace as a whole. It is not clear whether Stanhope or Dubois was the initiator of the scheme, but Stanhope was to take the lead in trying to effect it. Both men felt an equally pressing need to get the other powers to accept their new alignment. Dubois's main concern was Spain: he wanted Philip V to acknowledge the Orleanist succession in France but he also had to appease pro-Spanish groups at the French court. Stanhope also wanted to conciliate Madrid because of British trading interests, but he was less immediately concerned with Philip than with maintaining good relations between Britain and the Emperor.

Soon after reaching agreement with France Stanhope rapidly assumed direction of British foreign policy. He was able to do so because the opposition of his Whig colleagues in London, Townshend and Walpole, to George I's anti-Russian policies, contributed to their fall from power early in 1717. Energetic and persuasive, often to the point of bullying, Stanhope was to conduct an imaginative diplomacy over the next few years, based on frequent personal visits to foreign courts: Robert Walpole called him 'the knight errant of English diplomacy'. It was initially his presence in Paris at crucial times which largely kept the new Anglo-French *entente* intact. Despite his past career as a soldier, he preferred to try to solve European problems through negotiation. In this way he succeeded in stabilising the Hanoverian dynasty and at the same time pleasing the City merchants who felt war damaged their trade. He worked on the assumption that Britain could benefit from friendship with France and Spain as well as from alliance with Austria and the Dutch, and he hoped to reconcile the new Anglo-French *entente* with the old Grand Alliance system. As a Whig he was determined to maintain Britain's traditional relations with the Emperor and the Republic, because ultimately the real foreign danger to Britain came from France and the Jacobites: if France ceased to be conciliatory and returned, alone or with Bourbon Spain, to an expansionist policy, then Austrian and Dutch help would be needed. Stanhope could never afford to forget that the secretariat of the French council for foreign affairs and their diplomats abroad were hostile to the new direction of French policies under the Regent and were sympathetic to Philip V. He was also continually reminded by George I's Hanoverian ministers that Austrian support was just as necessary for the King in Germany as that of France. On the other hand, Stanhope grasped that co-operation with the Dutch and the Emperor would not achieve such an effective muzzling of the Jacobites or a settlement of Mediterranean and Baltic problems. It seemed only wise to capitalise on the Regent's desire for friendship in order to neutralise the adventurist and pro-Spanish ministers in France, to strengthen the new dynasty in Britain, to further Hanoverian ambitions in the north and to resolve Austro-Spanish differences before they led to further general war. French diplomatic and financial support would also be very useful in exerting pressure on Russia, Sweden and Prussia, as well as on Spain and Savoy. Stanhope was to realise, as did his successors in control of British policy, that the joint diplomatic and military strength of Britain and France could bend all Europe to their will. If there was a British preponderance in Europe after 1714, it was one built on this Anglo-French co-operation, an association which Britain usually led.

In trying to reconcile Austria and Spain, it seemed at first more important to Stanhope and Dubois to conciliate Charles VI rather than Philip V, who was still presenting a fairly moderate front. This appeared especially necessary because Austria's Turkish War had begun very successfully and there was a danger that Charles VI might soon use his victorious armies to resolve his grievances in Italy, if not actually against Spain itself. Consequently, at the close of 1716 Dubois and Stanhope agreed on a project which Stanhope drafted in the form of a treaty to be signed by Austria, Spain, the Dutch and the Anglo-French allies. This project, which came to be known as Stanhope's 'peace plan for the south', called on Charles VI and Philip V to recognise each other's territories, and at the same time it provided for further guarantees of the British and French successions. To satisfy what appeared to be the Emperor's main territorial grievance, Savoy was to be forced to hand over Sicily to him.

Despite the Austrian court's suspicions of the new Anglo-French association, it accepted the peace project in principle in January 1717. Unfortunately, although Philip V's position in Spain had been confirmed by the plan, he was to prove intractable. In fact Spain, and the adventurist policies pursued by different ministers there, was to be the main obstacle to European peace over the next decade and a half. Throughout the early months of 1717 Madrid resisted all the diplomatic efforts of Dubois and Stanhope. This was not surprising as the peace plan offered Spain nothing territorially, at a time when Philip was determined to regain the lost Mediterranean empire and was beginning to listen to his wife's ambitions for their first son, Don Charles (Don Carlos), who had been born in 1716. His chief minister, Alberoni, who had by now received a cardinal's hat, was already well advanced with plans for an attack on Austrian Sardinia. Alberoni hoped that the conquest of the island, at a time when Austrian troops were still engaged in the Balkans, would strengthen Spain's bargaining position and might even encourage France to join in an all-out war on the Emperor. He was working towards demanding the return of Naples and Sicily to Spain and, possibly, the succession to Parma and Tuscany for Don Charles. In August 1717 matters came to a head when Philip V ordered Alberoni, who wanted to delay the expedition, to dispatch a fleet to Sardinia. This was soon overrun by Spanish troops, and the reconquest of Spain's former Italian empire now seemed possible. But this Spanish success was almost totally eclipsed by a great Austrian victory over the Turks and the capture of Belgrade on 5 August. There was an obvious danger that Prince Eugene and his army would be sent to Italy and a full-scale war follow with Spain.

Stanhope desperately wanted to avoid such a clash, and he continued to hope that he could persuade the Spaniards to accept the Anglo-French peace project without the need to use force against them. He knew that any conflict with Spain would be unpopular with commercial groups at home and would put an intolerable strain on Britain's alliance with France. He felt it was vital for Britain to work closely with the Regent who was facing mounting pressure to abandon the *entente* and intervene on Philip V's side. Largely because of Dubois's influence – he had by now been admitted to the council for foreign affairs as well as remaining the Regent's private adviser –, Orleans stuck by the *entente*. It seemed far more important to maintain peace and achieve an Austrian as well as an Anglo-Dutch guarantee of his family's rights to the French throne than to further the interests of his Spanish rival. Yet Orleans could not ignore the domestic pressures or the strengthened position of Philip V after the conquest of Sardinia. The terms offered in the 'peace plan for the south' clearly had to be raised for Philip's benefit. That this was the only way to bring Spain's agreement was recognised by Stanhope as much as by Orleans and Dubois. Even before the Spanish expedition to Sardinia Dubois had considered offering Philip the island. Now the French suggested, with Stanhope's eventual consent, that an attempt be made to capitalise on Elizabeth Farnese's undoubted influence on her husband. Philip was therefore offered the succession of first Parma, and then of Tuscany as well, for Don Charles. By this sop to Elizabeth it was hoped Spain would abandon her direct claims in southern Italy: a Bourbon–Farnese prince in central Italy could also be expected to be independent of Madrid and to limit Austrian supremacy in the peninsula. As further concessions to Philip V, Charles VI was to have to renounce Spain and its titles formally and to surrender Sardinia to Victor Amadeus of Savoy in return for Sicily. To save the Emperor's face and to soften the blow of the successions to Parma and Tuscany, these duchies were to be recognised as fiefs of the Empire, and the cities of Pisa and Leghorn (Livorno) detached from Tuscany and turned into Imperial vassal republics. Philip V himself was to have to recognise Charles VI's Italian possessions and titles unequivocally.

Negotiations were conducted with Spain throughout the winter of 1717–18, but with no success. The Spaniards complained that Spain herself had still not been offered any territory and that there were insufficient guarantees for Don Charles's eventual succession to the duchies. But Madrid had no intention of agreeing to the amended project in any case, because it was confident of further military success: the increased offers had merely whetted Spanish appetites. Alberoni was preparing for a full-scale war in Italy. The largest Spanish navy since the battle of Lepanto in 1571, some 300 ships, and an army of 33,000 were assembled in the eastern ports, and it was hoped to seize strategic points in Naples, Sicily, Leghorn and Genoa. At the same time Alberoni was attempting to create a wide-ranging alignment of the Jacobites, Russia, Sweden and the Turks, to confront Britain, France and Austria. By spring 1718 there were two power blocs in Europe: the more homogeneous grouping of the *entente* powers and Austria, together with the reluctant Dutch, opposed to the very nebulous association conjured up by Alberoni. Although he was very optimistic about his diplomatic ventures, Alberoni's real hope was always that the prospect of actual war would divide his enemies, especially because of the pressure from Spanish sympathisers at the French court and the merchant community in Britain. In June 1718, therefore, despite desperate diplomatic representations by Britain, the Spaniards landed troops on Sicily as a preliminary to attacking the Italian mainland.

Despite this development in the Mediterranean, Stanhope and Dubois were able to persuade the Regent to sign a treaty with Britain in July 1718, which embodied the terms of the 'peace plan'. The treaty gave both Madrid and Vienna three months to accept the plan or have it forced on them. But the Austrian court was no more eager to accept than that of Spain. The new terms, especially over Parma and Tuscany, had caused alarm in Vienna, since they clearly threatened their recently won supremacy in Italy. Prince Eugene had declared Austria would 'run all risks, rather than suffer a son of the Queen of Spain ever to possess' Tuscany. Signature of peace with the Turks on 21 July 1718 (see p. 117) made the Emperor more confident. Charles VI himself and his Spanish advisers, who bitterly resented having to make a final renunciation of Spain, were also toying with the idea of seizing Parma and Tuscany and going on to take Sicily and Majorca. However, these notions were really illusions: Austria was in fact in a very difficult position, especially while the bulk of her troops remained in the Balkans. Lacking a fleet of her own, she desperately needed British naval help against Spain in the Mediterranean. The British made it plain that this would not be forthcoming without her signature of the 'peace plan'. On 2 August 1718 Charles VI was persuaded by his ministers to sign the treaty with Britain and France. This now came to be known as the Quadruple Alliance – quadruple because the Dutch were expected to sign, although they did not in case doing so damaged their trade with Spain. The way the treaty had been drawn up and signed, with Britain and France dictating the law to the Emperor and to Europe, was a significant pointer to the future course of diplomatic relations. Charles VI was to be increasingly faced with the choice in the coming years of accepting the dominance of the *entente* powers or retreating into isolation. He was largely to choose isolation as Britain and France co-operated even more closely together.

The Quadruple Alliance was an attempt to complete the work of the peace of Utrecht and of the Triple Alliance of 1717. Charles had finally to abandon his ambitions in Spain, while Philip had to renounce Italy and the Southern Netherlands. Victor Amadeus had to hand over Sicily to Austria, receiving Sardinia and the title of king in exchange. The successions of Parma and Tuscany were assigned to Don Charles, and it was suggested that neutral Swiss garrisons be established there to protect his rights. The alliance also included yet further guarantees of the Anglo-French successions. The manner in which the alliance tried to settle the outstanding problems between all the western powers and to guarantee their thrones provides ample reason for describing the treaty as an early collective security agreement.

Once Charles VI had signed the alliance it was up to Spain to join or to have it forced on her. The British fleet had already sailed for the Mediterranean (June). After Stanhope had failed in a personal visit to Madrid to avert hostilities, even offering to return Gibraltar at a future date, Admiral Byng destroyed the whole Spanish fleet off Cape Passaro (11 August 1718). But Philip V and Elizabeth Farnese refused to accept that their Italian ambitions were ruined and that they should sign the Quadruple Alliance. Britain, for her part, was reluctant to follow up Passaro by outright war to impose the treaty: the French might back away if actual conflict were necessary, and war could only damage British trade with Spain and benefit the Dutch, who steadfastly stuck to their neutrality. Spanish intransigence, however, left no alternative but war. In the event the Quadruple Alliance held together very well. Orleans's timidity was overcome when he saw that he would have both Britain and Austria on his side: in January 1719 Dubois, who had just been created secretary of state for foreign affairs, was able to join Britain in declaring war on Spain.

The Anglo-French declaration still did not bring Philip and Elizabeth to heel, nor did the dispersal by storms of a Spanish fleet attempting a Spanish–Jacobite invasion of Scotland. This attempted invasion in 1719 produced the strange spectacle of France's offering troops to protect George I. Despite this clear sign of the closeness of the Anglo-French connection, British ministers felt it politic to refuse the offer and to depend on Austrian and Dutch help, which in the event was not needed. In April 1719 it was Spain's turn to be invaded, when a French force advanced into the Basque provinces. This French occupation of northern Spain, threatening another Catalan revolt against Madrid, British attacks on Spanish shipping and the obvious failure of Alberoni to create a European coalition, gradually persuaded Philip and Elizabeth to give way. Yet it was not till December 1719 that they dismissed Alberoni, using him as a scapegoat for Spain's defeats, and in January 1720 joined the Quadruple Alliance. The three months' deadline given them to join had been continually extended during the war. The details of the treaty, particularly the thorny question of garrisons in Parma and Tuscany, were put off for decision at a congress which was expected to meet shortly. This congress was also intended to discuss the return of Gibraltar, which, after Stanhope's offer of 1718, was assuming more importance among Philip's ambitions. Stanhope himself felt the fortress had low strategic value, and he called it both 'useless and dangerous' because of how it soured relations with Madrid. He was quite willing to exchange it for an area with more apparent commercial importance, such as Hispaniola or Florida. As parliament might well oppose its return to Spain, no immediate decision could be made and referring the question to the future congress was a way out. This congress, which eventually met at Cambrai in 1724, and a subsequent one at Soissons, were not forerunners of the early-nineteenth century 'Congress System'. The congresses of Cambrai and Soissons were called merely to resolve problems left over from short periods of minor warfare and were a convenient device to shift difficulties to a future date rather than allowing them to prevent the conclusion of peace: they were not intended to establish a system of regular consultation among the powers.

British naval and financial resources, backed up by French military power, had together managed to preserve the essential features of the Utrecht peace settlement, with only minor territorial changes in the Mediterranean. In carrying out his 'peace plan for the south', Stanhope had laid the path which European diplomacy was to follow in western and southern Europe over the next decade or so: problems were to be solved by diplomatic co-operation and agreement among the great powers. Ostensibly, this settlement and the parallel one in the north (see pp. 90f.) were a brilliant success for the personal diplomacy of Stanhope. Britain's diplomatic lead had been accepted, and she had managed to remain allied to both France and Austria, while strengthening the new Hanoverian dynasty. But in fact Anglo-French diplomacy had only defused one crisis, not solved the Italian problem: Austrian and Spanish–Farnesean ambitions would continue to clash in the peninsula, and Spain still harboured other grievances resulting from the Utrecht peace.

The real obstacle to permanent peace remained the ambitions of the Spanish royal couple. Spain's failure in 1718–20 had convinced the King that the Anglo-French defence of the Utrecht settlement meant that he had to abandon his plans for the direct conquest of Spain's former possessions in the Mediterranean and Italy. Therefore, constantly declaring, 'I want nothing for myself', he transferred his Italian ambitions to the children of his second marriage, Don Charles and Don Philip. The Utrecht principle that Spain herself was not to hold anything directly in Italy was not to be called in question again, since in the settlements of the 1730s and 1740s (see Chs. 5 and 6), territories were to be ceded to the Bourbon–Farnese family and not to Spain.

Austria was the power which seemed to have gained most from the Quadruple Alliance, with the exchange of Sardinia for Sicily, which was now reunited with Naples. But the Emperor's power in Italy had been extended through British naval help and French goodwill: once these were withdrawn his position there would be unsteady. The poor showing of Austrian forces in Sardinia and Sicily in 1719–20, when they attempted to expel the Spaniards, was a bad portent for the future. Charles VI himself bitterly resented the way the Quadruple Alliance seemed to have been imposed on him by the *entente* powers, and he was to prove determined to make as many difficulties as possible in the years ahead over executing the terms of the treaty. The Emperor's territories had by 1720 reached their greatest extent. At the treaty of Passarowitz (Požarevac) with the Turks two years before in 1718, the Sultan had been forced, after defeats at the hand of Prince Eugene, to cede northern Serbia with Belgrade and the Banat of Temesvár. The forward policy pursued by the Porte since the humiliation of Peter the Great on the River Pruth had been brought to an equally humiliating close. Although the Turks kept their gains from Venice in southern Greece, the Austrian advance southwards seemed to be continuing irresistibly. Austria was now on the borders of the Danubian principalities and within striking distance of the Black Sea as well as the Adriatic (she already had a port at Trieste) and Aegean Seas. The capture of Constantinople itself did not seem too wild a possibility for the future. In the event, however, Austria's internal weaknesses, which Charles VI did little to solve, and her continued involvement in the west, meant that she was to advance no further in the Balkans, and even to lose ground to the Turks in the 1730s (see pp. 154ff.). Another disappointment with the peace of Passarowitz was to be the commercial treaty annexed to it, which allowed Austrian shipping down the Danube to trade with Constantinople and the Black Sea ports. As with so many of Charles VI's commercial ventures its expectations were not to be fulfilled.

THE COLLAPSE OF THE QUADRUPLE ALLIANCE SYSTEM, 1720–1724

Spain's signature of the Quadruple Alliance in 1720 in the event failed to solve the problems left over from the Spanish Succession War. The general wish for a permanent settlement proved short-lived, as did the fragile unity achieved by Stanhope's energetic 'shuttle diplomacy'. The congress to consider the differences glossed over in the Quadruple Alliance was not held at Cambrai till 1724. But by then a realignment of the powers was under way.

In 1720 the stability of both France and Britain, whose co-operation was so crucial to the maintenance of European peace, was badly shaken. Their diplomatic dominance was temporarily weakened, and this probably allowed the two restless powers, Spain and Austria, more freedom of action in the coming years. In summer 1720 the French Mississippi Company collapsed and with it the whole financial system created in France since 1716 by the Scottish financier, John Law. The Regent's need for cash to finance his recent foreign policy had made Law almost indispensable, and he had come to control the collection of taxation as well as monopolising French overseas trade through his company. The Mississippi crash and the subsequent flight of Law badly shook the confidence of the regency, but in the event Orleans survived. Dubois, whose influence had sunk as Law's star rose, recovered, becoming a cardinal in July 1721 and *premier ministre* early in 1723.

Britain suffered a similar financial crisis in 1720. In the autumn the South Sea Company collapsed. The close connection of the court and ministers with the company destroyed the existing Whig ministry and rocked the Hanoverian dynasty itself. By February 1721 Stanhope had died, and Charles Townshend and his brother-in-law Robert Walpole were back in power. Now began the long ascendancy of Walpole, but the political stability his Whig administration was ultimately to bring was not immediately seen. The new ministry was at first preoccupied with a struggle for control of foreign policy between the two secretaries of state, Townshend and Carteret, and this further weakened Britain's international position in the early 1720s. Carteret was largely isolated in the cabinet, but, as a fluent German speaker, he enjoyed more of the confidence of the King and his Hanoverian ministers. He was the real heir of Stanhope, preferring to co-operate with both France *and* Austria, whereas Townshend was prepared to abandon Austria and to work with France and Spain. Their quarrels, which lasted till Carteret's removal from the ministry in 1724, effectively prevented Britain from directing the Anglo-French *entente*, and British policy was reduced to *ad hoc* responses to events.

These divisions allowed Dubois to assert temporary French leadership of the *entente* until his death in August 1723: it was French rather than British diplomacy which finally brought peace in the north at Nystad in September 1721 (see p. 92). In the early 1720s there was a shift in emphasis in French policy: a growing independence from Britain, more overt hostility towards Austria and closer relations with Spain. As the young Louis XV approached his majority Orleans's obsession with the succession of his own family, and consequently his fear of Philip V, decreased. In Madrid Philip V was proving less aggressive and more anxious for friendship between the two Bourbon courts. The Spanish King and his wife realised that they were more likely to gain support for their ambitions from France rather than from Britain, especially as Philip was now as anxious for the return of Gibraltar as for expansion in Italy.

The Spaniards had been the one power eager to have the projected peace congress meet at Cambrai. They aimed to secure agreement for their own troops, rather than neutral Swiss soldiers, to garrison Parma and Tuscany so as to ensure Don Charles's eventual succession. Britain in particular was anxious to delay the congress, as she feared the succession issue would cause further conflict with the Emperor, and there was also the certainty that Spain would demand the return of Gibraltar there. Dubois was no more eager for it to open, but he signed a Franco-Spanish defensive alliance (on 27 March 1721) without British participation. This guaranteed the treaty of Utrecht and the Quadruple Alliance, assured Spain of diplomatic support over Gibraltar and, in a secret article, promised French help at the future congress for the entry of Spanish garrisons into the Italian duchies.

In making the alliance Spain had hoped France would abandon Britain and wholeheartedly commit herself to Spanish ambitions. But

Dubois, while determined to be more his own master, refused to destroy his own creation the *entente* and instead sought British accession to the new Franco-Spanish alliance. He was convinced that the association with Britain was essential, not just because of Orleans's succession (which was now a less pressing issue) but to prevent the possible re-creation of the Grand Alliance and the threat of war this might bring. The British were willing enough to join because the Spaniards had acted obstructively and resentfully towards them since signing the Quadruple Alliance. British merchants, on being read-mitted to Spain, found tariffs raised regardless of the treaties of 1715 and 1716. Philip had also pressed strongly and incessantly for the return of Gibraltar. Although British ministers were prepared to con-sider this and continued to underestimate the value of the fortress, parliament was implacably opposed. To mollify Spain, in May 1721 George I wrote to Philip V informally, promising to ask parliament eventually to restore it. This allowed Britain to join the Franco-Span-ish treaty, which was converted into a triple alliance, signed at Madrid on 13 June 1721. By joining, Britain appeared to be ready to support Spain at the coming congress. This, and George's promise over Gibraltar (never to be honoured), had enabled Dubois to win Spain's tacit recognition of British possession of Gibraltar and Minorca and the restoration of the previous commercial privileges.

The new alignment was to last three years. It grew stronger in 1722: in the January Philip's heir by his first marriage, the Prince of Asturias, married Orleans's daughter, and the five-year-old Spanish Infanta, Philip and Elizabeth's daughter, came to France to be edu-cated. It was intended she would eventually marry Louis XV who was now twelve. The Anglo-French connection was also confirmed and strengthened in the same year, when Dubois warned London of the unsuccessful Atterbury Jacobite plot. By creating the recent triple alliance Dubois had effectively transformed Stanhope's Anglo-Franco-Austrian system into a French–Spanish–British one. This would prevent war and safeguard French interests in the same way, but it could also adopt a much tougher approach to Austria. Dubois was, at bottom, as hostile towards her as other French statesmen, particularly because of her swollen territorial size. He now hoped to be able to restore French diplomatic ascendancy in Europe: French activity and success in the northern courts and in Spain in 1721 already seemed to show France was resuming her traditional leadership. For their part, the British hoped Spain, by signing the Triple Alliance, was sincerely accepting both Utrecht and the Quadruple Alliance. Britain, moreover, was coming to prefer associating with the two Bourbon powers because of her increasing annoyance with Charles VI: he was proving unco-operative, and even hostile, not only over the Italian duchies but also towards Hanoverian interests in the German Empire. Now that Britain and France had forced Spain to accept the Quadruple Alliance and the Emperor had received Sicily, he knew the western powers no longer had any hold over him. The Triple Alliance of 1721 was therefore seen, not only by Dubois but also by the British ministers, as a way of exerting pressure on Austria as well as deterring Spain from further independent adventures in Italy.

Despite the agreement of Britain and the two Bourbon powers, it was three years before the congress of Cambrai met. The British continued to be nervous in case Spain raised the Gibraltar question, but the chief problem was clearly the contrariness of Charles VI, now freed from the immediate threats of the Turkish and Spanish wars. There were interminable petty and tenaciously fought disputes – in these Philip V was as guilty as Charles VI – over the formal renunciations of the Spanish and Austrian titles: both the Emperor and the Spanish King continued to use each other's titles, despite what they had promised in the Quadruple Alliance. The Emperor also made use of his claim that Parma and Tuscany were imperial fiefs, and it was not till January 1724 that he formally accepted Don Charles's succession rights. The congress of Cambrai could then proceed. However, Vienna still intended to limit the concessions they had been forced to make in the Quadruple Alliance and their overriding concern was to prevent the entry of Spanish garrisons into the Italian duchies, since this would clearly reduce Habsburg influence in the peninsula.

If this obstructiveness was irritating, Austrian actions elsewhere seemed menacing, especially to the ministers of George I. It was becoming clear that Charles VI was trying to restore Imperial authority and influence in Germany, where there had been a definite decline since 1714. This policy was encouraged by the determined and fiercely Catholic Imperial vice-chancellor, Schönborn, who was angry at the scant regard paid to the Emperor by George I of Hanover and Frederick William I of Prussia during their recent struggle with Sweden in north Germany. George I's accession to the British throne seemed to have given him, as elector of Hanover, a dangerous independence from the Emperor's authority. Charles VI's ministers were also alarmed at what Prince Eugene described as Prussia's 'great army', which had been continually expanded since Frederick William became king. Austrian concern had been heightened by the co-operation between Hanover and Prussia which had developed after 1719. This had created a large and militarily strong, Protestant bloc in north Germany, made more dangerous by its close connections with Britain and France. Schönborn pressed Charles to reassert his authority by working with the Catholic and smaller princes and by hindering any further growth in Hanoverian or Prussian power. When minor incidents involving the persecution of Protestants occurred in the Palatinate and Mainz, Schönborn openly sympathised with the Catholic rulers. This was done regardless of the supposed impartiality of the Emperor, who probably did in fact want religious peace. At the same time Vienna deliberately held up Imperial approval, despite repeated requests, to Sweden's cession to Hanover of Bremen and Verden and to Prussia of Stettin.

It was far easier for Charles to bully George as elector of Hanover in Germany than as king of Great Britain elsewhere. Consequently, the less Charles got his way with Britain and France over Italy, the more he listened to Schönborn's pleas for trying to increase Imperial authority in the Empire. Inevitably, Hanover and Prussia drew more closely together and sought links with the other German princes and France. Increasingly George I, with his Protestant British kingdom overseas, came to appear as the natural leader for aggrieved Protestants in Germany. These quarrels were the occasion of more bad temper rather than action, but they did lead to a growing polarisation and confrontation between Austria and the north-German Protestant powers in the early 1720s.

Austria's increasing truculence substantially reflected Charles VI's own character: as he grew older and more confident he assumed more control over policy. It was his own very real and personal interest in his former Spanish lands in Italy which had made him so obstinate over the successions to Parma and Tuscany. Similarly, his interest in the former Spanish Netherlands led to further problems with the western powers. The Emperor, unusually for a Habsburg but largely because of his experiences while in Spain, had an enthusiasm for industrial and commercial enterprises. This had caused him to try to develop industry and trade within the Austrian and Bohemian lands. The trade clauses of Austria's treaty of Passarowitz with the Turks (see p. 118) provided a good opportunity and gave a great impetus to a commercial policy in the Balkans and Mediterranean. A council of commerce and an Eastern Company were set up in Vienna, while Trieste and Fiume (Rijeka) were declared free ports to encourage trade with the Levant. The Emperor had also set his heart on becoming a maritime power and from 1720 a small Austrian commercial fleet appeared in the Mediterranean. Unfortunately the new ports had little success, being too far from the main shipping routes for them to supplant Leghorn, Venice and Genoa, while the Eastern Company lacked the necessary network of consuls and factors. Far more promising were the developments in the Southern Netherlands.

The Barrier treaty of 1715 had turned the Southern Netherlands into what amounted to a military and economic satellite of the Dutch and, to a lesser extent, of the British. One-third of the revenues went to support the Dutch 'barrier' garrisons, while Dutch and English goods benefited from favourable tariffs. The closure of the River Scheldt, imposed by the Dutch since the late sixteenth century, meant overseas trade could not be pursued from Antwerp. After 1715, however, largely through local initiative, ships had made occasional voyages from Ostend to Far Eastern as well as European ports. Charles

VI realised the Netherlands were useless to him unless they were developed commercially. In December 1722 he therefore founded the Ostend Company to trade with the West and East Indies and to form colonies. Inevitably the Dutch and English East India Companies were jealous of this newcomer, especially as it was initially highly successful, with profits on voyages often reaching 80 to 100 per cent.

The formation of the Ostend Company was yet one more blow to the system of co-operation by Britain, France and Austria created by Stanhope and Dubois. By 1722 the Quadruple Alliance, which had been falling apart since 1720, was no more. Almost all Charles VI's recent actions had antagonised George I as elector or king as much as they had annoyed the Bourbon powers. George could already depend on friendship with Prussia and France, and now the Ostend Company produced co-operation with the Dutch. It was the Dutch who had taken the lead since 1718 in protesting in Vienna that such trade was forbidden by the peace settlements of Utrecht and Westphalia and in harassing Ostend ships. The weakness of British policy in the 1720s is illustrated by their failure to bring pressure to bear on the Emperor over Ostend and in leaving it to the Dutch. However, George as elector adopted a far more belligerent line towards Charles VI in Germany, and relations between Hanover and Austria were to remain strained till 1731.

Hostility between Britain and Austria was certainly novel, but it was not really surprising. Previous Anglo-Austrian co-operation had been based on joint opposition to Louis XIV's policies, and the two countries had little else in common. Economically, British textiles were competing with Silesian ones in central Europe, and the Southern Netherlands were proving a cause of commercial conflict. Their political systems and religions were directly contrary to one another, and, but for the French danger, the Austrian court would have sympathised with the exiled Stuarts. Essentially, both considered the other a convenient ally against France. Now that France no longer appeared a threat, particularly to Britain, Austria's roles as the linchpin of a continental bloc against France had become temporarily redundant. Indeed by 1723 the British were coming to fear Austria as the main danger to the European balance and to interpret Charles's attempts to get his own way by being unco-operative as proof that he intended – in the words of the Hanoverian minister in Vienna – to become 'the arbiter of Europe'.

This view was largely groundless: Austria's recent territorial gains had led to an exaggerated estimate of Habsburg power. The Emperor Charles VI had failed to introduce the fundamental administrative and financial reforms which the monarchy desperately needed. In fact he was already becoming increasingly concerned about the future of his territories. His heirs were his daughters, and he feared another war of succession because of the novelty of a female succession. Therefore, between 1720 and 1723, he persuaded most of the diets in his territories to agree to the succession rights of his own daughters before those of his elder brother's daughters. This order of succession was regulated in a document known as the Pragmatic Sanction. When his nieces (Joseph I's daughters) married the Saxon and Bavarian electoral princes in 1721 and 1722, each had to renounce her succession rights. International guarantees for the Pragmatic Sanction now also began to be sought. Although most British ministers had been sympathetic, on the whole, believing it was as necessary for European peace to stabilise the Austrian as well as the British and French successions, the French consistently opposed a guarantee of the Pragmatic Sanction in case the Austrian monarchy was strengthened. George I's Hanoverian ministers and Townshend similarly interpreted it as part of an attempt to increase Habsburg power in Germany and Europe. It was this fear of Austria which was one of the reasons for George I's signing the alliance of Charlottenburg with Prussia in October 1723, though its main purpose was to contain Russia.

UNEASY PEACE IN THE NORTH, 1721–1725

The treaty of Nystad opened up a long period of uneasy peace in northern Europe. Russia controlled the eastern shores of the Baltic and seemed intent on further expansion, while George I dominated the west. The British King did so not only because of his Hanoverian electorate and the British fleet but also because of the close relations he had maintained with Denmark from the last years of the Northern War. George's interests both as king and elector appeared to demand the containment of Russia, and since 1716 he had pursued a consistently hostile policy towards the Tsar (formal diplomatic relations were broken in 1719). British supplies of naval stores, which were essential for her naval supremacy, seemed to have been imperilled by Peter the Great's conquests. The Tsar could also be expected to try to undermine Hanover's own much strengthened position in Germany, where George had gained Bremen and Verden and continued to occupy Mecklenburg. Peter still acted as protector of the exiled Duke of Mecklenburg, who had of course married his niece. However, what was potentially more explosive than this was the engagement of the Tsar's daughter Anna to Charles Frederick of Holstein-Gottorp (1721). The Duke, who was now a puppet of Russia, was to be the focus of much of the diplomacy of these years. He claimed to be ruler of Schleswig, which George as elector of Hanover had guaranteed to Denmark when he purchased Bremen from her. In addition, Charles Frederick's claims on the Swedish throne – he was the son of Charles XII's elder sister – gave Peter a dangerous lever in Stockholm. At the same time Russia continued her *de facto* protectorate over Poland, where Augustus II's power had never recovered from his earlier humiliations. Peter's arbitration of a settlement (1716) between the Polish King and his nobility, which severely limited the size of the royal army and increased aristocratic power, had begun Russia's long role as guarantor of the Polish constitution. Although Russian troops had been withdrawn in 1719 because of Austrian and Hanoverian pressure (see p. 89), they could return at any time, and Poland provided an open door to central Europe for Russia. In Poland, as elsewhere round the eastern Baltic, Russia's influence was all-pervasive in the final years of Peter the Great.

In the years immediately after the peace of Nystad Britain made a determined effort in Copenhagen, Stockholm and Berlin to keep the northern powers away from Russia and to isolate her. The British even tried to stir up the Turks to divert Peter's attention from the Baltic: throughout the 1720s they were to adopt the traditional role of France in encouraging Turkish intervention in eastern Europe, usually against Russia but sometimes also against Austria. On the whole Britain could depend on France's diplomatic support in pursuing this policy. Although Dubois adopted a more independent role than when Stanhope was alive and would have been quite willing to consider friendship with Russia, he did not want to offend the British.

Anglo-Russian relations reached crisis point in 1723 and followed a pattern which was to recur almost annually till the end of the decade. In July false reports reached the British that Peter the Great's fleet had put to sea to force either Denmark or Sweden to accept the claims of the Duke of Holstein-Gottorp. The British secretaries of state, Townshend and Carteret, were as concerned as George's Hanoverian advisers. Money was therefore voted in parliament to increase the navy, and then on 10 October George and Frederick William I of Prussia concluded the treaty of Charlottenburg, promising each other mutual support. This alliance was both the culmination of George's Protestant and anti-Austrian policies in Germany (see pp. 121f.) and a counter to the threat from St Petersburg.

Russia did not undertake a Baltic adventure in 1723, and it is doubtful if Peter ever intended to help Charles Frederick by force. It is more likely that he hoped to use the Schleswig claim as a way of frightening the Danes into removing dues on Russian shipping passing through the Sound. However, in 1724 the Tsar succeeded in matching the alliance of Charlottenburg by making a treaty with Sweden, which agreed to joint diplomatic action (if possible, with the Emperor as well) to restore Schleswig to Charles Frederick. This move particularly worried Townshend, who feared that Frederick and Ulrika of Sweden, who had no children, might abdicate, and that the Swedes, under Russian pressure, would elect Charles Frederick as their successor. Townshend also managed to persuade himself that there was a danger of Russo-Swedish naval co-operation which was likely to lead to an attack on Hanover or even on Britain herself.

British fears of Russia in northern Europe in the years after Nystad were largely groundless. Russia's energies were chiefly directed elsewhere, in the region of the Caspian Sea, the termini of the Asian caravan routes. As part of his general policy of transforming his empire into a vast Eurasian trading power, Peter aimed at forcing the trades in silk and other oriental goods to use Russian rivers. In 1722 he began a short and successful war against the Shah of Persia to seize vital areas. This ended in September 1723 with the cession of Baku to Russia. During the war the Turks moved into Georgia and Armenia, where they established themselves to prevent further Russian expansion.

COLD WAR IN EUROPE, 1724–1728

The late 1720s saw rapidly changing alliances and almost continuous confrontation between the powers in western Europe, largely over the issues which the Quadruple Alliance had failed to solve. Serious military conflict was prevented mainly by the Anglo-French alliance, which managed to survive despite important changes in leadership in 1723–24. Dubois, the joint architect of the *entente*, died in August 1723. His policy of peace and friendship with England had ensured stability in France during Louis XV's minority; he had prevented the revival of the Grand Alliance and safeguarded the Orleanist succession. By the time of his death he was also gaining more control over the *entente* and had improved France's relations with Spain, while isolating the traditional enemy, Austria. Although the Regent Orleans also died soon after Dubois (December 1723), there was no change in French policy. The new first minister, the Duke of Bourbon, concluded that France, with its thirteen-year-old king, still needed peace and should continue her alliances with Britain and Spain.

Soon after these changes in France, Townshend and Robert Walpole engineered the fall of Carteret (April 1724). Under Townshend's leadership British foreign policy now developed a firmer line. Britain remained committed to the French alliance, but Townshend was himself to show growing hostility towards Austria, partly because of the Ostend Company but mainly because of his fears of an increase in Habsburg power in Germany. The resulting Anglo-Austrian friction soon became as important a cause of instability in Europe as the ambitions of Madrid and the rise of Russia.

In April 1724 the congress of Cambrai opened at last, but it dissolved in the October having completely failed to solve the problems left over from the Quadruple Alliance. The negotiators, in Carlyle's words, had been 'busied, baling out water with sieves', and the congress left the powers angrier than before. The Spaniards had unsuccessfully pressed Charles VI to allow their garrisons into Parma and Tuscany and reminded the British about George I's unfulfilled promise over Gibraltar. Dutch protests about the Ostend Company had embittered relations between the Maritime Powers and the Emperor. The negotiations had been further complicated by Philip V's temporary abdication in favour of his son Louis and resumption of the throne six months later in August 1724 at the youth's death. Philip's action was but one symptom of growing mental instability. Sometimes convinced he was a corpse or a frog, he wore his clothes to rags, bit the carpets or himself and scratched his wife. Elizabeth's patient forbearance increased her influence over him. Her authority was now at its height and she used it to subordinate Spanish policy to her children's interests in Italy.

The Cambrai congress convinced Philip and Elizabeth that cooperation with the British and French, which Spain had pursued since 1720, had been futile. They were now to adopt a policy which provoked a crisis lasting till the end of the decade. Quite unexpectedly they approached Charles VI directly to exploit both his diplomatic isolation and his differences with the Maritime Powers over the Ostend Company. They intended to conclude marriage alliances for their two sons, Don Charles and Don Philip, with the Emperor's daughters, and hoped these would eventually bring their children control of the Habsburg hereditary lands and most of Italy. As bait for this ambitious Farnese dynastic policy, Spain could offer her guarantee for the Pragmatic Sanction and commercial concessions for the Ostend Company. Consequently a Dutch adventurer, Ripperda, was sent secretly to Vienna in January 1725. The Austrians responded, seeing a chance to escape isolation and to build a new system revolving round Vienna. But they were prepared to give little away themselves, and the talks might have failed but for an incident which gave a rude shock to the Spanish royal couple's pride.

Louis XV's chief minister, Bourbon, was determined to get the King, who was now fifteen, married as soon as possible: an heir would strengthen the dynasty and ruin the claims of Bourbon's rival, the new Duke of Orleans, to the succession. All groups at the French court were now agreed that the engagement to the Spanish Infanta, who was only seven, had to be broken off and a mature bride found. Unfortunately, Bourbon handled the affair ineptly. Instead of preparing Philip and Elizabeth for what was not meant as a hostile act, he simply bundled their daughter back to Spain in February 1725. Six months later Louis was married to the daughter of the exiled King of Poland, Stanislas Leszczyński. Madrid was naturally enraged and pushed for a quick agreement with Austria for revenge against the western powers.

On 30 April/1 May 1725 Ripperda signed three treaties in Vienna. By these Philip and Charles VI finally renounced each other's thrones and lands, thus settling the most important remaining issue from the Spanish Succession War. Philip also renounced the French throne and guaranteed the Pragmatic Sanction. The Emperor promised to invest Don Charles with Parma and Tuscany at the death of the ruling princes, but he refused to allow Spanish garrisons there beforehand. He also evaded definite commitments over a marriage alliance. The two powers promised mutual assistance in case of attack, and Charles pledged his diplomatic support to persuade Britain to return Gibraltar and Minorca. Finally, they concluded a commercial treaty by which Spain promised to allow the Ostend Company to trade in any part of her empire except the Americas, and to give the Emperor's subjects the same privileges as those enjoyed by the Maritime Powers.

The Emperor had clearly gained most. In return for vague promises, he had received substantial concessions in areas dear to him. Concern about the future of his own dynasty was becoming his main worry, and he intended this alliance to be the basis for wider European acceptance of the Pragmatic Sanction. He had wanted neither to further Spanish ambitions nor to create a war situation. Unfortunately, he misjudged Spanish adventurism and the reaction of the western powers. Although Spain had gained little that was tangible, there was public rejoicing in Madrid over the treaty, since it seemed a slap in the face to France. At Versailles the court was dumbfounded and there was real fear of attack: the new alliance appeared to be directed as much against France as against the Maritime Powers. The French consequently turned to Britain for help and passively accepted the leadership of Townshend. Though he mostly encouraged growing public fears in London about the Ostend Company to secure parliamentary and Dutch support, Townshend himself saw the Vienna alliance as a real threat. He believed it would undermine the diplomatic predominance of the Anglo-French *entente*, which was essential for the preservation of European peace and of the Protestant succession itself. His earlier antagonism towards Charles VI's forward policy in Germany led him to see Austria as the main culprit, and he seriously feared Austria was intent on establishing her hegemony in Europe.

Townshend's fears were compounded by a new, and once again largely imaginary, Baltic crisis. Peter the Great died in February 1725 and was succeeded first by his wife Catherine I (1725–27) and then by his young grandson Peter II (1727–30). The great Tsar's death and the subsequent struggles for the throne were to take much of the dynamism and drive for territorial expansion out of Russian policy till the late 1730s. But this was not immediately apparent to the western powers, who were more impressed by the huge size of the Russian army (210,000 in 1727, and with 100,000 irregulars) and continued to fear renewed Russian territorial expansion westwards, particularly after the marriage in May 1725 of Charles Frederick of Holstein-Gottorp to Peter's daughter Anna. The Tsaritsa Catherine was known to support Charles Frederick's claims to both the Swedish throne and Danish Schleswig, and this endangered the system which had existed in the Baltic since 1721.

In summer 1725 Europe was gripped by a serious war crisis mainly caused by Townshend's exaggerated reaction to rumours of Russian naval preparations at Reval and to Spain's decision to mobilise her army and navy. By over-reacting he inflamed the situation further. Convinced that conflict with Russia and the Austro-Spanish allies was inevitable, he took military precautions and set out to create a counter-alliance system. In doing so he re-established British diplomatic ascendancy in Europe, once again on the basis of close co-operation with the more pacific France. On 3 September 1725 Townshend negotiated the signature by Britain–Hanover, France and Prussia of the alliance of Hanover. The Dutch, still furious about the Ostend trade, were *de facto* members from the start, although they did not formally accede till a year later. The intention was to contain Austria, Spain and Russia, and all the parties guaranteed one another against attack. Britain and France also promised to support Prussian claims to the succession to the Rhenish duchies of Jülich–Berg, and this was sufficient at the time to encourage Frederick William I to continue his policy of alignment with Hanover against the apparent Catholic–Austrian threat in Germany. The alliance was an impressive achievement for Britain and particularly for Townshend. It averted any military threat to Hanover, while the British navy could be relied on to deal with the Spanish and Russian fleets. The French were equally satisfied with the alliance as it gave them security from what they felt was the very real prospect of an Austro-Spanish attack.

Unfortunately the result of the alliance of Hanover was to polarise European diplomacy. The Russians who had in fact hoped for a negotiated settlement over Schleswig were now driven to conclude that only force could extract Anglo-French agreement to Charles Frederick's claims. Moreover, the two unnatural allies, Spain and Austria, instead of submitting, were pushed into closer co-operation. On 5 November 1725 they signed a military convention for mutual protection: this and the previous agreements are usually called the First Treaty of Vienna. Charles VI agreed in principle to the dynastic marriages Spain wanted, and the two states even agreed to partition France if there were a war. The Emperor promised to begin raising troops, and Spain was to pay him subsidies.

Ripperda and Elizabeth Farnese hoped that the new alliance would be a prelude to a European war which would benefit the Queen's own family, while Philip intended to use it to cancel Britain's commercial privileges and to seize Gibraltar. Ripperda was therefore allowed to try to assemble a European coalition, similar to the one dreamt up by

Alberoni, to attack the western powers. However, these schemes were really doomed from the start, because Austria, despite Townshend's suspicions, had no further territorial ambitions. She was now largely concerned with protecting herself, safeguarding the Habsburg succession, preserving the Ostend Company and avoiding war. Charles VI was at best half-hearted in his commitment to Spain. He had no real wish to conclude the dynastic marriages and still did not want Don Charles to have the Italian duchies. He considered the alliance with Spain as primarily a defensive one and hoped for Spanish subsidies for his troops. The Emperor also realised that he needed other allies now that the alliance of Hanover had been formed. Urgent talks were therefore begun with both Saxony and Russia and efforts made to rebuild an Imperial party in Germany. In summer 1726 mutual fear and hostility towards Britain produced a preliminary Austro-Russian treaty and then a defensive alliance (August), which included a Russian guarantee of Charles's Pragmatic Sanction. The Russian court had been eager to sign: their hopes that the western powers would accept the Duke of Holstein-Gottorp's claims had been dashed, and they now wanted to force him into Schleswig with Austrian help. The new alliance proved durable, becoming almost a permanent feature of European politics, mainly because of its value to both Austria and Russia against the Turks. The Austrians had been the first power to see the use which could be made of Russian strength outside eastern Europe and to try to make Russia a regular member of the European states system.

The Russian alliance was largely the work of Prince Eugene, whose influence in Vienna was recovering after a period of eclipse in the early 1720s. Eugene wanted Austria to build a new grouping of powers based on alliances with Russia and with Prussia. He grasped that if his court could overcome its dislike of Protestant Prussia and gain Frederick William I's support, the position of the alliance of Hanover in Germany would collapse. Eugene recognised that it had been the co-operation between the Prussian King and George of Hanover–Britain which had caused a disastrous decline in the Emperor's authority within the Empire. He now rightly anticipated that the recent Austro-Russian alliance would have an immediate influence on Frederick William. The Prussian King was basically unwarlike and was known to be very afraid of Austria's Russian ally because of the exposed position of East Prussia. The King himself was becoming disillusioned with the alliance of Hanover, and this came to a head in August 1726, when the Dutch joined it. In doing so they forced the allies to abandon the clauses promising support for Frederick William's claims to Jülich–Berg, as they did not want Prussia on their borders. Moreover, Frederick William's 'German' conscience had always been disturbed by his alienation from the Emperor: he welcomed the attentions of an Austrian envoy, Seckendorff, who fitted well into the barrack-room atmosphere of the Prussian court and was supported by one of the King's ministers in Austrian pay, Grumbkow. Almost with relief Frederick William made the secret treaty of Wusterhausen with Charles VI in October 1726, which was followed by a further alliance in 1728. In return for a Prussian guarantee of the Pragmatic Sanction, Charles VI gave vague promises over the Jülich–Berg succession. (Austria was still reluctant to countenance further Prussian expansion.) Prussia had now effectively dissociated herself from the alliance of Hanover, and Austria's success in Berlin was followed by expensive subsidy treaties with several minor German princes which effectively neutralised the Empire.

Actual European conflict came nearer when Britain tried to intimidate the Austrian–Spanish–Russian alignment. Fleets were sent to the Baltic, Mediterranean and Caribbean in 1726, and from then till 1729 Britain was on a continuous war footing. Outright war was avoided partly by Franco-Dutch attempts to restrain the bellicose Townshend, but also because neither Austria nor Russia wanted to initiate military action. Charles VI knew his territories were highly vulnerable. He also recognised that his finances were too weak to raise substantial numbers of troops on his own, especially as he now realised that Spanish military and financial help would be insignificant (Spain had promised 3 m. gulden a year but only paid 2 m. altogether). In fact, the tenuous Spanish alliance was being seen in Vienna by 1726 as of apparently little value. The ministers with the most influence now, Eugene and Starhemberg, much preferred the alignment with Russia and Prussia, especially as they had not been responsible personally for making the alliance with Spain.

Almost from the start of the crisis the Austrians would have been prepared for a diplomatic settlement, and their Russian ally was to prove as unwilling to challenge the western powers militarily. When the British fleet blockaded the Baltic port of Reval from May to September 1726 to discourage Russian moves over Schleswig, Catherine I's government was duly impressed and remained passive. At the same time British and French diplomacy co-operated in Stockholm and Copenhagen and managed to bring first Sweden and then Denmark into the alliance of Hanover (March–April 1727). The accession of the two Scandinavian powers in some part compensated for the loss of Prussia, and by the beginning of 1727 the Hanover allies were clearly in the ascendant. In the meanwhile the opposing grouping of the Vienna alliance was changing its shape: an eastern bloc of Austria, Prussia and Russia (with tacit Saxon support) was emerging, while the extraordinary Austro-Spanish association was gradually falling apart and Spain going her own way.

It was Spain, in spite of her weakness and impending isolation, who forced a military confrontation and the outbreak of a minor Anglo-Spanish War in 1727. The dispatch of a British squadron to the

Caribbean in 1726, in an unsuccessful bid to prevent Spain's treasure fleet from leaving Portobello, merely made her more bellicose. Although the new Spanish chief minister, Patiño, felt peace was essential for Spain's economic recovery, Philip and Elizabeth were determined to punish the British. For, though Anglo-Spanish differences were not to blame for the original crisis, Britain had clearly taken the lead in trying to curb Spain's latest diplomatic venture. In December 1726, therefore, Spain cancelled British commercial privileges and in February 1727 began a leisurely and unbloody siege of Gibraltar. Britain responded by naval action against Spanish shipping, although neither state formally declared war. The Spanish royal couple, who had clung to the Austrian alliance, hoped the siege of Gibraltar would encourage Charles VI to declare war on Britain and France. But this minor Anglo-Spanish conflict did not develop into a wider struggle because of the reluctance of both Austria and France to become involved. France was determined to prevent war. Dislike for Britain and sympathy for Bourbon Spain remained strong at the French court, but the desire for peace was stronger. It was increased by France's financial weakness at this time and by the advent of Cardinal Fleury to power in June 1726 after the fall of the Duke of Bourbon.

Louis XV dismissed Bourbon because he had tried to undermine the influence of the King's tutor, Fleury. Lampooned as a one-eyed ruffian, Bourbon had been openly greedy and an obvious blunderer. His successor Fleury was already seventy-three when he replaced him, and he was to remain in power till he was nearly ninety. Although he was never formally *premier ministre*, there was no doubt of his control over domestic and foreign policy. He achieved office through his influence over the teenage King, but he kept it by his own skill and success. Subtle and determined, he followed fundamentally cautious and pacific policies; in many ways he resembled Britain's Robert Walpole, who also grasped the value of peace. Fleury gave France stable and effective government, while fostering the rapid growth of the navy and of commerce. He was a partisan of the *entente* with Britain, but only as long as it served French interests and did not involve France in war. On the wider international stage he was gradually to restore France's political leadership and establish his own personal dominance.

Fleury's accession to power was to lead to a shift towards France in the balance of the Anglo-French *entente*, but at the beginning he was at a disadvantage. France's financial weakness demanded peace at almost any price, while Bourbon's ineptness had alienated Spain and made France heavily dependent on Britain. Fleury had to follow a delicate policy of exerting enough French force to deter Spain and Austria from risking war, and at the same time restraining the bellicose Townshend from extending Britain's minor conflict with Spain into a wider one with the Emperor. To a great extent he shared Townshend's exaggerated fears of Austria: he constantly tried to avoid guaranteeing the Pragmatic Sanction, at least without adequate territorial compensation for France.

Given the desire for peace in both France and Austria, the European crisis could have been easily resolved but for Townshend's aggressiveness and Spain's refusal to compromise. Townshend was to respond reluctantly to the siege of Gibraltar with a short naval war against Spain and, more enthusiastically, by raising a mercenary army in Germany to frighten Charles VI. He considered Austria rather than Spain Britain's real enemy. In March 1727 diplomatic relations between Britain and Austria were broken off, and the Maritime Powers then began to seize the Ostend Company's shipping. War seemed very close, as all the European powers began to arm. Although France herself raised an extra 100,000 men and Fleury had assured Britain of French support over Ostend, the Cardinal actively sought to defuse the dangerous situation. He realised Charles VI did not want war and was more willing to compromise than Spain, and he rightly calculated that if Spain could be completely isolated, she would eventually have to fall in line with what Britain and France wanted. In the early months of 1727 Fleury therefore concentrated his diplomatic efforts on Vienna.

The Austrians agreed to negotiate rather than risk immediate war. Their military preparations had proved chaotic and, although they were no longer isolated, the majority of the German princes clearly wanted neutrality, while the Russian alliance appeared at risk on the death of Catherine I in May 1727. Consequently, after Fleury had warned he would help the Maritime Powers suppress the Ostend Company by force, Charles VI signed the Paris preliminaries on 31 May 1727. He made major concessions: he suspended the company for seven years and abandoned his commercial agreement with Spain. Fleury now aimed at persuading the other powers to sign these preliminaries, to discuss further points at a congress to be held at Soissons and then to conclude a definitive treaty.

Charles's signature of the Paris preliminaries ended the immediate danger of conflict on the Continent and was soon followed by the conclusion of the Anglo-Spanish War. Realising Austria had abandoned her, desperately short of money and unsuccessful in her siege of Gibraltar, Spain had to compromise. She therefore accepted the Paris preliminaries, lifted the siege in June 1727 and restored British commercial privileges. This brought the naval war to an end (convention of the Pardo, 6 March 1728).

Fleury had now established a reputation as a peacemaker. He could claim his diplomacy had saved France from war, divided Austria and Spain, ended the Anglo-Spanish War and maintained the relationship with Britain. However, Townshend could equally argue that his own tough approach had forced Spain and Austria to back down: he certainly intended to continue in this fashion. He could also claim that British belligerency had paid off in the Baltic as well, where another British squadron had been sent in 1727. This naval pressure, together with the death of Catherine I (May 1727), had ended Russia's thoughts of installing Charles Frederick in Schleswig by force. The accession of the twelve-year-old Peter II (May 1727–January 1730) made Menshikov, Peter the Great's general, the real ruler and destroyed the influence of Charles Frederick, who was expelled from Russia in July 1727. Continual struggles at court were to cause Russia to pursue a more isolationist role, stressing the defence of the status quo and abandoning the forward policy with its threat to Denmark. This suited Ostermann, the chancellor from 1725 to 1745, who largely controlled foreign policy. He hoped for a *rapprochement* with Denmark as well as Prussia, although he wanted to maintain the Austrian alliance, which he felt was vital because of the Turks and was a way of preserving Russian influence in Europe. The Russo-Austrian alliance was to remain the basis of Russian foreign policy till the Seven Years War.

Russia's more conciliatory attitude helped to lessen Anglo-Russian tension, especially as the British gradually grasped that Russia wanted to encourage rather than damage their Baltic trade. The two countries came to realise they were natural economic partners. The death of the anti-Russian George I in 1727 and the accession of George II (1727–60) also helped reconciliation. Diplomatic relations, which had been severed in 1719, were restored by the appointment of a consul-general to Russia in 1728 and then by proper representation in 1731. The long period of British and Russian co-operation in Europe which was to last for half a century, was just beginning.

THE DECLINE OF THE ANGLO-FRENCH *ENTENTE* 1728–1731

The armed confrontation between the powers which had begun in 1725 was to last till the end of the decade. But of more ultimate significance was the simultaneous realignment of the powers and, in particular, the steady weakening of the Anglo-French *entente*. By the early 1730s the *entente* was to be no more.

Spain's formal signature of the Paris preliminaries (March 1728) meant that the congress of Soissons could meet. Like Cambrai this proved a non-event. The congress (June 1728–July 1729) was no more than a facade, for Fleury effectively kept the negotiations in his own hands at Versailles. During the congress Austria again became isolated from all the western powers. Britain and the Dutch Republic, supported by Fleury, insisted on the final suppression of the Ostend trade, while the final collapse of the short-lived Austro-Spanish *rapprochement* predictably led to the revival of the old differences between Vienna and Madrid. Spain, for her part, now moved towards the western powers. Having failed to defeat Britain in the recent undeclared war or to overcome the British refusal to have Gibraltar discussed at Soissons, Spain concentrated once more on ensuring Don Charles's succession in Italy. This latest turn in Spanish policy also reflected Elizabeth Farnese's undiminished control over her husband. The Queen increasingly fretted about her own and her children's future if Philip should die. A solution of the Parma and Tuscany issue seemed vital, and she therefore turned to Britain and France for an alliance to force Austria, by military action if necessary, to back down in Italy.

Fleury welcomed Elizabeth's new approach. The birth of a dauphin (September 1729), which seemed to settle the French succession, had strengthened his own position *vis-à-vis* Spain. But the Cardinal was as determined to avoid war as ever and was equally intent on including Britain in any agreement. It was to be the British, however, who were most responsive to this new swing in Spanish policy, especially as they had not wanted the recent war with Spain. Townshend was still anxious to complete the humiliation of Austria, and he made the running in the negotiations with Madrid. Reconciliation was easy enough now that Spanish ambitions were once again directed towards Italy. In November 1729 Britain managed to effect the Seville Treaty, a defensive alliance between Spain, France and the Maritime Powers. The treaty tacitly confirmed British possession of Gibraltar and Minorca, renewed British trading concessions and cancelled those given to the Ostend Company. In return Britain and France finally agreed to enforce the introduction of 6,000 Spanish troops into Parma and Tuscany.

The treaty of Seville seemed to have restored the international situation to what it had been nearly five years before when Ripperda first approached Vienna. But now Spain had far stronger Anglo-French commitments over Italy, and the new treaty amounted to an ultimatum to Charles VI. Although Austria was not without allies her position was in reality weak: Charles VI's army and finances were still wholly inadequate, he lacked effective support from his Russian and Prussian allies and French influence was beginning to recover among the German princes. None the less, the Emperor appeared intent on resisting the treaty of Seville by force. Austrian troops were sent to Italy to prevent Spanish garrisons being installed in Parma and Tuscany. Although, given the poor state of the Habsburg army, there was a great deal of bluff in this action, when the reigning Duke of Parma died (January 1731) Charles VI was determined to prevent

Don Charles's succession: he therefore immediately occupied Parma with his own troops.

Townshend, once the Seville Treaty was concluded, had intended to carry out its terms, even if this meant war with Austria. But he was to fall from power before he could do this. His costly and bellicose policies, and the seemingly endless crisis they had produced since 1725, were finally to alienate the pacific Walpole, who had had to defend them in the House of Commons. In May 1730, he forced Townshend to resign. Walpole was now in effective control of British policy and was to embark on the difficult task of reconciling Austria and Spain while maintaining the Anglo-French alliance. He chose to do this by a direct approach to Vienna behind the backs of the French. He seems to have feared the French might spoil the negotiations if they were involved, but he also seems to have believed that Fleury in the event would put up with unilateral British action. His willingness (unlike Townshend or the French) to pay Charles VI's price for agreement – acceptance of the Pragmatic Sanction – made reconciliation possible with Austria. Prince Eugene, who had by now largely resumed control of Austrian policy, welcomed the restoration of the traditional alliance with Britain, believing it would once again provide security against the Bourbon powers. On 16 March 1731 the Second Treaty of Vienna was concluded between Charles VI and George II as king of Great Britain and elector of Hanover. (The Dutch joined the following February.) In making the treaty the two rulers ended six years of confrontation between their states and tried yet again to solve the problems which had faced the powers since the peace of Utrecht–Rastadt. Besides guaranteeing each other's possessions, George II guaranteed the Pragmatic Sanction and Charles VI agreed to suppress the Ostend Company and accept Hanoverian control of Bremen and Verden. The Emperor, moreover, at last agreed unequivocally to Don Charles's succession to Parma and Tuscany and the entry of Spanish garrisons. Because of this Spain was able to accede to the Second Treaty of Vienna in July 1731. British ships then transported both the Spanish garrisons and Don Charles to Italy later in the year. In March 1732 he entered Parma as duke: it seemed as if the long crisis over the duchies had finally been settled peacefully and Elizabeth Farnese's ambitions satisfied.

Walpole had preserved peace and had also scored a great diplomatic triumph. Britain's naval supremacy in the Mediterranean, based on Gibraltar and Minorca, had been confirmed at a time when the danger from Russia in the Baltic had disappeared. Her trading privileges from Spain had been renewed and the rival Ostend Company had been destroyed. The Austrian alliance had been added to the one Britain already had with France. Although Fleury, who was now isolated, refused to join the Second Treaty of Vienna because of the guarantee of the Pragmatic Sanction, he was forced to accept the *fait accompli*.

Yet the settlement was a very fragile one. The Emperor resented having to allow Don Charles into Italy. The treaty also merely whetted Elizabeth Farnese's appetite, while her husband still hankered after the return of Gibraltar and Minorca and the cancellation of the trading concessions.

Of greater importance was France's reaction to the Vienna treaty. French passivity and loyalty to the *entente* had been essential for Walpole's success. But the Vienna treaty, and the way it had been negotiated, were unacceptable to Fleury, who was to feel less inclined to co-operate with Britain in the future. The treaty seemed to have directly harmed France by its guarantee of Charles VI's Pragmatic Sanction and the integrity of his monarchy. In some measure the treaty also appeared to have revived the Grand Alliance because of the union of Austria with the Maritime Powers. Although Walpole had not intended to separate Britain from France, in making the treaty this is what had happened: the decade and a half of diplomatic co-operation between Britain and France was now coming to an end. From now on Britain would lack the French support which had helped sustain her diplomatic ascendancy in Europe since 1716. This was at a time when the French had covertly grown much stronger. While Britain, Austria and Spain had suffered great financial strain so as to remain under arms during the long diplomatic crisis from 1725, France had managed better, once the inept Bourbon had gone, because she already maintained a large standing army. By the 1730s with an adult king, her succession secure and her economy and administration on the mend, France could once more stand on her own feet. She no longer needed British support and could even contemplate fresh military expansion.

CHAPTER FIVE

The recovery of France, 1731–1739

The shifting alliances of the 1720s solidified after the Second Treaty of Vienna into a new pattern, one in which France emerged again as the leading power and Fleury as Europe's leading statesman. The balance and European peace which had existed in the generation after Utrecht had rested on the Anglo-French *entente* and Britain's willingness to interfere on the Continent. The collapse of the *entente* and a deliberate British retreat into isolation under Walpole were quickly followed by the War of the Polish Succession (1733–35). This involved the continental powers in the first serious fighting in western Europe for almost twenty years. The conflict was ostensibly over Poland and allowed Russia to reassert her dominance in eastern Europe, but its effects elsewhere were probably more significant. France regained a predominant position throughout the Continent, while Austria suffered a corresponding steep decline in prestige.

THE EUROPEAN STATES SYSTEM AFTER THE SECOND TREATY OF VIENNA

The Second Treaty of Vienna in 1731 (see pp. 136–7) signalled the end of the Anglo-French *entente* and the era of co-operation between the two powers. The secret Anglo-Austrian negotiations before the treaty and its signature by both Spain and the Dutch left France isolated in the face of the apparent reconstruction of the Grand Alliance. Above all the guarantee of the Emperor's Pragmatic Sanction seemed to threaten France. Rather than accept and join in such a guarantee, Fleury was willing to let the *entente* with Britain collapse. Already in December 1731 the French government instructed its new minister in London that the two countries' interests were too far apart for them to 'deliberate together upon the affairs of Europe'.

Even without the shock of the Vienna treaty the *entente* would probably have ended. It is surprising that a system enjoying so little general support, even among diplomats, should have lasted so long. The *entente* had been created and then sustained by the weakness of the two dynasties, but the latter were now secure enough. George II's peaceful succession in 1727 and the stability of Walpole's long ministry were paralleled by the birth of a dauphin in 1729 and the dominance of Fleury. The Cardinal's ascendancy after 1726 was accompanied by the restoration of the monarchy's prestige within France and the country's financial and economic recovery. Commerce expanded so rapidly, both in the Atlantic and Mediterranean, that it seemed France might soon overtake Britain as a trading nation. France rediscovered her self-confidence and began to feel capable of pursuing policies without continually fretting about Britain's reaction. After 1727 the secretary of state for foreign affairs was the anti-British and anti-Habsburg Chauvelin. The British tended to blame him for difficulties which developed in relations with France. However, although Fleury himself had certainly seen the advantages of co-operation with Britain, he was far less of an Anglophile than Robert Walpole believed. Chauvelin was never more than Fleury's instrument, and his appointment showed France was regaining her diplomatic independence. Fleury found it useful in getting his own way to allow Chauvelin to adopt a hostile and uncompromising attitude and then to appear conciliatory himself. France's increasing independence was demonstrated in the early 1730s by quarrels with Britain over Dunkirk, Nova Scotia and the West Indies. These had always been below the surface, but they were now allowed to emerge.

Similar doubts about the Anglo-French relationship also appeared in London. There had always been those who had believed the *entente* unnatural, and others who came to realise that France was now the main threat to the expansion of British trade, particularly in the Americas. But it is all too easy, with hindsight, to exaggerate the significance of British hostility towards France in the 1730s. The disputes which took place were all minor ones and similar disputes had happened at times in the 1720s as well – even a minister like Chauvelin was not a complete novelty. Overt hostility only occurred when the British realised France's growing power in Europe, the extent of her commercial and naval development and finally her support for Spain in 1739–40.

France's greater independence and self-confidence did not lead initially to her challenging Britain. Her policy instead followed the well-worn path against the Austrian Habsburgs. Charles VI was seen as the real villain of the Second Treaty of Vienna and the main threat to France. The Emperor in fact had won definite advantages from the treaty, despite having to abandon his commercial ambitions and to accept a Farnese prince in central Italy. He was no longer isolated and, through the guarantees given to the Pragmatic Sanction, had achieved confirmation of the huge increase in Austria's size which had occurred during his reign. Of course the monarchy's structural weaknesses meant that Austria's size did not truly reflect her actual power. The Emperor himself by now had no aggressive ambitions and his chief concern was the integrity of his inheritance and the succession. After the birth of his youngest daughter in 1724, he had to accept that his wife could bear no more children and that – as he had feared from the early 1720s – there would be no son. His eldest child Maria Theresa would therefore have to inherit the hereditary lands. (The Imperial title of course was not hereditary and, as a woman, she could not be elected to it.) As he reached middle age (he was forty-five in 1730) the need for international guarantees, of the sort which Europe had grown used to since Utrecht over the British and French successions, became more urgent. Spain had guaranteed the Pragmatic Sanction in 1725 and again in 1731, Russia in 1726, Prussia in 1728 and then the Maritime Powers and Hanover in 1731/32. Following the Second Treaty of Vienna, which included the Anglo-Dutch guarantee and which strengthened his position in Germany by ending Hanoverian hostility to him, Charles persuaded the Imperial Diet to recognise the Pragmatic Sanction on 11 January 1732. Rather ominously Bavaria and Saxony, where the Elector and Electoral Prince were married to the late Joseph I's daughters, voted against it. But at this stage they seemed of little importance.

A parallel problem for Charles VI was choosing a husband for the teenage Maria Theresa and, just as important, persuading the German electors to accept him as the next emperor. Habsburg pride could not stomach a match with another major European family: Charles's house would appear to be absorbed by another. Instead he favoured one with a minor family where the opposite would seem true. As early as 1723 he had really decided on Francis Stephen, who became duke of Lorraine in 1729 and whose family had been traditionally protected by the Habsburgs. As France would inevitably violently oppose the union of this frontier duchy with Austria, almost from the beginning Charles realised Francis Stephen would have to renounce Lorraine if he married Maria Theresa. Unfortunately, he never made this clear to Versailles.

France was the only major power not to have recognised the Pragmatic Sanction and she was potentially the most dangerous. Fleury would not guarantee the integrity of the huge Habsburg inheritance, particularly with a Habsburg–Lorraine marriage in prospect, without major territorial concessions. His recent pacific policies, in contrast to those of the belligerent Spanish Bourbons, had lulled Austria and Europe into a false sense of security. However, after the Second Treaty of Vienna, he determined to seize the first opportunity to reduce or at least prevent any further extension of Habsburg power. Throughout the 1720s many French statesmen, including Chauvelin, had looked forward to a war to dismember Austria. But those actually in control had been restrained by France's internal weakness and their connection with Britain. Consequently the French governments had used the diplomatic creations of these years defensively, rather than offensively, against both Spain and Austria.

Similar considerations of defence induced Fleury, in the wake of the Second Treaty of Vienna, to encourage his more bellicose subordinate Chauvelin to assemble a bloc of states which would look to Versailles for political leadership. But the Cardinal was also prepared before long to use this grouping in a more offensive way against Austria if the chance arose. The creation of a pro-French bloc was made easier by Britain's gradual retreat into neutrality under Walpole's influence. The prospect of future gains at Austria's expense also made several smaller states willing to follow a French lead. In Germany Bavaria was openly hostile to Charles VI, while Cologne, Saxony and the Palatinate were unlikely to help the Habsburgs in a future conflict. In December 1732 Charles Emmanuel, who had succeeded two years before as duke of Savoy and king of Sardinia, approached Chauvelin and suggested France could have his lands west of the Alps if she helped wrest Milan from Austria. However, Fleury and Chauvelin concentrated their chief efforts on Spain. The birth of the Dauphin had ended Philip's aspirations for the French succession, and it was now possible to consider the kind of intimate relationship with the Spanish court promised by the accession of a Bourbon in Madrid. France's approaches encouraged Elizabeth Farnese to hope at last for French support for a full-scale assault on the Emperor. Although her son Charles now had Parma and the expectancy of Tuscany, she also wanted Mantua for him and Naples and Sicily for her younger son Philip. But she was very wary of making an agreement: Fleury's past behaviour suggested he would draw back from actual war and her children would gain nothing. She personally detested the Cardinal and continually cursed his name. In fact she refused to conclude a Franco-Spanish alliance till France was actually at war with Austria late in 1733.

Conflict between France and the Habsburgs could very well have developed over German or Italian issues, but on 1 February 1733 Augustus II, Elector of Saxony and King of Poland, died. His death produced the crisis which led to war.

THE GREAT POWERS AND THE POLISH ELECTION OF 1733

Augustus the Strong's ambitious plans at his election to the Polish throne (in 1697) had all been disappointed. Schemes to make Poland an absolute hereditary monarchy had been abandoned amid the humiliation of the Great Northern War. Power remained in the hands of a few Polish–Lithuanian magnates. Although the country had escaped partition, it had fallen into dependence on its eastern neighbour. Peter the Great effectively turned Poland into a satellite: she served as both a bridge to and a barrier against the west. After Peter's death, the alliance between Austria and Russia in 1726, which Prussia soon joined, left Augustus even less room for manoeuvre. The three eastern powers were beginning their long period of deciding the fate of Poland among themselves.

The internal confusion in Russia after Peter the Great died in 1725 slackened the pace of expansion, but the accession of Anna as tsaritsa in 1730 and her successful maintenance of her absolute power brought more strength and continuity to Russian policy. Its direction stayed in the hands of Ostermann, who was given the title of 'first cabinet minister' in 1734. His main aim was to consolidate and extend Russian influence among their immediate neighbours, but he and Anna's chief advisers were Germans who believed their policy should take account of all the European powers. Ostermann himself had promoted the Austrian alliance of 1726 to defend Russia against her chief enemies, the Ottoman Empire and Britain. He convinced Anna of its lasting value and after the Second Treaty of Vienna he hoped Britain could be brought into a grouping with Austria, Prussia and Russia, especially as he was now coming to fear the increase in French influence in Germany and northern Europe. He wanted to end the long period of hostility with Britain and believed British naval power would complement Russia's continental alliance with Austria. This system would safeguard Peter the Great's Baltic conquests and contain any crisis which arose in Sweden, Poland or the Balkans. For their part the British now realised the benefits of friendship with Russia. The decline of the Anglo-French *entente* brought to a close the co-operation between the western powers at the Scandinavian courts, which had been directed largely against Russia. After 1731 the British were more suspicious of French activities there than those of Russia, and gradually British and Russian envoys began to work together instead.

As part of a general effort to increase their influence in Europe, the French after 1731 began to try to revive their relationships with Denmark, Sweden, Poland and the Turks. In the seventeenth century these connections had been used to contain the Austrian Habsburgs. They were now intended to be exploited against Austria's Russian ally as well. During the 1730s the main rivalry in the Baltic changed from an Anglo-Russian to a Franco-Russian one, as the French became as keen on checking Russian power as Austrian. They wanted to destroy what they saw as an Austro-Russian domination of northern and eastern Europe. However, the French had little success at Copenhagen.

Anna's accession had finally ended Russian support for Charles Frederick of Holstein-Gottorp (see pp. 124ff.), and Denmark responded in 1732 by an agreement with Russia and Austria. This brought an Austro-Russian guarantee of Danish possession of Schleswig and Denmark's recognition of the Pragmatic Sanction. In Stockholm the French supported the Hat party in the Riksdag, since the Hats favoured an adventurist foreign policy and believed French help essential for Sweden to regain the Baltic provinces lost to Russia in 1721. But the dominant influence for most of the 1730s was the Cap party and its leader Count Horn who wanted peace and friendship with Russia and Britain. Consequently the British worked tacitly with Russia to counter the French.

Both Russia and Britain were by now well aware of their common commercial interests. The Russian nobility benefited from the sale of naval stores to Britain, and the British, who had an increasing appetite for the latter, could pay for them with colonial goods, textiles and bullion. Ostermann hoped to use a favourable trade treaty as a lever to persuade Britain into a political association with Russia and Austria, which could be used against France. But despite Walpole's interest in agreement over trade and Anglo-Russian diplomatic co-operation in the Baltic, neither a commercial nor a political treaty had been concluded before the outbreak of the War of Polish Succession in 1733. Walpole had set his mind against further political alliances and was keeping to the path he had said he wanted to follow as early as 1723: 'My politics are to keep free from all engagements as long as we possibly can.'

The question of Poland was largely forced on Anna's ministers, since they had been busy planning a war of conquest against the Ottoman Empire. But Ostermann's attempts to persuade Austria to help against the Sultan were rebuffed in 1732: Vienna did not want a further war in the Balkans and believed co-operation over the future of Poland more important. They were concerned about the Polish succession, but they were also alarmed at Augustus II's ambitions in the last months of his life. Despite his failures in Poland and his extravagant court and life style, his electorate of Saxony was well administered and supported a well-equipped army, 30,000 strong. During the crises of the late 1720s he had largely aligned himself with Austria and Russia. But in 1731 he began to respond to Chauvelin's offers of subsidies and suggestion that he join Bavaria and France in a partition of Habsburg territory. This would benefit Augustus' son who had married a daughter of Joseph I. However, Augustus's relations with France were ambivalent. He wanted his own son to succeed him in Poland and would need Austrian and Russian support. He knew the French had been committed, since Louis XV's marriage (1725), to support their own queen's father, Stanislas Leszczyński.

In September 1732 Austria, Russia and Prussia tried to anticipate the crisis which would inevitably ensue when the sixty-two-year-old Elector-King died. Because of Augustus's recent fickleness, and to scotch any idea of the crown becoming hereditary in the Saxon family, the three powers agreed to support a dependable nonentity, Emmanuel of Portugal, as candidate for the Polish throne. This frightened Augustus into trying to persuade his eastern neighbours to let his own son succeed as hereditary ruler by offering what amounted to a partition of Poland: Polish (or West) Prussia but not Danzig to Prussia, Lithuania without Vilna (Vilnius) to Russia and Zips to Austria. However, before the powers could respond, he died on 1 February 1733 and the expected international crisis followed.

France intended to support Stanislas Leszczyński's candidature and had secretly encouraged his supporters in the past. It was partly a matter of Bourbon family pride, especially as it would improve the image of Louis XV's marriage to the lowly Maria Leszczyńska, but also the chance had now arrived to attack the Austro-Russian dominance of eastern Europe. It soon became clear that Leszczyński's own popularity as a native Pole would win him the election for the throne. However much the eastern powers bribed and blustered, they had to accept that Emmanuel was bound to lose and they faced the real threat of a French puppet in Warsaw. They therefore switched their support to the new Elector of Saxony, who at least had some following in the Polish Diet. Charles VI took the opportunity to induce the Elector, another Augustus, to guarantee the Pragmatic Sanction. Although Frederick William I of Prussia followed the Austro-Russian lead, he did so reluctantly for he still preferred a Portuguese prince to his Saxon neighbour.

Confident of French help against foreign interference, the Polish Diet in September 1733 once more elected Stanislas Leszczyński their king. The nobility hoped to destroy Saxon and Russian influence and make the new King even more a figurehead than Augustus had been. But the eastern powers could not, of course, accept this show of independence. Russia was particularly angry at the threatened loss of her satellite. But she also feared Warsaw would become the central link in a possible future chain of pro-French powers stretching from Stockholm and Copenhagen to Constantinople. Austria, too, felt she had been defeated by the election, as she had openly co-operated with Russia and had moved her troops into Silesia to put pressure on the Poles. But it was a Russian army which invaded Poland and helped Saxon troops force Leszczyński to flee to Danzig late in September. A new Diet was convened and, under Russian military pressure, elected Augustus III king on 5 October. He immediately showed his dependence on Russia by giving Courland to the Tsaritsa Anna's favourite, Biron.

THE WAR OF THE POLISH SUCCESSION, 1733–1738

The future of Poland, and ultimately its very existence, was to be an international issue for the rest of the century. But the War of the Polish Succession, which now broke out, although it was to confirm the Saxon Augustus as king, was fought largely in western Europe and over issues far removed from Poland. The war was essentially one for the re-establishment of French ascendancy in Europe. Fleury, who was still very much in control of French policy, had little choice about supporting Leszczyński in Poland: France had openly backed him, and her honour could hardly suffer the ignominious ejection of the Queen's father. Chauvelin had continually threatened the eastern powers throughout 1733 and found strong support from a growing war party at court, nobles starved of war since before Louis XIV's death. However, Fleury was not 'juggled…into war', as Frederick the Great believed. He exploited the unavoidable Polish crisis for France's direct benefit. At an early stage Fleury realised that France was almost powerless to help Stanislas Leszczyński in Poland. Instead he deliberately used the small-scale struggle there as an excuse to attack Austria in western Europe where France herself could gain. The Cardinal saw a chance to humble the Habsburgs with the minimum of risks and without France's appearing the aggressor. If the quarrel could be portrayed as essentially one over Poland and the war kept short and limited, the Maritime Powers would be unlikely to intervene and Austria would be isolated in the west. Fleury's real aim in the conflict was kept secret: the acquisition of Lorraine. He had warned Vienna in 1728 that France might annex the duchy if its duke, Francis Stephen, married Maria Theresa. In July 1732 the French were discussing doing so if the marriage were announced. It is likely that from the start of the Polish War Fleury never wanted Leszczyński to have the Polish throne, but intended him to be compensated with Lorraine. Moreover, to get the powers to accept such a transfer demanded that Louis XV's father-in-law should first be beaten in Poland and denied its crown.

On 20 May 1733 the French council of state had decided in principle to go to war with the Emperor. During the following months Fleury allowed Chauvelin to complete the coalition he had been trying to build over the past couple of years with Spain, Savoy and some of the German states. It was aimed primarily against Austria but indirectly against Russia as well. Chauvelin's efforts to direct it against the British were resisted by Fleury, who was determined not to involve the Maritime Powers and thereby risk resurrecting the Grand Alliance of Louis XIV's last wars.

The coalition was speedily assembled by French diplomats. They had least success in Germany, where all that could be achieved was Bavarian neutrality through a subsidy treaty concluded in November

1733. However, in Italy, Charles Emmanuel of Savoy made an alliance with France (September) and was promised subsidies and 40,000 French troops to help him seize Milan from Austria. Expansion along the Po valley had now become the real focus of Savoyard ambitions: Charles Emmanuel described Milan as 'an artichoke to be eaten leaf by leaf'. Savoy itself was the only Italian state important enough to count with the European powers. Both Charles Emmanuel and, before 1730, his father Victor Amadeus had struggled to increase their country's military strength. Only Prussia devoted more of its resources to the army. In peacetime, Savoy's forces numbered 18,000 men, but their magazines were stocked for a wartime strength of 60,000 men. The artillery had been reformed and the treasury had funds for two years' campaigning. Both father and son realised that conflict between France, Austria and Spain offered Savoy a chance to expand. However, although the major states felt her support was worth buying in times of war, when they themselves decided to settle their differences, as in 1718–20 and again in 1735–38, Savoy was effectively ignored. A month after the Franco-Savoyard alliance, and when hostilities had actually broken out in Italy, France and Spain concluded the First Family Compact (pact of the Escorial, 7 November 1733). The justification for this was the proposed Habsburg–Lorraine marriage which, with the Pragmatic Sanction, was claimed to threaten the European balance. Louis XV guaranteed Parma and Tuscany to Don Charles and promised to help his brother Don Philip seize the Habsburg possessions of Naples and Sicily. The alliance therefore aimed primarily at destroying Austria's position in Italy and advancing Elizabeth Farnese's children. However, it contained clauses which were potentially threatening to Britain and which could ultimately benefit Spain herself. The pact guaranteed France and Spain's territories in Europe and overseas, promising mutual help in case of attack. In addition, Louis XV promised to help Spain in the future to recover Gibraltar from Britain, if necessary by force; the Spaniards agreed in return that if Britain intervened in Italy they would reduce British commercial privileges in Spanish America and Spain and give some of these to France. Under the leading minister, Jose Patino (1726–36), Madrid was trying to encourage her own merchants. He intended to prevent the British abusing these privileges and eventually to suppress them. Although the French hoped this would benefit their merchants at Cadiz, Patiño himself did not want to subordinate Spanish interests to France, and even after the Family Compact he tried to act independently. However, a degree of Spanish dependence on France was the inevitable result of the 1733 treaty.

The first Family Compact was not immediately followed by the two Bourbon powers pursuing a joint policy. The French were opposed to any substantial growth in Farnese power in Italy, and this was to cause continual quarrels during the coming war. Moreover

Fleury, at least at this stage, did not want to put into effect the clauses of the treaty concerning Britain. Nevertheless, the Family Compact was a turning-point in Franco-Spanish relations outside Europe and eventually was the basis for co-operation to halt British expansion. During the previous twenty years France had failed to support Spain because of uneasy Franco-Spanish relations and because of the restraints imposed by the Anglo-French *entente*. The two Bourbon monarchies, however, had genuine mutual interests in promoting the Cadiz trade and suppressing British contraband trade. They also wanted to restrict Britain's further aggrandisement in the Americas, where it was feared her ultimate aim was to expel the French colonists and seize all Spanish America. The territorial threat was made plain in 1733 when the British founded Georgia, a move which menaced French Louisiana as much as Spanish Florida.

The War of the Polish Succession broke out in western Europe a month before the Franco-Spanish pact was signed. On 10 October 1733 France declared war on Austria, and her armies immediately moved into northern Italy and across the Rhine. Lorraine was seized, and a Franco-Savoyard army occupied Milan before the end of the year. Early in 1734 Spanish troops landed and quickly overran Sicily and Naples, where Spain was still popular and the Austrian administration had alienated the population. At the same time the French seized Philippsburg on the Rhine.

These remarkable victories of the French–Spanish–Savoyard coalition were won with hardly any Austrian resistance. In part this arose from surprise attacks launched later than the normal campaigning season. Above all, however, Charles VI had been taken completely unawares by the outbreak of war in the west: he had felt secure from attack because of his alliances with Russia, Prussia and the Maritime Powers. Bartenstein, who was the minister who now largely conducted the Emperor's foreign policy, lacked an overall view of Austria's European position and had concentrated exclusively on the Polish question. Moreover the chancellor, Sinzendorff, continually assured Charles that France under Fleury would never go to war. The Austrians had miscalculated disastrously over both the security afforded by their alliances and the attitude of Fleury.

Austria henceforth had to fight a defensive war with no hope of regaining her initial losses. But the enemy coalition did not add to its spoils of 1733 and 1734, principally because of Fleury's determination to limit the war. Although he had allowed Chauvelin and the war party their head, he retained real control. He refused to turn the struggle in Poland into a major war in the east by encouraging the Swedes or Turks to intervene. Under 2,000 French troops were sent to help Leszczyński, and consequently by mid-summer 1734 he was forced to abandon Danzig, where he had taken refuge. In the west Fleury intended to pursue a holding operation till peace could be made: he refused to throw France's full weight behind the war or to countenance a major struggle in Germany and co-operation with Bavaria for the possible partition of the Habsburg lands. Because of this Bavaria maintained her neutrality. Above all Fleury rejected demands at court to attack the Austrian Netherlands since this would probably have caused the Maritime Powers to intervene. If he allowed a lengthy and extensive war to develop which alarmed all Europe, then the coalition's victories would be endangered. Fleury therefore kept Chauvelin's far-ranging schemes in check in case they led to the renewal of the Grand Alliance which had humbled France in the past. His determination to prevent its revival had been a pressing reason for allying with the Maritime Powers previously, and it was to be reflected in his future policies. His ultimate aim now was a rebirth of French power, but not one based on the pattern of Louis XIV's military preponderance as Chauvelin and the war party at court wanted. Instead he wanted what Louis had worked for in 1714–15: co-operation with Savoy, Bourbon Spain and some German princes and then eventual reconciliation with Austria to separate her from the Maritime Powers and, additionally in Fleury's case, from Russia. Europe would be at peace under the domination of French diplomacy.

Fleury successfully prevented the intervention of the Maritime Powers in this war. Besides personal assurances in London and at The Hague of his own goodwill, he took positive steps to quieten their fears. Not only were the Austrian Netherlands left alone, but he followed the pattern of 1715–16 by approaching the Dutch directly and agreeing to a declaration of neutrality for this sensitive area. Still loaded with debts and with their army run down, the Dutch desperately wanted this reassurance. These measures had a similarly reassuring effect in Britain, where both George II and the leading secretary of state, Newcastle, had wanted to intervene. George as elector of Hanover was one of the few German princes to assist Charles VI in campaigns along the Rhine in 1734–35. But his chief minister, Walpole, refused to honour the alliance with Austria: he argued that the terms of the 1731 treaty of Vienna were inoperative since Austria had brought the conflict on herself by her actions on Poland and could not claim to have been attacked. Although Britain, as well as the Dutch, had supported Augustus's candidature for the Polish throne, it was easy to argue that the French had acted defensively over Leszczyński's rights: even if Austrian troops had not entered Poland, by massing his forces on the borders to intimidate the Diet, Charles VI had acted as an accessory to the Russian aggression.

Walpole's arguments over the terms of the Second Treaty of Vienna were largely semantic: he had no intention of going to war, treaty or no treaty. He maintained, with some truth, that the Republic's neutrality meant that the Dutch would snatch up British trade with Spain if Britain intervened against the Bourbon powers. This argument had often been used by Stanhope and is an interesting comment on why the Maritime Powers felt they had to act together. Above all, however, Walpole's decision for neutrality reflected his passionate belief that the well-being of the country, especially of its trade and its dynasty, as well as his own political survival, demanded peace. At a time when he was involved in a crisis over the Excise Bill in parliament and was also preparing for the 1734 election, any increase in the land tax to pay for war was unthinkable. Walpole's personal influence was sufficient to prevent the King and his other ministers taking the country into war, and consequently he could make his famous boast to Queen Caroline at the end of 1734: 'Madam, there are fifty thousand men slain this year in Europe, and not one Englishman.'

Although Britain had nothing to gain immediately from intervention, her failure to do so was to lead to a great increase in French power and a decline in Austrian influence, which would ultimately threaten British security. As Walpole knew of the contents of the First Family Compact, the eventual danger to Britain was not hidden from him. Yet he allowed France to achieve diplomatic hegemony over Europe and, at the same time, to escape from the semi-dependence on Britain which had restricted her for more than a decade. The Bourbons were not to express any gratitude for British neutrality, while the Austrians were to see it as yet another instance of Britain's bad faith.

Charles VI proved incapable of coping by himself with the limited war Fleury pursued in 1734–35 along the Rhine and in Lombardy. The Austrian monarchy failed to recover from the initial shock of the attack and its military disasters. The finances collapsed into the usual chaos, while Eugene of Savoy, who had managed to bring some order into Austria's previous wars, was now senile. The vote by the Imperial Diet in February 1734 to help was ignored by Bavaria, Cologne and the Palatinate. Only the missing subsidies from the Maritime Powers would have enabled Charles to hire enough troops from those German princes willing to help. Prussia was ready to supply a large force, but the Emperor dared not accept because he feared Frederick William would inevitably present his bill for territorial compensation in Germany.

Russian forces were fully occupied in Poland till 1734 and when they could move westwards in 1735 it was too late. Moreover, in agreeing to send troops to the Rhine, Ostermann forced Charles VI to promise to help Russia in case of war with the Turks in the future. For their part the Austrians encouraged further Russian negotiations with Britain for a commercial treaty as a way of bringing the latter into the present war. An Anglo-Russian commercial treaty was eventually signed in December 1734. The agreement reduced tariffs on British textiles and ensured their commercial supremacy in the Baltic at the expense of the Dutch. Although it contained a declaration of friendship, Walpole had refused to be drawn into a political alliance.

In the immediate context of the Polish Succession War the Anglo-Russian treaty had no importance: Charles VI still lacked significant outside help in his struggle against France and her allies. As late as May 1735 the Emperor and his closest adviser Bartenstein pathetically deluded themselves that the Maritime Powers would intervene. But they then finally accepted that peace had to be concluded. Fleury made no difficulties, fearing the dispatch of Russian troops to Germany would extend the war and might ultimately cause Anglo-Dutch involvement. He hoped to use the peace as the basis for a *rapprochement* with Vienna which would first undermine Austria's relationship with Russia and what was left of that with the Maritime Powers, and then bring her into dependence on France. Together with the maintenance of the Family Compact with Spain, this *rapprochement* would create a continental balance very different from that presided over by Britain since Louis XIV's death. France would now usurp Britain's role as the diplomatic arbiter of Europe.

In August 1735 Fleury sent his agent, La Baune, in secret to Vienna, and on 5 October a preliminary treaty was signed. Agreement was reached quickly on the two issues which Fleury believed had made friendship impossible in the past: Lorraine and the Pragmatic Sanction. In return for Lorraine Fleury would guarantee the Pragmatic Sanction and the integrity of the Habsburg inheritance. However, he was prepared to soften the impact of the cession of the duchy. Lorraine was not to go immediately to France but to Stanislas Leszczyński, who was to leave it to his daughter, the French Queen, and to her heirs. (In this way it passed to France in 1766, and was to be, except for Corsica, her only major gain of the eighteenth century.) To make this possible Fleury had to fashion an Italian settlement very different from what he had initially promised his Savoyard and Spanish allies. Yet another game of musical chairs was played with the Italian states. Tuscany was to go, at the death of its present duke, not to a Farnese child but to Francis Stephen as compensation for Lorraine. Although the young Duke of Lorraine was reluctant to surrender his own duchy, he did so on the blunt warning from Bartenstein, 'No renunciation, no archduchess.' (His marriage to Maria Theresa followed in February 1736.) Parma was given directly to Austria, but she had to cede Naples and Sicily to Don Charles in return. His younger brother Philip received nothing, while Charles Emmanuel of Savoy–Sardinia had to make do with a further slice of Milan.

In this way a solid block of Habsburg territory was formed out of the rest of Milan, Parma and Tuscany in northern Italy. (Tuscany was to be held by Francis Stephen in secundogeniture: it should be inherited not by his direct heir but by a younger son.) However, the enlargement of Savoy and the creation of the Farnese kingdom in the south meant Habsburg hegemony in the peninsula was now over. The territorial settlement itself was to prove no more lasting than previous Italian ones. The inordinate ambitions of the Farnese family remained: Elizabeth felt robbed of Parma and Tuscany, especially as Parma was her ancestral home, and she was determined to secure them for her younger son, Don Philip. Spain herself had gained nothing directly, and clauses in the peace treaty were specifically framed to prevent the re-creation of a Spanish empire in Italy. The treaty forbade the union of the kingdom of the Two Sicilies (as Naples and Sicily were usually called) with Spain, and insisted it also be held in secundogeniture. (The same proviso was also made in 1748 when Don Philip received Parma. See p. 253 for Don Charles's eventual succession to Spain as Charles III.)

Spain and Savoy reluctantly agreed to Fleury's preliminary treaty in February 1736, and the final peace treaty – the Third Treaty of Vienna – was only signed by France and Austria on 2 May 1738, three years after hostilities had ceased. The Maritime Powers also agreed to sign in September, to be followed in April 1739 by Philip V and Don Charles, now King of the Two Sicilies. All the western powers had thus confirmed the settlement of Lorraine and Italy as well as guaranteeing Charles VI's Pragmatic Sanction.

Skilful diplomacy, with limited military effort, had secured a considerable success for France. The future absorption of Lorraine would strengthen France's eastern frontier and complete the work of French diplomacy since 1648. A branch of the Bourbon family now reigned in Naples, while the relentless territorial expansion of the Habsburgs had been reversed and the monarchy weakened. The conflicts of western and central Europe had been resolved, as Fleury had intended, between Versailles and Vienna, and then accepted by the other powers. The Third Treaty of Vienna was an effective answer to the snub Fleury had suffered through Walpole's manoeuvres and his treaty of 1731. France had become once again, in the words of Frederick the Great, 'the arbiter of Europe'. Yet her conduct had left all the belligerents with some grounds for satisfaction, in that they had all gained something. The obvious exceptions were the unfortunate Poles who had had to accept a second Saxon king. Almost in passing, the peace settlement confirmed the election of Augustus III, and therefore tacitly acknowledged Russian supremacy in Poland.

In his wish to use the peace settlement as a basis for a *rapprochement* with Austria to preserve European peace, Fleury found willing collaborators in Charles VI and Bartenstein. However, his own secretary of state, Chauvelin, was hostile, preferring to dismember Austria rather than be reconciled with her. Fleury consequently feared a reversal of policy if Chauvelin succeeded him on his death, and he therefore forced the secretary's dismissal in February 1737. Chauvelin had been useful as *persona grata* in Madrid in persuading Spain and Savoy to accept the peace. For Fleury it now seemed high time to show the war party at court who was in control.

Chauvelin's dismissal was welcomed in Vienna. By 1738 Charles VI and Bartenstein had come to see a *rapprochement* with France rather than a return to the association with the Maritime Powers as offering the best chance to implement the Pragmatic Sanction. They were very embittered against the British and Dutch and were intent on pursuing a pacific policy presenting no risks, at least outside the Balkans. In effect, Austria became for a year or two almost a dependant of France. This was shown clearly in the peace mediated by France between the Emperor and the Turks at Belgrade in 1739 (see pp. 156f.). Although this brief Franco–Austrian *rapprochement* foreshadowed the later Diplomatic Revolution, it differed from it in two important respects. The 1738 *rapprochement* was not an actual alliance. Whereas the later agreement was to entail France's furthering of Austrian ambitions, this one was the other way round – Austria was helping to prop up French ascendancy.

By the time of the Third Treaty of Vienna Charles VI had done all that was possible through paper treaties to ensure his daughter's succession, for only Bavaria had not given a guarantee. However, the election of his son-in-law Francis Stephen as his successor as emperor was still problematic. It would depend in large measure on the attitude of France, who after the recent war enjoyed a position of dominance within the Holy Roman Empire similar to that of the late seventeenth century. The British, who with the support of the French *entente* had been so powerful there in the 1710s and 1720s, had declined in importance because of Walpole's passivity and Fleury's actions. (George II was also less active in Imperial affairs than his father had been.) British policy in Germany had vacillated between the Protestant anti-Habsburg stance of the 1720s, pro-Habsburg moves after 1731 and then indifference. France, on the other hand, had consistently tried to extend her own influence since the early 1730s. She had developed close relations with Bavaria, Cologne, Mainz and the Palatinate and was also beginning to undermine the firm alliance between Frederick William I and Charles VI which had existed since the later 1720s (see pp. 130f.).

During the negotiations for the European peace settlement Fleury had done his best not to antagonise Britain. The dismissal of Chauvelin (1737) made relations easier and Fleury proposed renewing the former alliance. However, no agreement could be reached on the terms, and by 1738–39 the Cardinal felt strong enough not to need one: the final peace had been signed with Austria, an alliance concluded with Sweden (November 1738) and peace mediated between Austria and the Turks (September 1739). France's new friendship with Austria and the maintenance of the existing relationship with Spain effectively isolated and weakened Britain: she was largely ignored in the peace negotiations of the late 1730s.

The balance in Europe had shifted decisively in favour of France. To some extent this seemed justified by domestic developments. Contemporaries were well aware of the apparent contrast between the success of France – and in some respects of Spain – in achieving administrative and economic stability, expanding commerce and the navy, and the difficulties which crowded in on Walpole's administration in the late 1730s. The triumphs of Fleury's diplomacy and French economic advance were beginning to awaken fears in Britain similar to those which had led to the struggle with Louis XIV. There was growing concern at the pace of French commercial development compared with Britain's. British trade in the years 1735–40 showed a definite decline (exports fell from £13½m. in 1735 to £9m. in 1740). France, on the contrary, seemed to be forging ahead at Britain's expense, particularly in the Levant, Italy and Spain. Expansion of French trade with Cadiz meant a corresponding increase in the indirect trade with Spanish America. French exploitation of the Newfoundland fisheries and the forests of North America for furs challenged British exports to Europe, while French West Indian sugar was capturing the bulk of the market in northern Europe. There were also alarming signs that France was becoming a major naval power once more and had recovered from the low point reached during the Spanish Succession War. Merchant ships could easily be converted to privateers in wartime and the crews used to man warships. Fortunately for Britain the French merchant marine had not grown as fast as French trade, and was probably still only one-sixth of the size of Britain's. On the other hand, by 1739 France had fifty capital ships, usually better designed and built, compared with Britain's eighty.

France under Fleury, largely through diplomacy rather than military force, had regained the paramount position in Europe which her population and resources justified. This had been accompanied by a corresponding decline in British influence. The Anglo-Austrian alliance had collapsed, while trade disputes with Spain were leading to a deterioration in relations (see pp. 159ff.). Walpole's desire for neutrality had produced an aimlessness in British diplomacy in sharp contrast to his deliberateness in 1730–31. Britain's earlier dominance had been based on France's willingness to co-operate. This had now disappeared, but Walpole himself seems to have shown little appreciation of the value of the Anglo-French *entente*. He had helped to destroy it by his move towards Austria in 1730 and had then allowed Fleury to pursue policies separate from Britain, policies which led to the Family Compact with Spain and then to the reconciliation with Austria. As Louis XIV had grasped at the end of his life, agreement between the Bourbon powers and Austria denied Britain the chance to intervene on the Continent.

Walpole was largely unconcerned by these developments, especially while France showed no open hostility towards Britain. However, in the late 1730s Fleury's success was to encourage the two Bourbon powers to challenge Britain overseas and to try to pursue those clauses of the First Family Compact of 1733, aimed at Britain (see p. 146). None the less, the struggle which broke out between Britain and France in the 1740s was not caused by a conscious British realisation of the clash of interests with France and an attempt to resolve them: it was rather that the British were responding to France's alignment with Spain outside Europe and her return to a policy of military domination of the Continent. It was France, not Britain, which adopted a forward policy after 1739.

THE AUSTRO-RUSSIAN WAR AGAINST THE OTTOMAN EMPIRE, 1735–1739

From the beginning of Anna's reign Russian ministers had been determined on war with the Turks, who with their Crimean Tartar vassals still controlled all the northern shores of the Black Sea. The crisis in Poland had merely diverted Russia, and success there encouraged plans for expansion southwards. This inevitably entailed a defensive stance in the Baltic, and on the whole Russia followed this approach for the rest of the century.

Anna's influential war minister, Münnich, had reformed her army and now wanted to win glory for himself by leading a war against the Turks. He was supported by Ostermann, who believed that the deposition of Sultan Ahmed III (1730) heralded the collapse of the Ottoman Empire. This seemed confirmed by the disasters inflicted on the new Sultan Mahmud I's armies during the Turkish–Persian War of 1731–36. The war itself tied down the bulk of Ottoman troops and provided an ideal opportunity for a Russian attack. The Russians intended to conquer lands round the Black Sea, which would allow them to develop maritime commerce there, and then, in Münnich's words, to plant 'the Tsaritsa's standards…in Constantinople'. This was ambitious but not totally impractical, despite the vast distances involved, because of the firmer Russian control established over the nomadic steppes of the Ukraine after the defeat of the Cossack leader Mazepa with Charles XII at Poltava (1709).

Although the initiative was taken by the Russians, the Turks themselves were quite willing to accept the challenge. Russian success in Poland, as during the wars against Charles XII and later in the 1760s, posed a real threat to Turkish control of the Danubian principalities of Moldavia and Wallachia. The Turks were also rather contemptuous of Russian military power after their humiliation of Peter the Great on the Pruth (1711). Their own army, despite its failures against the Persians, was being reformed, especially its poor artillery, by the Frenchman Bonneval who had been a general in the Austrian army. The reform was encouraged by France, who wanted to use the Turks as a check on both Russia and Austria.

Excuses for further war between Russia and the Porte existed in disputes over the wild borderlands in the Caucasus. The immediate pretext was provided by Tartar troops crossing part of these mountainous regions claimed by Russia, in an attempt to attack Persia from the north. In autumn 1735, once it became clear that war was over in western Europe, Münnich dispatched a large raiding party into the Crimea. Although most Tartar bands were fighting the Persians in the Caucasus, the expedition failed: cold and hunger brought about an ignominious retreat. None the less, the following April (1736) Anna formally declared war on the Sultan.

Over the next two years Russian armies concentrated on the area north of the Black Sea. They occupied the Crimea and the country round Azov, only to be forced out by the extremes of weather and by Tartar horsemen cutting their communications. Russian military organisation and supply services proved consistently poor. However, Münnich eventually made a decisive breakthrough in 1739 by massing his troops further west against the Turkish satellite Danubian principalities. Facing Turkish forces which were already stretched by war with the Austrians in the Balkans since 1737 (see p. 156), Münnich avenged Peter the Great's defeat: he crossed the Pruth, took the Moldavian capital of Jassy (Iaşi) and was poised for further advance southwards.

The Turks did not direct their main military effort against the Russians once they became free of the Persian War in 1736. Instead they concentrated on the Austrians who intervened on the Russian side the following year: at this stage the Porte still considered Austria the more dangerous enemy. Austrian intervention had not been decided on easily. Vienna had ignored the Balkans since the peace of Passarowitz, but the involvement of their Russian ally in war and appeals for assistance forced a change in policy.

The wretched state of their army and finances after the war against France made the Austrians understandably reluctant to embark on a fresh one. Yet by autumn 1736 they had decided to intervene as soon as possible. The Austrian government felt it was essential to maintain a close alliance with St Petersburg, especially as the Russians had been prepared to provide them with troops at the end of the Polish Succession War and appeared their one dependable ally. The majority of Charles's ministers, including Bartenstein, hoped to make up for their losses in Italy by gains in the Balkans. They expected to repeat their earlier victories there. Vienna also feared that Münnich's armies,

155

despite recent failures, would soon achieve total success and allow Russia to expand dangerously towards the Danube. Already the future Austro-Russian rivalry in the Balkans was looming on the distant horizon. In July 1737 Austria declared war: Fleury's evident desire for a *rapprochement*, which seemed confirmed by Chauvelin's dismissal, reassured Charles VI about his western frontiers.

Enough troops were raised and equipped to support campaigns in southern Serbia, Wallachia and western Bulgaria, but the war proved an utter disaster. Largely this came from the ineptness of the Austrian generals – Eugene was now dead and had trained no successors – but also because of problems of supply and the dispersal of their army into small and vulnerable units. Charles VI himself wrote in despair that 'whenever the army meets the enemy it is too weak to cope; if we reinforce it, then it starves'. Moreover, the Austrians were facing the bulk of the reformed Turkish army. Consequently, Austrian expeditionary forces were beaten back ignominiously in 1737 and 1738; and in 1739 the Turks besieged Belgrade, Austria's great gain from the last Turkish War, although they stood little chance of taking it.

By 1739 military disaster had made the Austrians desperate for peace, especially because of the rapid Russian advance through Moldavia. They therefore thankfully accepted Fleury's offer to mediate. The Cardinal, while stressing his friendship towards Charles VI, intended to mediate for the benefit of the Sultan and to try to destroy the Austro-Russian alliance. He believed the latter was a barrier to French influence in eastern Europe, as France's recent impotence in Poland had shown. Austrian defeats gave Fleury the chance to prove to the Emperor that he had more to gain from a partnership with France than with Russia, even in the east. In this way he hoped to isolate Russia and prevent any further increase in her power. At the same time it was essential to bolster up the Ottoman Empire, especially as French influence in Poland had been substantially reduced.

Both the Russians and Turks were as eager as the Austrians for peace and quickly accepted French mediation. The Turks were naturally appalled at Russian military success, while Anna's government now feared a Swedish attack on St Petersburg from across the Finnish border – the pro-French Hats had come to power in Stockholm in 1738. All three protagonists therefore gave the French minister, Villeneuve, full powers to conclude peace in negotiations held at the camp of the Turkish grand vizier outside the besieged city of Belgrade.

On 18 September 1739 the peace of Belgrade was signed. Austria was forced to return most of the gains she had made in 1718: western Wallachia, northern Serbia and Belgrade itself, although the city's fortifications were to be demolished. However, she kept the lands north of the Sava and Danube as well as the Banat of Temesvár. Russia had to restore all her recent conquests except Azov, which was to be unfortified, and an area of the steppe between the Dniester and Azov inhabited by the Zaporozhian Cossacks. Russia therefore still lacked direct access to the Black Sea, and she was specifically forbidden to have merchantmen or warships on it. The disputed areas of the Caucasus were declared independent of either side.

The Turks had managed by themselves to turn back what had appeared almost irreversible Austrian expansion in the Balkans and to limit further advance till the late nineteenth century. Villeneuve achieved just as great a diplomatic triumph in cancelling out Münnich's military successes and largely restoring Ottoman control around the Black Sea. However, unlike in the Balkans, the frontiers there had not been settled and would have been difficult to stabilise in any case because of the nomadic Cossacks and Tartars. Having lost little territory, or rather suzerainty over the mobile populations there, the Turks had gained a breathing space to recover, one which was to last for thirty years before a further Russian advance.

The extent of France's prestige victory in 1739 cannot be exaggerated. She had managed to maintain her *rapprochement* with Austria while appearing her protector against the Turks. At the same time the Porte felt France had saved it from the Russians. French influence at Constantinople, which had decreased as that of Britain rose after the peace of Karlowitz in 1699, had now been triumphantly reasserted. As a reward French commercial privileges in the Ottoman Empire were increased by a treaty in May 1740. This treaty helped consolidate the dominance of French economic interests in the eastern Mediterranean.

The war had reaffirmed, in a particularly humiliating way, the collapse of Habsburg power, while the peace of Belgrade had shown Austria's new dependence on France. Yet Fleury had failed in one of his aims in mediating the peace: the Austrians still clung to their alliance with Russia, whose military reputation and international importance had both been enhanced by Münnich's victories. But Russia had achieved little return in territory for the outlay in men and resources. Moreover, the confidence of the Russian court was badly shaken by the results of the war and the successes of French diplomacy. French influence was in the ascendant at Vienna as well as Constantinople, and in Sweden the pro-French Hats were in power. The Hats wanted to regain part of the Baltic provinces and had suggested a league with Denmark and France to attack Russia during the Turkish War, but neither the Danes nor Fleury had been interested. None the less, after the peace of Belgrade the Russians felt alarmed enough to consider an accommodation with France similar to the one made by Austria. France herself hoped to bring Russia into her orbit and for this purpose sent a new minister, La Chétardie, to St Petersburg, where he made almost a triumphal entry late in 1739. While Ostermann remained in power, the Russian chancellor was determined to resist such a change in policy. But the death of Anna in 1740 and the *coup d'état* of December 1741, which deposed the child Tsar Ivan VI and brought Elizabeth to the throne with the assistance of La Chétardie, seemed to promise further success for France. With these triumphs in eastern Europe, the recovery of France, the central development of the 1730s, seemed complete.

CHAPTER SIX
A new pattern, 1739–1763

For a generation after 1739 the European powers fought one another with a ferocity unknown since the War of the Spanish Succession. At stake was not only the future shape of Europe but also control of a great part of the world overseas and, in particular, its trade. The struggle undermined the dominance of European politics by British and French diplomacy, which had been the main feature of the generation after the peace of Utrecht. At the same time Russia was brought decisively onto the European stage, Prussia became a great power and Austria's very right to be one was questioned. Two basic issues emerged: that between Britain and France overseas and that between Austria and Prussia in Europe. The traditional primacy of continental issues in the relations of the powers was slowly undermined by extra-European ones. Although many statesmen, even in Britain and France, remained blind to the latter, it is symptomatic of the change that the first conflict was purely colonial in nature.

THE WAR OF JENKINS' EAR

In 1739 Britain went to war against Spain in a manner reminiscent of the days of Hawkins and Drake. Once again British seamen and merchants tried to seize control of all trade with Spanish America. This attempt led to a wider conflict with France for dominance of all the commerce between Europe and the outside world. Unlike in the earlier brief Anglo-Spanish wars of 1718–20 and 1727 Spain was not the aggressor and her ambitions in the Mediterranean were not the cause. During the War of the Polish Succession Philip V and Elizabeth Farnese had been largely absorbed in finding thrones in Italy for their two sons. Their bitterness at how Fleury dictated peace after 1735, without enough regard for them, led the King and Queen to try to

159

court British goodwill once more and to stifle their annoyance over Britain's commercial privileges and possession of Gibraltar and Minorca. However, at the same time, they encouraged Patiño's efforts to improve the navy and the administration of the American colonies. This was bound to be resented in Britain, where in the mid 1730s there was growing discontent among traders over the situation in the Caribbean and a desire to destroy completely Spain's trading monopoly with her American colonies. Large cracks had already been opened up in this monopoly. The South Sea Company's agents had exploited the cover of the *Asiento* and annual ship to carry on more trading than was allowed under the terms of the treaty of Utrecht (see p. 65). More important was the blatant, direct illicit trade conducted by Britain and her colonies, especially the merchants in Jamaica. In fact the Spanish colonists, starved of industrial goods from Spain and unable to dispose of all their colonial products there, welcomed these interlopers or smugglers, who often included Dutch traders from Curaçao.

Madrid and its colonial governors had continually tried to suppress the illicit trade. Lacking enough royal ships and faced by vast expanses of sea to patrol, they employed the notorious *guarda-costas*, coastguard ships, to stop and search any foreign vessels found in or near Spanish-American waters. Based mainly on the Caribbean islands and depending on prizes to survive, these *guarda-costas* often acted as little more than pirates. They preyed on British ships trading legitimately with Jamaica as well as on the smugglers and they often maltreated captured crews. Between 1713 and 1731 they seized ten British ships per year; as the Spanish government tried to conciliate British, the number fell to five per year from 1734 to 1737. Since this merely encouraged the smugglers, the Spanish governors made a determined effort in 1737, when an alarming twelve ships were taken.

The merchants, illicit and legitimate, of London, Bristol, Liverpool, Glasgow and Jamaica (the 'West India interest') began a furious campaign for government action in 1737, and this rose in intensity over the next two years. They were backed by a jingoist public opinion, demanding commercial imperialism, while the parliamentary opposition discovered in this a fine opportunity to attack Walpole and his pacific policies. Demands for justice for British traders and an end to Spanish searching of their ships developed into cries for a commercial and colonial war on Spain and the resolution of the unsatisfactory situation created after Utrecht. At a time of stagnation and decline in British trade they held the simple mercantilist belief that Britain's survival demanded she grab as much as possible of a fixed amount of world trade. That war would inevitably destroy the very profitable British trade with Spain itself was ignored, probably because this trade was dominated by Catholics and Jews. There were also some demands, as yet far less strident, for war with France as well and claims that she was Britain's real enemy and rival in the

Americas. There were those who pointed out that French commerce, unlike British, was forging ahead, particularly in the West Indies. In fact, although few grasped it at the time, what was really at stake, as the future showed, was control of the whole Caribbean trading area, British, Spanish and French. The plantations developed on the West Indian islands and parts of South and North America in the late seventeenth and early eighteenth centuries had created a vast storehouse for tropical products – sugar, rum, tobacco, cotton, wood and dyes – and a demand for West African slaves and European manufactured goods.

The political temperature was considerably raised in March 1738 when a Captain Jenkins showed a suitably horrified House of Commons his unfortunate ear, which he claimed had been lopped off by a *guarda-costa* captain and which Jenkins had kept pickled in a jar. There were immediate demands for war. Walpole, who knew war would force up the land tax and undermine his position in parliament pleaded for moderation. In 1738 and the early months of 1739 he tried to reach agreement with Spain over the trade question and the subsidiary problems of the border between Britain's colony of Georgia and Spanish Florida and the British claims to cut the logwood needed for manufacturing dyes on the Honduras coast. Spain wanted to compromise but not at the cost of sacrificing her trading monopoly. The agreement patched up between Spain and Walpole in January 1739, the convention of the Pardo, stood no chance of acceptance by the British public. Concentrating on compensation for vessels lost, it ignored the Spanish practice of searching legitimate shipping and evaded the crucial issue: Spain's intention to go on suppressing smuggling. Walpole finally had to yield before the clamour from outside and even from within his own government: war was declared in October 1739. It was one purely for commercial gain: at the declaration stocks rose.

Sooner or later France would inevitably become involved. Although Fleury had characteristically urged moderation on Spain, his policy by now was moving towards commercial and colonial conflict with Britain. During 1739 the two branches of the Bourbon family had joined more closely together by the marriage of Louis XV's daughter to Don Philip, the younger son of Philip V and Elizabeth Farnese. But Fleury had more practical motives: British victory and tough peace terms would damage French trade with Cadiz and probably threaten her invaluable sugar islands of Martinique, Guadeloupe and Haiti. He felt confident in facing up to Britain: together France and Spain probably had more capital ships (i.e. ships of the line) which were believed to be more seaworthy and better armed. In Europe Britain was diplomatically isolated, whereas France was in a strong position after the treaties of Vienna (1735–38) and Belgrade (1739). In 1740, therefore, Fleury sent a French fleet to the Caribbean with orders to help a Spanish attack on Jamaica. This action could only have been intended to lead to war between France and Britain.

In the event the Anglo-Spanish War, or the War of Jenkins' Ear, was quickly overshadowed and enveloped by the outbreak of conflict in Europe from 1740, but it is doubtful if it would have been decisive in any case. The British could not decide whether to destroy Spanish trade and shipping or seize colonies; France's clear intention to intervene eventually added to this indecision. British operations against Caribbean and South American ports between 1739 and 1742 achieved little, and until the peace in 1748 further action was limited to raids on shipping and attempts to isolate Spain from her colonies. Distance, climate and disease proved the main obstacles, but the quality of the British navy had declined since Utrecht, and the Spaniards put up a spirited defence. Britain's one consolation was that France's expedition of 1740 ended in disaster, and this failure, together with the momentous events on the Continent in 1740–41, destroyed Fleury's plans for active co-operation with Spain outside Europe.

THE WAR OF THE AUSTRIAN SUCCESSION, 1740–1748

In October 1740 the Emperor Charles VI, the last male Habsburg, died unexpectedly. It was not anticipated that his death would lead to war or to the break-up of his territories, as had happened when Charles II of Spain died in 1700. The succession of his daughter, Maria Theresa, seemed secure: all the leading European and German states, except Bavaria, had guaranteed the Pragmatic Sanction and, more importantly, Maria Theresa enjoyed the goodwill of the major powers. Although the Russian Tsaritsa Anna had died three days before Charles, the regency for the child Ivan VI was pro-Austrian. In France Fleury wanted to avoid continental war and concentrate on the struggle with Britain overseas. Since 1735 he had worked to reduce Austria to a friendly dependency and had no intention of challenging Maria Theresa's position in the Habsburg territories. However, he hoped to see Charles Albert of Bavaria elected emperor rather than Maria Theresa's husband, Francis Stephen: French influence in Germany would increase and Francis Stephen be deterred from trying to recover Lorraine. Although Spain looked for further gains in Italy and both Bavaria and Saxony had claims to the Habsburg succession through marriages to the daughters of Emperor Joseph I, these states were not really dangerous without French support. At home Maria Theresa's succession went unchallenged throughout her provinces. Unfortunately, these still lacked any administrative unity and the one unifying force besides the church, the army, had been shattered and demoralised by Charles's last calamitous wars. The field army stood at 30,000 men – garrison troops brought the total to 70,000 – and could only be increased and improved by drastic domestic reform. The twenty-three-year-old Maria Theresa herself had been totally unprepared for her new role; her husband had few political or military talents; her ministers were largely old, timid and incompetent; she had no decent generals and her treasury was empty.

In December 1740 the blue-coated troops of the King of Prussia crossed into Maria Theresa's most northerly province of Silesia and began the War of the Austrian Succession. The attack was a complete surprise to her and to Europe. Prussia had no serious dynastic claims to any of the monarchy and had not been a traditional enemy. Under Frederick William I Prussia's large army, the King's unpredictability and flirtations with Peter the Great and the first Hanoverian ruler of Britain, had occasionally annoyed Vienna, but he inspired neither fear nor respect. In the international pecking order Prussia, which was still divided into three parts, ranked only a little above Bavaria or Saxony. Frederick William's only gain from the Northern War had been Stettin and its surrounds. He had spent most of his energies in his last years in trying unsuccessfully to persuade the European powers to recognise his succession rights to the small Rhineland territories of Jülich–Berg which adjoined his duchy of Cleves. From 1726 he had loyally supported the Austro-Russian alliance in Poland and the Empire. Yet in 1738 Charles VI had shown his contempt for him by agreeing with France and the Maritime Powers to exclude Prussia from the Jülich–Berg succession. Deeply wounded, Frederick William turned to France, and in 1739 Fleury promised support over Berg: by separating Prussia from Austria, French dominance over both powers, and in Germany, would be assured.

Frederick William I died a few months before Maria Theresa's accession. His son Frederick II, Frederick the Great, seemed likely to be less of a threat to the European order than his father. He enjoyed a good deal of sympathy outside Prussia because of the brutal upbringing he had received from Frederick William. Charles VI had interceded to save his life and had lent and given him money. A poet and musician, friend of Voltaire and French culture, he was expected to relax and humanise the savage, militarised Prussian state which squeezed 7 million thalers annually from his poor and largely agrarian country. He seemed unlikely to continue spending 5 million of these on the military or to maintain a war chest of 8 million thalers and an army of 80,000. The latter seemed absurd for a population of 2.25 million, when France's population was ten times larger and only supported an army twice the size. However, in reality the intellectual dilettante was also a callous, determined proponent of *Realpolitik*, who believed the logic of his father's administrative reforms and model army was territorial expansion. In this way Prussia's poverty and territorial fragmentation could be overcome and the state be transformed into one which made rather than followed events. Desire for revenge on Austria for the shabby treatment of his father over Berg (see p. 163) probably influenced him only a little. Without the opportunity provided by Charles VI's death, Frederick would hardly have contemplated military action. The accession of a young woman when Austrian finances and army were in chaos presented him with the chance to seize the rich province of Silesia. With a population of 1 million, many of them still Protestant, flourishing agriculture, ore deposits and famous textile industry, it would greatly increase Prussian strength and wealth. Bordering Brandenburg, Silesia formed a natural extension higher up the River Oder. Moreover, prudence suggested Prussia should seize it before the Elector-King of Saxony–Poland, Augustus III, was tempted to. By coming between Saxony and Poland Frederick weakened both and made them possible victims for future Prussian expansion. Although Prussia had some vague claims to small areas of Silesia, dynasticism played no part in Frederick's policies and he only presented them for form's sake. He congratulated his minister, Podewils, for concocting a legal justification for the attack: 'Splendid, that's the work of an excellent charlatan!' Frederick's view of international morality was that the ruler should unashamedly further the interests of his own state. In May 1741 he was to write: 'If we can gain something by being honest, we will be it, and if we have to deceive, we will be cheats.' Yet the King at this time was also impelled by motives a young ruler of an earlier age would have understood. He confessed later: 'My youth, hot headedness, thirst for glory...the satisfaction of seeing my name in the gazettes and then in history carried me away.' He was prepared to take risks and to fight for what he wanted, but he was no militarist and realised Prussia's standing army and full treasury allowed him to wage short wars for limited territorial ends. With luck in any case he might gain Silesia without a fight and he had no intention of provoking a partition of Austria or a general war. He counted on the passivity of the other powers and hoped Maria Theresa would yield. The regency in Russia would be wary of helping her Austrian ally actively, and Frederick believed it could be bought off with 'a mule laden with gold'. Above all Fleury's clear intention to help Spain at sea meant that probably neither France nor Britain would stand by Maria Theresa and might even bid for Prussian support.

After occupying Silesia in December 1740 Frederick offered to buy the province, but Maria Theresa contemptuously refused. Pride and obstinacy played a part, but clearly the cession of any of her lands would call into question the validity of the Pragmatic Sanction and encourage other claims on her inheritance. Moreover, it was easy enough for Frederick to seize an isolated province in the depths of winter but a different matter to keep it. Maria Theresa also expected the other powers would denounce him. At Versailles Louis XV declared that 'the King of Prussia is a fool', while Fleury called him 'a dishonest man and a cheat'. Unfortunately, others at the French court drew different conclusions, especially when Frederick won his first victory over the Austrians at Mollwitz in April 1741 and his actions encouraged others: Charles Albert of Bavaria claimed Bohemia and Austria, while Philip V of Spain demanded Tuscany and Parma for Don Philip. Fleury found himself faced by a group of young bellicose aristocrats, led by the ambitious Count Belle-Isle, who wanted to be rid of him and his cautious policies. They received some sympathy from Louis XV, who was now becoming impatient to free himself from the octogenarian Cardinal. Gradually Fleury lost ground to Belle-Isle and had to abandon plans to concentrate on a naval conflict with Britain. He had to accept French policy returning to the seventeenth-century tradition of territorial expansion at the expense of the Habsburgs. In fact no better opportunity to destroy the Habsburgs completely had ever presented itself.

This was the view of Belle-Isle, who by spring 1741 was at Frankfurt and acting in effect as French foreign minister. He aimed to win the Imperial election for Charles Albert and to create a coalition to break up Austria: the Southern Netherlands should go to France, Silesia to Prussia, Bohemia to Bavaria and the Italian lands to Savoy and the Spanish princes. In May he gave French blessing to the Spanish–Bavarian alliance of Nymphenburg, and a few weeks later he concluded French alliances with Bavaria and Prussia. Believing he could use both these states as pawns, he promised subsidies and French auxiliary troops for a full-scale attack on the Habsburg lands in central Europe. French diplomacy also tried to neutralise Russia by encouraging a Swedish attack across the Finnish border in August 1741. In the autumn Spanish troops landed in Italy, while French, Bavarian and Prussian troops, as well as those of another predator, Augustus of Saxony–Poland, attacked Maria Theresa's German and Bohemian territories. The fiction was maintained that France was not at war with the Habsburgs but merely acting as an auxiliary of Charles Albert. By the end of 1741 Belle-Isle was in Prague at the head of a Franco-Bavarian force, and both Bohemia and Upper Austria were occupied. Charles Albert had himself crowned archduke of Austria at Linz and king of Bohemia at Prague, and then in January 1742 he was elected Emperor Charles VII, the first non-Habsburg for 300 years. He was clearly a French puppet: both the Empire as an institution and the Imperial title, which had kept much of its prestige by its association with the Habsburgs, had been debased, probably irreparably. Belle-Isle appeared to have achieved French mastery of central Europe and to have gone far beyond Louis XIV's wildest dreams.

Austria none the less survived. This was because of divisions which appeared among her enemies and because of Maria Theresa's stubborn courage. Deserted by many of the Austro-Bohemian nobility and clergy, she turned to Hungary and threw herself on the chivalry of the rebellious and independent nobility. After wringing constitutional concessions from her, they raised a force of 20,000, mostly irregular cavalry, which saw her through the crucial winter of 1741–42. This support and her coronation as queen of Hungary restored her credibility in Austria and abroad. Equally important was Frederick II's desertion of his allies by a short armistice with Maria Theresa in October 1741 and a more durable one through the treaty of Breslau (Wroclaw) in July 1742. This was bought by the cession of most of Silesia, which was all Frederick wanted from the war. Maria Theresa had no intention of making this permanent, but realised she had to concentrate on the French and Bavarians in Austria and Bohemia as they threatened her very existence. The armistices had been the work of British mediation and the Queen could not resist their demands.

The outbreak of war on the Continent in 1740–41 had radically altered the situation for Britain. Fleury's plans for helping Spain overseas were abandoned and were only taken up again in 1744. The Spaniards also concentrated on grabbing what they could in Italy. Yet the British failed to take advantage of this in the New World and were drawn themselves into the European struggle. Walpole's attempts to preserve neutrality, as in 1733, proved impossible. It was clear to the other ministers and to George II that Austria's existence was at stake and that her destruction would raise the power of France and her German allies to a level which would threaten Hanover and ultimately Britain herself. They insisted Britain honour her guarantee of the Pragmatic Sanction and found Maria Theresa's cause popular in parliament. In June 1741 an Anglo-Austrian alliance promised British subsidies and 12,000 troops. The money was paid and British diplomacy tried to improve Austria's military situation, however bitter the pill for Maria, by arranging the successive armistices with Frederick. But the troops hired from Denmark and Hesse-Cassel were never sent. This was because when George II visited his electorate in summer 1741, he became so scared of a French attack that he insisted they remain to defend Hanover. Moreover, he even signed a convention with Louis XV to neutralise Hanover, promised to vote for Charles Albert as emperor and did so the following January. For the first time since the accession of the Hanoverians, the danger emerged of France's seizing the electorate and using it as a lever against Britain: this threat was to be a constant factor in Anglo-French relations over the next generation.

British policy towards the continental war became more decisive in February 1742 when Walpole fell. For the next two years control of foreign policy in the patched-up Whig administration lay with Carteret. Political opportunism had made him a fiery protagonist of the trade war with Spain. But Carteret was essentially a Whig of the old school, who thought in continental terms, feared French ascendancy and wanted to revive the policy of the Grand Alliance which had proved so successful against Louis XIV: Britain should build a coalition and supply it with cash and troops. French hegemony would be destroyed, Britain would regain her position as arbiter of Europe and achieve supremacy overseas. It was vital, therefore, to preserve Austria since she was needed to help check France. But Carteret was also determined to have Maria Theresa accommodate with Frederick of Prussia so that Austria could concentrate on France. The latter inevitably led to uneasy relations between Britain and Austria. Carteret encountered similar difficulties with his ministerial colleagues and parliament because he was determined to please George II by defending Hanover, seeing it as an essential part of a system against France.

The war turned dramatically in favour of the Anglo-Austrian allies in 1742, when Carteret persuaded first the Prussians and then the Saxons to make peace with Austria. Frederick had no qualms in deserting his allies and ending the First Silesian War (1740–42) in July. Having gained Silesia, he had no interest in furthering Franco-Bavarian ambitions, especially as he lacked the resources for a long struggle and needed peace to rebuild his army. This withdrawal enabled Maria Theresa to expel the French and Bavarians and even to occupy Bavaria. Although neither was officially at war with Louis XV, it now seemed possible for Austria and Britain to concentrate against France. Maria Theresa wanted to continue the war both to punish her enemies and to gain compensation for Silesia in Bavaria or in Alsace-Lorraine; Carteret had the less tangible aim of humbling France. The French, freed from the remaining passive influence of Fleury by his death in January 1743, intended to reassert their influence in Germany and restore their puppet, the Bavarian Emperor Charles VII.

Carteret's visions of repeating the victories of the Spanish Succession War were illusory. These had depended heavily on wholehearted support from the Dutch and most German states including Prussia. Now the Republic insisted on neutrality, and the lack of enthusiasm among the German princes, despite British subsidies, meant that Carteret's neo-Grand Alliance was a pale shadow of the original. In June 1743 George II in person led the so-called 'Pragmatic Army' of German mercenaries, paid for by Britain, to a surprise victory over the French at Dettingen near Frankfurt. Although he forced French troops from Germany, this battle proved to be no new Blenheim. George was too nervous of following it up with an attack on France in case Prussia re-entered the war and invaded Hanover. None the less, French power had been removed from Germany and Carteret was determined to expel her Bourbon allies from Italy as well. In September he forced Austria, under the threat of withdrawing the subsidies her army needed to survive, to sign the treaty of Worms with Charles Emmanuel of Savoy. The latter, following the traditions of his house, used the Habsburg–Bourbon struggle to extract promises from Maria Theresa of more of Milan as well as Piacenza. In return, with British cash and Austrian troops, he agreed to co-operate against France, Don Charles of Naples and the Spanish troops in Italy. By the end of 1743, therefore, through British subsidies and bullying Austria into distasteful concessions, Carteret had managed to destroy the predominant position in central Europe created by Belle-Isle for France in 1741. However, the anti-French grouping did not have the muscle to force Louis XV to accept this by attacking France herself. In creating his alliances Carteret had hardly considered non-European factors and did not try seriously to destroy France and Spain at sea or in the colonies, where Britain stood the best chance of success. He did not realise, any more than any other government or opposition politician, except possibly Pitt the Elder, that ultimately control of the world's trade was at stake.

Recent failures forced the French to make a long-overdue appraisal of their policies in 1743: Louis XV was now clearly engaged in full-scale war with Britain and Austria, although formally at peace with both. The King himself had no coherent ideas of his own except to increase his personal prestige and further the interests of the Bourbon family, but he had been battered by conflicting ministerial advice. Eventually he decided, largely in self-defence, to concentrate on those areas where France had been most successful in the past and which would directly threaten Austria and Britain: Italy, the Rhineland and the Southern Netherlands. No actual territorial gains seem to have been intended for France. In October 1743 he signed a close dynastic alliance with Philip V at Fontainebleau (the Second Family Compact), formulating a policy mainly for his Spanish relatives' benefit. France and Spain should co-operate in Italy to conquer Milan, Parma and Piacenza from Austria for Louis's Spanish son-in-law Don Philip; the two powers would renew their joint action against Britain overseas abandoned in 1741; and France would help Spain regain Gibraltar and Minorca and cancel the British commercial concessions. In spring 1744 war was at last declared against Austria and Britain. Franco-Spanish forces invaded Italy, but met with little success against Austria and Savoy. An attempt to invade Britain to restore the Stuarts was abandoned when a storm dispersed the French fleet. However, the French invasion of the Austrian Netherlands under Marshal Saxe, a natural child of Augustus the Strong of Saxony, was highly successful.

Saxe's campaign was helped, and allied attempts to counter it along the Rhine undermined, by Frederick the Great's re-entering the war. He invaded Bohemia in August 1744 to begin his Second Silesian War (1744–45). It was Maria Theresa's recovery, her occupation of Bavaria and an alliance with her previous enemy, Saxony, in December 1743, which pushed him into a new campaign to weaken Austria and gain further guarantees for Silesia. He feared that if the Austrian recovery continued, she might in time attack him to recover Silesia. With his finances restored and an army now 140,000 strong, he soon took Prague and forced the Austrians to evacuate Bavaria. Frederick's intervention was a serious blow to Carteret's anti-French policy: the Austrians now had to face a war on two fronts again, although the French had no intention of sending an army into central Europe once more. Carteret was also disappointed that the Dutch, despite the French invasion of the Austrian Netherlands, still refused to enter the war. At home his political position was crumbling. His ministerial colleagues, Henry Pelham, Pelham's brother, Newcastle, and Hardwicke, envied his close relations with George II and had to bear the burden of guiding his costly and unpopular subsidy policy through parliament. It was easy to claim that the British-financed 'Pragmatic Army' in Germany was defending Hanover and Austria rather than British interests: in parliament Pitt the Elder called Carteret the 'Hanoverian troop-master'. Yet it is difficult to see what else could have been done. George II was insistent on defending Hanover, and with only a trifling army of her own Britain had to contain France through foreign alliances and troops, which cost money. The imperialist war against Spain, and public enthusiasm for it, had died out after early failures in the Caribbean. None the less, in December 1744 Carteret had to resign. Newcastle largely took over responsibility for foreign policy, while Henry Pelham, the leader of the ministry, was at the Treasury.

The Pelhamite administration was faced with much the same problems as Carteret and tried very similar solutions. They showed no more appreciation of Britain's imperial interests, and they continued to view the war largely in European terms and the need to maintain a coalition against France. However, they were helped in making the struggle more necessary and intelligible to the public by the direction of the French war effort from 1744. Saxe's advances in Flanders brought home the French danger in a form not apparent since the days of the 'Sun King'; French support for the Stuart Pretender James reopened the question of the Protestant succession. The French decision to co-operate with Spain in the desultory war at sea reopened the struggle which had been developing in 1740–41 between Britain and France for overseas supremacy. Yet the importance of this for contemporaries should not be exaggerated. Since Fleury's death French ministers had no more real grasp of the importance of the struggle for empire than those in Britain. On both sides of the Channel the overseas struggle was undertaken hesitantly and with the minimum of resources. None the less, the clash of Anglo-French interests was now more direct and apparent and provided the main reason for the continuation of the War of the Austrian Succession beyond 1745.

In that year the war within Germany came to an end. In January the Emperor Charles VII died and Bavarian pretensions with him. An Austro-Bavarian peace was quickly signed in the April and soon afterwards Maria Theresa's husband was elected emperor as Francis I. Throughout the year the British tried to persuade the new Empress to come to terms with Prussia, using the old argument that France was her main enemy. Maria Theresa obstinately refused, declaring on one occasion she would 'rather give away my chemise and petticoat than Silesia'. But continual Prussian victories, culminating in the occupation of Austria's ally, Saxony, and the ultimate British threat to cut off the vital subsidies forced her to agree to peace. Frederick himself desperately wanted this as well. Anxious to rebuild his army and refill his war chest, he feared that the Russians, free from war with the Swedes since 1743 (see p. 176) and now firmly under Tsaritsa Elizabeth's control, would attack him to rescue Augustus of Saxony–Poland. He knew he could expect little help from France and none from Bavaria. On Christmas Day 1745 Austria and Prussia therefore concluded the peace of Dresden, where Frederick once more received Silesia. The treaty, coming after the peace with Bavaria, effectively settled the question of the Austrian succession. The war itself now became essentially a conflict between the Bourbon powers and Austria and Britain for and against French hegemony in western and central Europe.

The Austrians now showed more enthusiasm for fighting France. Their only hope for compensation for Silesia lay outside Germany, and in 1746 Maria Theresa concentrated all her forces in Italy, the Netherlands and along the Rhine. The British had grown desperate for this help because of the extent of French victories in 1745. Bourbon troops had won successes in northern Italy but above all in the Austrian Netherlands, where Marshal Saxe had made remarkable gains for France. His victory at Fontenoy over the Anglo-Austrian army in May 1745 was followed by the occupation of most of the province. This was facilitated by the withdrawal of the British regiments and those Dutch troops protecting the Barrier to suppress the Jacobite rebellion in Britain. For in July 1745 the Young Pretender, Charles Edward, landed in Scotland and began the 'Forty-five adventure, the greatest threat to the Hanoverian dynasty since its accession in 1714. Although it failed and Jacobitism died with it, the confidence of the English establishment was badly shaken and England's vulnerability clearly demonstrated. Fortunately, her naval power ensured the French could not dispatch direct military help, but the rebellion and French conquests in the Austrian Netherlands convinced the Pelhamite government and public opinion that the war was now one for Britain's survival, and that France had to be humbled.

The immediacy of the French threat made it more difficult than ever to consider the possibility of harming France seriously outside Europe. When the Anglo-French naval conflict broke out in earnest in 1745, the British fleets concentrated on protecting the British Isles, attacking the French in the Mediterranean, and then disrupting French external trade where possible, especially that with the West Indies. Neither government expressed much interest in the skirmishes between their North American colonists or the agents of their East India companies on the Indian subcontinent. However, in 1745 a largely colonial force, backed by the Royal Navy, took Cape Breton Island with its massive fortress of Louisbourg controlling the St Lawrence seaway into French Canada. A harassed British public opinion immediately seized on the victory and gave Louisbourg's retention great symbolic importance.

If national survival had become the motive for the war in Britain, what had it become for the French now that Bavarian and Prussian desertion had ruined their ambitions for control of Germany? Despite her success it is difficult to know what France wanted besides a vague yearning for hegemony. In Italy Louis wished to continue the close co-operation he had achieved with Philip V and to further the dynastic ambitions of Don Philip, the Spanish King's son and Louis's son-in-law. But quarrels with Spain over the territorial settlement made it impossible for the Bourbons to capitalise on military victories and Savoy's willingness for peace. As to the Southern Netherlands, there were suggestions from some French ministers that their forces should be withdrawn and the area neutralised, so as to reassure the Dutch and use them against Britain. Louis, however, although he seems to have had no intention of permanent annexation, preferred to follow Saxe's advice to achieve complete military conquest, and the bulk of French forces operated there till the end of the war.

THE PEACE OF AIX-LA-CHAPELLE, 1748

The conclusion of peace with Prussia in 1745 did not mean the end of the war for Austria. The direction of French military expansion obliged them to defend their own possessions in Italy and in the Netherlands. Although they increasingly considered the latter a burden, its loss would have been a further blow to Habsburg prestige. Italy offered the possibility of territorial compensation for the loss of Silesia and the greater part of Austria's troops was concentrated in the peninsula. By late 1746 her forces and those of Savoy, both heavily subsidised by Britain, had expelled most of the quarrelling Bourbon troops from the north. However, Maria Theresa was now beginning to believe the monarchy needed peace to begin wide-ranging domestic reforms. The Austrians, moreover, increasingly felt they were becoming British mercenaries in an Anglo-French war. In fact, as paymasters of Austria and Spain, the decision for war or peace did largely rest with the two western powers.

By 1746 Louis XV personally wanted peace despite difficulties over satisfying his Spanish relatives and Saxe's argument that once all the Austrian Netherlands were conquered France could dictate terms. However, indirect French moves for peace were wrecked by British intransigence. While Henry Pelham wanted an end to the war because of the financial burden, Newcastle, George II and his influential second son Cumberland insisted on continuing the struggle until France had been humbled. The popular conquest of Louisbourg, the final defeat of the Jacobites by Cumberland at Culloden in April 1746, success in Italy and the death of Philip V of Spain in the July, led them to ignore the situation in the Netherlands. They had high hopes that Philip's son, Ferdinand VI (1746–59), would conclude a separate peace. The new Spanish King had a pro-British, Portuguese wife and was known to hate his stepmother Elizabeth Farnese and her children. However, Spain still had her own unresolved differences with Britain, and Ferdinand personally wanted territory in Italy for his Farnese half-brother Don Philip so as to get him out of Spain.

In September 1746 Madras fell to the French East India Company and, more importantly, Saxe's advance in the Low Countries could not be staunched. By 1747 French troops had reached the Dutch border. In April France declared war on the Republic, which, despite the involvement of its Barrier fortress troops in the war, had hitherto struggled to maintain its neutrality. The resulting panic in Holland led to a revolution, reminiscent of that of 1672, the overthrow of the pacific oligarchic regime and the restoration of the stadtholdership under William IV. Newcastle, who shared the misconception of other eighteenth-century British ministers about the strength of the Dutch, deluded himself into believing they would now join in a new Grand Alliance. But the Dutch were no longer a real force in international relations. William IV was no William III, and the Dutch, whatever their regime, desperately wanted peace and a return to neutrality. They even appealed for British subsidies. When the great fortress of Bergen-op-Zoom fell to Saxe in September 1747, even the most bellicose British leaders concluded that only peace could save the Dutch from conquest. Maria Theresa would send her troops only to Italy and was suspected of spending British subsidies on building her palace of Schönbrunn. Although Britain had signed an agreement with Russia in 1747 for troops to be sent to the Republic the next year, the full cost would fall on Britain, which was paying £1.7 million in foreign subsidies in 1747. This was in addition to £6 million spent on her own army and navy. The Austrian Succession War was at least as expensive as that of the Spanish Succession had been. It was eventually to cost

Britain £43 million, of which £30 million was added to the National Debt. With the land tax at 4s in the pound, alarmists in the government raised the cry of national bankruptcy. Early in 1748, therefore, talks between the Maritime Powers and France began in earnest at Aix-la-Chapelle (Aachen).

Saxe's spectacular victories should have given France a strong bargaining position, but Louis XV and the country as a whole, which had suffered a food crisis in 1747, were as anxious for peace as the British. There were also straws in the wind for what was to happen in the next war, but they were signs which the British in their scramble for peace failed to grasp. During 1747 the French finance minister, Machault, had pleaded for an end to the struggle because the financial system was collapsing. The cause, besides the inbuilt weaknesses of the system, was the dramatic decline in customs' receipts as French foreign trade dried up. Initially the naval war had hardly affected French commerce: Canada was bottled up, but contact was maintained with the West Indies, while neutral Dutch ships still entered French ports. However, by 1747 British naval victories, and an effective blockade of the French coast, radically altered the situation. The Newfoundland fisheries were cut off and there were justified fears that the priceless sugar islands would fall into British hands. On the other hand British trade, which had declined after 1739, was now recovering and perhaps even expanding, as the navy achieved increasing control of trade routes. Versailles assumed Britain could continue the war indefinitely at sea despite her defeats on land. The occupation of the Netherlands and the conquest of the Dutch Republic hardly seemed grounds for prolonging a struggle which was crippling France's economy.

In their haste for peace neither France nor Britain took advantage of their strength in different spheres to prolong the negotiations. Although Louis wished to satisfy Don Philip, he wanted nothing for himself. An overriding concern about the financial situation and need to raise the British blockade made him agree to return the Netherlands without compensation. Britain showed a similar urgency for peace and felt the preliminaries, signed in April 1748, had saved her from ruin. Both Austria, who had tried in vain to interest the French in separate negotiations, and Spain had to fall in line with their paymasters and the definitive treaty of Aix-la-Chapelle was signed in October 1748.

This treaty confirmed the territorial status quo in western Europe: the Netherlands were restored to Austria and the Dutch allowed back as impotent custodians of the Barrier fortresses. Madras and Louisbourg were exchanged by Britain and France, the French once again expelled the Stuarts, guaranteed the Protestant succession and agreed to destroy Dunkirk's sea defences. As neither power wished to offend him, Frederick's possession of Silesia was guaranteed. A similar guarantee was given to Maria Theresa for her remaining lands, but she had to cede Parma and Piacenza to Don Philip and yet more of Milan to Savoy. The main territorial changes in a European treaty had applied yet again to Italy, but the peninsula now ceased to be a source of conflict among the powers until the Revolutionary Wars. Elizabeth Farnese's family ambitions had been handsomely satisfied and her direct influence disappeared in Spain, which no longer had any territorial ambitions in Italy after the death of Philip V. Austria similarly, although retaining Tuscany and most of Milan, abandoned her half-century attempt to dominate the area, and instead became absorbed in central Europe. In 1752 Spain and Austria reached a final settlement over Italy by the treaty of Aranjuez. France, which had largely intervened in Italy because of her relationship with the Spaniards, was uninterested in expansion there. The end of great-power conflict over Italy robbed Savoy of any further chance for her recent expansion which had fed on Habsburg–Bourbon rivalry. Unlike in Prussia her rulers lacked the confidence to strike out on their own.★

The settlement at Aix-la-Chapelle ignored the disputes which had caused the Anglo-Spanish War in 1739. Both British and Spanish governments had been reticent in the negotiations as they wished to conciliate each other. Moreover, their rivalry had been dwarfed by that which had now erupted between Britain and France and which had been by no means settled. The outcome of this conflict was vital to the economic development of both powers. If Britain had not ultimately succeeded in holding on to and expanding her overseas markets, particularly in the New World, her great economic advance during the eighteenth century would have been severely curtailed. Yet British ministers were far slower to realise the economic significance of the mid-century conflicts than public opinion, some members of parliament, government agents in the colonies and the colonists themselves. They similarly failed to grasp the extent of British success and French desperation in the naval struggle at the close of the Austrian Succession War. The Pelhamite ministry's priorities remained the containment of France in Europe, the defence of the British Isles and strategically sensitive areas on the Continent. Trade and colonisation could be left to individual initiative. In their eyes Louisbourg was not so much exchanged for Madras as for the Austrian Netherlands. Certainly they had grounds enough to worry about Britain's future role in Europe, given France's military successes and the disarray of the alliances used by Britain to contain her. The Dutch had proved useless, while the relationship with Austria had become increasingly strained. Something new would have to be worked out to replace or

★The duke of Savoy was now beginning to be generally known by his correct title of king of Sardinia. Although he had been promised Piacenza as well in 1743, his gains in 1748 were limited to more of Milan.

complement the moribund Grand Alliance to defend Britain, the Netherlands and Hanover.

France was in a similar paradoxical positon. Saxe's military victories had overshadowed those of Frederick the Great, while the anti-French coalition had achieved none of the success of previous ones and had ended the war in a shambles. At Aix-la-Chapelle an Austrian minister had declared: 'France has achieved her great aim, the humiliation of the house of Austria.' The truncated state of the Habsburg monarchy seemed to confirm this. Yet France had no tangible territorial gains from the war and puzzled Parisians coined the phrase, 'bête comme la paix' – 'stupid as the peace'. What had begun as a bid for hegemony in western Europe in the style of Louis XIV had proved beyond French resources, while even the later more modest attempt at expansion had had to be abandoned because of the collapse of trade and finances. The objectives of French foreign policy needed to be re-examined, particularly as her own alliances with Spain and Prussia were unsettled. With decisive leadership and realistic objectives, France could look forward to future success. Although less powerful than in the late seventeenth century, France was still the leading military power and had the potential to match Britain outside Europe.

For Austria the peace was little short of humiliating. Although Maria Theresa's succession had been confirmed and the bulk of her possessions preserved, three more years of war had led to losses in Italy as well as Silesia. Desperation for subsidies had reduced the Empress to a dependant of Britain. On being told the peace terms by the British minister in Vienna, she had exclaimed: '...Why am I always to be excluded from transacting my own business.' Austria therefore needed to regain control of her own policies, if she were to act as a great power. To achieve this a thoroughgoing reform of the army and of the administration and finances in Austria and Bohemia was undertaken in the late 1740s and early 1750s. Copying the reforms which had proved so effective in Prussia under Frederick William I, Maria Theresa's ministers tried to transform her monarchy into a more centralised and stronger state. Externally, the aims of the new Austria were to be concentrated on recovering Silesia and regaining a dominant position in Germany. The differences with Spain and even with France were to fade into the background. Although Maria Theresa's family had regained the Imperial crown, which seemed worth having because of the prestige which was still felt to go with it, the 'German mission' of defending the Rhine barrier against France and regaining lands lost to her, was finally abandoned.

By his conquest of Silesia Frederick the Great increased the resources and population of Prussia by almost a half. He spent the years after the peace of Dresden (1745) trying to assimilate the new province and expand his army and revenues. The army was his chief asset. Officered by the nobility, the *Junkers*, its manpower largely recruited from outside the country and from the least productive elements of Prussian society, it was trained to perfection and soon became the model for other European armies. Ultimately, control of Silesia and Frederick's own survival rested on these troops. International treaties might guarantee his conquest to him, but it could be snatched away just as cynically as he had seized it: his annexation had now set the pattern for international morality. However, Frederick himself judged the European situation was not ripe for further Prussian expansion; he also laboured under the disadvantage that no one really trusted him. But all had to take notice of Prussia which had become Austria's equal in Germany and a major force in European diplomacy through his political astuteness and military ability. Straddled across the north-German plain between the Oder and Elbe, Prussia's consent would be needed for any changes in Poland and Germany. The future of Germany, however, should not be seen solely in terms of Austro-Prussian rivalry. France still had plenty of scope, if she wanted, to follow her traditional policy of trying to make the German states, including Prussia herself, her satellites. Britain was also involved in German politics because of Hanover which had to be protected from French retaliation or Prussian expansion. Finally, German affairs were of increasing concern to Russia.

Russia had kept in the wings throughout the past war, at times apparently about to intervene on the Austro-British side but then drawing back because of her domestic troubles. Her expansionism and solidarity with Austria, so evident in the 1730s, had collapsed amidst the chaos following Anna's death (1740). In 1741 a Swedish attack on Russia had coincided with the successful coup against the child Tsar Ivan VI by Peter the Great's daughter, Elizabeth, who had Franco-Swedish support. Once on the throne, however, the new Tsaritsa had turned against her foreign friends and at the treaty of Åbo (1743) the over-sanguine Swedes were forced to yield more of Finland to act as a protective shield round St Petersburg. Elizabeth now moved gradually under the influence of her chancellor, Bestuzhev, to a pro-Austrian and British stance. Although Frederick II had not challenged Russian influence in Poland, his temporary occupation of Augustus of Poland's Saxon electorate (1745) was deeply resented. Prussia's emergence as a strong power in north Germany might challenge Russia's control of the eastern Baltic and would prove a barrier to further expansion westwards.

In 1746 Russia renewed her alliance with Austria, and this now had a decidedly anti-Prussian bent. Both feared future aggression from Frederick. While promising each other mutual help against attack from any power in the future, Elizabeth also in effect agreed, in a secret article, to help Maria Theresa regain Silesia if Prussia invaded either Saxony or Austria. This alliance of the two Empresses formed the basis of a growing determination by both powers to destroy Frederick himself. Complementary to it in Bestuzhev's system, was an alliance concluded with Britain in December 1747, one which George II's Hanoverian ministers had actively encouraged to protect Hanover from possible Prussian attack. In 1747, however, the main purpose in British eyes was to use Russia as a convenient source of mercenaries to save the Dutch from France, and the following January 30,000 Russians set out for the Republic in return for a £500,000 subsidy. The march of the Russians was an added incentive for France to make peace, and in the event they got no further than Poland. The menace of Russia in the background had made both Prussia and France uneasy during the war: now with Elizabeth securely in power, Russia was to play a far more telling, and often decisive, role in Europe.

THE UNOFFICIAL ANGLO-FRENCH WAR IN AMERICA, 1748–1755

Europe enjoyed less than a decade of peace after the treaty of Aix-la-Chapelle before being plunged into another general conflict – the Seven Years War – the last war before the wars of the French Revolution to involve all the major powers. Although the peace was little more than a truce between Britain and France, particularly in the colonies, in a similar way Austria and Prussia were unreconciled. Yet the new conflict was more than a continuation of the earlier one, especially with the intervention of Russia. The European system was now becoming one of five major states with competing interests. No power dominated as France had in the 1730s or Britain in the years after Utrecht. The rise of Prussia and the re-entry of Russia as a major protagonist forced statesmen to consider central and east European issues far more, and much of the diplomatic initiative after 1748 was to be taken by Austria and Russia. On the other hand, Spain and the Dutch Republic had now clearly left the ranks of the major powers and were to show a justifiable passivity.

Ferdinand VI of Spain was uninterested in foreign affairs; his minister, Carvajal, intended to use *détentes* with Portugal, Britain and Austria to give Spain the chance to concentrate on her domestic and colonial economy and become independent of both Britain and France. He settled differences with Austria in Italy (treaty of Aranjuez, 1752) and worked for a compromise with Britain. No more was said about Minorca and Gibraltar, and Carvajal hoped that the withdrawal of the *guarda-costas* and buying out the South Sea Company's rights for £100,000 in 1750, together with the confirmation of trading concessions with European Spain, would persuade the British to end their smuggling with Spanish America. The attitude of the new Spanish King was very similar to that of the Dutch, who also wanted to concentrate on their commercial interests and ignore European quarrels. Their army was too run down to contemplate war and it was now clear that neither Britain nor Austria could defend the Netherlands. Badly shaken by Saxe's victories, they were determined to conciliate France.

Anglo-French rivalry remained and was apparent to all after 1748, and it was to trigger off the actual renewal of war between the powers. Yet the two governments themselves had no wish for further war within or outside Europe. Louis XV's government still largely drifted without firm direction, but it intended to keep the peace and concentrated, under Maurepas and then (after 1754) Machault, on rebuilding the navy to put it on a par with Britain's. The loss of nearly half the merchant fleet in the last struggle made what public opinion there was non-imperialist and convinced that peace was preferable to war. France was also beset by domestic problems because of the revival of the Jansenist religious controversy and quarrels between the crown and the privileged orders over attempts to reshape the taxation system.

In London the Pelhamite ministry showed more unity of purpose and had a large majority in parliament, but it was equally pacific. While Newcastle largely directed foreign policy, the dominant influence until 1754 was his brother Henry Pelham at the Treasury. In the Walpole tradition Pelham believed war hampered trade, and he wanted to keep the land tax low and avoid adding to the National Debt Consequently, expenditure on the navy and army was cut, and he and parliament firmly opposed further foreign subsidies. Both would have liked to ignore Europe, but Britain could no longer afford to adopt the same detached and balancing attitude of the 1730s. Britain was directly involved in continental affairs because of the overt rivalry with France and the potential French threat to the Southern Netherlands and that of France and Prussia to Hanover. Outside Europe the extent to which the British, as well as the French, government could control events was limited. George II's ministers also had to contend with a volatile public opinion and parliamentary opposition.

British and French interests clashed outside Europe in India, the Caribbean and North America. Although the other areas helped increase the general tension, only North America was to be a major cause of the Seven Years War. The volume of trade with the whole Far East was very small: the monopolistic English East India Company only sent out a score of ships every year. Conflict which developed in southern India between the agents of the French and English companies after 1749 was discouraged from Europe, as neither government considered vital interests at stake.

The Caribbean islands were the most important overseas interest for both powers. Hundreds of ships sailed back and forth across the

Atlantic every year. A fifth of all France's external trade was with the West Indies. Although it made mercantilist sense to seize one another's islands and plantations, both governments showed themselves equally keen to avoid a clash. In effect, conflict in the Caribbean depended on their willingness to commit their navies, and before 1755 neither was prepared to do so. While control of the West Indies would be the most valuable prize in any struggle, it was not itself a motive for the coming war.

In North America, by contrast, a direct confrontation between the colonists was to drag their unwilling home governments into war. There the population of the English colonies had leapt sevenfold over the past half-century to about 2 million. Hungry for new land to settle, the colonists pressed relentlessly westwards. Unfortunately, as they crossed the Allegheny Mountains towards the Great Lakes they came up against the French. Although there were probably only 60,000 Europeans in French Canada and even less in the newer colony of Louisiana, they were more rigidly controlled by their governors. The latter were working to link together the two colonies with a chain of fortresses and alliances with Red Indian tribes to stem the westward tide of the British. They had decided advantages in the struggle with the British colonists which came to a head in the 1750s. The Indians preferred to co-operate with the French Canadians, who were largely trappers and hunters, rather than with the British who wanted their land to farm. The French had an efficient and centralised military organisation unlike the squabbling British colonists, and Louis XV's government was willing to send out substantial numbers of regular troops. Versailles recognised that the population of Canada was too small to defend itself, and that a large garrison was needed, because the British navy could always cut off the supply of reinforcements in wartime. Although Canada with its skins and furs was of marginal economic importance compared with the Newfoundland fishing banks, or the tropical agriculture of Louisiana and the West Indies, France looked on the defence of its oldest colony as a matter of national prestige and was determined not to leave the colonists in the lurch. None the less, although Louis's agents in Canada were pursuing a forward policy and the number of French troops there was being steadily increased, Louis XV himself continued to try to conciliate Britain. British naval supremacy made France's position a very precarious one, and to the end she put up with continual provocation in order to avoid outright war. It was the British who abandoned conciliation first.

The American colonies were of considerable economic value for Britain. The southern ones exported semi-tropical goods like tobacco and cotton, while the north was being seen as an alternative to the Baltic for naval stores. Both absorbed British exports and supplied the West Indies with essentials. None the less, George II's ministers in London flinched from a conflict in America. It was really despite themselves – because of lack of a firm and properly thought-out central policy and weak control of their colonists – that they became enmeshed in a colonial struggle which led to a direct Anglo-French war. Unlike in India neither government could simply instruct its trading company to stop fighting. In North America large groups of British and French were directly involved in what they believed was a life-and-death struggle. Once the British colonists came to blows with what proved a far more formidable French military power, the Pelhamite government could not abandon them, subject as it was to pressure from within parliament and outside.

The centre of the American conflict was in the northernmost reaches of the Ohio valley. There, near modern Pittsburgh, the French built Fort Duquesne in 1753 in a determined effort to block further migration westwards by the British colonists. This led to skirmishes with those from Virginia in 1753–54 in which the French and their Indian allies scored easy victories. These showed that only regular British troops could challenge the French and deny them control of all the lands stretching south as far as Georgia and Louisiana. The British government, no more imperialist than Versailles and as keen on peace and retrenchment, had to decide whether to abandon its tacit understanding with the French to prevent an escalation into open warfare.

In March 1754 the resolutely pacific Henry Pelham died: the Duke of Newcastle, who retained control of foreign policy, now headed the ministry. He proved timid in the face of rising demands for concrete help for the colonists and a tougher stand against France. These came from George II and his son, the commander-in-chief Cumberland, and from ambitious politicians such as Pitt and Henry Fox. Although political opportunism was involved, there was also genuine awareness of the real issues of empire and trade and concern that France's greater natural resources and home population would prove decisive unless Britain took immediate advantage of her naval supremacy. Responding to this pressure, Newcastle was drawn relentlessly into actions which made it impossible to back down.

Early in 1755 British regulars were shipped to America under Braddock to counter the steady build-up of French troops and with orders to seize French forts in the Ohio valley. The French response was to try to augment their Canadian garrison. Fearing that the French with a standing army ten times that of Britain would soon achieve total military supremacy, the British government ordered Boscawen and his squadron to prevent ships carrying French reinforcements from entering the St Lawrence. Evidently George II's government hoped for a brief colonial war in which Canada would be blockaded, Braddock take the Ohio forts and Versailles be forced to agree to a diplomatic settlement. Unfortunately, most of the French troopships gave Boscawen the slip in June 1755, while the next month Brad-dock's force was wiped out near Fort Duquesne. Versailles still wanted to compromise: its efforts at naval rebuilding were incomplete, although it had some 70 ships as against possibly 100 comparable British vessels. But Newcastle's ministry kept up the pressure because of the inevitable demands from public opinion and their parliamentary critics. To intimidate France by ruining her overseas trade, Newcastle ordered the seizure of French merchantmen. Although 300 ships had been captured by the end of 1755, the French did not retaliate but asked for compensation. Britain refused and formally declared war in May 1756 to the delight of the colonists and the war party in London.

THE DIPLOMATIC REVOLUTION

The rapid deterioration in Anglo-French relations in 1755 was the catalyst for a realignment of the European powers and a war crisis on the Continent. This could only happen, however, because of actual differences among these powers, particularly the implacable hatred of Austria and Russia for Prussia. This factor, together with Britain's continuing search for European allies to protect Hanover and the Southern Netherlands, changed the alliance system, which had survived the Austrian Succession War in a tattered form, into an essentially different one. This change was radical enough to have been called the 'Diplomatic Revolution'.

In the making of this revolution France played a largely passive role and in the process the threat of French hegemony, still a real menace in the 1730s and 1740s, became one which really worried only the British. Louis XV and his mistress, Madame de Pompadour, clearly wanted peace, but they placed their confidence in no particular minister so that diplomacy in practice lacked purpose. Their most important alliance of recent years, the Family Compact with Spain, had collapsed. The one with Prussia survived rather tenuously, Berlin instead of Munich becoming the focus of Bourbon influence in Germany. Contacts were also maintained with other German, the Scandinavian and Turkish courts, but no conscious attempt was made to weld this network of relationships into a strong pro-French bloc, which could be used against Austria or Britain to preserve peace or allow French expansion. Yet Louis himself devoted a surprising amount of time to diplomacy, directing his own 'king's secret' (*secret du roi*), which bypassed the secretary of state for foreign affairs and official channels. Secret diplomacy conducted by the ruler had been a recurrent theme from the Regent Orleans's time. To some extent this was an effect of the increasing importance of ministers and the decline in that of the monarch in the formulation of policy since the last years of Louis XIV's reign. In Louis XV's case it had really begun from 1743 when he started to discuss foreign policy privately with his cousin, Prince Conti. He hoped to have him elected next king of Poland and, in secret, instructed French diplomatic agents to further this. By 1752 his ambassador at Warsaw, Broglie, was at the centre of a web of correspondence between Louis and his diplomats. By now the aims of the 'king's secret' had gone beyond Conti's candidature to resurrecting the seventeenth century eastern barrier of Sweden, Poland and Turkey to check Russia as well as Austria. Its aims were not incompatible with France's real interests, given Russia's leanings to Britain and Austria since 1746. It might therefore have been more sensible to pursue it openly and vigorously. Instead France abdicated her diplomatic leadership of Europe, confined herself to royal subterfuge and had to respond to initiatives from elsewhere.

France's principal ally, Prussia, also played a passive role. A great part of Frederick II's energy was absorbed by internal reform after 1748. He still thought about further expansion, in Mecklenburg, Saxony and West Prussia, but he recognised he would have to wait for another chaotic situation like that of 1740. His widely scattered territories made Frederick, as he was very well aware, highly vulnerable to attack. Faced with the permanent hostility of Austria and the growing hatred of the Russian Tsaritsa Elizabeth, he needed both the security of the connection with France and of his own army ready to strike fast and hard: by 1756 he would have over 140,000 men backed by 13 million thalers in his war chest. Largely isolated, widely distrusted by the other powers and with a poorly informed diplomatic service, Frederick would be one for military rather than diplomatic initiatives. The initiative in Europe after the Austrian Succession War was to be taken by the Austrian, Russian and British allies.

Maria Theresa's reforms had impressive results: by 1756 she had approaching 200,000 men under arms throughout the monarchy, and for the first time Austria's dependence on others seemed to have been substantially reduced. Only events would show, however, whether the army would live up to expectations and how well the monarchy could support it. While the reforms were being carried through peace was essential, and the time clearly had to be spent reappraising Austria's external policies after the bitter experience of the last war. An attempt to rethink Habsburg diplomatic objectives was made at famous meetings of the privy council or conference in March and April 1749 by the young Count Kaunitz, the man largely responsible for the monarchy's foreign policy over the next half-century.

A typical product of the eighteenth-century Enlightenment, Kaunitz tried to approach diplomacy as an exact science, patiently calculating every move and its effects. As yet, however, he was a very junior member of the conference, which agreed at these meetings that Prussia had now become a greater menace than even France and the Turks. There was general agreement with Kaunitz's own description of Frederick II as their 'greatest, most dangerous and most irreconcilable enemy' and his insistence that the recovery of Silesia should be their chief aim. However, the other ministers saw no way that French hostility could be ended. Fearing further French attack and nervous of French strength, they concluded the old association with the Maritime Powers had to be kept up despite its drawbacks. Kaunitz accepted they had to keep Britain friendly, or at least neutral, but emphasised that the British would never help against Frederick and claimed they were neither the 'guardian of the dynasty' nor Austria's 'natural ally': only Russia could be this because of their common Turkish enemy. He therefore suggested the Habsburgs should base their policies on Russian friendship and try to accommodate with France, weaning her away from Frederick. Louis XV's neutrality and even his active alliance against Prussia should be bought by offers of territory in the Southern Netherlands or Italy for his son-in-law, Don Philip, the new Duke of Parma.

This bold plan appealed to Maria Theresa herself: it offered her the means to recover Silesia. But as her immediate concern had to be peace, she decided for the present to hold to the alliance with Britain as well as with Russia: to renounce the former prematurely would leave Austria dangerously isolated and lacking the subsidies she and Russia would need if war came. None the less, Maria Theresa was willing to test out his ideas and, despite her husband Francis Stephen's hostility towards France because of his loss of Lorraine, she tried to appease Louis XV and sent Kaunitz himself to Versailles as minister in 1750. Here he soon discovered the King's liking for secret diplomacy and desire for peace, but his mission proved a failure: the court and most ministers were hostile and wanted to retain the link with Prussia. When he was recalled to direct the Empress's foreign policy as chancellor from 1753, he accepted he would have to shelve his plan and be patient, although he seems to have become rather pessimistic about the chances of success. However, over the following two years his patience was rewarded, because the worsening relations between Britain and France in America and the obvious danger of war from 1755 allowed a dramatic change in the existing alliance systems.

The real, but unwitting, instigator of the change was not Kaunitz who wanted it, but the Duke of Newcastle, who did not. Much against his will Newcastle, whose interests lay in Europe not outside, was being dragged into a colonial conflict with France. Although he did not want war with her, he believed this to be inevitable, and in the years after Aix-la-Chapelle he worked continuously to find continental allies against France and Prussia. He realised Britain's vulnerability to a direct attack from France – the success of the Young

Pretender in 1745 was a dreadful warning of what a regular French force could do – and the need to defend the Austrian Netherlands and Hanover, where Britain had direct interests. Both areas could be occupied by France and held hostage to force the return of any gains made in a colonial war. Although the Southern Netherlands were clearly the most vulnerable and important because of their proximity, Hanover was not without economic or strategic value. However, the main factor here was George II's personal interest. The King and his Hanoverian ministers feared a Prussian as much as a French attack, either for Frederick's own gain or to help his French ally. They were convinced that only Russian power could restrain him, and from 1748 they had urged Newcastle to pay Elizabeth to station forces on Prussia's borders to intimidate Frederick. But Elizabeth's price was too high, and while Henry Pelham lived it would not be paid. Given the financial constraints on Newcastle's policy and Prussia's hostility to tentative British moves in her direction and her clear preference for friendship with France, he had to look for most of the years after 1748 towards the powers where tradition and common interest could be expected to have most appeal, that is to the 'Old System' of the Dutch and Austria, reinforced by some German states and, perhaps, Russia. This in any case fitted in with the Duke's own preferences.

Unfortunately the 'Old System' was almost played out. Newcastle mistook the Dutch for the power they had been fifty years before, as well as ignoring their desperate wish for neutrality. Similarly, he had no idea that Maria Theresa was feeling her way towards abandoning the British alliance, and he tried in a rather ham-fisted way from 1749 to bribe the German electors to elect her son Joseph as king of the Romans, which would allow him automatically to become emperor at his father's death. Newcastle hoped at the same time to recruit the electors for a coalition against France and Prussia. But by 1752 he had to abandon the scheme because Henry Pelham refused to let him meet the soaring costs.

Maria Theresa herself had not liked the scheme as it smacked of outside interference in the Empire. When Kaunitz became chancellor (1753) he was willing to maintain good relations with Britain, believing that friendship was of some value. But he was determined this must not come in the way of a future accommodation with France. He also intended that the connection with Britain should cater for Austria's needs against Prussia rather than Britain's against France: Austria would no longer serve essentially British interests by defending the Southern Netherlands and acting as a diversion against France. However, he shared George II and his Hanoverians' concern over the Prussian danger to Hanover, and he co-operated tacitly with them in pressing Newcastle to try once more for a subsidy treaty with Russia to curb Frederick and to protect Hanover and Austria from Prussia and France. But the Russians continued to ask too much, and these negotiations dragged on inconclusively from 1753 to 1755.

The relations between the powers began to take more definite shape in 1755, and the period of indecision after 1748 came to an end. The imminent outbreak of war between Britain and France forced the other powers to decide what they would do. Having resolved to act firmly in America by the dispatch of Braddock and Boscawen (see pp. 180–81), the British were desperate for definite continental support in case France compensated for her weakness at sea by invading the Southern Netherlands and Hanover, or by asking Prussia to attack the latter for her. Both areas might be used as bargaining counters or even bases for invading Britain herself.

British appeals to Austria faced Kaunitz with both a dangerous situation and an opportunity. Austria might all too easily be drawn into a war to protect Britain and revert to the dependent relationship of the 1740s. Kaunitz's plans for a shake-up of the European alliance systems and a coalition against Frederick would be stillborn. He therefore refused even to defend Austria's own province of the Southern Netherlands, insisting it was an Anglo-Dutch problem – as it was – and urged Britain to make arrangements herself to protect it and Hanover by subsidy treaties with the German states and Russia. At the same time he was determined Austria herself should not go to war with France who posed no threat to her now, but instead should accommodate with Louis XV and try eventually to persuade him to co-operate against Prussia. However, while Louis could be expected to welcome accommodation and the neutralisation of Austria, he would be even less likely than Britain to countenance or help an attack on Prussia to regain Silesia. Kaunitz had set himself an apparently impossible task, but he was convinced it was essential: although he could depend on Russian support, since Elizabeth was growing increasingly hostile to Frederick, he felt French help as well would be necessary to destroy him.

In the Austrian conference in June 1755 Kaunitz proposed a careful approach, so as not to frighten off the French, by first offering them Austrian neutrality during the coming Anglo-French War. Austria should then try to persuade France to join an alliance with her, Russia and the other Bourbon monarchies. The proposal was to be larded with offers to support Conti's election in Poland, the cession of Luxemburg to Don Philip in return for Parma and agreement to France's garrisoning Ostend and Nieuport during war with Britain. Silesia was not to be mentioned yet. By late August 1755 Kaunitz could instruct the young Austrian minister in Versailles, Starhemberg, to exploit Louis's weakness for secret diplomacy by trying an unofficial approach. Starhemberg was to do so through Madame de Pompadour, whom Kaunitz had cultivated during his own embassy.

Louis responded: he was personally attracted to agreement with the other major Catholic power and admired Maria Theresa. At the same time he disliked Protestant Prussia's agnostic ruler, who had personally affronted him by assuming he was his equal and by ill-advised remarks about his mistress. A simple *rapprochement* would bring France herself clear advantages: the standing threat from the Habsburgs in the Netherlands, Germany and Italy would be lifted and Britain robbed of her traditional ally and the cornerstone of all the previous anti-Bourbon coalitions. Agreement seemed to offer what Louis wanted most: peace in Europe. Even so, Starhemberg's talks during the autumn with a protégé of Madame de Pompadour, the Abbé de Bernis, achieved little. Louis was probably too timid to push for agreement against the known anti-Austrian feelings of almost all his ministers, who had been kept out of the negotiations. Moreover, there was an understandable nervousness about falling between two stools and offending Frederick just as war seemed about to break out between Britain and France. But for mistakes made by Britain and by Prussia the Franco-Austrian *rapprochement* might never have happened.

By summer 1755 it was clear in London that Austria would neither defend her own Southern Netherlands nor help Britain against France. All efforts to raise a sizeable mercenary army from the German states had also failed. Unaware of Starhemberg's talks, Newcastle expected Austria would eventually return to the fold but realised he had to take other immediate measures. He pursued vigorously the subsidy negotiations with Russia and, for the first time, began a serious attempt to gain Frederick. Both powers responded, especially Russia and her importance in the background to the Seven Years War was crucial. Bestuzhev, the Tsaritsa Elizabeth's chancellor, intended both to destroy Prussia and contain France. Already enjoying close relations with Austria, he wanted similar ones with Britain. He saw her value essentially as a provider of subsidies and as a power sharing the same hostility he felt towards France as well as towards Prussia. In fact, relations between Russia and France had been very poor since Aix-la-Chapelle, when Louis had insisted on excluding Russia from the peace negotiations. Their respective ministers had competed at Stockholm, Warsaw and Constantinople, and one purpose of the 'king's secret', according to Broglie, was to push Russia back 'into her vast wastes'. Yet there was a pro-French party in the St Petersburg court led by Bestuzhev's enemy, the vice-chancellor Vorontsov, while the Tsaritsa had some affection for France. What all parties at St Petersburg agreed on was hostility towards Prussia.

Elizabeth herself had been nettled by the reports of Frederick's tactless jokes about her weakness for strong drink and strong men. Bestuzhev was obsessed by loathing for Prussia: he believed she had assumed the role played by Sweden in the seventeenth century and, backed by French power, was barring Russia from her rightful position of hegemony in eastern Europe. He wanted to partition Prussia with Austrian and Saxon–Polish help and reduce the rump state to the Russian satellite she had been under Peter the Great. Silesia would be returned to Austria and East Prussia ceded to Poland, who would give Russia Courland and all lands east of the Dvina and Dnieper. This fitted in well with Kaunitz's own plans, but until 1755 he had tried to restrain Bestuzhev. Aware of both Austrian and Russian financial weakness, he was convinced they must first secure French help and subsidies or at least neutrality. As a second best they would have to be sure of British help. Bestuzhev, with his fear of France, preferred the latter and until 1755 had hoped for British money to maintain a permanent force for use against Prussia.

By summer 1755 Bestuzhev's hopes appeared to have been realised. A harassed British government, faced by the prospect of the colonial and naval struggle spreading to Europe and feeling abandoned by Austria, accepted it must pay what Newcastle called Russia's 'very monstrous' price. In September 1755 a convention was agreed – it was never in fact ratified – promising mutual help in case of attack and providing for an annual British subsidy of £100,000 for the upkeep of 50 Russian galleys and 50,000 troops in Livonia. If these troops were actually deployed to help George II, a further £40,000 a year would be paid. Bestuzhev was to receive £10,000 for himself. However, while he intended the agreement to be the first step towards attacking Prussia, the British considered it in purely defensive terms: if France or Prussia attacked Hanover the Russians would come to the aid of the electorate.

The British not only intended that their convention with Russia should deter Frederick from attacking Hanover but also, equally important, that it should frighten him into agreement with Britain. During the summer of 1755 Newcastle had become convinced the latter was essential because of Austria's refusal to help: agreement with Frederick would safeguard Hanover and Germany and might allow Britain to limit the war with France to one overseas. It would also make it unnecessary to activate the additional and expensive clause of the Anglo-Russian convention, one which was bound to evoke strong criticism from those in parliament who were against foreign subsidies. This reasoning of course ignored Russia's designs against Prussia and assumed, as usual, that European politics could be shaped to suit Britain's needs.

Frederick responded to the Anglo-Russian agreement precisely as Newcastle had hoped. Throughout the early 1750s the Prussian King had considered friendship with France essential and natural. Believing that permanent Bourbon–Habsburg rivalry meant he could always depend on her and that the French alliance would always be there for the taking, he had written in his *Political Testament* in 1752: 'Silesia and Lorraine are two sisters, Prussia having married the elder and France the younger. This marriage forces them to pursue the same policy.' Consequently, he had never seriously considered agreement with Britain, and in fact relations had been very bad with George II, exacerbated by a series of minor, but acrimonious, disputes. The Hanoverian Elector-King had often seemed a greater threat to Frederick in the Empire than Austria, and for his part George and his Hanoverian ministers were openly hostile. Yet fundamentally the differences between Britain and Prussia amounted to little more than their association with the main enemies of the other, with Austria and Russia and with France.

By 1755 Frederick began to revise his views as he saw Britain and France clashing more fiercely in the colonies. He feared being involved in a war for France's sake and not his own. At the same time he had no doubt that Austria and Russia – together with Saxony, which was now effectively their satellite – were determined to attack him as soon as they could. While confident against Austria, he was haunted by the menace of Russia whose limitless manpower had not been deployed against him in the last war. It also now seemed that the British in their search for help against France and Prussia were being forced into subsidising his enemies. Even if Austria and Russia did not attack him, there was the danger France would drag him into her war with Britain and then into a wider conflict with Britain's Austro-Russian friends. He would have to bear the brunt of the fighting against the latter while France concentrated on her own borders and overseas. All Frederick's fears seemed to be borne out by Britain's negotiations in St Petersburg and her agreement of September 1755. However, Newcastle had already offered him a possible escape route by opening simultaneous negotiations with him.

The British proposed an Anglo-Prussian convention to neutralise Germany: this would safeguard Hanover by removing the direct threat from Prussia and France and might possibly preserve peace on the Continent. (Although the rise of Prussia offered Britain a viable alternative to Austria as an ally against France, the Duke of Newcastle still wanted to maintain the traditional relationship with Austria and even hoped eventually to reconcile Prussia to it.) For his part Frederick was receptive, as the British treaty offered him a way of weakening the hostile coalition gathering round him. He was also convinced that the Russians in their greed for British gold would follow any lead from London and would abandon their hostility towards him at Newcastle's bidding: he greatly exaggerated the influence of British diplomacy at the Russian court. The Austrians would thereby be rendered isolated and powerless. At the same time he hoped, and perhaps convinced himself, that the French would not be offended by the treaty, since by neutralising only Germany it left Louis XV free to concentrate on the Southern Netherlands or overseas. Consequently, Britain and Prussia signed the convention of Westminster on 16 January 1756. Here they agreed in a very vague formula not to attack one another and to prevent foreign troops entering Germany: this would deter a French attack on Hanover and a Russian one on Prussia. Frederick – in an attempt to please Louis XV – had insisted the Southern Netherlands be specifically excluded and thereby left it open for the French to undertake a war on the Continent at a point where it would still directly threaten the British Isles.

The agreement was not an alliance for mutual help but a makeshift arrangement to ensure the neutrality of Germany and avoid the war there which both parties feared. Neither expected it to have the consequences it did. George II himself considered it just another convention to safeguard his electorate, similar to those made with Prussia in the last war. Newcastle, thinking wholly of the French threat and totally blind to the importance of Austro-Prussian hostility, deluded himself into believing Frederick could soon be drawn into a system with Austria and Russia to contain France. He even told the Austrians that they were now safe enough in Germany to send troops to defend the Southern Netherlands. Inevitably this cut no ice in Vienna, where the convention of Westminster was seen as undermining its plans for action against Prussia. In fact, the effects in France and Russia were to further these plans.

Frederick's bland assumption, or hope, that the French would not take offence was quickly and painfully disappointed. Versailles was enraged: the parvenu Prussian King, who had deserted France twice in the last war, was once again showing his bad faith by abandoning her when war with Britain was breaking out and even dictating to Louis where he could wage war by neutralising Germany. On 4 February 1756, Louis's council, without even considering the advantages of a neutralised Germany, decided angrily not to renew their alliance with Prussia, which was due to expire in the spring. As France was now isolated in Europe, the secret, and so far fruitless, talks with the Austrians were taken up seriously and openly by Versailles. In Kaunitz's words, the Anglo-Prussian convention 'was the decisive event in the salvation of Austria'. Yet the Austrian chancellor proceeded warily: he had no intention of becoming involved in the Anglo-French War and also realised France might be frightened off if he suggested military co-operation against Prussia. However, Louis XV wanted to punish Frederick publicly and saw the immediate advantages of a treaty with Austria, and on 1 May 1756 France and Austria signed a defensive alliance, known as the First treaty of Versailles. Louis XV and Maria Theresa promised each other 24,000 men in case of attack. Although the Anglo-French War, which finally broke out officially the same month, was specifically excluded, Maria Theresa promised her neutrality and to help Louis actively if an ally of Britain attacked France.

The Franco-Austrian alliance marks the real 'Diplomatic Revolution': it ended the centuries-old enmity between the French and Austrian ruling families and announced their breach with their former allies. As it stood, the alliance served French interests well and was similar to the *rapprochement* wanted by Fleury in the 1730s, since the other Bourbon powers, Spain, Naples and Parma, were to be invited to join. It had an immediate effect in The Hague, where it reinforced Dutch determination to keep out of the Anglo-French War. On 14 June in return for a Dutch promise of neutrality in the war with Britain, Louis XV himself promised not to invade the Southern Netherlands. The Austro-French alliance had therefore destroyed the 'Old System' of the Grand Alliance in its Anglo-Dutch as well as Anglo-Austrian dimension. France seemed sure of continental peace and of being able to concentrate her resources overseas. The dramatic success of her navy in seizing Minorca from Britain in June 1756 appeared to promise a far more evenly matched maritime conflict than before. France therefore had every reason to congratulate herself over the new alliance, and not for one moment did Louis and his ministers fear that its mutual assistance clauses would be invoked: Frederick would surely not dare attack Austria and risk war with France.

The alliance brought the Austrians similar immediate tangible gains. At a stroke the historic threat from France in Italy and Germany as well as through her connection with the Turks had been removed, while the recent Franco–Prussian alliance, which had come close to ruining the monarchy in the last war, had been broken up. Moreover, the French had promised support if Frederick attacked Austria. Kaunitz was therefore some way towards his ultimate goal of a European coalition against Prussia. However, over the coming months Versailles resisted efforts to persuade them to join an anti-Prussian coalition with Austria and Russia, despite an offer of the Southern Netherlands for Don Philip of Parma if Maria Theresa regained Silesia. While Louis himself might have agreed, his ministers still hoped to balance between the two German powers while concentrating outside Europe against Britain. Kaunitz, however, was prepared to be patient. He seems to have hoped Frederick himself would blunder and allow Austria to secure the more far-reaching alliance with France Kaunitz needed if the planned war of revenge was to take place. His minister at Versailles, Starhemberg, wrote: 'We shall succeed sooner or later in our great scheme and perhaps the King of Prussia himself will be our most effective helper.' Frederick's fears and actions were in fact to do Austria's work for her.

The Prussian King had badly miscalculated on the effects of his convention with Britain, not only on France but also on Russia. The news of the Anglo-Prussian convention of Westminster produced as much anger in St Petersburg as at Versailles: Britain had betrayed Russia by associating with her chief enemy and intended victim. Russia's own recent convention with Britain was now as good as dead: Elizabeth had no intention of letting George II buy her troops to use against any power but Prussia. As the Tsaritsa was also ready to restore relations with France, the influence of the pro-British Bestuzhev collapsed. His enemy, the equally anti-Prussian and pro-Austrian but also pro-French Vorontsov, now came to the fore.

In March 1756 a special Russian Imperial council was set up to plan and execute war against Prussia with Austrian, and possibly French, help. The army, 330,000 strong, began to mobilise and the Austrians were encouraged to mobilise as well. But Kaunitz applied the brakes, for the same reason as before: the two powers' financial weakness made French subsidies and the support of a third army against Frederick essential, and, as yet, they did not have this active French support. During summer 1756 he managed to persuade Elizabeth to delay attacking Frederick till early the next year.

Frederick only slowly realised that this attack was to be delayed. During the spring and summer Russian troops had massed in the Baltic provinces, while in July Austrian troops had also been concentrated in Bohemia, either to prevent a Prussian surprise attack or to goad Frederick into one. His signature of the convention with Britain had produced an alarming sequence of events which he could never have imagined: he had lost his alliance with France, Russian hostility had been increased and his only friend was Britain, a non-continental power, with which he had concluded no formal alliance. Over him loomed the threat of an Austro-Russian attack, which France seemed willing to condone, although not, as yet, to help. His diplomatic efforts had rebounded on him and only desperate measures seemed to offer a chance of escape. Henceforth military considerations tended to be uppermost in his mind.

By as early as mid-June Frederick was convinced he would be attacked by Austria and Russian in the spring of the following year, and he therefore decided to strike first. He was probably psychologically incapable of patiently riding out the crisis and preferred to act instead. None the less, he waited till late August before pouring his troops into Saxony, which he considered an Austro-Russian dependency and a probable base for an attack on him as well as the key to Bohemia. The delay until late summer meant that neither Russia nor France could help Saxony or Austria that year. Rapid Prussian victories might well break up the coalition against him and actively discourage France from honouring her defensive alliance with Austria. In fact, however, his action was to push Louis XV solidly behind Maria Theresa, particularly as the French King's son was married to a Saxon princess. France would probably not have made this decisive break with her past but for Frederick's invasion of Saxony. Together with the other continental states the French court was outraged by this latest piece of Prussian aggression.

The invasion enlarged the coalition against Prussia by ensuring France would participate, a step which Kaunitz had felt essential for success and himself had failed to achieve. On the other hand the Austro-Russian union was already in being and would have attacked Frederick sooner or later with or without French help. War at some date was inevitable. The invasion of Saxony was a gamble which could have ruined Prussia, but it was one Frederick had to take if the new Prussia with its control of Silesia were to survive. The more he delayed, the greater the danger his enemies would come closer together and complete their military plans. He had to use his advantages, a full treasury and an army permanently ready for action, to their maximum effect in a short war. His enemies had to be robbed of the chance to match his forces and involve him in a long war. In the event they were to manage both.

THE SEVEN YEARS WAR IN EUROPE, 1756–1763

Frederick II's invasion of Saxony (29 August 1756) had been a victory for military over diplomatic considerations. From a purely military point of view it was a considerable success. The Saxon forces were surrounded and forced to surrender (October 1756) and the Elector of Saxony was permitted to retire to his Polish territories, where he remained until the end of the war. Saxony was treated as a Prussian province throughout the Seven Years War, and suffered increasingly brutal exploitation. The considerable strategic threat of an Austrian invasion through Saxon territory (the Prussian capital, Berlin, was only some 30 miles from the border) had apparently been removed. From a diplomatic point of view, however, Frederick's attack on Saxony was far less successful, since it completed the anti-Prussian coalition Kaunitz wanted. The enmity of Russia and France had previously been one of Frederick's most important securities; the Prussian invasion of Saxony gave the two states a common interest which they would otherwise have lacked and inaugurated a period of political partnership. In the autumn of 1756, the most important component in Kaunitz's intended coalition was his defensive alliance with France (First treaty of Versailles, 1 May 1756). Frederick's aggression not only made this treaty operative: it brought France into the struggle, and was also used by Kaunitz to complete the anti-Prussian coalition. In January 1757 Russia acceded to the First treaty of Versailles and the following month concluded a new, offensive alliance with Austria against Prussia. The Austrian chancellor's skilful diplomacy then produced the Second treaty of Versailles (1 May 1757), an offensive alliance between Austria and France. This decisive agreement transformed France's role in the continental war. There was, however, no formal Russo-French alliance: Russia was united to France only by virtue of their respective treaties with Austria, and this was to prove a significant weakness in Kaunitz's coalition. The anti-Prussian league was completed by the adherence of Sweden (March 1757) and by the dispatch of contingents of soldiers from the Empire.

The military and economic resources of his enemies were considerable and Frederick II appeared to be facing overwhelming odds. In 1756 the strength of the Prussian army was around 143,000 men; Austria alone had some 177,000 men under arms. Kaunitz was never able, however, to use the apparently massive superiority of the anti-Prussian coalition to achieve a decisive victory. The explanation for this is largely to be found in the nature of the coalition, irresistible on paper but grievously weakened in practice by the absence of a unifying common purpose. Sweden's contribution was limited to some desultory manoeuvring in West Pomerania, while the contingents from the Empire were of limited military value. The main burden of the war fell on the three principals, Austria, Russia and France; but at different times their military efforts were reduced by other factors.

The basic problem was that the three allies each saw the war in a different light, and no amount of diplomacy was able to disguise this fundamental weakness. For Austria the war was, and always remained, a struggle to regain Silesia, and Habsburg military operations concentrated on the slow reconquest of this province. The traditionally cautious tone of Austrian military planning made the kind of swift, decisive stroke needed to defeat Frederick all but impossible. For Russia, the Seven Years War came to be primarily a war of territorial expansion in the eastern Baltic. The Russian military machine was, traditionally, cumbersome and slow-moving; its operations were at times hamstrung by deficiencies in the supply system and also by the illness of the Tsaritsa Elizabeth. Since her successor, the Grand Duke Peter (the future Peter III) was fanatically pro-Prussian, his accession would bring an immediate reversal of Russian foreign policy. Consequently, the periodic and serious illnesses of Elizabeth inevitably weakened the Russian war effort against Prussia by encouraging Russian commanders in their innate caution. France, for her part, increasingly regarded the struggle with Britain as more important. Her political and military commitment to the continental war was considerable in its initial stages, as the Second treaty of Versailles pledged French resources on a significant scale to the war in Europe. But France's expectation of an early Prussian defeat proved unfounded, and the steady accumulation of French reverses overseas reduced enthusiasm for the continental war at the French court. The advent of Choiseul to overall power in December 1758 was followed by a considerable reduction in the French commitment to the war in Germany (Third treaty of Versailles, March 1759).

The difficulties caused by the divergent aims and faltering enthusiasm of the principals in the anti-Prussian coalition were increased by the inevitable tensions of wartime co-operation. The fundamental problem was that the Diplomatic Revolution had made temporary partners out of old and sometimes bitter enemies – most notably in the case of France and Russia who were now obliged to sink their traditional rivalry in eastern Europe in the cause of defeating Prussia. These basic antagonisms were never satisfactorily reconciled and the military failures of the coalition caused them to re-emerge. Further tension arose from the difficulties of coalition warfare, which was a novel experience for all the allies. Each state expected its partners to commit their resources to its own distinct objective.

These basic weaknesses were highlighted and exacerbated by the early successes of the Prussian army. Frederick's response in 1757 to the critical situation he faced, as yet without any British help (see p. 196), at the same time as the anti-Prussian coalition was taking shape, was to go on to the offensive against the Austrians. He won a bloody victory at Prague (6 May 1757), where Prussian losses were greater than those suffered by the Austrians, and suffered an equally costly reverse at Kolin (18 June 1757). The autumn of 1757 was, for Frederick, the first crisis of the Seven Years War: the Austrians forced him back into Saxony, the Russians invaded East Prussia and the French advanced on his western flank, having earlier forced the surrender of the Hanoverian army under Cumberland which had been sent to protect George II's electorate from France (convention of Kloster-Seven, 8 September 1757). This desperate situation made Prussia's predicament fully apparent in the first year of the war and forced Frederick to reformulate his strategy. Abandoning his outlying provinces he now fought along interior lines. He pursued a war of mobility, striking first against one foe and then the next, trying to prevent Prussia's enemies combining their armies and thereby exploiting their immense numerical superiority. This was to become Frederick's characteristic strategy during the Seven Years War. It was seen to spectacular effect in the closing months of 1757 when the Prussian King retrieved a desperate situation first by smashing the Franco-Imperialist forces at Rossbach (5 November) and then, after a forced march, winning a remarkable victory over a much larger Austrian army at Leuthen (5 December).

Frederick's victories at Rossbach and Leuthen proved to be of immense significance in the long term. Above all, they encouraged Britain to repudiate the convention of Kloster-Seven and to provide effective support at last for Prussia's struggle for survival. France, discouraged by defeat, seriously contemplated a unilateral peace with Prussia. Austria's defeat at Leuthen had the predictable effect of reinforcing the traditional Habsburg preference for manoeuvre rather than battle. Austria henceforth aimed at exhausting Prussia's resources rather than defeating Frederick outright, a surprisingly defensive strategy in view of her desire to reconquer Silesia. The main burden of the campaigns of 1758 and 1759 was borne by the Russians who inflicted several serious reverses on Frederick (most notably at Kay and Kunersdorf in the late summer of 1759) but never followed these up, in part because of the failure of the Austrians to provide military assistance when this was most needed. As French resolution continued to weaken, Austria was increasingly forced to depend upon her Russian ally. However, the Tsaritsa Elizabeth's designs on East Prussia (which she was intent on annexing or exchanging for some Polish territory) were deeply suspect in Vienna, since the Austrians had no wish to see any strengthening of Russian power in central Europe. Russo-Austrian military co-operation was never wholehearted and Frederick was able to struggle on. Yet his resources were reduced each year, his position grew increasingly desperate and his central task of preventing the Austrians and Russians uniting their forces became more difficult with every campaign. But by the end of 1759 a military stalemate had emerged which saved Prussia from extinction, and Frederick retained his knack of winning the important battles – as in the second half of 1760, when he retrieved an apparently lost position by defeating the Austrians first at Liegnitz (15 August) and then at Torgau (3 November).

These two reverses effectively ended Habsburg hopes of recovering Silesia. The Austrian government, in spite of the administrative reforms of 1749, was simply unable to raise the men and, more especially, the money to defeat Frederick. Vienna henceforth sought peace, and in 1761 set about the further internal reforms that the Seven Years War had shown to be necessary. Austria, however, was unable to conclude a unilateral peace with Prussia. The Russian Tsaritsa, Elizabeth, remained determined to eliminate the Prussian state as a political rival, and this prolonged the war for a further two years. Although Frederick's position remained critical, he was never faced by the major attack which might have proved decisive, and he was finally saved by the death of the Tsaritsa at the beginning of January 1762. The reversal of Russian policy which had long seemed imminent now took effect. The new ruler, Peter III, withdrew from the war and signed a peace treaty with Prussia (May 1762); Sweden followed suit in the same month; and, before long, a Russo-Prussian alliance was taking shape, with the aim of securing for the Tsar his patrimony of Schleswig by a war on Denmark. Peter III in his turn was swept from the throne (July 1762) by a palace coup engineered by his wife Catherine. But Russia's new ruler, though she refused to ratify the alliance negotiated with Prussia, remained neutral for the rest of the war. In the second half of 1762 Frederick was thus able to concentrate entirely on the Austrians, who were soon happy enough to conclude the peace of Hubertusburg (15 February 1763) on the basis of the status quo ante bellum.

Prussia's survival seemed to many contemporaries to border on the miraculous, and certainly there was real heroism in the behaviour of Frederick and his soldiers. The King's own contribution was immense: his inventive strategy, his powers of leadership and his obstinate refusal to admit defeat sustained Prussia in the darkest periods of the Seven Years War. The resilience of the Prussian soldiers and the remarkable ability of the Prussian bureaucracy somehow to raise the money, men and munitions to keep the war going were scarcely less important. But Prussia's survival was also in considerable measure, due to the weakness and divisions within the opposing coalition. The alliances that fought the Seven Years War were tenuous and uncertain affairs, reflecting the considerable shock to the established political order provided by the Diplomatic Revolution of 1756, and this was seen in the military performance of the anti-Prussian coalition. In particular, France and Russia were long-time rivals for influence in eastern Europe, yet the needs of the war against Prussia forced them to attempt to suppress this antagonism in the interests of defeating Frederick. Their success in doing this was, understandably, limited and their partnership disintegrated, amidst mutual recrimination, in 1761.

Anglo-Prussian relations during the Seven Years War were similarly troubled, and their partnership ended acrimoniously in 1762. The convention of Westminster (see p. 189) was in no sense an Anglo-Prussian alliance, and, in the early part of the war, British ministers were uncertain whether to support Frederick. But after Pitt took control in mid 1757 London's commitment to the Prussian cause increased significantly, and a subsidy convention (the only formal link between the two states during the war) was concluded in April 1758. Though no alliance was ever signed, Britain was Prussia's political partner and contributed significantly to Frederick's survival. The annual subsidy of £670,000 for four years, more significant assistance in the shape of a British-financed 'Army of Observation' in western Germany, whose operations protected Frederick's flank for much of the war, and the imperceptible psychological support that came from the knowledge that Prussia was not fighting alone, were all provided by this link with Britain. Anglo-Prussian relations, however, remained harmonious only for the central years of the war, when their mutual dependence and the magic name of Pitt were strong enough to hide the divergent interests of the two states. The 'breach' of 1762, significant chiefly for Frederick's enduring conviction that he had been 'deserted', merely showed that the two powers no longer needed each other. Britain's support for Prussia was essentially opportunistic, a way of protecting Hanover and of tying down French resources on the Continent. The spectacular successes of Britain overseas during the Seven Years War ultimately made the link with Berlin redundant.

THE SEVEN YEARS WAR OVERSEAS

The Seven Years War was perhaps the first truly world war, extending to European possessions overseas in a way that the War of the Austrian Succession had never done. For Britain and France this war was the latest and, as it proved, decisive round in their struggle for colonies and commerce. The war began badly for Britain: a series of disconcerting defeats in 1756–57 exposed the lack of leadership in London and revealed the need for a coherent British strategy. These early French successes in turn contributed to the instability of English politics. It was the second half of 1757 before the Pitt–Newcastle ministry which ultimately won the war, was sufficiently secure to give its full attention to the struggle with France. The dominant voice in this ministry was William Pitt the Elder who emerged, almost overnight, as a great war leader. Pitt's single-minded aim was to destroy French power, and he reinforced this by unusual energy – the real basis of his reputation as an administrator – and complete self-confidence. Imposing his overall view of the war, he was largely content to leave the detailed implementation of his plans to the relevant government departments; Lord Anson at the Admiralty, in particular, deserves a far greater share of the credit than he has traditionally received for Britain's triumphs. Nor was Pitt's overall plan wholly novel: it refined and developed the Admiralty's experience of previous eighteenth-century wars with France. This strategy was essentially that of containing and keeping France occupied in Europe while defeating her overseas.

Britain's strategy during the Seven Years War thus successfully exploited the basic weakness in the French position: even the apparently greater resources at the disposal of Louis XV were not sufficient for France to participate in a continental war against Prussia in Germany and simultaneously fight Britain overseas. Despite this France remained committed to the continental war, albeit to a diminishing extent, and Pitt sought to prolong and strengthen Frederick II's resistance by means of the annual subsidy between 1758 and 1761 and, more significantly, by the British-financed 'Army of Observation' in Germany. This British aid to Prussia also served the vital purpose of protecting Hanover, which might otherwise have been overrun all too easily by the French and used as a bargaining counter in subsequent peace negotiations. An original and effective element in Pitt's strategy was a series of amphibious 'hit-and-run' attacks against the French coastline. These combined operations forced the retention in western France of units which could have been employed in Germany. Although Britain's commitment to the continental war was always comparatively small in financial and material terms, strategically it was decisive since it enabled British resources to be concentrated on the struggle overseas. 'America', as Pitt phrased it, 'had been conquered in Germany' by a strategy that was in full operation from 1758 onwards.

The central element in this strategy was Britain's continuing dominance at sea, a mastery that was confirmed by the decisive British victories in 1759 off Lagos and in Quiberon Bay. England was superior to her rival in the essential foundations of sea power, possessing a larger merchant navy, better dockyard facilities, an adequate and regular supply of naval stores, more trained seamen and better leadership: the decisive advantage which this conferred was made evident by the Seven Years War. For most of the war, the French fleet did not put to sea, unable or perhaps simply unwilling to escape the blockade of France's Atlantic and Mediterranean ports by British squadrons. This acceptance of British naval supremacy, which was as much a matter of poor French morale as of material deficiencies, was strategically decisive. The inability of France to send supplies and reinforcements to her colonies left these possessions exposed to attack by British forces, whose superiority in numbers and in resources was, before long, translated into an impressive series of victories. The years 1758–62 saw spectacular British gains overseas: French colonial power in North America and India was all but destroyed; in West Africa and the Caribbean it was severely undermined.

Pitt concentrated first on North America, where French resistance had already been weakened by a serious quarrel between the military commander and the civilian governor, and by near-famine conditions. The British blockade prevented essential food supplies from France reaching the troops in Canada. Successful amphibious operations led to the capture of Louisbourg (1758) and Quebec (1759), while the conquest of Canada was completed by the taking of Montreal in 1760. In 1758, French trading posts in West Africa (notably in Senegal and on the island of Gorée) were captured in an attempt to disrupt the supply of slaves necessary for the French plantations in the Caribbean. Between 1759 and 1762 a series of successful combined operations destroyed France's position in the West Indies, with the capture of Guadeloupe, Martinique and the 'neutral' islands. (Dominica, St Lucia, St Vincent and Tobago had been declared neutral and not to be settled by the peace of Utrecht in 1713.) In India, the situation was complicated by the existence of a confused, triangular struggle for influence between the English, the French and the native princes, but the final outcome was substantially the same: Clive's somewhat fortuitous and small-scale victory at Plassey (23 June 1757) opened the way to English dominance over the subcontinent, and by the end of the war British power in India was securely established.

The entry of Spain into the Seven Years War in 1762 enabled further additions to be made in this catalogue of British triumphs. Pitt had by this time resigned (in October 1761, following his failure to obtain the support of his ministerial colleagues for a pre-emptive British declaration of war against Spain), but his strategy continued to be employed and, almost inevitably, to bring further triumphs. Spain had remained neutral for much of the war, despite Spanish alarm at the tide of British successes, which appeared to be destroying the colonial equilibrium established by the peace of Utrecht in 1713, and annoyance at the inevitable wartime disputes with England over neutral trade. This neutrality had been carefully cultivated by British diplomacy and protected by Ferdinand's pro-English minister, the expatriate Irishman Richard Wall. The accession of the implacably anti-British Charles III in 1759 gradually undermined this neutrality, and this development was certainly encouraged by the French foreign minister, Choiseul. Eventually, a Franco-Spanish alliance was signed in August 1761 (the Third Family compact, see p. 253) and Spain entered the war on the side of France in January 1762. The results of this intervention were little short of disastrous, as Spain's military and naval weakness immediately became apparent. The successful and well-tried formula of combined operations enabled Britain in 1762 to capture Havana, the focal point of Spain's empire in the Caribbean, and Manila in the Philippines. Spain made no difficulty about acceding to the peace which was now concluded between Britain and France.

Anglo-French peace negotiations had been conducted intermittently since 1759, but the early discussions had broken down because of Pitt's Carthaginian terms and his apparent lust for new conquests. By 1760–61, however, war-weariness was increasing in Britain, aroused by the seemingly high cost of the victories and focused on the commitment to the war in Germany. The accession of a new king, George III, in 1760 and the advent of his minister-favourite Bute, both of whom were intent on courting popularity by giving the nation the peace it desired, provided a fresh impetus to a settlement. The resignation of Pitt in October 1761 removed a considerable barrier to the conclusion of a treaty with France. The terms of the peace of Paris (signed on 10 February 1763) were less severe than Pitt would have imposed, but they were still eloquent testimony to the extent of Britain's victory. France was totally excluded from the mainland of North America (retaining only a precarious foothold in the Newfoundland fisheries by her possession of the islands of St Pierre and Miquelon), while her position in India was effectively destroyed; only in the West Indies did the French avoid substantial territorial losses. The Seven

Years War had thus decisively established Britain's maritime and colonial supremacy, and it had done so mainly at the expense of France. Britain also regained Minorca, which she had lost to France at the beginning of the war. Her gains from Spain were limited to Florida, and the French had compensated Charles III for this by ceding Louisiana to him previously.

CHAPTER SEVEN

Diplomacy and the European states system

Diplomacy, in its broadest sense, is almost as old as human history. The sending of representatives for official purposes was familiar to the ancient and medieval worlds. But resident embassies and continuous political relations – the characteristics of the modern European states system – only really began in the decades around 1500. In the second half of the fifteenth century the Italian city-states started to appoint permanent ambassadors, and in the sixteenth century this emerging network of resident embassies gradually spread outside Italy, until it embraced the majority of western and central European states. These permanent missions were intended not only to promote closer contacts but also to provide the news of political events on which policies could be formulated. Resident embassies were part of the monarchical and bureaucratic states emerging at this time: the more elaborate machinery for foreign affairs corresponded in some ways to that developed for domestic matters. But this trend towards resident embassies throughout Europe was certainly not linear or unbroken. The sixteenth and the first half of the seventeenth centuries saw a disruption in the tentative steps towards permanent diplomatic representation. This was because of the difficulties of Protestant embassies in Catholic countries and vice versa during this period of numerous and widespread religious conflicts. The next decisive developments came about during the long personal rule of Louis XIV (1661–1715).

A network of embassies and minor missions, linking most of the major European capitals and many of the smaller courts as well, was permanently established during the second half of the seventeenth century. Louis XIV took the lead in this exchange of diplomats and the other states (especially the Maritime Powers) quickly followed him, largely to counter French power. Resident diplomacy was thus finally established during the reign of the 'Sun King'. Louis XIV's France, however, did not merely complete the institutional framework of the European states system: it also created the diplomatic traditions and practices of the next two centuries. In diplomacy, as in government and in culture, seventeenth-century France led the way. The greater bureaucratisation evident within France extended into the diplomatic service: Louis XIV's foreign policy depended on his ambassadors much as his internal government depended on his intendants. Until 1815 and even beyond, French methods and techniques in diplomacy were the model for the rest of Europe. While France's diplomatic service was always the most regulated and hierarchical, other states before long acquired more formal, although often different, machinery for formulating policy and conducting negotiations. This dominance of French practices was the result of the military ascendancy of Louis XIV's France, the resources she had to spend on foreign subsidies and financing her diplomatic service, and the parallel successes of her diplomats. As his reign wore on, the amount of business transacted and the range of states involved in negotiations increased at a significant pace. By 1700 regular diplomacy and permanent embassies were established throughout Europe as the twin foundations of the modern states system, and there were to be comparatively few changes before 1815.

The most obvious consequence of this dominance was the gradual replacement of Latin by French as the language of diplomacy. Only in the peace negotiations in 1713–14 did the Habsburgs agree to the use of French in formal agreements. But, thereafter, French rapidly became the first language of most diplomats. It was not only used in international negotiations and in treaties, it was also employed between diplomats and even, occasionally, in formal correspondence between foreign ministers of other states and their ambassadors. French was the official language of Prussian diplomacy from June 1740 onwards, and in the second half of the century Austrian diplomats frequently preferred it to German. British diplomats used it extensively in George I's reign as a common language between them and their German sovereign. In this and other instances broader cultural questions were also involved. The position of French as the universal diplomatic language merely reflected its dominance, in the eighteenth century and beyond, as the principal language of monarchical and aristocratic society.

The growing predominance of French was linked to the emergence of diplomatic corps in the capitals of Europe during the *ancien régime*. Diplomats sent to one particular state were increasingly forming a distinct community, conscious that they were united by several important common interests. In particular, they were coming to realise that any attack on the rights of one ambassador was an affront to the whole diplomatic corps. By the second half of the seventeenth century it was widely accepted that the immunity of a diplomat and his household was necessary in order to ensure permanent relations between states. The only significant exception was at Constantinople,

where until the nineteenth century a foreign envoy was always likely
to be arrested and imprisoned in the Castle of the Seven Towers on
the outbreak of a war between his own state and the Ottoman Empire.
Everywhere else a diplomat could expect to be expelled or allowed
to withdraw unmolested on the declaration of hostilities; Napoleon's
infringement of this principle was widely resented (see p. 304).
Diplomatic immunity, based on the concept of extra-territoriality, was
becoming securely established, though the precise extent of this in-
violability was everywhere a matter of interpretation and dispute.
Debts contracted by diplomats were the most frequent source of
such difficulties. In a similar way, it was now generally accepted that
although diplomatic correspondence sent by the ordinary post might
be opened and copied, diplomatic couriers were inviolate. Incidents
such as the blatant robbery of a French courier in the Dutch Republic
in 1684 were very unusual. As couriers were expensive, diplomats
tended to resort to writing the more secret parts of their dispatches in
code.

By 1700 there was a generally recognised hierachy both of states
and of the level of diplomats exchanged. It was agreed that the European states were not all equal in rank – irrespective of their political
power. Rulers of Catholic states allowed some measure of pre-
eminence to the Pope, and monarchies were recognised to be superior to dukes, minor princes and republics: the Dutch had endless
problems in securing due recognition, even from their allies. Beyond
this slim measure of agreement lay endless quarrelling over precedence, which was not as irrelevant as it might seem because it reflected a state's reputation. In a similar way, there was agreement
that only the major states had the right to use ambassadors, though
this privilege seems to have been eroded in the course of the eighteenth century. Envoys came next in importance to ambassadors:
they were cheaper, they did not have to be nobles and they were also
a convenient and recognised way of avoiding a dispute over precedence, for an envoy was surrounded by less elaborate ceremonial.
Ambassadors and envoys constituted the diplomatic *élite* and were
clearly far above the lower rank of diplomats, the residents and secretaries of embassy, who often had by far the best knowledge of
foreign courts, where they tended to serve for several years. In the
course of the eighteenth century this hierarchy was complicated by
the increasing use of other titles, in particular minister plenipoten-
tiary, but the basic distinction remained.

By the later seventeenth century permanent and resident embassies
were all but universal in Europe. The major states all maintained
reciprocal representation in peacetime: in war, or when relations
became acrimonious, these diplomats were withdrawn or the level of
representation was lowered, usually to that of secretary of embassy.
The two principal exceptions were Russia and the Ottoman Empire,

and both these states came to be integrated into this network, in different degrees, during the eighteenth century. In the course of the Great Northern War (1700–21) Russia emerged very rapidly from her previous isolation. The first permanent Russian diplomats were sent to the major European capitals during the conflict. Previously, Russian rulers had been very reluctant to permit permanent foreign embassies in Moscow, and they themselves had sent very few, and usually temporary, missions abroad. Closer relations had only been maintained with neighbouring states, above all Poland, where the first permanent embassy had been established in 1688. This diplomatic isolation had simply expressed the intense traditionalism of old Muscovy and its deep suspicion of foreigners, while on the European side the lack of permanent diplomatic contacts reflected Russia's limited importance before 1700. The Great Northern War dramatically changed this situation and Russia's quest for allies and for European technology led to closer links with the west, while Peter the Great's victories over Sweden gave Russia a new-found importance in European eyes. Peter rapidly created a western-style diplomatic service and established permanent embassies throughout Europe. By 1725 there were no fewer than twenty-one permanent Russian missions (including consulates) abroad. This number declined slightly during the eighteenth century, but Russia henceforth maintained substantial and permanent links with the European states despite problems over language and ceremonial.

The other new member was the Ottoman Empire, though its entry occurred rather later and initially proved less complete. The Ottoman impact on early modern Europe had been considerable, yet it was the final decade of the eighteenth century before the first permanent Ottoman embassies were established in European capitals. Until then the Porte had sent individual missions for specific purposes, such as the signature of a peace treaty, after which they returned to Constantinople. The absence of permanent resident Ottoman embassies reflected a basic assumption of superiority: diplomacy was unnecessary during the centuries of Ottoman power. Contact was futile, for nothing was to be learned from the infidels who ought rather to appear as supplicants in Constantinople – Lord Macartney's mission to China in 1793 received the same treatment. However, many European states maintained diplomats at the Porte, often for commercial reasons, though they operated under peculiarly complex and difficult conditions. By the end of the eighteenth century, and in particular after the defeats in the wars of 1768–74 and 1787–92, the Ottoman Empire came to be involved in the European states system: it needed military and financial aid and political alliances, and its weakness made it increasingly the focus for the ambitions of the great powers. The growing involvement which resulted, the need for greater knowledge of events in Europe and the desire of the great reforming Sultan, Selim III (1789–1807) to modernise his state by learning from the west, produced in 1793 a formal decision to establish permanent embassies in western capitals. The first was set up in London the same year, and in the next few years Ottoman diplomats were also sent to Paris, Berlin and Vienna. But the Ottoman network of embassies was never extensive and was crippled by lacking the regular courier service possessed by other states.

Diplomacy under the *ancien régime* was essentially a temporary employment for aristocrats and amateurs rather than a career. In the lower posts of residents and secretaries of embassy, which were separated by an increasingly well-defined hierarchy from ambassadors and envoys, there is some evidence of a growing careerism. But there were few professional diplomats in the ranks of ambassadors and envoys. These were drawn almost universally from the higher nobility and, occasionally, from leading churchmen, though the employment of clerics soon became rare. This aristocratic dominance followed the principle that ambassadors represented their sovereign; rulers therefore sent the men most capable of glorifying themselves. The employment of noblemen also reflected a general desire not to offend a recipient by using diplomats of a lower status. The only significant exceptions to this aristocratic monopoly of European diplomacy were the Dutch Republic and England, whose rather different social structures were mirrored in their choice of diplomats. Both employed noblemen, but some Dutch diplomats were members of the Regent oligarchy and some British ambassadors lacked titles.

The top aristocrats tended to be sent to the most important embassies: Rome (for Catholic states), Paris, Madrid and, in the eighteenth century, Vienna and London. In a similar way there was a certain reluctance on their part to go to the more remote corners of Europe, such as Constantinople, St Petersburg and Warsaw. Ambassadors drawn from the aristocracy often took only one or two important missions. Few of these men had any previous diplomatic experience, for their status was an effective barrier to accepting any of the lower-level posts which would have provided experience. The inexperience of many ambassadors was in theory compensated for by the inclusion of more experienced diplomats in their retinue. But, here again, the privileged world of the eighteenth century frustrated good intentions. An ambassador would usually select his own secretaries and other assistants and draw them from the circle of his own family and friends. It is not surprising that such haphazard recruitment should often produce inadequate staff. The size of embassies depended on the importance and formality of particular courts, but an ambassador's retinue could be surprisingly large; in Rome, for example, the Spanish and French ambassadors often had households numbering 100 or more. Once again, personal and national prestige dictated that ambassadors should often have extravagant and expensive staffs with them.

Only a small part of the cost was borne by the ambassador's government. Diplomats were everywhere expected to spend their own money in the service of their monarch and this reinforced the aristocratic domination of major embassies.

The existence of a permanent diplomatic network by the end of the seventeenth century and the increased volume of negotiations inevitably raised the question of the training of diplomats. The need for this was certainly recognised, but there were comparatively few attempts to train young men for a diplomatic career. The most notable of these was the Académie politique (the famous 'School for Ambassadors') founded by the French foreign minister, Torcy, in 1712. The origins of this were twofold. The Académie politique was part of the increasing bureaucratisation of French government apparent in the latter part of Louis XIV's reign. It also reflected Torcy's awareness of the shortcomings of French diplomacy and, in particular, the absence of good secretaries of embassy. The fact that these secretaries were usually employed by individual ambassadors rather than the French government, had inevitably produced insecurity and a lack of suitable candidates. Torcy aimed to replace this system of patronage, with all its deficiencies, by a trained cadre of diplomats. It seems clear that he hoped that it would eventually be possible to train not only secretaries of embassy but all French diplomats, even the highest ambassador. The Académie politique opened in 1712 with six students, each of whom received 1,000 *livres* a year and a promise of subsequent employment. Six further students, unpaid, were added for a time after 1714. But the Académie never recovered from the political eclipse of its founder, Torcy, in October 1715, and it disappeared in 1720.

The Académie politique was the most famous of a handful of attempts to train diplomats during the *ancien régime*. The training of Papal diplomats at the Pontifical Ecclesiastical Academy began in 1701 and was more or less continuous thereafter, while the founding of the Regius Chairs of Modern History at Oxford and Cambridge in 1724 was partly inspired by a wish to produce trained recruits for the British diplomatic service, though it failed to do so. Frederick II founded a training school to produce secretaries and residents for the Prussian diplomatic service in 1747 but within a decade it had collapsed. There were several similar attempts in eighteenth-century Russia. Peter the Great found a chronic shortage of suitable personnel for diplomatic posts, when he tried to create a western-style diplomatic service during the Great Northern War. He therefore sent young Russian noblemen abroad to study, particularly western European languages. In 1779 Catherine II sought to overcome an identical shortage by attaching one or two young men, at her own expense, to Russian embassies as a kind of diplomatic apprenticeship, while in 1797 Paul I laid down that thirty noblemen should be trained by the College of Foreign

Affairs. Napoleon also attempted to systematise the training of diplomats and did succeed in producing some improvement in their quality, especially in his final years in power. These various attempts embodied the orthodoxy of the day about the necessary subjects which a trainee diplomat should study. Diplomatic theorists and practical statesmen agreed that a knowledge of 'public law' (later called international law), recent European history, particularly diplomatic history, and foreign languages, especially French, were essential: this was, for example, the curriculum at the Académie politique, while the principal obligation on the new Regius Professors of Modern History was the teaching of modern languages.

The Académie politique and similar attempts at the training of diplomats are primarily interesting for the evidence they provide of the recognised deficiences in established practice. They had little contemporary impact and, with the minor exception of the Pontifical Ecclesiastical Academy, all soon collapsed. The *ancien régime* had no professional diplomatic corps, which were only to emerge in the course of the nineteenth century. The explanation for this is twofold. In the first place, the near monopoly over the higher posts enjoyed by the aristocracy in itself militated against extensive training. Secondly, there was little incentive to enter the world of diplomacy when there was no career structure, the top posts were reserved for aristocrats and promotion was usually a matter of favour and patronage. Diplomacy was a notoriously insecure profession. Failure in a negotiation could wreck a career, while a diplomat could often be forgotten or his position undermined while abroad. Not many people actually sought a diplomatic career, regarding service abroad as an honourable exile, a 'gilded relegation' (in the words of the Dutch statesman John de Witt) to be exchanged for a suitable post at home as soon as the opportunity offered. Pay in the diplomatic service was notoriously bad and frequently delayed. It offered far worse prospects than the readily available posts in the emerging bureaucracies of the continental states with their opportunities to supplement the meagre salary by a system of fees. The quality of diplomats produced in this haphazard way was variable and usually poor. At most they might glance through some old dispatches bearing on relations with the state to which they were being sent, though the elaborate instructions which they received at the beginning of a mission did something to make up for these deficiencies.

The duties of a diplomat were not very extensive. Diplomacy was, superficially, simply a matter of representing your own sovereign, and for this it was enough to be a nobleman. Beyond this, the role of diplomats would obviously depend on whether a ruler or his minister kept negotiations in their own hands and dealt with ambassadors accredited to their court, or entrusted these to their own envoys. The conduct of actual negotiations, though ostensibly the purpose of diplomacy, was comparatively infrequent. It occupied little of a diplomat's time, which was largely taken up by comparatively routine tasks. In any case, really important negotiations would often be handled by a special mission. The other duty of a diplomat, besides representing his monarch, defending his interests and those of his subjects (particularly merchants) was to provide information for the policy-makers at home.

A diplomat was expected to gather as much information as he could about the state to which he was posted and, in particular, about its armed forces. Napoleon, who had a low view of diplomats and diplomacy, declared: 'Ambassadors are, in the full meaning of the term, titled spies.' To be effective it was essential for a diplomat to be accepted into the society of the court to which he was accredited. Much of an ambassador's time was spent on the social round. By keeping his eyes and ears open he might obtain useful information. The other, less frequent, source of information was bribery or espionage. This aspect of a diplomat's duties is one reason for the widely held but exaggerated view of the importance of 'secret diplomacy'. Since diplomats often sought to attribute their own failure to extensive bribery by a rival, such excuses have too often been taken at face value. However, there is no doubt that, at certain times and places, money was the principal basis of diplomacy. In Poland during the generation before partition, or in Sweden during the 1660s and 1670s as well as in the 'Age of Liberty' (1718–72), rival diplomats spent lavishly to build up a party in the intense domestic political struggles. But usually expenditure was on a much more modest scale and took the form of pensions or gratifications to courtiers or statesmen. Such gifts were not seen as corrupt and were intended not to influence a particular decision or to obtain information but to cultivate people already well intentioned. Presents on the conclusion of a treaty were also expected as the norm.

The importance of espionage has tended to be exaggerated. Every state maintained a secret office or *cabinet noir* which tried to intercept and copy the diplomatic correspondence of their rivals. Skilled decipherers were available to crack the codes (almost always numerical ones) employed by diplomats. The Austrian *cabinet noir* was particularly energetic and made life difficult for diplomats in Vienna, though its efficiency occasionally left something to be desired. On one occasion the British minister Sir Robert Murray Keith had to protest formally that he sometimes received copies of dispatches from London while the originals were sent to Kaunitz! In any case, most diplomats were aware that their dispatches were intercepted, often by postmasters in the countries through which these letters passed, and either exploited this or avoided it by using couriers during important negotiations. And while the eighteenth century was not lacking in spectacular coups – as when the entire correspondence of the British ambassador in Constantinople from 1770 to 1775 was betrayed to his French rival – the gains from espionage were very small compared to the time and money expended on it.

Foreign policy throughout this period was overwhelmingly monarchical, although Europe's rulers often delegated some degree of control to a chief minister. Leading ministers were almost always primarily concerned with diplomacy because of the complete dominance of foreign affairs. The precise mechanisms for the control of foreign policy obviously varied from state to state, but the general tendency, particularly in the eighteenth century, is clear: an evolution towards more specialised departments of increasing size, responsible for the conduct of diplomacy, 'foreign offices' in all but name. In this, as in the matter of diplomatic services, France led the way. A more elaborate foreign office emerged during the second half of Louis XIV's reign, particularly during the ministry of Torcy (1698–1715), the King's last foreign minister. At Louis's assumption of real power in 1661, a single coach would have sufficed to transport the minister who controlled French foreign policy and his handful of assistants. But by 1715 Torcy and his retinue would have needed twenty such coaches, so many specialised personnel (permanent officials, archivists, translators, cryptographers, clerks) had been added. The French foreign office remained supreme until the end of this period, providing a model for other states.

The eighteenth century saw the emergence, in all the major states, of similar specialised departments and ministers whose responsibilities were primarily for foreign affairs. This was both a response to developments in France and one dimension of the general administrative evolution of continental states in this period; it also reflected the increased volume of diplomacy being conducted. But it was not until the last quarter of the eighteenth century that this development was complete. Even then, the functional division of responsibility was usually incomplete. Many of the officials in the embryonic foreign offices were still devoting a good deal of their time to transacting essentially domestic business, while other departments of state retained control over minor aspects of foreign affairs. This was especially the case in England where the secretaries of state were as responsible for domestic as for foreign affairs until 1782. Yet the trend towards more specialised departments for diplomacy is unmistakable. In this the remote state of Russia led the way. Peter the Great's energetic policies abroad and his attempt to promote closer contacts with the West resulted in the emergence of a large and specialised foreign office. In 1719, during the major administrative reorganisation at the end of Peter's reign, the old Posolskii Prikaz ('Department of Embassies') was replaced by the College of Foreign Affairs, which during the eighteenth century acquired increasingly specialised departments. The foreign offices of France and Russia grew faster than those of any other state, but broadly familiar if less complete developments are to be found elsewhere. In Spain a specialised ministry of foreign affairs evolved during the reign of Charles III (1759–88) and a similar, if far less complete, trend was visible in Poland and Sweden during the final quarter of the century. For much of this period, the control of British foreign policy was divided on a geographical basis between two secretaries of state, but in 1782 unified direction was established with the creation of the office of foreign secretary. Yet the machinery for the control of Britain's diplomacy always seemed primitive when compared to the increasingly elaborate foreign offices of the major continental states. The British foreign office had under twenty permanent officials in the 1780s compared with over seventy in its French counterpart.

Foreign policy everywhere reflected the ambitions and concerns of Europe's rulers. Diplomacy was in the hands of a tiny *élite*, for only in Britain and the Dutch Republic could parliamentary or public opinion occasionally exert any influence on policy. The motives behind these rulers' foreign policy were changing significantly in this period. In the sixteenth and seventeenth centuries, religion and dynastic interest had been the dominant issues. By 1648 however, religion was fast ceasing to be an important factor in international relations and for the eighteenth-century great powers it was always a marginal consideration. It might be a useful propaganda weapon but, except within the Holy Roman Empire, religion was no longer an important issue in politics. The eighteenth century also saw some decline in purely dynastic motives behind foreign policy. Until the 1740s, the principal justification for territorial claims, at least in western Europe, tended to be dynastic rights, commemorated in the names of the major wars, such as those over the Spanish succession and the Austrian succession. The personal whim of a ruler could never be excluded, for there were in practice so few restraints on his action, and certainly the reputation of a monarch and his state was always a significant dimension of international relations. But purely dynastic considerations were becoming less significant in the eighteenth century. Nor, in this period, was nationalism ever really a factor in relations between states. It was also only in the 1790s that ideological motives became part of foreign policy, as members of the anti-French coalition increasingly aimed to reverse the political changes introduced in France by the Revolutionaries, which they regarded as a threat to their own security. Instead, eighteenth-century international relations were dominated by considerations of *raison d'état*.

The doctrine of *raison d'état* ('reason of state') was simply the argument of necessity as the basis for the political conduct of states. Self-interest was – as it has perhaps always been – the dominant motive behind foreign policy. The result of the general acceptance of this was the competitive states system of the eighteenth century where, as one well-informed publicist wrote in 1760: 'In the end everything depends on power.' Force was an essential, if unspoken, element in international relations. The effectiveness of a state's diplomacy was directly linked to the size and reputation of its permanent standing army. 'The spirit of monarchy', wrote Montesquieu, 'is war and aggrandisement.' Rulers and statesmen strove ceaselessly to increase the power, and therefore the wealth, of their state. State power was everywhere measured in terms of territorial extent and population, which in turn determined revenue and the size of the army. Economic advantages were similarly usually sought only for the increase in state power which they produced. Additional territory was everywhere the aim of policy. Catherine II remarked in 1794, as Poland was finally being removed from the map of Europe, 'who gains nothing, loses'. This cynical opportunism and perpetual search for territorial gain was everywhere justified by the doctrine of *raison d'état*. The result was to make the eighteenth-century states system resemble the state of nature postulated by Hobbes, a competition of all against all, where violence was the only law.

The same self-interest, however, also provided a mechanism for restraining this struggle: the balance of power. This gave some stability in a states system dominated by a violent competition for supremacy. The idea of the balance of power existed at two distinct levels in the eighteenth century: theoretical speculation and practical politics. In the first place there was widespread discussion among publicists (particularly in Britain) and philosophers about the desirability and practicality of a balance of power, which since the advent of Newtonian physics was viewed increasingly in mechanical terms. Rousseau, for example, saw it as a self-regulating mechanism for continuing harmony between states. The naive optimism and frequent superficiality of much Enlightenment thinking was shown in the frequent assumption that the balance of power would be a way of advancing the widespread plans for permanent peace. But the argument, on the whole, went against the advocates of a balance of power. It proved very difficult to defend such a notoriously vague and imprecise concept against intelligent sceptics such as J. H. G. von Justi, for whom it was only a chimera. In any case, the contemporary impact of such speculation on the European states system was mimimal. But the maintenance of a balance of power was also the objective of many statesmen.

The treaty of Utrecht (1713) declared its purpose to be 'to confirm the peace and tranquillity of the Christian world through a just equilibrium of power (which is the best and most secure foundation of mutual friendship and lasting agreement in every quarter)'. This was the first occasion on which a peace settlement had referred directly to the balance of power. In practical terms the balance of power meant simply that no one state, or alignment, should become too powerful;

and that if it did, the other European states would join together to reduce its power. It was both instinctive reaction and conscious policy, and as such it was not new to the eighteenth century. The idea of a balance of power originated in later-fifteenth-century Italy, as a means of preventing Venice from becoming too dominant. In sixteenth and seventeenth-century Europe statesmen thought more of localised balances than an overall balance of power, which only really established itself after 1714, once Europe became more of one political system. In the eighteenth century, these local balances, particularly in Italy, Germany and around the Baltic, were essential components in a European-wide balance of power.

The new European equilibrium was complex and difficult to uphold. In the first place, there had previously been a simple equilibrium with only two major components: France had opposed the Habsburgs of Spain and Austria, while the states of the second rank joined one side or another. But the eighteenth century saw the emergence of several new great powers: by 1763 five can be recognised – Britain, France, Austria, Prussia and Russia. Secondly, the extension of Anglo-French rivalry to territories overseas meant that, for the first time, the balance of power acquired a colonial dimension. For both these reasons its maintenance became more difficult. Yet, at the same time, the near-equality of the great powers (with the exception of Britain because of her immense colonial and commercial gains) made the balance of power more important as a restraint. Any gain by one state was a matter of concern for all the other powers because of their near-equality. In this way the balance of power came to operate against the smaller, weaker states. For if a state could not be prevented from making a territorial gain, the principle of equilibrium required that other states should make an equivalent gain. This idea was most forcefully expressed in the three partitions of Poland at the end of the eighteenth century. As the author of *The Political State of Europe* (first published in 1750) wrote: 'The struggle for the balance of power is, in effect, the struggle for power.'

Much of the thinking about the European states system in this period was static, a matter of habit and reflex assumptions rather than constructive statesmanship. The minds of rulers and diplomats ran along familiar grooves; any variations in the established pattern were seen as positively unnatural. They thought more in terms of enmities than of alliances. The fixed points of international relations were the well-established, permanent and seemingly ineradicable rivalries. Chief among these were the struggle between Habsburg and Bourbon which lasted until 1756, and the new rivalry between England and France (often aligned with Spain) which began in 1689 and was all but continuous until 1815. Further east, hostility between Austria and the Ottoman Empire, and the parallel antagonism between Russia and the Ottomans largely endured throughout this period. In the Baltic,

Russo-Swedish rivalry was similarly permanent, while from the 1740s the struggle between Austria and the rising power of Prussia, in Germany and in central Europe generally, became a dominant and permanent theme of continental politics.

The alliance of traditionally hostile states was certainly rare enough to be unusual. This was why contemporaries were so surprised by the alliance of such hereditary foes as France and Austria in 1756 that they styled it a 'Diplomatic Revolution'. In a similar way the long period of Anglo-French co-operation between 1716 and 1731 (see Ch. 4) was widely seen as an unnatural and probably temporary variation from the established pattern. Throughout most of the period the foreign policies of the European states were based on these assumed rivalries, and it proved difficult for any statesman to ignore them – as witness the obstacles to the attempted Anglo-French *rapprochement* in the early 1770s (see pp. 255–7). Only in the wholly unusual circumstances of the wars of 1792–1815 between France and Europe (see Chs. 10 and 11) did these hostilities temporarily take second place, and even then old antagonisms were for long a significant barrier to effective co-operation against the Revolution and Napoleon. The struggle against France did produce some unexpected if temporary alignments, such as the Anglo-Spanish alliance of the War of the First Coalition and even, at the end of the 1790s, a short-lived Russo-Turkish *rapprochement*.

Alliances founded on these fixed rivalries proved most enduring; statesmen sought such alignments on the *ad hoc* basis that 'the enemy of my enemy is my friend'. The longest alliances were founded on shared hostility: towards the Turks and then against Prussia in the case of the Russo-Austrian alliance (1726–62, renewed in the 1780s) or against Britain in the case of the periodic Franco-Spanish alliances of the eighteenth century (especially the Third Bourbon Family Compact of 1761–90). Shared hostility towards France was sufficient to keep the intrinsically unstable alignment of Britain, Austria and the Dutch Republic (the 'Old System' of alliance) together in three wars between 1689 and 1748. But some of the most perceptive and successful statesmen were hostile to alliances *per se*, even if they were stable and enduring. Frederick II of Prussia, for instance, declared in his *Political Testament* of 1752: 'Policy lies in profiting from favourable events, rather than in preparing them in advance. This is why I advise you not to conclude treaties formed in anticipation of uncertain events....'

It is perhaps not surprising that the diplomacy of the *ancien régime* should have attracted the censure of the Enlightenment. Some of the *philosophes* attacked its ruthlessness and selfish competitiveness, and condemned the attention given by governments to external affairs: the *Primat der Aussenpolitik* ('primacy of foreign policy') was to give way to a concentration on internal reform. Such vague idealism had little contemporary impact. Vergennes, France's foreign minister from 1774 to 1787, is generally alleged to have been more influenced by the Enlightenment than any other statesman, but it is extremely difficult to see where his actual policies were indebted to the *philosophes*. His much-vaunted refusal to seek further territorial annexations can be more convincingly explained by his awareness of France's weakness. The early stages of the French Revolution saw reformers within the assembly take up the *philosophe* critique of the old style diplomacy, to the extent of arguing that 'France should isolate herself from the political system of Europe'. Yet within a few years the Revolutionary leaders were pursuing a foreign policy more grasping and aggressive than anything the *ancien régime* had seen. One of the few statesmen to attempt the kind of foreign policy advocated by the *philosophes* was the notoriously unsuccessful Marquis d'Argenson, who briefly controlled French foreign policy in the 1740s. And even he acknowledged the futility of idealism in foreign affairs. 'A state', he wrote in 1739, 'should always be at the ready, like a gentleman living among swashbucklers and quarrellers. Such are the nations of Europe, today more than ever; negotiations are only a continual struggle between men without principles, impudently aggressive and ever greedy.' Such conduct was necessary for survival in the competitive states system of eighteenth-century Europe.

CHAPTER EIGHT

Partition diplomacy in eastern Europe, 1763–1795

THE EUROPEAN SYSTEM AFTER THE SEVEN YEARS WAR

The separation of continental and colonial issues reflected in the two peace settlements of Hubertusburg and Paris persisted for the next generation. Only in the 1790s, in response to the aggression of Revolutionary France, did European diplomacy again acquire a basic unity. Until then, the eastern powers and the western states seemed almost to exist in separate political worlds. Britain concentrated on the maritime and colonial struggle with France and her ally, Spain (see Ch. 9), while Russia, Prussia and Austria were preoccupied with eastern European questions and exhibited an increasing appetite for territorial gains at the expense of their weaker neighbours. Such a separation had been implicit during the Seven Years War, which had been essentially two distinct conflicts, united principally by France's inability to break free from her initial commitment to the anti-Prussian coalition. France long remained trapped between her growing desire to concentrate the bulk of her resources on the maritime struggle with England and the involvement in continental affairs which geography and political tradition suggested was necessary. The principal theme in French foreign policy throughout the next two decades was hostility towards Britain, and this was primarily expressed overseas; this, in turn, restricted Versailles's role in European affairs.

France had lost more than any other state by the Seven Years War: her substantial territorial cessions by the peace of Paris emphasised the low point her international prestige had reached by 1763. Her wretched performance in the war surprised contemporaries, for whom France had long been the leading military power in Europe, and this decline was not speedily reversed. The years after the Seven Years War saw significant attempts at military reform, but it was to be the 1790s before French armies again became formidable. Fundamental to France's eclipse was her financial weakness, which had been exacerbated by the immense cost of the recent war. France's political prestige had been dented by her defeats, while the period of wartime co-operation with Russia, though acrimonious and short-lived (the partnership had broken up in 1761), had involved an abdication from France's traditional role as patron and friend of Poland, Sweden and the Ottoman Empire. Attempts to regain this influence in eastern Europe after 1763 proved unsuccessful. France's political decline, and the concentration of limited resources on the struggle with England, reduced her impact on European diplomacy. Versailles ostensibly had a continental policy throughout this period, but this was something of an illusion. It was always a policy of weakness, since France could never support her objectives by force. Superficially, France maintained her wartime alliance with Austria until at least the end of the 1770s, though increasingly this existed more in name than in fact. After the Seven Years War the Franco-Austrian alliance was a confession by both states that neither had a credible political alternative.

France's gradual disappearance as an effective force on the Continent was less evident at the time than it appears in retrospect. Contemporaries were accustomed to French political leadership of Europe and they failed at first to appreciate the transformation that was taking place. The continuing activities of the *secret du roi*, the largely unsuccessful and short-lived attempts by Choiseul to resume an anti-Russian policy after 1766, and the apparent continuation of the Franco-Austrian alliance all helped to perpetuate the idea that France remained active in Europe. By the early 1770s, however, and the first partition of Poland, France's withdrawal was becoming apparent. Versailles's diplomacy was increasingly disregarded by the eastern powers as they became aware of this decline. It was to be the aim of d'Aiguillon and, in a different way, Vergennes to recover this lost influence, but they were unsuccessful (see pp. 256ff.). Only in the 1780s, with the ending of the War of American Independence, could France once again play a significant part in European affairs (see pp. 265ff.). The eclipse of France for two decades after the Seven Years War was an important factor in the swing to the east apparent at this time. It was also partially responsible for the minimal role played by Britain in European politics in the period up to the mid-1780s.

The virtual disappearance of Britain from any active role in Europe was surprising, coming as it did in the aftermath of the most successful war she had ever waged. Nor was it, initially, a matter of deliberate calculation. Britain's isolation was not the result of a conscious policy but of the failure of her diplomacy, which for some time after 1763 in fact aimed at securing alliances with major states on the Continent. This search for allies was largely a matter of habit and political tradition, but it now proved less successful than in the past. After the bitter dissolution of the wartime partnership in 1762, relations with Prussia were so bad that no alliance could be concluded for a quarter of a century; the one attempt, in 1766, was a fiasco. Approaches to Austria and Russia were more frequent in the generation after 1763 but no more successful. Only in the later 1780s did Britain emerge from this diplomatic isolation. In fact, France's political decline had largely undermined the traditional basis of British foreign policy: the exploitation of the French threat, whether real or imaginary, to the 'liberties of Europe' or 'the balance of power' to construct an alliance system on the Continent to protect England's own security. British ministers were slow to perceive this transformation and, in particular, they failed to understand that a price would now have to be paid for a continental alliance. Nor, apart from long-term considerations of security, did Britain appear to have much need of an ally before the later 1770s. Her problems in these years were internal and colonial: ministerial instability and the growth of radicalism at home, and the rising tide of opposition and, ultimately, rebellion in the American colonies. It was not clear exactly how a continental alliance could aid in their solution. Until the American revolt in the mid-1770s, Britain's power remained substantially undiminished. Her prestige and political influence on the Continent did decline, but less dramatically than those of France.

The severely diminished role of Britain and France after 1763 contributed to a new pattern in European affairs. Although the territorial *status quo* on the Continent had been restored by the peace of Hubertusburg, the Seven Years War had significantly modified the relative power and prestige of the belligerents, and this helped to produce new diplomatic alignments. In the first place, the war had confirmed Prussia's claim to be considered a great power. The successful seizure and defence of Silesia in the 1740s had elevated her to a position of equality with the Habsburgs in Germany; Frederick's survival, against overwhelming odds, in the Seven Years War raised Prussia to the first rank of European states, perhaps the leading power on the Continent after 1763. It was a position that rested on seemingly insecure foundations. Prussia was a small, exposed and thinly populated country, apparently lacking the material resources necessary to be a great power; but, for the moment, the personality of its ruler, Frederick II, seemed amply to compensate for these deficiencies. The almost total exhaustion of the Prussian lands, which effectively prevented Frederick II playing the role in European politics to which his victories and his reputation had entitled him, was not immediately apparent.

The other power to gain significantly as a result of the Seven Years War was Russia. She had, indeed, made no conquests, but her prestige had been considerably increased by her victories over Frederick's armies. Russia had been the leading power in the coalition in the second half of the war (until her withdrawal early in 1762) and this ensured that she could never again be ignored by the other European powers. Russia was a permanent, and increasingly important, component in the European states system after the Seven Years War; she had now permanently entered the ranks of the great powers. Her new-found importance also reflected the exhaustion of Prussia and Austria after 1763 and the diminishing role of France in European affairs. No other state was in a position to challenge Catherine's political leadership after the war, though her own preoccupation with domestic affairs in the 1760s and 1770s reduced Russia's role in continental politics. Her position was considerably strengthened, during the next generation, by the continuance, though in a muted form, of Austrian resentment towards Prussia. This antagonism ensured that (until the 1790s) Catherine II could always choose one of the two German powers as an ally. Russian support would obviously be decisive in any renewed Austro-Prussian struggle, and the conclusion of an alliance with St Petersburg was a principal aim of both Habsburg and Hohenzollern diplomacy.

For Austria, the war had been a major disappointment: the apparently overpowering coalition assembled by Kaunitz had failed to produce the expected victory. Heavy sacrifices in men, money and material resources had been made to no avail. Prussian possession of Silesia had to be accepted by Vienna after 1763. In their hearts the Habsburgs could never renounce this valuable province (and in the years ahead Kaunitz produced a variety of ingenious if improbable plans for its peaceful recovery): in their heads they knew that its reconquest was not practical politics, particularly given the obvious weakness of the Habsburg state. Vienna now accepted Prussia's position of equality in the Holy Roman Empire, and in Europe generally. In another significant, if less important sense, Austria's position in Germany had been weakened by the Seven Years War. In order to defeat Prussia – a German state whose ruler was an elector – Vienna had allied with France, the hereditary enemy both of the Habsburgs and of the Empire. This action undoubtedly offended and alarmed many of the German princes (particularly the Catholic rulers in southwest Germany) on whose loyalty and support Austria had traditionally depended, and this was later to be important when the Habsburgs tried to acquire Bavaria. Austria's European position was undoubtedly weaker in 1763 than it had been in 1756. Her resources were all but exhausted, her administration near to collapse. By the closing stages of the war it had become apparent that further and wide-ranging reforms were necessary, and these were begun even before peace was signed. The conclusion of a Russo-Prussian alliance in April 1764 was merely to emphasise Vienna's predicament.

European diplomacy in the immediate aftermath of the Seven Years War was in an unusually fluid and volatile state. The alliances that had contested the war had been the product of an unexpected and somewhat accidental realignment of the powers in 1756–57, and the war had done little to give permanence to the new alignments. Two of the wartime partnerships (those between France and Russia and between England and Prussia) had broken up; the Franco-Austrian alliance, characterised by friction and mutual disappointment during the Seven Years War, struggled on into peacetime, largely for the want of any obvious alternative. Only the Franco-Spanish alliance, concluded in 1761, appeared to be at all secure in the immediate aftermath of the war, and it was sustained principally by mutual dependence in the continuing struggle against Britain overseas. The shock to the established political order which the Diplomatic Revolution had represented was still apparent at the end of the Seven Years War. The resulting uncertainty was intensified by a certain general hesitancy over the conclusion of new alliances, in case it led to a further costly and destructive war similar to that produced by the last bout of alliance diplomacy in 1756–57.

A clearer focus was given to post-war diplomacy by the Polish crisis of 1763–64 and, in particular, by the Russo-Prussian alliance which it produced. Poland had been ruled since 1697 by the Electoral House of Saxony, but real power belonged not to the elected monarch but to his Russian patron. Since the early eighteenth century, the Polish state had been a satellite of Russia. The death of Augustus III of Saxony–Poland (ruler since 1733) on 5 October 1763 came at an inopportune moment for St Petersburg. Catherine II was only slowly, and with some difficulty, consolidating her own hold on the Russian throne and restoring some order to the government. As a woman, a foreigner – by origin she was a minor German princess – and a usurper, her position in Russia was, for some time, insecure. The security of Russia's western frontier dictated the continuance of St Petersburg's invisible empire in Poland and this, in turn, made the election of a pliable king essential. There was the danger that should a third Saxon king be elected, it might suggest that the Polish throne was hereditary and thereby weaken Russian influence in Warsaw. This was appreciated by Catherine II, who was determined to secure the election of one of her former lovers, the Polish nobleman Stanislas Poniatowski. The Tsaritsa was, however, fearful of French opposition and Ottoman intervention and needed foreign support to guarantee the election of Poniatowski. In the previous election in 1733 Russia's partner had been Austria; now it was to be Prussia. Frederick II skilfully exploited this situation and, by suggesting that he might be on the point of signing an alliance with the Ottoman Empire, forced Catherine to conclude the alliance which he believed to be essential to protect Prussia's future security.

The Russo-Prussian treaty of 11 April 1764, a defensive alliance to last, in the first instance, for eight years, was a considerable diplomatic triumph for the Prussian King. Frederick, as he confessed on one occasion, 'feared Russia more than he feared God', and this had always been central to his foreign policy. Russia's contribution to the Seven

Years War and, in particular, the heavy defeats she had inflicted on
Prussian armies strengthened this anxiety. Frederick certainly feared
Russia more than any other state after 1763 and he had therefore
sought an alliance with Catherine II. Russia would, perhaps, have
made such an alliance in any case, but the 1764 treaty was concluded
on terms of near-equality and there is no doubt that Frederick gained
rather more from it. Alliance with Russia protected Prussian security:
it effectively neutralised Austria (since Vienna could not contemplate
a war against a combination of Russia and Prussia) and thereby gave
a certain stability to international relations in eastern Europe. It also
left Frederick free to undertake the vital task of internal reconstruction
and recovery made necessary by the devastation of the Seven Years
War. The Hohenzollern lands had suffered considerable losses of population and economic resources during the war, and this was an
important factor in Prussian foreign policy after 1763. Prussia was
simply too weak to risk another war, and in recognition of this Frederick II pursued an essentially pacific policy throughout the second
half of his reign.

Prussia's preoccupation with internal reconstruction mirrored the
situation in the Habsburg lands and, to a lesser extent, in Russia. The
severe burdens and considerable destruction of the Seven Years War
ensured that after its conclusion domestic reform and reorganisation
came to be the principal objective of all the participants. The traditional primacy of foreign affairs was undermined after 1763 as states
acknowledged, perhaps fully for the first time, that internal strength
was a necessary precondition for a successful foreign policy. The
widespread attempts at reform in the generation after 1763 – the age
of 'Enlightened despotism' – were, in the major European countries,
motivated principally by the desire to strengthen the state and, specifically, to finance the enlarged standing armies that were now universal. In the Habsburg lands, for example, the significant reforms
during the second half of Maria Theresa's reign and the hectic decade
of Joseph II's personal rule (1780–90) were undertaken primarily with
the intention of strengthening the financial basis of Austrian power.
The measures reflected the Cameralist doctrine that the best foundation for a strong state was a prosperous population that was able, and
willing, to pay its taxes. A broadly similar pattern can be seen in
Russia, where a complicating factor was Catherine II's need, in the
early years of peace, to consolidate her own hold on the Russian
throne.

This concern with internal affairs was reflected in the distinctive
orientation of Russian foreign policy for a decade and a half after
Catherine II's accession in 1762. The 'Northern System' of Nikita
Panin was based on the shared conviction of the Tsaritsa and Panin
(the minister responsible for foreign policy after October 1763) that
a long period of peace was necessary, during which the Russian

administration (which had all but collapsed under the strain of the Seven Years War) could be rebuilt and, in particular, the finances restored. Panin's projected system was defensive in nature and it implied that St Petersburg had no immediate territorial ambitions. It aimed to protect Russia's vulnerable western flank, particularly against the wiles of French diplomacy; an exaggerated fear of France – and a corresponding hostility towards Versailles – was the basis of Panin's diplomatic outlook. The 'Northern System' gradually took shape largely in response to events in Poland (see p. 219) and Sweden. Russia feared an attack from Swedish Finland, particularly since her capital, St Petersburg, was close to the vulnerable north-western frontier. Russian observers always saw a connection between the restoration of absolutism in Stockholm and renewed Swedish aggression; St Petersburg's policy was long conditioned by memories of the career of Charles XII. Russia therefore sought to maintain the Swedish Constitution of 1720, with its severe restrictions on monarchical authority and its elaborate system of checks and balances which made Sweden far less of a danger to her neighbours.

Russia's anxiety about French intrigues in eastern Europe, her need for security against the possibility of renewed Swedish aggression and her desire to maintain the traditional protectorate over Poland were the principal origins of the idea of a 'Northern System'; its basis was the Russo-Prussian alliance of 1764. In conception it was to be a grandiose series of alliances: Russia was to unite not only with Prussia but also with Denmark and Britain, while Sweden, Poland and Saxony were to be brought in as 'passive' members by pledging themselves to remain neutral in any future war in northern Europe. Austria, St Petersburg's principal ally since 1726, was now to be discarded as Panin's policy took shape. In practice, however, the 'Northern System' was a much more limited affair; it was always more a matter of aspirations than of alliances. A Russo-Danish alliance was duly concluded in 1765 and the ties uniting St Petersburg and Copenhagen were considerably strengthened by a second treaty two years later. Britain, however, though she genuinely desired a Russian alliance (to improve her own diplomatic position), would never agree to the subsidy demanded by St Petersburg as the price of its conclusion and, in time, Panin and the Tsaritsa both came to doubt whether England would ever again be a real force in continental politics. Frederick II, though a founder member, was determined that he should be Russia's only important ally, and he was fundamentally opposed to the extensive alliances envisaged by the 'Northern System'. The central importance of his own alliance with St Petersburg for Prussian security, however, inevitably restrained his opposition. Yet Panin's system, though only partially realised – it was really never more than a triangular alliance of Russia, Prussia and Denmark – nominally remained the basis of Russian diplomacy until the later 1770s and it always had a certain utility, though it offered no protection against Russia's main enemy, the Turks. It helped to stabilise international relations in the eastern half of the Continent. Moreover, the existence of the 'Northern System' was an important restraint on Austrian policy, and in practice forced Kaunitz to continue his wartime alliance with France. There was no real alternative as far as the Habsburgs were concerned, now that Vienna's traditional alliance with Russia had been broken.

The 'Northern System' ran counter to – and was ultimately undermined by – the most obvious characteristic of continental diplomacy in the years after the Seven Years War: the tendency of the major states to expand at the expense of their weaker neighbours. The appetite for new territory which the major states now revealed was, to a significant extent, the corollary of their widespread preoccupation with internal reform as a means of strengthening the state. Contemporaries assessed political power in terms of population and wealth; it therefore followed that an increase in territory would automatically increase a state's potential power. The search for new territory which resulted, was not confined to the great powers of eastern Europe. The Swedish King Gustav III (reigned 1771–92) dreamed all his life of conquering Norway, then ruled by the King of Denmark. France secured the expected reversion of the duchy of Lorraine (provided for by the Third Treaty of Vienna of 1738 – see pp. 150f.) in 1766 on the death of Stanislas Leszczyński; and two years later she acquired the strategically important island of Corsica, in the western Mediterranean, by a thinly disguised purchase (and at a bargain price) from the Republic of Genoa. These acquisitions by France, while undoubtedly important, were, however, far less significant than the major territorial changes in eastern Europe in the period 1763–95. These changes took the form of forcible cessions of territory from Poland and the Ottoman Empire. Both states had, by the second half of the eighteenth century, declined from their previous greatness; both lacked an effective central administration and proved all but powerless to resist successive encroachments on their territory by the major states; both presented a compelling target for their powerful and voracious neighbours.

THE FIRST PARTITION OF POLAND, 1763–1772

The first victim was Poland. The weakness and internal divisions of the faded power of Poland, whose elective king was effectively controlled by the magnates, had long suggested that it might become a victim of the powerful states that surrounded it. The existence of the famous *liberum veto*, which enabled any member of the Polish Diet to exercise a personal veto over legislation, and the intervention of foreign powers, usually by their support of the various factions that constituted Poland's political life, ensured the permanence of this weakness. As a result the Polish state had long been unable to introduce necessary financial and military reforms. This internal weakness, however, did not make partition inevitable: it merely ensured that the Republic could not resist the first seizure of her territory carried out in 1772–73. The origins of the first partition are rather to be found in the critical political situation which existed in south-eastern Europe by 1770 and this, in turn, was related to the response of Poland's neighbours to events there since 1763.

In 1763–64, Catherine II, with Prussian help, had secured the election of her candidate to the Polish throne and thereby, it was assumed, perpetuated Russian influence in Poland. It had been intended that the new King, Stanislas Poniatowski, should be a puppet ruler, but he had proved to be more independent of Russian control than had been anticipated. In particular, he sought to introduce financial and military reforms which would have strengthened the Polish state. Any such initiative was unwelcome to St Petersburg, since the continuance of Russia's invisible empire demanded that Poland be kept weak and divided. In order to safeguard this protectorate Catherine now intervened actively in her neighbour's internal affairs. The Dissidents (Poland's non-Catholic subjects) provided a convenient cloak for this intervention. By posing as the defender of their religious freedom, Catherine was able to frustrate Stanislas Poniatowski's attempts at reform. Russian troops were sent into Poland to supervise the Diet of 1767–68, which guaranteed the religious freedom enjoyed by the Dissidents; these privileges and the preservation of the constitutional *status quo* were then enshrined in the 'Perpetual treaty' of March 1768 between Russia and Poland. This latest Russian intervention, however, provoked armed Polish resistance. With the formation of the confederation of Bar (in the extreme south of Poland, close to the Turkish frontier) in February 1768, St Petersburg was faced by a serious guerrilla war and a corresponding fear that France might aid Russia's opponents.

Russia's growing military control of Poland had been watched with considerable alarm in Constantinople, since in any future war Polish assistance to Russia would threaten the Sultan's province of Moldavia and generally undermine Ottoman strategy. Russian activities in the Crimea (an Ottoman vassal state) and Catherine's promises of assistance to some of the Sultan's Orthodox subjects in the Balkans were also resented by the Turks, but it was the situation in Poland which caused most alarm. French diplomacy was active at the Porte in these months, though whether it did any more than confirm Ottoman ministers in their Russophobia is doubtful. The double violation of Ottoman territory at Choczim (Khotin) and Bender (Bendery) by Russian troops pursuing Polish confederates brought matters to a head and on 6 October 1768 the Russian resident in Constantinople was imprisoned in the Castle of the Seven Towers, a symbolic action which in Ottoman eyes amounted to a formal declaration of war.

Russia was unprepared for the outbreak of this latest war with the Ottoman Empire. Until the very last it had been assumed in St Petersburg that war could be averted by the traditional means of extensive bribery in Constantinople. Russian troops were heavily committed in Poland and this, together with innate Ottoman lethargy, delayed the first serious fighting until the autumn of 1769. After some initial, and disconcerting, Ottoman opposition, Russian forces carried all before them in 1770–71. The Danubian principalities (Moldavia and Wallachia) were soon occupied, the Crimea was conquered and the Turkish fleet was destroyed at the battle of Chesmé (July 1770). The extent of these Russian successes was reflected in the continual reformulation of Catherine's terms for peace, which increased with each new triumph. By the closing months of 1770 the Tsaritsa's demands amounted to freedom of navigation for her ships on the Black Sea (a traditional Russian aspiration), the independence of the Crimea (whose Tartar Khan, hitherto, had ruled as an Ottoman vassal), the acquisition of a considerable amount of territory around the Sea of Azov, and (as an indemnity for the war) control of Moldavia and Wallachia for twenty-five years. The tide of Russian victories, moreover, suggested that Catherine might actually be able to impose these ambitious demands on a defeated Ottoman Empire.

Austria and Prussia were particularly alarmed by the threat of such a considerable extension of Russian power in the Balkans and around the Black Sea. This concern found expression in the limited Austro-Prussian *rapprochement* that emerged in 1769–70, symbolised by the meetings of Joseph II and Frederick II at Neisse (August 1769) and Neustadt (September 1770). The situation in south-eastern Europe had previously done much to bring Russia and Austria together; it was now beginning to divide them. Austria resented the arrival of Russian influence in an area traditionally seen as a Habsburg preserve, but she was all but powerless to oppose this. Frederick II was also alarmed by the prospect of such an increase in Russian power, since it would destroy the territorial balance in eastern Europe and might eventually undermine his cherished alliance with Catherine. The Prussian King was becoming increasingly anxious that Russian expansion in the Balkans and the prospect of easy gains for the Habsburgs might eventually produce a Russian–Austrian alliance. In the short term, Russia's victories were a serious threat to the existing territorial, and therefore political, balance. Any gain by one state, it was believed, needed to be compensated by broadly equivalent gains for the other powers, if the balance were not to be upset. This was certainly one element in the diplomacy of the first partition. Prussia and Austria both aimed to restrict Russia's gains from the Ottoman Empire, but neither wished to go to war for this purpose.

The danger that a general European war might be provoked by the conflict in south-eastern Europe appeared considerable. French diplomacy was active in Poland and at Constantinople, and the anti-Russian tone of Versailles's policy was fully apparent. Austria's opposition to Russian expansion was equally evident. The obvious danger, as contemporaries saw it, was that one or other state would enter the war on the side of the Ottoman Empire. This, in turn, would activate the two principal defensive alliances that existed in the late 1760s, between Russia and Prussia and between France and Austria, and thereby bring about a general European war. The danger of this was, perhaps, more apparent than real; yet this fear was widespread and was an element in diplomacy at this time. And by 1770–71, it seemed that only a general European war could check the Russian advance in the Balkans.

Frederick's solution to this apparent impasse was a three-power partition of Polish territory. The Prussian King had long appreciated the potential strategic value of West (i.e. Polish) Prussia to the Hohenzollerns; its acquisition would unite the central core of his territory with the isolated duchy of East Prussia. Frederick also understood, however, that the acquisition of Polish Prussia would be a matter of considerable difficulty, and the cautious tone of his foreign policy after the Seven Years War inevitably reinforced the belief that any such gain would probably be a matter for a future Prussian king. The precise origins of the plan for a tripartite seizure of Polish territory are unclear. A scheme which bears a striking similarity to the partition implemented in 1772 had earlier been put forward, nominally by a retired Danish diplomat, Count Lynar, but more likely by Frederick himself. But it had been rejected, after discussions with St Petersburg, as impracticable in 1769. The Prussian King's renewed interest in the possibility of a partition was the product of a visit by his brother, Prince Henry, to Russia in 1770–71. A series of conversations at the Russian court revealed Catherine's potential appetite for Polish territory. Frederick II now began to work on a broad diplomatic front, in an attempt to prevent a general European war by means of a partition of Polish territory in which Russia and Austria would also participate.

Russian support for the scheme was soon obtained. The preservation of Poland's territorial integrity was an important part of Panin's 'Northern System', and this remained the official basis of St Petersburg's foreign policy. But some of Russia's military leaders had been pressing since the very beginning of Catherine's reign for a 'rectification' of the Russo-Polish frontier and, specifically, for the annexation on strategic grounds of Polish Livonia. The acceptance of their arguments was facilitated by the continuing military resistance in Poland in 1769–71 (where the remnants of the opposition to Russia continued to wage a guerrilla war) and by Catherine's anxieties at the apparently warlike pose adopted by Austria. Peaceful gains in Poland seemed preferable to the general European war which might result if she tried to impose her massive demands on the Turks. By October 1771, the Tsaritsa, rejecting the contrary advice of Panin, was persuaded to support Frederick's plan for a partition. Austrian acceptance proved rather more difficult to obtain, and Kaunitz revealed considerable ingenuity in 1771–72 in his attempts to frustrate Frederick's scheme. It was not that the Habsburgs lacked the appetite for new lands; on the contrary, the Austrian seizure and formal annexation of the county of Zips and of three districts in the Tatra foothills in 1769–70 revealed Vienna's willingness to take lands from Poland. The initial occupation of Zips, an area on the Polish–Hungarian border to which the Habsburgs had a very dubious claim, was carried out at Kaunitz's suggestion in 1769 in order to prevent the warfare in Poland spilling over into Habsburg territory. Frederick II instituted a similar military cordon on his border with Poland in the same year. But the formal incorporation of the area was the work of a military clique at the Habsburg court and, perhaps, Joseph II. The annexation of Zips was opposed by Kaunitz who feared that it might provoke partition: as, indeed, it did. This action by Austria provided the excuse for further and more important seizures of Polish territory.

The difficulty about partition, as far as Kaunitz was concerned, was the notion of a tripartite division, since this would have benefited not only Austria but Russia and, worse, Prussia as well. It was essentially for this reason that Vienna was long opposed to any idea of partition, since the Habsburgs desired a unilateral gain to compensate for the loss of Silesia and, at the same time, were determined to prevent any further increase in Prussian strength. But Habsburg policy was ultimately determined by the simple fact that Vienna was not strong enough to fight a war to restrain Russian expansion in the Balkans. The defensive alliance signed with the Ottoman Empire early in July 1771, but never ratified, was a mere stratagem. Kaunitz had no intention of fighting on the side of the Sultan. Nor, of course, could Austria watch while Prussia and Russia made substantial territorial gains, since this would further weaken the relative position of the Habsburgs in central Europe. This political logic finally convinced Kaunitz that Austria must, as the least of several considerable evils, participate in the proposed partition. Maria Theresa's stubborn opposition to the partition, which she long believed to be nothing short of a crime, was eventually overcome by the arguments of Kaunitz and Joseph II, and Vienna then indicated to the other eastern powers her willingness to join in.

This belated and reluctant acceptance that partition was unavoidable did not, however, prevent Kaunitz from seeking an enlargement of Austria's intended share. The diplomatic initiative had now passed decisively to Vienna, for the other two eastern powers, having committed themselves to the seizure of Polish territory, by a convention signed in February 1772, needed the consent of Austria to complete the partition and to guarantee its permanence. The Austrian chancellor skilfully exploited this opportunity in the spring and early summer of 1772 to secure a significant increase in the extent of Habsburg acquisitions. The precise shares of the partitioning powers were then laid down in a series of conventions between Russia, Prussia and Austria signed in St Petersburg on 5 August 1772. Russian bayonets and the threat of further annexations were sufficient to persuade the Polish Diet to ratify these conventions (30 September 1773).

The first partition deprived Poland of almost 30 per cent of her territory and 35 per cent of her population. The Habsburgs acquired Galicia, Russia made substantial gains in Polish Livonia and White Russia, while Frederick II secured the coveted prize of Polish Prussia (which now became West Prussia). Austria acquired approximately 83,000 square kilometres of territory and some 2,650,000 inhabitants by the first partition, while Russia's share amounted to 92,000 square kilometres and 1,300,000 inhabitants and Prussia's to 36,000 square kilometres and 580,000 inhabitants. Prussia's gain was, however, much more important than these figures might suggest. In fact, Frederick II, though he was unable in 1772 or in the years immediately following to extend his share to include Danzig and Thorn (Toruń), and thus secure complete control of Polish trade down the Vistula, gained most from the first partition. The acquisition of West Prussia created for the first time a solid block of Hohenzollern territory stretching across northern and central Germany. For the Prussian King, moreover, the partition was a considerable personal triumph: he had induced Russia and coerced Austria to accept his policy, and he had avoided the general war which he dreaded. Catherine II had acquired the largest territorial share and strengthened her western frontier. But this was poor compensation for the ending of the undivided control over Poland which Russia had traditionally exercised, for the Tsaritsa had been forced to admit that Prussia and Austria should henceforth have a voice in the destiny of Poland. Austria had, on the surface, made the most valuable gains, in terms of economic resources (Galicia contained important salt-mines) and population; but the first partition was in reality a defeat for Habsburg policy.

The first partition was of considerable significance for the relations of the great powers. It revealed, in the first place, the indifference of Great Britain to events in eastern Europe and the declining interest and, more obviously, authority of France in continental affairs. The diplomacy of the partition made clear, perhaps for the first time, the political division of Europe into two separate and largely self-contained spheres. The first partition also significantly affected subsequent relations between the three eastern powers, since their complicity gave them a common interest for the future. At the time, the partition was Frederick's diplomatic masterpiece, but in the long term it can be seen to have created a potential threat to Prussian security: it brought together Russia and Austria, whose separation Frederick had always regarded as the basis of his security, and threatened the continuance of his fundamental alliance with Catherine II. For the moment, Panin's 'Northern System' continued to be the official basis of St Petersburg's foreign policy, but the events of 1772 in Poland and in Sweden (where the King, Gustav III, carried out a *coup d'état* in August) had been a mortal blow to this system (see p. 235); while in Vienna the prejudices of Maria Theresa were a powerful barrier to any Austrian *rapprochement* with Russia. Yet a realignment in the relations of the eastern powers became increasingly probable as the 1770s progressed. Austria seemed at the time the principal loser by the partition. Vienna's substantial gains were little compensation for the visible diminution of the power of France (still Austria's only ally), the renewed western advance of Russia and the further strengthening of Prussian power and Frederick's personal prestige – developments which all seriously threatened the Habsburgs' position in Germany and in Europe generally. The cession in 1775 of the Ottoman province of the Bukovina (provided for by the secret Austro-Turkish treaty of 1771) did not significantly increase Habsburg power in eastern Europe, nor did it diminish Austria's appetite for new territory.

The first partition of Poland had highlighted the brutal acquisitiveness of continental diplomacy after the Seven Years War, an acquisitiveness sanctioned by contemporary thinking about the balance of power (see pp. 211–2). By the later eighteenth century there was general agreement that if one state was about to make territorial gains, then the other great powers should join in and demand equal, or equivalent, shares. In this way, the balance of power became a threat to the existence of the smaller states. Poland had been deprived of one-third of her territory and remained an obvious target for the territorial appetite of her neighbours. Nor had the first partition done much to restrain Russia's appetite for Ottoman territory and Catherine II was able to make substantial gains by the peace of Kutchuk–Kainardji in 1774, though she was careful to take these around the Black Sea and not in the Balkans (see p. 235). The partitioning powers had justified their action by the plausible argument that Polish 'anarchy' was a threat to the peace of Europe. The first partition of Poland, however, was primarily a result of the territorial ambitions of the neighbouring powers, ambitions which were aroused, rather than satisfied, by the initial seizure of Polish territory.

HABSBURG ATTEMPTS TO ACQUIRE BAVARIA, 1777–1785

Austrian participation in the first partition of Poland had been belated and extremely reluctant, since the principle of approximately equal gains for each of the eastern powers which it enshrined was anathema to Vienna. The Habsburgs had accepted after 1763 that Silesia was, at least for the foreseeable future, part of Prussia and that no further attempt could be made to recover it during Frederick II's lifetime. Maria Theresa and Kaunitz could never completely abandon Silesia, but they were now reconciled to its loss and concentrated instead on possible 'equivalents' (which would have to be unilateral gains) for the lost province in order to restore Habsburg primacy in Germany. The most obvious target was the small and now politically insignificant but prosperous and fertile electorate of Bavaria, which also attracted the Habsburgs on purely strategic grounds. Bavaria lay directly to the west of Austria and had served as the access for foreign invasions in 1703–4 and again in 1741–42. Possession of Lower Bavaria, and in particular the lands round the Inn, would give the Habsburgs control of the upper Danube; it would create a solid wedge of territory running from Bohemia to the Tyrol (with the exception of the small archbishopric of Salzburg) and would help link up the German lands with the Habsburg possessions in Italy. The strategic value of Bavaria to the Habsburgs was obvious, and since the end of the seventeenth century a variety of unlikely schemes for rounding off Habsburg territory in the west by its acquisition had been entertained intermittently in Vienna. As the eighteenth century had progressed, these schemes had become increasingly linked with the idea of some kind of exchange involving the Austrian Netherlands (obtained in 1713), which were seen in Vienna as a distant and expensive distraction, particularly when Habsburg foreign policy came to concentrate, from the 1740s onwards, on the struggle with Prussia.

The question of Austria's acquisition of Bavaria was given a new urgency in the aftermath of the Seven Years War by the fact that the ruling Wittelsbach house seemed about to die out and by the steadily increasing influence in Vienna of Joseph II. Joseph had become emperor on the death of his father in 1765, and his growing importance in Vienna was matched by a considerable appetite for new territory. The Elector, Max Joseph, had no direct heirs, and the opportunity his death would present for Austria was very real; indeed, it had been largely with this in mind that the new Emperor had earlier married (as his second wife) the Elector's sister, the wretched Maria Josefa. From the later 1760s onwards Joseph II was loudly advocating the acquisition of Bavaria, though he found little positive response in Vienna. Kaunitz was certainly aware of the potential value of the electorate, but he also understood, far more clearly than did the

Emperor, the obstacles in the way of acquisition. Max Joseph's increasing age and Joseph II's steadily growing voice in Habsburg policy, together made the matter more urgent by the mid-1770s, and the Elector's death (30 December 1777) brought the issue to a head.

The designated successor to the Bavarian lands was Charles Theodore of the Palatinate, and here a further opportunity presented itself to Vienna. Charles Theodore had no direct heirs, but he was the father of a large brood of natural children and the resources of the Palatinate were insufficient to provide for them; he was, in any case, somewhat reluctant to leave his pleasant court at Mannheim. The Habsburgs' trump card was their ability to find positions for Charles Theodore's children in the Imperial bureaucracy and this promise was sufficient, in the immediate aftermath of Max Joseph's death, to secure an agreeement by which Charles Theodore ceded most of Lower Bavaria (the strategically important area amounting to a third of the electorate) to the Habsburgs whose troops immediately occupied it. The convention further seemed to suggest that Upper Bavaria would in turn be ceded to Austria. This arrangement appeared, superficially, a considerable Habsburg coup, but Vienna's hopes were dashed by the severe opposition which now emerged.

Austria's nominal ally, France, not only refused all assistance (even if Austria were attacked) but actually informed Prussia of this refusal. The French foreign minister, Vergennes, was on the point of intervening on the side of the American colonists in their struggle with Britain (see pp. 258ff.) – the Franco-American treaties were signed on 6 February 1778 – and had no intention of becoming involved in a continental war. He was, in any case, anxious to see the continuance of the equilibrium in central Europe which had been confirmed in 1763, and this would obviously be undermined by a unilateral territorial gain for the Habsburgs. The principal opponent of Austrian schemes, however, was the King of Prussia. Frederick had a vested interest in preventing anything that would strengthen the Austrian state and was able to exploit the considerable latent opposition to the Habsburgs that Joseph II's aggressive and overbearing policies had aroused within the Empire. The King also managed to persuade Charles Theodore's legal heir, Duke Charles Augustus of Zweibrücken, to protest to the Empire that *his* rights of succession in Bavaria had been violated by the agreement between Austria and the Palatinate, and this protest was viewed sympathetically by many of the smaller German princes, alarmed by Joseph II's policy. After some frenetic diplomacy in the first half of 1778, Austria found herself isolated, abandoned by France and opposed by many of the smaller Imperial states as well as by Frederick II.

The Prussian King was determined to frustrate Austrian policy, and Vienna's diplomatic isolation gave him his chance. France, as Frederick knew, would not assist her nominal ally, while he himself was still the ally of Russia. The contrast with the situation a decade before (see p. 224ff.) was considerable, and when Austria seemed to be intent on retaining her acquisitions in Bavaria the Prussian King invaded Habsburg territory (July 1778). The war which followed, the War of the Bavarian Succession (1778–79), was pure Gilbert and Sullivan: neither Austria nor Prussia nor Saxony (who had her own claims on Bavarian territory and joined the war against the Habsburgs) really wanted a war and both sides sought – successfully – to avoid actual battles. The principal struggle of the rival armies was against disease and hunger and this gave it the nickname of the 'Potato War', in commemoration of the Prussian soldiers who were reduced to digging potatoes out of the soil in order to survive. Negotiations for peace began in the same month as the military manoeuvring in Bohemia and Moravia: Maria Theresa's pacifism, her realistic awareness of Habsburg weakness and her bitter memories of the destructive impact of the last war against Prussia, all made her determined for peace at almost any price. The Empress-Queen initiated negotiations behind her son's back and she was supported by Kaunitz who was also anxious for an early settlement. Negotiations dragged on inconclusively throughout the second half of 1778, complicated by Frederick II's insistence (ultimately successful) that his claims to the territories of Ansbach and Bayreuth must be settled at the same time. It was only in the spring of the following year that peace was concluded, under Franco-Russian mediation at Teschen (Cieszyn). Habsburg gains by the peace of Teschen (May 1779) were not negligible, amounting as they did to a small area in south-east Bavaria, the Innviertel, an acquisition which had the important effect of joining up the Tyrol with the main core of Habsburg territory in central Europe. This first attempt to acquire Bavaria, however, proved a considerable reverse for Habsburg policy.

The principal lesson which Joseph II drew from this failure was the absolute necessity of obtaining an alliance with Russia, for Catherine now gave the law to the rest of the Continent. In 1778–79 the Tsaritsa, who did not wish to see any change in the territorial balance in Germany (which favoured Russia), had given diplomatic backing to her ally, Prussia, and this support had been an important factor in Frederick II's vigorous opposition to Habsburg schemes. Catherine's mediation of the peace of Teschen revealed Russia's new-found importance in German affairs. As the Emperor recognised, it would be necessary to destroy the Russo-Prussian alliance, which had effectively neutralised Austria since the end of the Seven Years War, before Vienna could pursue an active policy. However, Maria Theresa retained final control over Habsburg diplomacy and she was unwilling to countenance any alliance with Catherine. Her death on 29 November 1780 gave Joseph complete control over Austrian policy and he immediately set out to ally with St Petersburg. Catherine II was, by this time, becoming increasingly committed to an expansionist policy in the Balkans (see pp. 235ff.) and an alliance with Austria was logical in view of this; the long-lived Austro-Russian alliance concluded in 1726 had been largely based on shared hostility towards the Turks. The formal conclusion of an alliance, however, proved to be a matter of considerable difficulty. The basic problem was Catherine's claim to an imperial title which Joseph, as Holy Roman Emperor, could not concede. The resulting impasse meant that no formal treaty could be signed. These difficulties explain the unusual form the Austro-Russian treaty eventually took: in May and June 1781, Joseph and Catherine exchanged private letters laying down reciprocal obligations. These amounted, in effect, to a treaty of defensive alliance, aimed particularly at the event of an Ottoman attack on Russia. For the moment, however, this Austro-Russian alliance remained secret.

The new alignment represented a reversal of Habsburg foreign policy since 1763. In the 1760s and 1770s, Vienna had been alarmed by Russian expansion in the Balkans and had tried unsuccessfully to restrict Catherine's gains. Joseph now sanctioned further Russian expansion in return for the Tsaritsa's support for Habsburg policy in Germany and, perhaps, his own ambitions in south-eastern Europe. But the new alliance was always flawed. Each state intended it to serve different ends. For Joseph the treaty was directed against Prussia, for Catherine the target was the Ottoman Empire. The Russian alliance was also a tacit rejection of Austria's previous dependence on France, though the original treaty concluded in 1756 nominally remained in operation. After 1780, Joseph II took a more positive role in the formulation of foreign policy than his mother Maria Theresa had ever done. He retained Prince Kaunitz as his foreign minister, in spite of periodic and sometimes serious disagreements over policy. Kaunitz's experience and his unrivalled knowledge of European affairs were certainly valued by the Emperor, and the old Chancellor's avidity for power, and its rewards, enabled him to accept both the apparent ending of the French system soon after Maria Theresa's death and the need to discuss policy more fully than he had done in the past. The most significant modification of Kaunitz's outlook which was apparent in the 1780s, was a greater willingness for war, caused principally by his realisation that Frederick II would not live much longer and that Prussia would be far less formidable under his successor.

The early years of Joseph II's personal rule (1780–90) were dominated by the Emperor's impetuous attempts at internal reform, and it was not until 1783 that he again turned his attention to the acquisition of Bavaria. Towards the end of 1783, Joseph II finally committed himself fully to Catherine's forward policy in the Balkans and received in return a promise of Russian support for his own ambitions towards Bavaria. In April 1784 the Emperor began seriously to work for the exchange of the Austrian Netherlands for the remainder of Bavaria.

Charles Theodore, who had been ruling rather reluctantly as elector of Bavaria since 1779, was to be offered a royal title to persuade him to accept the scheme. The obstacles to any such project were formidable, as soon became clear. Charles Theodore's agreement in principle was soon obtained, but the details of the arrangement proved very elusive. Nor could the Bavarian Elector's heir, Duke Charles Augustus of Zweibrücken, be induced to give his consent.

The attitude of France (still Austria's ostensible ally) was critical, both because of the proposed change on her northern frontier and because of Versailles's effective control over the Duke of Zweibrücken. Vergennes's views for long seemed ambivalent, but in reality he was always opposed to the scheme. Franco-Austrian relations were, in any case, rather acrimonious at this point, principally because of the Emperor's strenuous efforts to force the opening of the River Scheldt to non-Dutch shipping. This closure had been part of the Westphalian settlement in 1648, and Joseph believed that if he could bring it to an end it would revive the economic prosperity of the Austrian Netherlands; the Emperor also resented the restraints on his sovereignty implied by the closure. *Force majeure* was used in an attempt to coerce the Dutch and a war with Holland almost broke out late in 1784, but France gave diplomatic support to The Hague and Joseph was forced to abandon his scheme. He attempted to win French support for the more important question of the Bavarian Exchange by concessions over the Scheldt. France, however, feared the consequent strengthening of Habsburg power in Germany, and for this reason refused her consent to the project. Nor, despite Joseph II's expectations, did Russia provide much more than token diplomatic support. In addition, Austrian diplomacy proved inept in 1784–85: Joseph II's impatient temperament was ill-suited to the delays inevitable in any negotiation and the whole episode was eloquent testimony to the Emperor's lack of finesse in foreign policy.

The Chancellor, Kaunitz, soon lost his initial enthusiasm for the scheme as the formidable obstacles became clear. By spring 1785 even Joseph II was prepared to admit that the project was impossible. It only remained for Frederick II, alarmed by continuing but erroneous rumours of an imminent exchange and fearful of the diplomatic isolation facing him because of the Russo-Austrian alliance, to form the *Fürstenbund* ('League of Princes') with Hanover and Saxony on 23 July 1785. This was later joined by other German princes who resented and were alarmed by Joseph II's attempts to expand Austrian influence, and it proved a significant barrier to any future attempt at Habsburg expansion within the Empire. The wheel had turned full circle. In 1740 Frederick II had inaugurated his reign with a piece of unprovoked aggression that had thrown Germany and Europe into turmoil. He was now the sponsor of a union to preserve the territorial status quo within the Empire.

The failure of both of Joseph II's attempts to acquire Bavaria was a significant diplomatic defeat for the Habsburgs. Considerable opposition, and lasting unease, inside and outside Germany, had been aroused by Austrian territorial ambitions, and Vienna's prestige was undoubtedly damaged by the two episodes. In a more general sense, the failure of Joseph's Bavarian projects also reveals the near-impossibility of substantial unilateral gains of territory in the context of later eighteenth century diplomacy. Prussia's opposition in 1778–79 was the clearest expression of this general unwillingness of the great powers to permit any one state to make a unilateral territorial gain. Only in the Balkans were such acquisitions possible. The weakness of the Ottoman Empire and the relative strength of Russia and, perhaps more important, her considerable freedom of action ensured that such gains could only be prevented by a full-scale European war.

RUSSIAN EXPANSION IN THE BALKANS, 1772–1792

The first partition of Poland had arisen out of the mutual desire of Prussia and Austria to find a means of limiting Russian gains at the expense of the defeated Ottoman Empire in the war which had broken out in 1768; but in practice the acquisition of Polish territory did very little to satisfy Catherine II's appetite for new lands in the Balkans. Even the considerable danger of a war against Sweden in the winter of 1772–73, in the aftermath of Gustav III's *coup d'état* (August 1772) which restored royal absolutism in Stockholm, did not seriously divert the Tsaritsa from her growing preoccupation with the situation on her southern frontier. The intensity of Austrian opposition persuaded Catherine to abandon her hopes of including Moldavia and Wallachia in the final settlement, but otherwise her war aims (see p. 224) were pursued intact. The easy Russian victories in the war against the Sultan had revealed to St Petersburg the extent of Ottoman decline and the resulting opportunity for Russian expansion in the Balkans. The extent of these emerging territorial ambitions became fully evident when Catherine's terms for peace were announced. The scale of these demands largely caused the collapse of prolonged Russo-Turkish peace negotiations in 1772–73. Military operations were resumed in the spring of 1773. Russian troops took the offensive and won several victories before they were checked and turned back in the early summer. Catherine II was then distracted by the great peasant–Cossack rising led by Pugachev which broke out in the autumn of 1773. By the end of the year this had spread to much of eastern and south-eastern Russia and presented a very serious threat to the government. But the Tsaritsa, against the advice of many of her ministers, continued to insist on military victory and a dictated peace over the Turks. This proved to be less difficult in practice than many observers in St Petersburg had believed. There was now considerable war-weariness in Constantinople, and a further series of Russian victories in the first half of 1774 was enough to force the Ottoman Empire to make peace. The Turkish negotiators were aware of Catherine's increasing difficulties with the Pugachev rebellion and they skilfully exploited these to reduce Russian demands. Nevertheless, the Tsaritsa still managed to obtain most of her war aims by the treaty of Kutchuk–Kainardji concluded on 21 July 1774.

The terms of Kutchuk–Kainardji reflected Russia's spectacular military successes in the Russo-Turkish War of 1768–74. In the first place, Catherine II made considerable territorial gains to the immediate north of the Black Sea: the Kuban and Terek areas of the Caucasus, the strategically important cessions of Kinburn and the fortresses of Kerch and Yenikale in the Crimea (which together controlled access into the Sea of Azov), along with important territory between the mouths of the Bug and the Dnieper. The port of Azov, ceded to Russia in 1739 on the proviso that it should remain unfortified, was now confirmed as Russian and the restriction removed. The limited foothold on the northern littoral of the Black Sea, which these gains conferred, was of considerable significance, but these territorial acquisitions and the large war indemnity were less important in themselves than Russia's other gains. Catherine's ships were granted freedom of navigation on the Black Sea, and Russian merchant ships could now pass freely through the Straits into the Mediterranean. The Tsaritsa was also permitted to build an Orthodox church in Constantinople. The further privilege of protecting this church 'and those who serve it' was ambiguous and would prove of immense significance (as a potential lever for Russian intervention in Ottoman internal affairs) in the nineteenth century. Finally, the khanate of the Crimea, a vassal state of the Sultan since the mid fifteenth century, was given the independence it did not want. It was widely assumed that this would only be a prelude to full annexation by Russia.

These fears at first proved unfounded, for Catherine II was not yet intent on annexation. The later 1770s were a confused and essentially transitional period in Russian foreign policy. The earlier orientation embodied in the 'Northern System' had been seriously questioned by the outbreak of the Turkish War in 1768 and then effectively undermined in 1772 by the partition of Poland and by the re-emergence of royal absolutism in Sweden. Thereafter, Panin fought a losing battle to maintain his influence over the Tsaritsa. His principal rival was one of Catherine II's former lovers, Potemkin, whose star was visibly rising at the Russian court in the later 1770s. Potemkin was a vigorous advocate of further expansion and colonisation in the south, and his position as governor-general of the territories acquired in 1774 enabled him to effect his consciously imperial designs. His continuing personal influence over the Tsaritsa and the undoubted appeal of his schemes to Catherine's imagination, proved stronger than Panin's strenuous opposition. By 1779, Catherine seems to have been convinced by Potemkin's arguments: her grandson, born in the same year, was christened 'Constantine' to symbolise the vague but definite ideas of dramatic southern expansion which came to be associated with the so-called 'Greek Project'. This aimed at the expulsion of the Turks from Europe, the restoration of a 'Byzantine Empire' ruled by Constantine, and (less certainly) an independent principality in the Balkans for Potemkin himself. It is a matter of considerable doubt whether the 'Greek Project' was ever the formal basis of St Petersburg's policy in south-eastern Europe; but Russian desire for further expansion in the Balkans was undoubted.

The most obvious first step, as Potemkin ceaselessly argued, was the Crimea. Since 1774 Russia had sought to maintain the Crimea as independent but, at the same time, firmly under her influence, and she had been prepared to intervene militarily to ensure a friendly regime. Catherine's policy towards the Crimea after 1774 was strongly reminiscent of her treatment of Poland in the 1760s. Russian troops first established Sahin Giray as khan and then suppressed an uprising against him. The Ottoman Empire was resentful of Russia's growing control, and the Sultan was urged to intervene by the growing number of Crimean exiles in Constantinople. But Ottoman weakness severely restricted its capacity to act effectively and the Porte was in fact forced to acknowledge Russia's control of the Crimea by the convention of Aynali Kavak, signed early in 1779. This turned the Khan into a Russian puppet.

Open annexation, however, and further expansion in the south, both required a change in Russia's foreign policy. Panin's Prussian alliance had to be replaced by one with Vienna, and this only became possible once Joseph II began his personal rule (November 1780). The conclusion of the secret Russo-Austrian alliance in May–June 1781 (see pp. 232f.) was an essential preliminary to the full emergence of an expansionist Russian policy in the Balkans. Until the early 1780s, St Petersburg had aimed only at maintaining the Crimea as a satellite. But this policy failed because of Sahin Giray's unwillingness to accept the role Russia intended for him. His own ambitious and aggressive policy produced a further rebellion against his authority and renewed Russian military intervention. By the end of 1782 the Crimea had been effectively conquered by Russian troops under Potemkin, who now convinced Catherine II that there was no real alternative to outright annexation, and this was formally proclaimed on 19 April 1783.

The value of the alliance with Austria secretly concluded two years before now became apparent. The Russian annexation of the Crimea was the most significant territorial change in south-eastern Europe in the generation after the Seven Years War, and it was widely recognised as a decisive gain – especially in the context of Russo–Ottoman relations. Catherine II now possessed adequate naval bases and ports on the Black Sea and could launch a further, sea borne attack directly against Constantinople whenever she wished. The threat of further Russian expansion at the expense of the helpless Ottoman Empire was certainly appreciated by the other great powers, but effective support for the Turks was not forthcoming. Concerted diplomatic action would have been extremely difficult, in view of the fundamental antagonisms which divided Britain from France, and Austria from Prussia. Nor was any single power able to give effective support to the Sultan. Britain was not as yet seriously concerned at the extent of Russian expansion in the Balkans. In any case, the definitive treaty ending the War of American Independence was not signed until September 1783 and this effectively prevented her playing an active part in continental diplomacy and made her reject out of hand the French foreign minister Vergennes's tentative suggestion of co-operation against Catherine. France, traditionally the friend of the Ottoman Empire, was most hostile to the annexation of the Crimea, but Catherine II's well-timed disclosure (in the summer of 1783) of the existence of the previously secret Austro–Russian alliance intimidated Vergennes (who in any case doubted whether the Ottoman Empire was worth preserving) from action against Russia. Frederick II was neutralised by the same disclosure. The Tsaritsa's bold use of her secret treaty with Joseph II effectively prevented any great-power opposition and was instrumental in securing international acceptance of a major and, of more importance, unilateral Russian gain.

The acquisition of the Crimea gave new impetus to Russian expansion and this, in turn, produced considerable tension between St Petersburg and Constantinople. The interests of the two states came into conflict in the Danubian principalities and, more particularly, in the Caucasus, where a fierce struggle for influence followed Georgia's acceptance of a Russian protectorate in 1783. Russia's support for the Sultan's Orthodox subjects in the Balkans and the activities of Russian consuls (whom the Sultan had been forced to admit to Ottoman territory in 1781) also caused considerable resentment at the Porte. Particularly menacing, when viewed from Constantinople, was Catherine's apparently systematic exploitation of her recent acquisitions: the creation of a Russian Black Sea fleet emphasised the vulnerability of the Turkish capital to attack by sea, for it was only a day's sailing from Sevastopol, while the full incorporation of the Crimea into the Russian administrative system in the mid 1780s suggested the importance of the region in the Tsaritsa's eyes. The extent of Russian ambitions, particularly after Potemkin was placed in sole control of policy towards Turkey (October 1786), inevitably increased Ottoman resentment and desire for revenge over the humiliating loss of the Crimea. In the spring of 1787, Catherine's spectacular imperial progress down the Dnieper and through the Crimea produced a new crop of alarming rumours about Russian intentions, while the presence in her suite of her ally, Joseph II, inevitably increased its anti-Turkish appearance. The war party at the Porte, which had been gaining strength throughout the 1780s, now acquired the upper hand and, in August 1787, war was declared on Russia.

Austria fought on Catherine II's side in the Russo-Turkish War of 1787–92. The Austro-Russian alliance of 1781 had not brought the political advantages which Joseph II had anticipated; in particular, Russia had failed to provide diplomatic backing for Vienna's attempt to acquire Bavaria in 1784–85. Yet the alliance with Catherine II remained the basis of Austrian policy. Habsburg involvement in the Turkish War, however, was not simply a matter of Joseph II's acknowledgement of an unavoidable obligation to an ally: it was also closely linked to Vienna's policy towards Prussia. Kaunitz's traditional hostility to the latter had revived in the mid 1780s; it had been intensified by Frederick II's success in forming the *Fürstenbund* (see p. 233). The Austrian chancellor's dreams of revenge were encouraged by the increasingly poor health of the Prussian King, who died in August 1786. The expected death of the formidable Frederick II had allowed Kaunitz to look forward to a war of revenge against the new, and far less formidable, Prussian ruler, the future Frederick William II. In any such conflict, Russian support would obviously be essential. The Austrian chancellor was anxious to prevent a Russo-Turkish war, since this would distract Catherine II from the situation in Germany. He was also afraid of further Russian gains at the expense of the apparently helpless Ottoman Empire, since these would threaten Habsburg interests in south-eastern Europe. There was also the danger of a future revival of the Prusso-Russian alliance that had only broken down in 1780, since Catherine's heir, the Grand Duke Paul, was known to be pro-Prussian.

The Ottoman declaration of war on Russia in August 1787 again posed the fundamental problem of Habsburg foreign policy in the later eighteenth century: that of reconciling Austria's need for Russian support in Germany against Prussia with her fundamental opposition to further Russian expansion in south-eastern Europe. Kaunitz eventually concluded that, both in order to maintain the Russian alliance and in the hope of restricting Catherine's gains, Austria had to assist St Petersburg in the Turkish War. The Emperor, Joseph II, who retained the decision for peace or war, was unconvinced by Kaunitz's arguments. He would probably have preferred to remain at peace, and, indeed, he had vainly tried to restrain Russian aggression; yet he accepted that in practice Austria had little alternative to fighting alongside Catherine. In September 1787, barely a month after the

Ottoman declaration of war, Vienna acknowledged that the *casus foederis* under the alliance with Russia existed.

The formal Austrian declaration of war was delayed until 9 February 1788 in the hope that a surprise attack might lead to the capture of the strategically important city of Belgrade. In fact, the Austrian campaign of 1788 was a disaster from start to finish. Joseph II personally assumed command of the Habsburg forces, only to show himself a fitting successor to the long line of incompetent Austrian generals. An ill-judged attempt to establish a defensive screen against the Turks stretching from Croatia to Moldavia was unsuccessful; the Ottoman army broke through this and ravaged Habsburg territory before withdrawing in the autumn. Russia's campaign was similarly unsuccessful. As in 1768, St Petersburg was unprepared for the war and the first full year of fighting was indecisive, though in December 1788 Potemkin captured the fortress of Ochakov. Russia's position, moreover, was considerably complicated by Sweden's declaring war on her in July 1788.

Russo-Swedish relations had been tense since Gustav III's *coup d'état* in 1772, yet this new conflict was unexpected. The Swedish declaration of war was the culmination of Gustav III's growing hostility towards Russia in the late 1780s. It also reflected his hope that a short and successful war would strengthen his position within Sweden, where aristocratic opposition to his absolutism had assumed considerable proportions. The Swedish King hoped to recover some of the territories in Finland ceded to Russia in 1721 and 1743. Gustav's bold plan was not achieved fully; but any Swedish attack was a serious matter for Catherine II, since the Turkish War meant that there were relatively few Russian troops in the north, and the capital, St Petersburg, seemed at the mercy of Swedish forces. In the event, the Tsaritsa was saved by the emergence of severe internal opposition to the Swedish King which she herself had encouraged. Gustav III's aristocratic opponents had been further enraged by the declaration of war, since the King had not consulted the Riksdag as he was constitutionally obliged to do; at the same time, a nascent separatist movement in Swedish Finland, which had emerged in the past few years, came to the fore. These two strands of opposition now coalesced in the so-called league of Anjala which paralysed the operations of the Swedish army in the autumn of 1788. Though Gustav's political skill enabled him to overcome his domestic opponents, Sweden's war effort was blunted. Simultaneously, Russia's ally Denmark declared war on Sweden (August 1788), but pressure from Prussia and, unofficially, from two British diplomats quickly forced her to make peace. Only in the spring of 1789 was the Swedish King free to resume the war, and he was soon strengthened by a subsidy treaty with the Ottoman Empire (July 1789). Catherine was now forced to concentrate on the naval war in the Baltic. A further year's fighting produced no clear-cut result, though Russia seemed to be gaining the upper hand, and in August 1790 the two states signed peace at Verela (Värälä) in Finland. Essentially, this settlement restored the territorial status quo of 1788. Catherine's increasing preoccupation with the Turkish War and with the situation in Poland (see pp. 244ff.) made her desire peace with Sweden and this was reflected in two important concessions. Russia recognised the Swedish constitution of 1772 (which had restored the powers of the monarchy) and, significantly, she undertook never again to interfere in domestic Swedish politics.

The brief Swedish War, though it distracted Russian attention, did not seriously affect Catherine's prosecution of the war against the Ottoman Empire. The campaign of 1789 had in fact ended triumphantly for the Russo-Austrian alliance, though this had seemed unlikely at the outset. Joseph II, discouraged by failure in 1788 and by the poor performance of his ally Russia, dogged by ill-health and alarmed by discontent among the Hungarian nobility, determined on peace. Though Kaunitz urged the need to continue the war, the Emperor (after consultation with Russia) had initiated peace negotiations with Constantinople in the closing weeks of 1788. These were making some progress until the situation was transformed by the death of the Sultan Abdul Hamid I (who had ruled since 1774) on 6 April 1789. His successor, the warlike Selim III, immediately renounced any thought of a negotiated peace and, on a wave of popular enthusiasm, the Ottoman Empire renewed the war. The campaign of 1789 was a triumph for the Russian and Austrian forces. The Ottoman army was shattered in two defeats at Fokshany and Martineshti, and these opened the way for a series of dramatic allied successes: Belgrade, Akkerman, Bucharest and Bender were all captured in October and November 1789. Neither the serious rebellion which broke out in the Austrian Netherlands in October 1789 nor growing Prussian diplomatic support for the Turks seemed major obstacles to a triumphant Austrian peace; but the death of Joseph II in February 1790 rapidly produced a complete reversal of Habsburg policy. The new Emperor, Leopold II (1790–92), abandoned any idea of significant territorial gains at the expense of the Ottoman Empire. Instead, he sought a *rapprochement* with Prussia, and he achieved this by the convention of Reichenbach (27 July 1790). This was an armistice which provided for the calling of a general peace conference, and it marked Austria's effective withdrawal from the Turkish War. Leopold's principal concern was to damp down the flames of rebellion in the Austrian Netherlands and in Hungary. He was also suspicious of Catherine's growing ascendancy in eastern Europe and his brief reign was to see Habsburg foreign policy resume an anti-Russian direction. For the moment, peace was the limit of Leopold's ambitions and, after lengthy and difficult negotiations, this was concluded at Sistova (August 1791), by which Austria returned almost all her conquests to the Ottoman Empire.

The effective withdrawal of Austria and Sweden from the war in the summer of 1790, together with the increasing ambivalence of Prussian policy, seemed to give Catherine a free hand in her struggle with the Turks. But the early months of 1791 saw instead a genuine if short-lived crisis, with the threat of a general European war. This was produced by a British attempt, periodically encouraged and assisted by Prussia, to prevent further Russian expansion. Since the early stages of the Russo-Turkish War the Triple Alliance of Britain, Prussia and the Dutch Republic, which had emerged in 1788 (see p. 269), had vainly tried to restrain Russia and had given diplomatic support to the Ottoman Empire and Sweden. The impact of these posturings had hitherto been negligible, not least because Britain had been almost as suspicious of Prussian ambitions as of the threat Russia posed to the European balance of power. But in 1791 Britain moved decisively into the anti-Russian camp. The prime minister, William Pitt the Younger sought to repeat his diplomatic brinkmanship, which had been so successful in defeating both France over the Dutch Republic in 1787 and Spain over Nootka Sound in 1790 (see pp. 267ff.). The rapid deterioration in Britain's relations with St Petersburg had commercial and political causes. The ending of the Anglo-Russian commercial treaty in 1786 and its replacement by a Russo-French agreement, was resented by Britain, where the idea of substituting Poland for Russia in the map of British trade was gaining ground. It was believed that Poland could become a cheaper and more satisfactory source of naval stores and other raw materials, as well as a market for British goods. This belief required that Russia should not attain an even more dominant position in eastern Europe. At the same time, there was growing concern in London at Russia's ascendancy and the prospect that this would be consolidated by a victorious peace with the Turks. The urgings of Prussia and of the Russophobe British envoy in Berlin, Joseph Ewart, who exerted considerable influence on Pitt, encouraged Britain to move into outright opposition to Russia.

Britain aimed to impose a peace based on the *status quo ante bellum* on Catherine II and then to construct a 'federative system' of alliances in northern Europe to safeguard this settlement. Pitt's diplomatic offensive against Russia in the early months of 1791 culminated in a British ultimatum at the end of March. Unless Catherine would immediately agree to British demands and, in particular, would not try to annex the port and fortress of Ochakov and the territory extending east to the Dniester, Russia would be attacked by a British fleet in the Baltic and a Prussian army in Livonia. But Pitt's plans were supported by very few of his cabinet colleagues and there was widespread press, public and parliamentary opposition which the Russian ambassador in London skilfully helped to orchestrate. Within a few days Pitt had to abandon his 'Russian armament', and in the summer Britain and Prussia both agreed that Catherine could make whatever gains she wanted from the Turks. The collapse of Pitt's policy was complete. This episode has a certain symbolic importance, for it was the first occasion on which Britain adopted her classic nineteenth-century pose as protector of the declining Ottoman Empire against Russian expansion. But at the time it revealed only the impossibility of obtaining support for a British foreign policy not founded on opposition to the Bourbons. There was no enthusiasm for a war against Russia, still widely seen in Britain as a 'natural ally', particularly over the distant and seemingly unimportant Ochakov (which most British ministers would have been hard put to place on the map). Pitt's failure also confirmed the very limited influence which British diplomacy could exert on events in eastern Europe in the generation after the Seven Years War.

Russia was thus left free to impose her own terms on the Ottoman Empire, for France, traditionally the friend of the Porte, was no longer a force in European politics after the outbreak of the French Revolution in 1789 and Prussia was now intent on a *rapprochement* with Russia as the prelude to a further partition of Poland (see pp. 245ff.). Peace was, as usual, dependent on prior military victory. Only the famous storming and capture of Ismail by the Russians under Suvorov (December 1790) had redeemed the previous year's campaign: but 1791 brought further significant Russian victories and these, together with the lack of foreign diplomatic support, forced Constantinople to accept Russia's offers of peace. Military operations were suspended in August 1791 and, after lengthy negotiations, peace was signed early in the following year. By the treaty of Jassy (9 January 1792), Russia acquired the fortress of Ochakov and the territory lying between the Dniester and the Bug, gains which secured her position on the northern shore of the Black Sea. The Porte was forced to recognise the Russian annexation of the Crimea and had to confirm the provisions of the treaty of Kutchuk–Kainardji. These gains were undoubtedly significant, yet they fell some way short of Catherine's war aims. This reflected the growing dominance of Poland in Catherine's thinking, for as during the Russo-Turkish War of 1768–74 there was a close link between events in the Balkans and the fate of Poland. The principal victim of the shifting alliances of the war was not the Ottoman Empire but the Polish state.

THE DESTRUCTION OF POLAND 1772–1795

The first partition did not make the final destruction of Poland as a state inevitable; on the contrary, it seems to have served as a salutary shock to the Polish political nation and it certainly provided an impetus to a series of significant, if limited, educational and administrative reforms in the years after 1772. Russia retained control over Poland, however, for the Polish King and many of the magnates concluded that the only secure course of action for the future was absolute submission to St Petersburg. In the 1770s and 1780s Stanislas Augustus Poniatowski continued to reign in Warsaw, but the Russian ambassador, Stackelberg, ruled. This rule, however, proved to be fairly tolerable, largely because Catherine II was preoccupied elsewhere: in the 1770s with the Pugachev revolt and the reform of provincial administration, in the 1780s with relations with the Ottoman Empire. This induced the Tsaritsa to lead Poland on a looser rein than in the 1760s and she even approved the modest measures of reform. It was symptomatic of the changing nature of St Petersburg's control that Russian troops were withdrawn in 1780, sixteen years after they had entered Poland.

There appeared to be little reason why Catherine II should contemplate further annexations after 1772: her acquisitions by the first partition had strengthened Russia's western frontier and her control of Poland remained intact. The Tsaritsa's appetite for new territories was to be satisfied by Turkish, not Polish lands. Nor was Austria attracted by the prospect of further gains at the expense of Poland: she would, in fact, have been quite prepared to have given up those made in 1772, if a satisfactory exchange could have been arranged. The Habsburgs remained fundamentally opposed to any further territorial gains by Prussia and this ruled out any future partition, given the prevailing assumptions about the need for roughly equivalent gains for each of Poland's neighbours. The Prussian state, in fact, was the principal threat to Poland's territorial integrity after the first partition.

Prussia had been disappointed that her acquisitions in 1772 did not include the towns of Danzig and Thorn, with their control of trade down the Vistula, and Frederick II had made considerable, if ultimately unsuccessful, attempts to extend his gains to include these two towns in the immediate aftermath of the first partition. In a second way, moreover, the original partition had been incomplete: the acquisition of the province of West Prussia had, in itself, been welcome, but it had left the problem of the western tip of Poland ('Great Poland'), a diamond of territory pointing directly at the heart of Brandenburg and separating Silesia and West Prussia. The first partition had not solved Prussia's fundamental geopolitical problems: it had merely posed them in a new form. For these reasons, the acquisition of Danzig, Thorn and at least part of Great Poland possessed considerable attractions for the Hohenzollerns. While the cautious policy that characterised Frederick II's final years militated against a further direct attempt at territorial aggrandisement, with the accession of a new king, Frederick William II, in 1786, these ambitions came to the front of Prussian policy. Hertzberg, minister to Frederick II and then to Frederick William II, had as early as 1778 put forward his own scheme by which Prussia would acquire the desired territories as a result of an exchange that was as ingenious as it was improbable. The 'Hertzberg Plan' was first enunciated at the time of Austria's initial attempt to acquire Bavaria (see pp. 229ff.) and it reflected this circumstance. In return for being permitted to acquire Bavaria, Austria was to return Galicia (gained by the first partition) to Poland, which, in gratitude, would then reward Prussia by the cession of Danzig, Thorn and Great Poland. The scheme itself was, intrinsically, implausible, but the territorial aspirations which it embodied were real and were an important element in Prussian foreign policy after the accession of Frederick William II. The 'Hertzberg Plan' was modified to take account of the new situation created by the outbreak of the Russo-Turkish War in 1787 (Austria was now to receive Turkish territory, rather than Bavaria and Russia was also to make gains in the Balkans), but its basic objective, that of further, and peaceful, Prussian expansion at the expense of Poland, remained unshaken.

The origins of the second partition of Poland (carried out in January 1793) lie in the territorial ambitions of Prussia and in the situation produced in Poland and in Europe generally by the new Russo-Turkish War. Once again the fate of Poland was closely linked to events in the Balkans, though the *dénouement* was rather different from what it had been in 1771–72. Russia's involvement in a war against the Ottoman Empire, together with the Swedish attack the next year, inevitably distracted Catherine's attention away from Poland. The reforms which Russia had been prepared to sanction had been piecemeal in nature. In particular, St Petersburg would not allow any substantial increase in the size of the Polish army. Russia's control over Poland in the 1780s, though less obvious than in the years immediately before the first partition, was still considerable and it was felt to be humiliating by an increasing number of Poles. Catherine's involvement in her Turkish War was seen by many energetic, self-confident and, perhaps, patriotic members of the political nation in Warsaw as a chance to throw off the Russian yoke and St Petersburg's irksome constitutional guarantee. The meeting of the 'Great Diet' (the four-year Diet of 1788–92) saw the overthrow of the Russian protectorate. This period of patriotic enthusiasm and intense political debate (partially inspired by contemporary events in France) culminated in the celebrated constitution of 3 May 1791, which transformed Poland into a hereditary constitutional monarchy and abolished many of the internal causes of her weakness, in particular the famous *liberum veto* and the right of confederation.

These political changes were, in many ways, remarkable, but their survival ultimately depended on the attitudes of Poland's neighbours and, in particular, Russia. Poland's new rulers recognised the necessity of international support and, in view of the alliance between St Petersburg and Vienna, they calculated that the most likely source of such assistance would be Prussia. Berlin's foreign policy under the new King, Frederick William II, was puzzling, inconsistent, a prey to court faction and at times contradictory; it was also calculated to deceive. Frederick William II aspired to play a decisive role on the European stage. He recognised the opportunity which the outbreak of the Russo-Turkish War presented to Prussia and dreamed of placing himself at the head of a great alliance system. His position was consolidated by the emergence in the summer of 1788 of the Triple Alliance of Prussia, Britain and the Dutch Republic (see p. 269), though his influence in this alignment was less than that of Pitt. But until the collapse of the Triple Alliance in 1791, after the crisis over Ochakov, Prussia worked within the framework provided by this league. The objective of Prussian policy remained consistent: the acquisition of Polish territory. But the means by which this could be secured were variable. The two principal strategies were co-operation with the Poles against Russia, in the expectation of a unilateral cession of territory from Poland, and co-operation with Russia against Poland with the aim of realising a modified version of the 'Hertzberg Plan' or bringing about a new partition. In some degree these two strategies were pursued simultaneously, and this was the source of much of the uncertainty surrounding Prussian policy. During the Russo-Turkish War the first of these strategies dominated Berlin's diplomacy. But in 1791 Prussian policy went into reverse and Berlin henceforth co-operated closely with Russia over Poland.

Catherine's preoccupation with the war with the Turks, and the additional problems for Russia after Gustav III's declaration of war in July 1788, created a situation favourable to the development of Prussian ambitions. Ostensibly, Berlin's policy sought to encourage the growing Polish freedom from Russian control which was becoming apparent during the four-year Diet and to pose as a friend of Poland, in the obvious hope that Prussia could acquire a dominant influence there. Central to this strategy was the alliance Prussia offered to Warsaw at the very beginning of the Diet in 1788 and finally concluded on 29 March 1790. This Prusso-Polish treaty was essentially a conventional defensive alliance containing a reciprocal guarantee of territories; it reflected the absence of any alternative source of foreign support for the Poles, who were always anti-Russian rather than pro-Prussian in sentiment. And, in any case, the fate of Poland would ultimately depend on the attitude of Catherine II.

Poland's emancipation from Russian control between 1788 and 1791 had enraged the Tsaritsa. Catherine was alarmed at the measures passed by the four-years Diet and especially the Constitution of 3 May 1791, in part because they seemed imitations of events in France which she abhorred. Her fears of Jacobinism were real. The heightened ideological conflict of the 1790s, unleashed by the French Revolution, led her to believe that she was combating Jacobinism in Warsaw. During the Russo-Turkish War she had, in effect, to turn a blind eye to the collapse of Russian authority in Poland. But she remained determined to reassert her control, for an independent and strengthened Poland would imperil Russian security in eastern Europe. It was always Catherine's intention to restore her own influence and she was able to exploit the growing European preoccupation with Revolutionary France to increase her freedom of action. By the winter of 1791–92 France's neighbours were becoming increasingly alarmed by the radical course of events in Paris and were moving towards intervention (see pp. 277ff.). Catherine encouraged Austria and Prussia to concentrate on the situation in France; her posturings against the Revolution were intended to free the field for herself in Poland. In the early 1790s the other European states were becoming involved with the French Revolution; but for Russia this was always of subsidiary importance until Poland had finally been partitioned. It was usually of secondary importance for Prussia also, given Berlin's desire for Polish territory, though Frederick William II characteristically could not make up his mind and in fact over-extended Prussia's scanty resources by pursuing an active policy in both eastern and western Europe. But for Austria the situation in France increasingly took priority because of family connections, geography and the position of Leopold II as emperor (see pp. 275ff.).

Leopold was always opposed to any further Prussian gains and he therefore tried to uphold the status quo in Poland. He worked to convince Catherine II that the new situation in Warsaw was compatible with Austro-Russian interests. The Emperor was thus a moderating influence on Russian policy, for Austria could not be safely ignored. But his death on 1 March 1792 removed this restraint and also intensified Austria's preoccupation with the French Revolution (see pp. 279ff.). Within two months the new Emperor, Francis, was at war with France, and Vienna turned decisively away from Poland.

The change in Austrian policy after Leopold's death was one of several factors freeing Catherine for decisive action. This could only follow the conclusion of the Russo-Turkish War which came about with the settlement at Jassy in January 1792 (see p. 242). In a similar way, the factional struggle at the Russian court in the aftermath of Potemkin's death (October 1791) was now resolved in favour of the group favouring military intervention in Poland. In the spring of 1792 Catherine set about restoring her authority in the traditional way. Her treaties with Poland in 1768 and 1775, by which she had guaranteed the constitutional status quo, provided a convenient pretext for intervention. The Tsaritsa first sponsored a confederation of some Polish noblemen. This was in fact drawn up in St Petersburg on 27 April 1792 but it was dated '14 May Targowica' to foster the illusion that it had arisen on Polish soil. The confederation then served as a cloak for Russian military intervention. Russian troops crossed into Poland on the night of 18–19 May under the pretext of supporting the confederation of Targowica. While these units were moving towards the Polish border, news reached St Petersburg that France had declared war on Austria (20 April 1792), which in turn brought Prussia into the war with the Revolution. This further strengthened Catherine's position over Poland. The Poles were largely unprepared for this latest Russian military intervention: it had been widely believed in Poland that Catherine would not risk antagonising Prussia and Austria and would in fact accept the new situation much as she had, two decades earlier, accepted the *coup d'état* in Sweden. This hope, and the expectation of support from Prussia, were quickly shown to be illusions. The ramshackle Polish army was no match for the numerically far superior Russian forces, and in July 1792 Poland, in the person of the King, Stanislas Augustus, submitted to St Petersburg's control. The emigration of a considerable number of Poles who had played a prominent part in the upheavals of the past few years shows the extent of this defeat. Henceforth the decisive voice in Polish affairs would again be that of Catherine II.

The precise intentions of the Tsaritsa at this point are by no means clear. A return to the situation before 1788 would perhaps have suited her best; yet she was certainly not wholly opposed to a further partition and she was also obliged to take some account of the views of Prussia and, less certainly, Austria. The signature of defensive alliances with Vienna and Berlin (July–August 1792) further strengthened Catherine II's hand, as she could now make a clear choice for a political partner between the two German powers. The attitudes of these two states towards Poland in the second half of 1792 were somewhat different. Ever since spring 1792, Frederick William II had looked towards a further partition and the new territory this would bring him. The unexpected resistance put up by the armies of the French Revolution to the Prusso-Austrian advance in the autumn (see p. 281) increased the desire for Polish territory, since this would compensate for the disaster in the west. The Prussian King was also anxious to prevent, if at all possible, the re-establishment of Russia's sole control over Poland.

The death of Leopold at the beginning of March 1792 produced a reversal of Habsburg policy, which had hitherto been opposed to any further partition. By June Francis had agreed that Prussia and Russia could make further gains in Poland provided Austria was allowed to carry through the exchange of the Austrian Netherlands for Bavaria. This was, of course, the old and deeply cherished Habsburg plan; its failure in 1784–85 had not dampened Vienna's enthusiasm for its realisation, and it had surfaced periodically during the Russo-Turkish War. At this point, however, its re-emergence was principally the work of the two ministers now responsible for the conduct of Habsburg diplomacy, Spielmann and Cobenzl, and there was considerable opposition at court in Vienna to this initiative in Austrian policy.

In the autumn of 1792, the fate of Poland was decisively affected by events in western Europe, where the war against Revolutionary France had begun. The defeat at Valmy (20 September 1792) and the disastrous retreat which followed (see p. 281) further increased the Prussian King's desire for Polish territory, since this would do something to salve the wound inflicted by the armies of the French Revolution. The failures of the allied forces also exacerbated the existing tension between Berlin and Vienna over the fate of Poland, for the Prussians believed that the Austrians had failed to provide enough support against France. The situation was brought to a head by Prussia's announcement in the last week of October that her price for continuing the war against France was an indemnity in the form of Polish territory. Austrian policy at this critical juncture was hesitant and contradictory. Spielmann and Cobenzl remained commited to the Netherlands exchange, but their policy continued to encounter considerable opposition in Vienna and was, in any case, effectively undermined (at least temporarily) by France's conquest of most of the Austrian Netherlands after her victory at Jemappes (6 November 1792). The dramatic successes of the French Revolutionary armies forced Austria to accept that, for the foreseeable future, war with France had to be her main priority, and Prussian support was essential to the success of this struggle. Austria was thus forced to accept Prussian demands for Polish territory, though any exchange involving the Netherlands was, for the moment, impossible.

Catherine II had, until now, played a masterly waiting game, resisting Prussia's considerable pressure for a new partition, since she herself was not yet fully committed to further acquisitions. Her final decision to force through a partition, which became apparent in mid December 1792, reflected her desire to keep Prussia in the anti-French coalition (Catherine was hostile to the French Revolution) and, more especially, her growing anxiety at developments within Poland, where the pro-Russian regime of the men of Targowica was increasingly unable to control the country. The formal justification of the second partition was the desire to combat the 'same spirit of insurrection and dangerous innovation' that had gained the upper hand in France and 'was ready to break out in the kingdom of Poland'. Catherine was clearly alarmed by the spectre of Jacobinism in Warsaw. In mid-December 1792 she announced her willingness to see Prussia occupy the territory Frederick William II was demanding and then announced her own terms. The scale of these was breathtaking and certainly amazed the Prussian King, but Frederick William had no intention of haggling over a scheme which gave him his demands in their entirety. After very brief negotiations, the formal Russo-Prussian treaty of partition was signed in St Petersburg on 23 January 1793. Catherine in effect dictated her own terms: Russia acquired some 250,000 square kilometres (principally comprising the districts of Minsk, Podolia, the western Ukraine and the eastern regions of Volhynia) with a population of over 3 million people; Prussia, by contrast, acquired far less, some 58,000 square kilometres (Great Poland, with the cities of Danzig, Thorn, Posen (Poznań) and Kalisz), and around 1 million new subjects. Austria was not officially informed of the second partition until March 1793 and received only a vague and specious promise from the partitioning powers to assist in bringing about the Bavarian exchange at some future date.

Austria's defeat was total. The initial mistake of Spielmann and Cobenzl in resurrecting the exchange project had been compounded by their dogged refusal to abandon it when circumstances changed dramatically and by the dilatoriness, timidity and indecision with which Habsburg policy had been conducted. The inexperience of the new Emperor Francis was of considerable significance during these months. His dismissal of the two ministers (27 March 1793) and their replacement by Thugut brought a greater realism and a new sense of purpose to Habsburg policy, but by then it was simply too late.

The second partition of Poland was an immense triumph for Russia; Prussia, though her share of the spoils was proportionately far less, had made an additional important territorial acquisition; Austria, however, had suffered another diplomatic defeat, a further shift against her in the political balance in eastern Europe. Poland, the helpless victim, had suffered a mortal blow. In 1793 she was deprived of half her territory and people, and was now a rump of 212,000 square kilometres with a population of some 4 million. The resistance within Poland to this brutal loss was strong and vocal, and it was only with considerable difficulty (and with the help of Russian bribes and soldiers) that the ratification of the formal treaties of partition were forced through the Diet of Grodno in the summer and autumn of 1793. A further series of measures passed at this Diet dismantled the new constitutional regime of 3 May 1791 and restored the evils that had contributed so much to the weakness of Poland, above all the elective monarchy and the *liberum veto*. Finally, a Russo–Polish 'treaty' of 16 October made Poland once again a Russian protectorate.

The second partition can be seen in retrospect to have been decisive, yet there was nothing inevitable about the final extinction of the Polish state two years later. In the aftermath of the second partition, the attitudes of Poland's neighbours remained contradictory. Prussia clearly desired a further, final partition. Austria, equally clearly, was opposed to any additional annexations yet, at the same time, vigorously resented her exclusion from the second partition. Russia's attitude was ambiguous and perhaps undecided. Catherine II, who now held the political initiative, may well have seen the necessity of a further partition as a final solution to the Polish question, for the situation created by the second partition was intrinsically unstable. Catherine's troops remained in Poland, while the Tsaritsa also supervised the Polish army and directed Polish foreign policy.

The re-imposition and, indeed, strengthening of Russian control intensified the mounting indignation and resentment within the rump of Poland and focused the vague plans previously discussed for a general Polish insurrection against Russia and Prussia. This was started on 24 March 1794. Its heroic leader, Kosciuszko, achieved a hard-won but important victory over the Russians at Raclawice (4 April 1794) and Warsaw evicted its Russian garrison. Within a few weeks the rebellion had spread to much of the territory Poland retained in 1793. The Polish rising was periodically weakened by the emergence of severe internal divisions (particularly the fundamental split between the conservatives and the radical 'Polish Jacobins') and, given the infinitely superior resources of its enemies, it was perhaps always bound to be defeated. Yet the makeshift Polish army caused Russia and Prussia considerable problems in the spring and summer of 1794, winning some notable victories. Russia now faced a full-scale war in Poland, and it was only the arrival of powerful Russian reinforcements that finally broke Polish resistance. The Russian victory at Maciejowice (where Kosciuszko was wounded and captured) on 9 October seriously weakened the rising. Three weeks later, Suvorov's forces stormed the Praga suburb of Warsaw, massacring the civilian population, and this action quickly produced the surrender of the terrified capital. By the closing weeks of 1794 the Polish insurrection had been crushed.

The origins of the third partition lie in the response of Prussia and, especially, Russia to the 1794 rising. The early successes of the Polish insurgents greatly alarmed Catherine II, who called on Prussia for military support. Frederick William II remained intent on a final partition and he had already decided to intervene. He was therefore delighted to respond to the Tsaritsa's appeal. The entry of Prussian troops into Poland (May 1794) effectively decided the issue of partition, for (as St Petersburg recognised) Prussia was not going to evacuate this newly occupied territory. Catherine II soon acknowledged that a further partition was the logical solution, since it seemed unlikely that Poland could ever be pacified, and Russia's success in finally suppressing the rebellion gave the political initiative to the Tsaritsa. Meanwhile, Austria, resentful at her exclusion in 1793, had no intention of being excluded again and quickly announced her acceptance of a final partition. By the end of June 1794 the obliteration of Poland had been agreed by the eastern courts. Negotiations to determine the precise distribution of territory continued throughout the year, while the Polish rising was being suppressed, and each power sought to pre-empt a final settlement by occupying as much Polish territory as it could.

These negotiations were considerably more complex and extended than those for the two previous partitions. Austria and Prussia were, in the first place, already on thoroughly bad terms. This reflected Vienna's annoyance at its exclusion from the second partition. It also testified to the difficulties of the unsuccessful war against Revolutionary France, and Prussia's belief that Austria had not played a full part in this struggle. A more fundamental difficulty during these negotiations was the fact that, for the first time, the frontiers of the partitioning powers were actually to come into contact; strategic considerations and, in particular, the question of 'natural' (or merely defensible) frontiers had to be taken into account. The discussions between the three courts in the second half of 1794 in fact produced a deadlock. Russia and Austria quickly agreed on their respective shares and hence on the need to restrain Prussia's territorial appetite. Frederick William II, however, remained intransigent; in particular, he refused to give up the city of Cracow (Kraków) and its surrounding region, long coveted by Austria but occupied by Prussian troops in 1794. The Austrian and Russian shares were set out in a secret treaty signed on 3 January 1795, which also had the character of an alliance directed against Prussia. The impasse remained, however, and Frederick William II, fearing a war against Russia and Austria, now withdrew from the coalition against France (treaty of Basle, June 1795: see p. 285). The Prussian state was now too weak to contemplate further fighting and in August 1795 Frederick William recognised this and agreed to the Russo-Austrian scheme for partition. Some minor Austrian concessions were enough to satisfy Berlin, and Austro-Prussian and Prusso-Russian treaties were signed on 24 October 1795. The third partition had now been carried out. It remained only for further treaties signed on 5 December 1796 and 26 January 1797 to arrange the final details of the obliteration of Poland. By the third partition, Russia acquired Courland, Lithuania, Podlesia and the western portion of Volhynia; Austria obtained Little Poland along with Lódź (Lublin) and Cracow; and Prussia took the remaining Polish territories, including Warsaw. Poland had ceased to exist as a state; to underline this, the partitioning powers solemnly undertook never to use the name of the vanished kingdom in the future.

The three eastern powers all made vast territorial gains from the partitions (see map 6), but these did not prove permanent. Within two decades Poland was first partially restored by Napoleon and then repartitioned at the congress of Vienna, when the bulk of what had formerly been Polish territory passed into Russian hands (see Ch. 11 and 12). Poland, the third largest continental state before 1772, had thus been removed from the map of Europe within a generation, and this inevitably produced a lively and continuing debate over the reasons for partition. The explanations advanced can be grouped under two principal headings: internal weakness and external pressure. The former has recently received greater emphasis, and it is certainly clear that the administrative, political and economic weaknesses of the Polish state were significant. Poland's development in the early modern period had been directly contrary to the general European pattern. Instead of the absolute monarchy, centralised administration and powerful standing army that were usual elsewhere, Poland had an elected monarchy largely at the mercy of the magnates, a weak central government and a small and backward army. But this dichotomy really only explains the ease with which Poland was obliterated. The actual partitions were brought about by her powerful and ambitious neighbours. The real villains were the three eastern monarchies, not the selfish magnates or the cowardly Stanislas Augustus Poniatowski. Poland's own weakness and her lack of defensible frontiers made partition considerably easier, as did the absence of outside support; the disappearance of France, a traditional friend of the Poles, from any active political role in eastern Europe after 1763 was of some significance. But it is by no means clear how either of the western powers could have resisted the successive encroachments on Polish territory. As Horace Walpole pointed out at the moment of the first partition, the British fleet could not easily sail to Warsaw.

Russia gained most from these territorial changes, and her relative position among the powers increased accordingly. Her annexations from Poland were at least equal to those of either Austria or Prussia, while she also made immense unilateral gains from the Ottoman Empire. By 1796, the year of Catherine II's death, Russia was securely established on the northern shore of the Black Sea and was poised for further attacks: attacks which the Sultan appeared unable to resist. The foundation of the port of Odessa in 1794 had signified Russia's intention to exploit her new and fertile southern territories and their considerable trading potential. The intense and continuing Russian pressure on Ottoman borderlands, at a time when Constantinople was already finding difficulty in controlling its outlying provinces, is the principal explanation for Russia's dramatic southern expansion. Nor were the other European powers able to resist this. The rivalry of Austria and Prussia worked to Russia's advantage, for it prevented effective co-operation against Catherine. In a similar way, the Anglo-French rivalry overseas, particularly before the 1780s, facilitated Russia's decisive westward expansion and her parallel emergence as the dominant power in eastern Europe and, perhaps, on the Continent: this was the principal political development of the generation after 1763.

CHAPTER NINE

Anglo-Bourbon relations in Europe and overseas 1763–1790

ANGLO-FRENCH RELATIONS AFTER THE SEVEN YEARS WAR, 1763–1774

Britain's victory in the Seven Years War, the latest round in the long Anglo-French duel for colonial and commercial hegemony, had been unusually decisive. In 1763, her maritime and colonial supremacy was firmly established: France was excluded from the mainland of North America, her position in India was almost destroyed and only in the West Indies had she escaped large territorial losses. The peace of Paris represented a serious and humiliating defeat for Versailles, and an early and determined French attempt to recover her losses seemed likely. The peace settlement, far from easing Anglo-French tension, increased it and itself constituted the main barrier to future good relations. For the next two decades, the principal aim of France, and of her ally Spain, was to undermine Britain's supremacy.

The succession of the French Bourbons to Spain had not created permanent political unity. On the contrary, Franco-Spanish relations had often been acrimonious. However, the accession of Charles III (1759–88) to the Spanish throne during the Seven Years War had proved a turning-point. For the first time, Spain had a king as hostile as the French court towards England. Charles III ('Don Charles') had previously ruled first Parma and then the kingdom of Naples (the Spanish secundogeniture in Italy) and the action of a British fleet in forcing him to withdraw from the War of the Austrian Succession by threatening to bombard Naples had made him a lifelong enemy of Britain. Two years after becoming Spanish king he signed a firm Franco-Spanish alliance, the Third Family Compact of August 1761, which brought about the ill-fated Spanish intervention in the closing stages of the Seven Years War (see p. 199), and this alignment continued for the next three decades. It was symptomatic of the dominance of colonial issues in Anglo-Bourbon relations that this Family Compact, unlike those of 1733 and 1743, was a response to overseas, rather than purely European, rivalries.

The defeats Britain inflicted on Spain in 1762–63 potentially threatened the stability of the alliance. Because of this (and also to persuade Madrid to accept an early peace settlement) France had ceded Louisiana west of the Mississippi to Spain in 1762 as compensation for likely Spanish losses at the peace, which in the event amounted to Florida. The Franco-Spanish alliance was always an unequal, and also an uneasy, partnership. The political leadership assumed by Versailles was resented in Madrid, as was France's systematic attempt to exploit Spain commercially. The precise strategy to be adopted against Britain also produced periodic disagreements. Moreover, each state – though agreed on hostility towards England – saw the alliance differently. Spain's extensive overseas empire, which was highly vulnerable to future British expansion, made her emphasise the defensive nature of the Family Compact. The French, however, wanted to use their relationship offensively and intended Spain's armed forces to play a significant, if minor, part in the eventual war of revenge against Britain. Yet this substantial difference of emphasis was blurred in practice because each needed the other's support against Britain, and this gave the partnership a remarkable degree of permanence. In particular, Spain was poorly equipped to face Britain's increasing challenge in the Americas after 1763, and France was the only source of assistance Madrid so obviously needed. For thirty years the Family Compact of 1761 remained a fixture in European politics. Only in 1790, in the crisis produced by the French Revolution, did the Franco-Spanish alliance break down.

The intense Franco-Spanish hostility towards Britain and desire for revenge were always tempered in practice by the realisation that the Bourbon powers were not strong enough to fight her and win. The essentially colonial nature of the Anglo-Bourbon conflict after the Seven Years War made sea power decisive and here, of course, Britain was clearly supreme. Consequently, for the next generation, relations between the three states were largely determined by their respective naval strengths. This was certainly appreciated by Choiseul, who had controlled French policy since 1758 and who concentrated on rebuilding the shattered armed forces of France and Spain immediately after the peace of Paris. Choiseul certainly did not neglect the French army, but in the early years of peace he focused attention and resources on the French navy, besides urging similar action on Charles III. Unfortunately, both states lacked the *matériel* (above all, timber), money and trained manpower to become major sea powers quickly. Moreover, Spain's political outlook was less aggressive than that of Choiseul, and her government and finances were in an even worse state than those of France. As a result, little real progress was made in rebuilding the Spanish navy. Choiseul's reconstruction of France's navy, however, was successful, but this work essentially paved the way for later French naval victories in the War of American Independence. In the short term, the Bourbon powers were unable to build sufficient ships to challenge Britain's mastery at sea, and consequently hopes of an early war of revenge had to be abandoned in the face of the naval realities: defence, not attack, was the basis of Bourbon policy at this time.

Britain's continuing naval dominance was reflected in the essentially moderate line taken by the Bourbon powers in a series of disputes in the 1760s. The war and the subsequent peace settlement had together produced several issues, minor in themselves but potentially inflammable, which dominated Anglo-Bourbon relations in the early years of peace. The most important of these were the 'Manila Ransom' (a sum allegedly due to Britain for not razing the Spanish city in the Philippines) and the perennial question of French fortifications at Dunkirk. While the British adopted a high-handed attitude and were willing to use naval blackmail, Choiseul was forced to follow an essentially conciliatory policy.

A new source of tension was provided by Britain's attempt to exploit her gains at the peace of Paris and to expand into the South Pacific, where France nurtured similar ambitions and Spain was already established. This triangular rivalry produced two disputes over the possession of the Falkland Islands (in the South Atlantic, but important as a staging post) in 1766 and 1770. The second of these brought an Anglo-Bourbon war nearer than at any time since 1763. The precise cause of this second crisis was the expulsion of the British colony at Port Egmont by a Spanish naval commander. Spain refused to make the restitution demanded by Britain, and war between Britain and the Bourbons was very close in the second half of 1770. Despite his conviction that France and Spain were not yet strong enough to fight England, Choiseul fully supported and, indeed, encouraged Madrid's firm stand. Whether Choiseul really wanted war in 1770 must remain doubtful, but Louis XV's belief that he did seems to have been central to the King's decision to dismiss him. The fall of Choiseul in December 1770 paved the way for a settlement early the following year. Once again the Bourbons, unable to challenge Britain's naval dominance, made concessions to preserve the peace. In 1771 Spain, while not abandoning her claim to the island, restored West Falkland to Britain and formally disavowed the action of the Spanish captain who had provoked the crisis.

The dismissal of Choiseul marked a turning-point in Anglo-French relations. His hostility had been considerable and deep-rooted; formal contacts between the two states during his ministry had been tense and frequently acrimonious; and only Britain's continuing naval superiority had prevented him from initiating a war of revenge. The early 1770s, however, saw a remarkable change. The fundamental causes of tension were still there, but new personalities and political priorities in both capitals produced several years of comparative harmony unparalleled since the final collapse of the Anglo-French *entente* in 1731. The initiative came from France. D'Aiguillon, who eventually succeeded Choiseul as foreign minister in summer 1771, shared Louis XV's well-known love of peace and immediately adopted a conciliatory attitude towards Britain.

D'Aiguillon's desire for better relations with Great Britain and the distinctly pacific tone of French foreign policy were initially prompted by France's preoccupation during the final years of Louis XV's reign (1771–74) with remedying the debilitating financial weakness of the French monarchy and solving the fundamental problems posed by the power of the *parlements*. This was paralleled in London where Lord North's ministry, which gave some much-needed stability to British politics after 1770, was similarly preoccupied with financial retrenchment and the problem of the American colonies. The resulting improvement in relations culminated, in 1772–73, in secret discussions for closer political co-operation and a possible alliance. After several hints from d'Aiguillon, it was eventually taken up on the British side by Lord Rochford (the secretary of state for the southern department) with the encouragement – briefly – of George III and perhaps (though this is unclear) Lord North.

D'Aiguillon based his policy on a superficial but fundamentally correct analysis of the rapidly decreasing influence of France and Britain in continental affairs. This had been apparent since the Seven Years War and especially in the early 1770s. The menacing turn of events in eastern Europe (see Ch. 8), where Russia seemed about to dictate peace to the Turks and where Poland was being partitioned with scant regard for the western powers, was particularly irksome to d'Aiguillon because of France's traditional influence at Constantinople and Warsaw. Discussions about some sort of political co-operation between Versailles and London went on intermittently – and always in secret – in 1772 and were briefly revived early in 1773, but ultimately to no avail. D'Aiguillon's proposal ran counter to the traditions and prejudices of British policy, and its considerable political logic was insufficient to overcome the growing official indifference to events in eastern Europe and the savage Francophobia of parliamentary and public opinion in England. The proposal was partly destroyed by France's encouragement and support for Gustav III's *coup d'état* which restored Swedish absolutism in August 1772. Versailles's part in this was fully known to British ministers (French diplomatic correspondence was intercepted in Hanover), and this was enough to end any thought of a *rapprochement*.

The failure of d'Aiguillon's proposals did not lead immediately to any worsening in relations. On the contrary, the harmony established in the early 1770s survived a brief but serious crisis in the spring of 1773 (produced by Britain's dread of general war and consequent refusal to allow France to send a fleet to the Baltic to support Gustav III against Russia) and substantially endured until the onset of the American War. Each desired peace because of its domestic problems. The government of Lord North was increasingly preoccupied with the rising tide of opposition in Britain's North American colonies, and it was the outbreak of rebellion there in 1775 which caused the next crisis in Anglo-Bourbon relations.

BRITAIN, THE BOURBON POWERS AND AMERICAN INDEPENDENCE, 1775–1783

Britain's territorial gains in 1763 created considerable problems. The need to assimilate, administer and defend the new acquisitions in North America produced policies that conflicted with the growing desire of many colonists for increased freedom from London's control, a sentiment which had been strengthened by the removal of the French threat in Canada during the Seven Years War. The origins of the American revolt lie beyond the scope of this present volume: suffice it to say that by 1775 colonial opposition had turned into open rebellion, and by the summer ministers in London reluctantly concluded that America would have to be reconquered militarily.

The logistical problems involved were immense. The theatre of war was 3,000 miles away by sea, and troops had not only to be transported across the Atlantic but supplied with munitions and food from Britain. From the outset, shipping was London's major worry. These problems were intensified by the nature of the struggle in which Britain was engaged. The conventional military wisdom of hitting the opponent's political or military centre of gravity was little use against an enemy whose strength lay in its popular support, its irregular warfare and a country substantially hostile to Britain's largely German soldiers. Victories in set battles would not in themselves defeat the American rebels. London's task was also complicated by the desire to avoid any action which might hinder a subsequent political settlement. The ambivalence of British ministers, and of their commanders in the field, towards a war against fellow Englishmen was always a considerable obstacle to British victory. Yet these various barriers to success, large as they were, were almost overcome. In 1775–76, Britain made a considerable military effort in North America, believing an early and decisive victory would force a settlement on the rebels. The campaigns of 1776 and 1777 saw substantial British gains, and colonial resistance would probably have been beaten and a political settlement imposed but for French intervention in 1778.

From the beginning of the rebellion American agents had sought French support, believing it essential for success. Since the accession of Louis XVI in 1774, French foreign policy had been in the capable hands of Vergennes, an experienced and perceptive career diplomat. Vergennes shared Choiseul's desire to humble Britain, though his hostility was more calculated: French policy throughout the War of American Independence was to aim at restoring the colonial balance of power, which had been tilted so decisively towards England by the peace of Paris in 1763, and in this way make possible an eventual reconciliation with London on French terms. Vergennes's policy was, essentially, a synthesis of those of his predecessors: Choiseul's war of revenge against Britain was to be the prelude to the political *rapprochement* attempted by d'Aiguillon. Louis XVI's foreign minister intended, in accordance with the tenets of mercantilism, to weaken British power by depriving her of her American colonies and the commercial and naval strength drawn from them. In this way, Vergennes hoped to restore the colonial equilibrium so that France could recover her traditional influence in Europe. For French policy aimed fundamentally at reasserting her European power. American independence for Vergennes was always a means to an end rather than an end in itself. He was alarmed at how the three eastern powers had come to dominate European politics since the end of the Seven Years War. The first partition of Poland and Catherine II's gains from the Russo-Turkish War of 1768–74 (see Ch. 8) were seen as expressions of the declining authority of France and ominous portents for the future. British supremacy overseas was forcing France to spend too much on the navy and restrict the sums available for France's army and for subsidies to other continental states – the means by which Versailles's authority in Europe could (Vergennes believed) best be restored. The considerable weakening of British power which the loss of the American colonies would represent and the subsequent Franco-British *rapprochement* should, in due course, allow France to cut expenditure on the navy. Vergennes's model was Fleury, who had also aimed to make France secure through co-operation with Britain. This curiously introspective analysis was flawed by its effectively ignoring France's crippling financial weakness (France would also have to spend on a war intended to make future reductions in naval expenditure!) and it considerably underestimated the actual dominance of Austria, Prussia and Russia over European politics.

Vergennes had immediately recognised the opportunity presented by the American revolt and, by spring 1776, he had secured Louis XVI's consent to the principle of French assistance to the colonists. This effectively ended the attempt at internal reform and, in particular, financial retrenchment associated with Turgot, who resigned almost immediately. For the moment, however, French support was limited to providing the colonists with money and arms. Political logic suggested that France should intervene directly, but the state of the French navy made immediate intervention impossible. As throughout the period since 1763, the level of naval preparedness ultimately determined Bourbon policy. Expenditure on the navy had been reduced after Choiseul's fall in 1770 and the fleet had suffered accordingly. However, the accession of Louis XVI soon led to the energetic Sartine's becoming navy minister and he strove successfully to remedy this situation. In addition, Versailles's commitment to the American cause was reflected in a considerable increase in naval expenditure.

At first, British ministers, preoccupied with the war in America, had tried to maintain the existing good relations with France, but France's obvious support for the colonists was difficult to reconcile with her ostensible neutrality, and relations inevitably deteriorated. The thorny question of American privateers using French ports produced a serious crisis in summer 1777 and it was clear that war could not be far off. By the beginning of 1778 Vergennes was convinced that the French navy was strong enough for war. On 6 February 1778 France signed treaties of friendship, commerce and defensive alliance with the colonists, an action which provoked a formal breach in relations with London in March. Britain and France were openly at war from July 1778.

A minor reason for Vergennes's delay in declaring war was his desire for the support of Spain and her fleet. The limited and essentially long-term success of Charles III's attempts at naval reconstruction had, by the mid-1770s, made Madrid's navy a significant factor in Anglo-Bourbon relations. Spanish policy towards the American revolt, however, was ambiguous. Charles III remained hostile towards England, and Spanish desire for revenge and, in particular, for the recovery of Gibraltar and (perhaps) Minorca was strong. But Madrid's attitude proved in practice to be less predictable than France had anticipated. In the first place, Spain resented having had repeatedly to follow the dictates of French policy, most notably in the Falkland Islands dispute in 1770–71. The Family Compact was still the principal component in Spanish policy, but it was no longer the only one. In the 1770s, Spain had increasingly looked to the western Mediterranean and to relations with the Ottoman Empire's dependencies in North Africa. In mid-1775 an attack on Algiers (the lair of many of the Barbary pirates who still preyed on Spanish shipping) proved a disastrous failure, and this fiasco inevitably tempered Spanish policy as a whole. During the early stages of the American revolt, moreover, Spain was preoccupied with relations with Portugal. Lengthy negotiations had failed to settle disputed colonial boundaries in South America and in 1776 Madrid had determined on force. The minor colonial war with Portugal which resulted (1776–77) made her more reluctant to undertake additional commitments. Above all, France retained comparatively few possessions in the New World and had much greater freedom of action, whereas Spain had an extensive colonial empire there. The fear that a successful revolt by Britain's colonists might produce rebellions against Spanish rule undoubtedly influenced ministers in Madrid, and this was the most likely reason for Spain's hesitant and limited support for the American cause. From summer 1776 onwards, Spain was secretly providing financial support on a small scale but for a long time this remained the limit of her help.

Vergennes intended to bring Spain openly into the war, but to do so he had to transform the essentially defensive Family Compact into an offensive alliance, and this proved difficult. The appointment of Floridablanca in February 1777 gave Spain a foreign minister more prepared to use the opportunity presented by the American rebellion; yet Madrid continued to be ambivalent, especially as France's refusal of aid during the brief war with Portugal aroused considerable resentment. Eventually, however, Spain was won over by a mixture of her own ambitions and Vergennes's arguments. In April 1779 she committed herself to the war against Britain by the convention of Aranjuez. This agreement considerably extended the scope of the Family Compact: it made Spain France's military ally, provided for a joint Bourbon strategy and prohibited either state from concluding peace until American independence was secured. It also specified the high price of Madrid's intervention: France undertook to help Spain regain Minorca and Gibraltar and acquire considerable territories in America, in particular Florida which had been ceded to Britain in 1763.

The entry of France and Spain into the war transformed Britain's struggle in American into a world war. The considerable problems of suppressing a distant colonial revolt were now dwarfed by those of waging war against the Bourbons all over the globe, and this without one continental ally to divert Bourbon resources to Europe. This completely reversed the situation which had obtained during the Seven Years War – and, indeed, in Britain's eighteenth-century wars against France generally –, when her victories overseas had been made possible principally by the French having to divide their war effort.

This reversal of the eighteenth-century pattern has usually been explained by Britain's undoubtedly inept diplomacy and failure to secure allies in the 1760s and 1770s. Superficially this is true, but her isolation was also caused by a fundamental change in the European states system. The dominance of the eastern powers, especially of Russia and Prussia (see ch. 8) left little scope for Britain, or France, in continental politics. Moreover, Britain's very success in her struggles with the Bourbons had also itself weakened her diplomacy. The threat, real or imaginary, presented by France had previously been exploited by British ministers to construct an alliance system which tied France down in Europe while Britain concentrated on the struggle overseas. Her triumphs in the Seven Years War had finally undermined the credibility of the British argument, since if anyone threatened Europe after 1763 it was Britain with her command of colonial trade and substantial empire overseas. British pleas for support against the supposed danger posed by France could now hardly be taken seriously and her isolation in the later 1770s reflected this fact.

The intervention of the Bourbons inevitably made the war in America itself less important for Britain. The surrender of Burgoyne at Saratoga (October 1777) had been a boost to American morale, and in the following years the rebels made further progress, but the real focus of the conflict now lay elsewhere. Britain was more concerned with countering French threats to her interests world-wide. Inevitably British naval power became crucially over-stretched and she was unable to blockade the enemy coastline as in previous wars. In autumn 1779 Britain even temporarily lost control of the Channel, but the resulting Franco-Spanish invasion attempt was a fiasco. French tactics at this point were surprisingly cautious and defensive. Intimidated by memories of previous British successes, France failed to take advantage of this favourable strategic situation to exploit Britain's exposed position. Much of France's naval activity was concentrated on the West Indies, where she captured some islands (Grenada, Dominica, St Vincent). But these French gains in 1778–79 were hardly decisive and must be set against the simultaneous collapse of French power in India and the failure to give real support to land operations in America. Britain's problems, nevertheless, increased as the war progressed.

The entry of the Bourbons and the extension of hostilities to European waters inevitably highlighted the perennial problem of neutral trade in wartime. It had been in Britain's interest to establish a strict interpretation of the rights of neutrals, and her dominance at sea had enabled her to impose her own views, particularly in the wars of 1739–48 and 1756–63. This had caused increasing resentment among the European powers. Since the beginning of the war in America, ships from the other European countries had sought to evade the British prohibition on trade with the rebellious colonies. The capture of some of these vessels by British warships and privateers had inevitably produced considerable diplomatic tension. But it was only in summer 1778, with the outbreak of hostilities between Britain and France, that the issue of neutral rights came to a head.

France's need of naval stores, and Vergennes's hope of isolating Britain, led French diplomacy to cultivate the neutrals by championing the liberal doctrine of 'free ships, free goods'. Some of the lesser European states, in particular Denmark and the Dutch Republic, possessed sizeable merchant fleets and protested strongly against British action in 1778–79. The leadership of the neutrals, however, came to be assumed by the somewhat unlikely figure of Catherine II. This was because the Tsaritsa wanted international prestige and increasingly wished to mediate in European disputes; it also reflected Russia's wartime importance as the principal source of vital naval stores and Catherine's resentment at the seizure of Russian ships and goods by the belligerents. By February 1780 the Tsaritsa had determined to lead a league of neutrals and to defend and define their rights – the two essential components in the Armed Neutrality, which emerged during the same year. This consisted of a series of conventions between Russia, Denmark, Sweden, Portugal and, eventually, the Dutch Republic (who joined in January 1781) aimed at upholding the most liberal interpretation of neutral rights, that of 'free ships, free goods'. The Armed Neutrality was more anti-British in effect than in original intention, and it aroused considerable resentment in Britain, doing much, in the longer term, to undermine the view of Russia as a 'natural ally'. Its short-term significance, however, was rather limited, and it did little more than feed Catherine's vanity.

The question of neutral rights was also the chief reason for the outbreak of the war between Britain and the Dutch at the end of 1780. A long period of co-operation against Louis XIV had made the two states traditional allies, and memories of this link influenced their policies long after changed circumstances had rendered it redundant. Both the political importance and the economic position of the Dutch had declined significantly during the eighteenth century. At least from the Seven Years War onwards, the Republic's foreign policy – if its international posturings merit that name – had been that of passive neutrality, and this continued during the early stages of the American revolt. Dutch neutrality was inevitably viewed in London as pro-American, particularly when the Dutch refused to provide the help in troops and ships which the British government claimed was due under previous treaties. Mounting tension over Dutch merchants insisting on trading with the colonists finally led to war, which was declared by Britain on 20 December 1780. This Fourth Anglo-Dutch War (1780–84) proved a disaster for the Republic. Her navy, as ever the victim of Dutch domestic politics, was in a deplorable condition and her colonies in the West Indies and Ceylon lay open to attack. The Dutch suffered enormous losses, particularly of shipping.

Dutch disasters, and the Fourth Anglo-Dutch War as a whole, were principally important for their impact on the Republic's internal politics (see pp. 267ff.), but the addition of another enemy, however weak, made Britain's naval predicament even worse. Indeed, Britain was largely saved from total defeat by the deficiencies of the enemy coalition. Spain was throughout France's ally not the Americans' (with whom she quarrelled over the area west of the Mississippi) and she pursued her own interests rigorously. She captured the island of Minorca after a lengthy siege in 1781–82, but another siege begun in 1779 failed to bring the prized possession of Gibraltar. By contrast, France's commitment to the American cause became more positive in 1781, when for the first time strategy was fully co-ordinated and produced dramatic results. The main French fleet now operated in North American waters, where it held off British reinforcements while the Americans forced the surrender of Yorktown (October 1781). The triumph at Yorktown virtually brought the fighting on the mainland to an end and made American independence a *fait accompli*, for British ministers now accepted that reconquest was impossible. British fortunes were everywhere at a low ebb in 1781, but Rodney's naval victory at the battle of the Saints (April 1782) put an end to a series of French conquests in the Caribbean and was the start of a significant British recovery in the final months of the war: a recovery reflected in the terms of peace. For all the belligerents by 1782 believed a negotiated settlement was necessary. Britain was prepared to recognise American independence, while the state of French finances demanded immediate peace.

The peace negotiations of 1782–83 were complex, reflecting the geographical extent of the war. Britain's enemies all had differing objectives, and the months of negotiation merely increased the incipient tensions among them. Spain's ambitions had not been diminished by her dismal military performance, and her intransigence seriously delayed the conclusion of the negotiations. She still expected to recover Gibraltar and also hoped for lands west of the Mississippi, although this obviously conflicted with American interests. The American representatives had, superficially, the simplest task, to secure formal recognition for their independence. But their position was weakened by their dependence on France and their task was further complicated by the territorial ambitions which they attributed – not always correctly – to their Bourbon allies. Spain's appetite for further expansion on the North American mainland was real enough, but the belief that France hoped to annex Canada was wrong. Vergennes in fact wanted Britain to keep it since this would strengthen France's future strategic position by forcing Britain to take account of North America. This French policy obviously conflicted with American ambitions in Canada. The negotiations, which began in autumn 1782, were dominated by Britain and France, who very quickly resolved the issues between themselves. This reflected their overriding need for peace. The desperate financial plight of the French monarchy (and of the Spanish), together with the recognition that victory at sea was now impossible, made France determined to reach a negotiated settlement. The objectives of Vergennes's foreign policy remained unchanged: a new balance between England and France as the prelude to an eventual political *rapprochement*. In 1782–83, moreover, the aims of British diplomacy temporarily coincided with those of France.

Britain was now willing to accept the loss of the American colonies and to patch up a peace with her other enemies. The resignation of Lord North's administration (March 1782) had made a settlement easier. The new government had not had to endure the defeats since 1775, and its survival largely depended on making peace quickly. The leading spirit in this administration and in the peace negotiations was the Earl of Shelburne, an enigmatic yet statesmanlike figure with the imagination to conceive of the settlement as more than a negative surrender. Shelburne's vision was twofold: generous concessions to the Americans to promote an eventual partnership, economic and political, with them – though he quickly recognised that such a reconciliation would not be achieved soon; and a future *rapprochement* with France to restore the Anglo-French political ascendancy in Europe, that had been effectively destroyed by the eastern powers. Here Shelburne and Vergennes's aims were very similar, as over their desire for a speedy settlement. Consequently the progress of the Anglo-French negotiations was remarkably smooth. Similarly, Shelburne's willingness to conciliate Britain's former colonists quickly produced the basis of an Anglo-American agreement. The chief obstacle to a general settlement was, predictably, the demands of Spain; but Howe's relief of the beleaguered British garrison of Gibraltar (mid-October 1782) eventually broke Madrid's stubbornness. The Spanish negotiator, Aranda, under French pressure, ignored his formal instructions and accepted terms which left Gibraltar in British hands.

The series of bilateral peace preliminaries between Britain and her enemies in the winter of 1782–83 were consolidated into a general settlement signed at Versailles on 3 September 1783. The peace of Versailles brought about surprisingly few territorial changes. France acquired the unimportant West Indian island of Tobago, the Senegal River and insignificant concessions in the Newfoundland fisheries. Spain received Minorca and Florida and vague promises that Britain would limit her wood-cutting settlements on the Honduran coast. The Dutch gave Britain the long-disputed trading station of Negapatam in Ceylon and the right of navigation among the Indonesian islands.

The principal beneficiary of this settlement was the new American Republic, whose independence was recognised by all the belligerents; British pressure ensured its frontiers to the north and west were more generous than France or Spain had intended. Britain's prestige was severely damaged by the loss of the Thirteen Colonies, but her successes in the final stages of the war and the parlous state of French finances meant her concessions to her Bourbon enemies were far less than had once seemed likely. The peace of Versailles largely restored the situation created by the peace of Paris in 1763 and thereby confirmed Britain's colonial and commercial dominance. Indeed, in one area – India – her position was now even stronger than two decades earlier. The Bourbons had not recovered the losses suffered in 1763 and Vergennes's strategy of undermining Britain's power by depriving her of the economic strength drawn from America also failed,

since Britain's near-monopoly of trade with her former colonies survived American independence. Bourbon policy was thus a considerable failure in real terms.

BRITISH RECOVERY AND BOURBON ECLIPSE 1783–1790

American independence was in itself a triumph for the Bourbon
powers and certainly France recovered something of her previous
international position. But the costs of intervention had been immense
and severely weakened both Bourbon states for the next decade.
Spain's substantial territorial gains hardly compensated for her
increasing financial chaos, and her foreign policy remained feeble
throughout the 1780s. On the other side of the Pyrenees, the financial
and political problems of the French monarchy, already serious
enough for a generation, now became acute because of the American
War. In 1783, the finances were the main focus of ministerial attention
and by 1787, with the summoning of the assembly of notables, the
situation was serious enough to remove France, at least temporarily,
from the ranks of the great powers. Vergennes's poor health and his
own increasing preoccupation with domestic affairs contributed to the
subdued tone of French foreign policy, which aimed only to preserve
continental peace and stability. The intended *rapprochement* with Britain was pursued in the early years of peace, and Vergennes's pacific
aims coincided with Britain's wish for reform and retrenchment. But,
though relations improved and a commercial treaty was signed in
1786, any prospect of a long-term realignment was wrecked by a new
crisis in 1787 over the Dutch Republic. The extent of the Bourbon
eclipse and the parallel British recovery was apparent both on this
occasion and three years later in an Anglo-Spanish colonial dispute.
First France and then Spain had to give way before a British show of
strength.

Britain's recovery was all the more remarkable in view of her
apparently desperate position in 1783. The recent war had seen her
fighting France, Spain and her traditional friend and ally, the Dutch
Republic, while the question of neutral trade in wartime had produced
the Armed Neutrality of 1780. The loss of America, moreover,
though not a serious blow to Britain's actual power, had certainly
lowered her prestige and her standing in Europe immediately after
1783. Defeat in America, however, had not altered the tenets of British diplomacy, which remained essentially a matter of automatic
opposition to the schemes of France and her ally, Spain. And in the
early years of peace there seemed ample evidence of Bourbon hostil-

ity. France continued to take an unhealthy interest in the prize British possession of India and was seeking to undermine the supremacy of the English East India Company by the foundation of a new French company. Tension remained between Britain and Spain over the perennial problem of the activities of British logwood-cutters on the Honduran coast. There was little in the early years of peace to alter the anti-Bourbon grooves along which British foreign policy traditionally ran.

The formal conduct of Britain's diplomacy lay in the hands of the inexperienced and incompetent Marquis of Carmarthen, foreign secretary from 1783–91. (The system whereby foreign policy was controlled jointly by two secretaries of state had been superseded by the creation of the foreign secretaryship in 1782: see p. 210). As he was a nonentity, foreign policy was always effectively controlled by the prime minister, William Pitt the Younger, who took office in December 1783 at the age of twenty-four. His priorities were peace and reconstruction and, though his economies did not extend to the navy, which was substantially rebuilt during the next decade, he was particularly anxious to avoid the cost of another war. Pitt, who was himself substantially ignorant of Europe, until 1786 largely abstained from diplomatic initiatives. The one area where British diplomacy was active in the early years of Pitt's ministry was in commercial negotiations. Britain negotiated with eight European countries, though a treaty was concluded only with France. Throughout the eighteenth century Anglo-French trade had been very limited, but in the peace of Versailles both states had agreed to conclude a commercial treaty. This had been an imaginative initiative on the part of Shelburne, but after his fall in February 1783 British ministers showed little enthusiasm for the project. Vergennes, however, was anxious for a commercial agreement, believing expansion of trade might alleviate the crisis in the French wine trade and improve the desperate state of French finances. France therefore proposed that trade should be established on a reciprocal 'most favoured nation' basis and this desire was exploited by Britain when Pitt's ministry took up the project in earnest in 1785–86. William Eden was sent to Paris and he skilfully negotiated a settlement largely beneficial to Britain. The commercial agreement signed on 26 September 1786 (the Eden treaty) abolished some tariffs between the two states and lowered many others. But its effects were not what French ministers had anticipated. British manufactured goods flooded French markets, while French agricultural products failed to penetrate the British.

The financial weakness of France and a common preoccupation with internal reform had made Anglo-French relations unusually harmonious by the mid-1780s. But any thought that the old animosities were disappearing was removed by the onset of another crisis in 1787, this time over the Dutch Republic. Dutch military disasters during the Fourth Anglo–Dutch War of 1780–84 had highlighted the short-comings of the Stadtholder, William V, and encouraged the urban patriciate to attack him. This strife between the Regent class and the House of Orange was similar to previous political struggles. But there was also a decisive new element: the Patriot movement. The Patriots had emerged during the Fourth Anglo-Dutch War, but while the Regents simply wanted to replace the Orangists in power, the Patriots were 'democratic': they sought to extend political participation to those groups traditionally excluded, especially the lower middle class. In the early 1780s the Patriot movement grew rapidly, acquired a rudimentary party organisation and, through the 'Free Corps' militia, an apparent military potential.

In the early stages, Regents and Patriots co-operated, but by 1785 this tactical alliance was becoming increasingly uneasy as the Patriot movement gained in strength and boldness. In autumn 1785 they expelled William V from The Hague, the centre of his power in Hol-land, and the following year they took control of Utrecht. The feck-less Stadtholder was incapable of providing decisive leadership; Frederick the Great had called him 'my booby of a nephew'. But this link with the Prussian royal family was a major political asset: his wife, Princess Wilhelmina, was the niece of Frederick II and sister of Frederick William II who became Prussian king in August 1786. This proved decisive in the crisis of 1787.

By mid-1787 there was complete political deadlock in the Dutch Republic. Patriots controlled three of the seven provinces, the Stadt-holder two and two were disputed. William V appeared helpless, even though the growing radicalism of the Patriots was producing a grad-ual *rapprochement* between Regents and Orangists. The real saviour of the House of Orange in the mid-1780s was to be the British minister at The Hague, Sir James Harris. Traditionally, British diplomacy had supported the Orangists while France had backed the Regents – as she still had in the early 1780s. But the British support for William V in the mid-1780s owed most to the initiatives of the ruthless and resourceful Harris, with Carmarthen in London merely following his lead. The British envoy was savagely anti-French and viewed the con-fused and localised political struggle in the Republic completely in terms of French intrigue. There was enough evidence to support his interpretation: the Patriots were now being supported by France, and in November 1785 after Vergennes had successfully defused a serious Dutch dispute with Austria over the Scheldt (see p. 233) a Franco-Dutch treaty of friendship and alliance had been signed. After the sig-nature of this treaty Harris moved on to the offensive against this growing French ascendancy. In the following months he set about rescuing William V and organising the Orangists. His tactics were a mixture of skilful bribery and intimidation; he risked civil war and contributed substantially to the crisis of 1787, for the Orangist counter-attack drove the Patriots to extremes.

Harris could act more ruthlessly as events moved to a climax partly because he was receiving growing support, and funds, from London as Pitt assumed more control over foreign policy and effectively superseded Carmarthen from late 1786. Largely under Harris's tutelage – the two met frequently in spring 1787 – Pitt increasingly recognised the French threat and had no wish to see France dominant in the Low Countries. By early summer 1787 Pitt had moved steadily towards outright resistance to France, sharing Harris's belief that Versailles was too weak to risk war. In fact, Harris, who had the common British failing of seeing all foreign policy solely in terms of Anglo-French rivalry, had exaggerated the extent of France's commitment and her actual control of the Patriots. His error became apparent when the crisis finally broke in the summer of 1787 with the arrest and temporary detention of Princess Wilhelmina by the Patriots.

The arrest of his sister drove the previously indecisive Prussian King to dispatch a series of ultimatums to the Patriots in the summer. Britain meanwhile concentrated on what she saw as the French threat. Ironically, her fear of France was growing – in September Pitt briefly mobilised for war – exactly when the French were trying to avoid a clash over the Dutch crisis. French diplomacy in the Republic was confused. France had been drawn to intervene principally by the enthusiasm of her network of agents in the Republic. She could not control the Patriots and was becoming alarmed at their radical political programme. Above all, French policy was ultimately determined, as it had been since 1783, by financial weakness: Versailles simply could not afford a new war with Britain. Montmorin, who had become foreign minister on the death of Vergennes at the beginning of 1787, briefly considered active support for the Patriots and with it the risk of war with Britain. But French weakness soon ruled this out and, once it was apparent that France would do nothing, Pitt left the field clear for Prussia's army to resolve the crisis.

Frederick William II finally decided to act on hearing (7 September 1787) of the outbreak of war between Russia and the Turks (see pp. 238ff.). This relieved him of any anxieties about Austrian intervention, for Joseph II would now have to aid his Russian ally. In mid-September 1787 a Prussian force of 25,000 men invaded the Republic. Faced with real soldiers the Patriot militia collapsed and, within a month, the power of the Stadtholder had been restored. Although the formal glory belonged to Frederick William II's soldiers, Pitt and Harris certainly contributed to the triumph and the main diplomatic benefits of the episode were gained by Britain. The whole episode revealed the utter impotence of the Dutch – the Republic was now treated like Poland or the Ottoman Empire – and the weakness and mounting internal problems of France, who had suffered a major defeat. In the autumn of 1787 events in the Republic seemed far less important to French ministers than their difficulties with the *parlement* of Paris.

The immediate effect of William V's restoration was to worsen Anglo-French relations by forcing France to declare publicly that she would not interfere in the Republic. Pitt, who had become more confident of his grasp of diplomacy after his success of 1787, now set about constructing an anti-French alliance of the old style, seeking treaties with the Dutch Republic and Prussia. Negotiations with both states began immediately after the restoration of the Stadtholder, but they proved more difficult and extended than had been anticipated. Pitt wanted an Anglo-Dutch alliance to consolidate the recent victory over France, to settle colonial disputes in the Far East and to prevent Prussia's gaining too much influence at The Hague. Although the Dutch also wanted an alliance, progress was delayed by the British insistence on resolving the colonial difficulties at the same time. Only when this was dropped was a defensive alliance concluded (April 1788). In the same month Prussia signed a similar treaty with the Dutch.

Discussions had also been in progress for an alliance between London and Berlin, but these proved difficult. This was because of Britain's suspicions about Prussia's wide-ranging ambitions in the Russo-Turkish War (see pp. 244–5). Pitt feared the threat they apparently posed to the territorial status quo and to the continental balance of power. He was therefore worried that an alliance with Berlin might drag Britain into a new continental war and thereby destroy her financial recovery. He would have preferred the security of a wider alliance with other powers, but overcame his reservations when it seemed (late May 1788) as if the volatile Prussia might joint France instead. As the Anglo-Prussian alliance was partly intended to prevent such a Prusso-French alignment, Britain now acted. Harris negotiated directly and successfully with Frederick William II, who was on a visit to the Dutch Republic: a defensive alliance was signed on 13 August 1788. This completed the so-called Triple Alliance of 1788, which was in reality a triangular series of alliances between Britain, Prussia and the Dutch Republic, not one treaty signed by all three.

The conclusion of the Triple Alliance and her earlier triumph in the Dutch Republic superficially marked Britain's return to an active role in Europe after a quarter-century of effective isolation. And the next few years saw a growing concern in London with the Continent. Pitt remained wary of the elaborate schemes of Prussia; he aimed to contain the war in the Balkans and, if possible, to maintain the existing territorial balance. Ultimately, this made British foreign policy anti-Russian, since it aimed to preserve the Ottoman Empire and to deny Catherine II further territorial gains. In 1791 Pitt tried unsuccessfully to force Russia to give up Ochakov (see pp. 241–2). But this short crisis revealed the limited influence of British diplomacy on the events of the Continent, especially in eastern Europe. Britain's brief anti-Russian role, moreover, was only possible because of France's virtual withdrawal from international affairs during the early stages of her Revolution. And this in turn allowed Pitt a further triumph in a new colonial dispute with Spain.

In spring 1790 a serious Anglo-Spanish dispute blew up and throughout the year another War of Jenkins' Ear was very close. The ostensible cause of the quarrel was a dispute over Nootka Sound on the west coast of what is now Vancouver Island. In 1789 a Spanish fleet had been sent to secure the coastline northwards from San Fran-cisco (the limit of Spain's settlements in California) and to establish a base in Nootka Sound. This expedition had seized four British ships in the Sound and destroyed a British trading post established there. Although the episode was trivial in itself, far wider issues were involved. The spectacular growth of Britain's 'empire of trade' after 1783 had brought it into conflict with the decaying Spanish empire on the American continent. British activities seemed to the Spanish government to be part of a sustained attempt to break into the Pacific. Spain had already tacitly abandoned her absolute claim to monopolise the Pacific by accepting Russian settlements in Alaska, but she was determined to assert her control over the long coast between Spanish California and Russian Alaska. The real issue was thus not the incident at Nootka Sound, but the wider problem of the Spanish claim to a territorial monopoly in north-west America, which conflicted with tentative British attempts to open up the Pacific and to share in its fur trade and in the lucrative and fast-growing whaling.

When the first news of the incident reached Europe in late January 1790 both states hoped for a peaceful settlement; at this stage it was believed that only one ship had been taken. But when the full extent of the seizures, together with the claim advanced by Spain to justify them, became apparent in the spring, Britain's attitude stiffened. Pitt adopted a bellicose stance which reflected his wider interest in overseas expansion and awareness of the economic and colonial potential of the region under dispute. He was supported by a popular demand for war, particularly after the publication in May 1790 of an exaggerated account of the episode by the owner of the British ships. Britain kept her fleet mobilised from May until the dispute was settled. The Span-ish government itself was left in no doubt that Britain was ready for a full-scale colonial war unless her demands were met. However, Pitt always wanted a wide-ranging agreement with Spain on all the colo-nial issues involved rather than merely to secure redress for the action of the Spanish fleet.

Britain's obvious willingness for war was the dominant factor throughout this crisis, and Spain could not resist the intense British diplomatic pressure. Her finances and armed forces were in no condition for war and Madrid could not rally France to her side. Louis XVI would have liked to uphold the Family Compact and support Spain but, though the issue raised considerable anti-British feeling in France, the whole matter became entangled and ultimately submerged in Revolutionary politics. The French assembly challenged the King's right to declare war and, consequently, Spain received no reply to her requests for assistance at the critical moment in summer 1790. By contrast, Britain was promised support in the event of war from her Dutch and Prussian allies. Weak and isolated, Madrid had to agree to release the captured ships and to pay compensation at the end of July 1790. But this failed to satisfy Pitt who sought trade and fishing rights and the abandonment of the Spanish claim to sovereignty over the whole area. The cabinet and the country were quite prepared for war in autumn 1790 and Pitt believed hostilities with Spain and France were likely. But the Spanish government's increasing disquiet at the radical course of events in Paris made them unwilling to accept French support, even when the assembly voted in August to arm forty-five ships of the line. The Spanish foreign minister, Floridablanca, therefore bowed to British demands. For the second time Madrid had had to give way to *force majeure*. An Anglo-Spanish settlement was signed at the end of October 1790, which brought Britain substantial gains: access to the long coastline between Alaska and California and Spanish acceptance that British whalers could fish in the Pacific. Pitt's brutal diplomacy offering Madrid the choice between concessions or war was thus successful over Nootka Sound, but was to fail humiliatingly over Ochakov the next year (see pp. 241–2).

The dispute over Nootka Sound confirmed what the second Falkland Islands crisis had revealed two decades before: Spain on her own was no match for Britain. Further Anglo-Spanish tension appeared inevitable because of continuing British expansion. But within three years the two powers were to be allied against France, yet one more of the diplomatic revolutions of the eighteenth century. The explanation was the unique impact of the French Revolution on the European states system.

CHAPTER TEN

Europe and the French Revolution, 1789–1802

THE OUTBREAK OF THE REVOLUTION

The outbreak of the French Revolution can be recognised, in retrospect, as one of the most decisive events in modern history: it was also to prove a significant watershed in the development of the European states system. By 1793 Europe was at war with the Revolution and this conflict was to last, with only one real pause (in 1802–3), until the final defeat of France in 1815. Yet it was some time before this struggle became the dominant theme in continental politics. The destruction of Poland and the fate of the Ottoman Empire remained important and, on occasions, overriding issues for the great powers throughout the War of the First Coalition (1793–97). By the later 1790s, however, the French Revolution had restored western and central Europe to the forefront of political calculations. The military successes of Revolutionary France gradually ended the political division of Europe into the two largely distinct spheres, which had existed since 1763. The legacy of the last generation – the political barriers between eastern and western Europe and the quarrels among the three eastern powers – was to prove an obstacle to concerted opposition to France throughout the 1790s.

The quarter-century from 1789 to 1815 was of considerable significance in the history of European diplomacy. Although there was continuity in the formal, institutional framework of international relations, there were several important innovations which did not, perhaps, become fully apparent until after 1815. The need to co-ordinate the military struggle against France eventually produced closer co-operation between the great powers and, finally, the notion of permanent consultation and concerted diplomatic action. The famous 'Congress System' of the years after 1815, with its implicit belief that statesmen could control and even shape events, rather than merely respond to them, had its origins in the long wars against France. The diplomacy of these years was considerably affected, perhaps even determined, by changing military fortunes. Months of patient negotiation could be wrecked by the outcome of one battle. Diplomacy in wartime posed new problems and European governments only slowly adjusted to its particular demands. Above all, international relations acquired a new, ideological dimension. The older dynastic and territorial motives behind foreign policy were soon supplemented, though never completely replaced, by the idea that the war between Europe and the French Revolution was a struggle between conflicting views of society and of political organisation. Increasingly, the other European states aimed not merely at the military defeat of France and the restoration of a territorial equilibrium – the conventional objectives of eighteenth century warfare. They also sought to reverse the political changes that had taken place in France during the 1790s and to restore a more familiar, and therefore less menacing, regime in Paris. The Younger Pitt spoke for Europe when he declared in 1794 that he had 'no idea of any peace being secure, unless France return to a monarchical system'. Such ideological considerations, however, only gradually came to dominate European diplomacy, for the French Revolution did not at first arouse the hostility of other governments, and few contemporaries were initially aware of the momentous significance of events in Paris and the French provinces from the summer of 1789 onwards.

The initial reaction to the French Revolution was far from unanimous. Particular responses were determined by local circumstances and by the proximity, or otherwise, to France. Europe's response was a variable blend of individual and private enthusiasm, official hostility and simple indifference. Considerable enthusiasm was immediately aroused in intellectual circles, particularly in Germany, where many writers interpreted events in France as the birth of a new era. The generation of Goethe and Kant, of Schiller and Wieland, was initially united in welcoming the Revolution. Similar support was to be found elsewhere in Europe. In England, for example, the existence of a movement for reform, particularly parliamentary reform, ensured that the French Revolution at first received considerable popular support.

In official circles reactions to the French Revolution were to be mostly indifferent and, occasionally, hostile. The only important state that was anxious from the very outset about the possible repercussions of events in Paris was Spain, where a determined attempt was made to isolate the Spanish people from them. The considerable French colony in the peninsula was kept under close surveillance; the periodical press was suspended in 1791; and stringent efforts were made to prevent the circulation of news from Revolutionary France. In several of the smaller German states, particularly Mainz and Trier, the early stages of the French Revolution led to similar concern to that in Madrid and brought to a precipitate end attempts at enlightened reform. For the most part, however, events in Paris were at first simply ignored by European governments. The period of internal confusion in France was widely seen as an opportunity for other states to benefit, as they usually did, from a rival's internal weakness. There was, in 1789–90, little serious anxiety: the revolutionary potential and infectious nature of developments in Paris were simply not appreciated at this stage. The disturbances in France, moreover, initially seemed to many observers to be less serious than the contemporary upheavals in Poland, the Austrian Netherlands and Hungary.

The danger of a general European conflict seemed considerable in 1789–91, but France would not be the cause of such a war. Catherine II was simultaneously involved in wars with the Ottoman Empire (as was Austria) and with Sweden. It was widely believed that Britain and her allies, the Dutch Republic and Prussia, might use force to restrain Russo-Austrian territorial ambitions against the defeated Ottoman Empire. France did not, at this time, occupy a prominent place in the political calculations of the other states. It was not until 1791–92 that the question of the French Revolution became a major issue in European diplomacy. For the moment, Europe's rulers had sufficient problems without giving more than passing attention to events in Paris. Moreover, they did not, as yet, feel particularly hostile towards the new regime in France. They welcomed the pacific foreign policy pursued by the Constituent Assembly during the first two years of the Revolution. Nor were they at this stage threatened by the kind of popular unrest within their own territories which might have aroused real anxiety about the dangers of revolutionary 'contagion' from France.

The French government, for its part, saw little threat from Europe until the middle of 1791. It was, in any case, preoccupied with domestic affairs. The dramatic events which signalled the outbreak of the Revolution – the fall of the Bastille, the 'abolition of feudalism' on the night of 4 August 1789, the march to Versailles and the symbolic return of the monarch to his capital – were followed by a lengthy and less spectacular, though no less important, period of political and constitutional change. A series of important reforms in local government, the agrarian measures made essential by the declaration that the feudal regime in the countryside had been abolished and certain religious changes (particularly the civil constitution of the clergy) occupied the early months and years of the Revolution. Measures such as these did not arouse much fear in the other European capitals. Nor had revolutionary violence reached such proportions as to produce general alarm. Above all, there had been no direct challenge to the continued existence of the monarchy in France nor any real threat to the safety of the royal family. For all these reasons, Europe paid comparatively little attention to the French Revolution in 1789–91. Nor were the moderate leaders in Paris greatly concerned with, or fearful of, events abroad. But in 1791–92 a significant shift in attitudes can be detected. The war which broke out in the spring of 1792 between France and the two German powers, Austria and Prussia, was to have primarily ideological causes.

THE ORIGINS OF THE WAR OF 1792

The *émigrés*, from the outbreak of the Revolution, had been the one group that had consistently advocated and sought to organise armed intervention from abroad. Until the spring of 1792 there were, in practice, few restraints on leaving France and a considerable number of noblemen, churchmen and army officers fled in the early years of the Revolution, either from fear for their own future or revulsion at recent events, or both. The first important *émigré* was the King's brother, the Count d'Artois, who left the French court immediately after the fall of the Bastille and took up residence, with the aristocrats who followed him, briefly in Brussels and then more permanently in Turin. Until the early months of 1791, the King of Sardinia's court was the focal point for *émigré* activity. Leadership of this group naturally devolved on Artois; political direction was provided increasingly by the former controller-general of finance, Calonne, who had himself fled before the Revolution (in 1787) and who came to Turin late in 1790. The 'Turin Committee' was busy in 1789–90, planning to rescue the King, plotting counter-revolutionary insurrections within France and seeking foreign assistance to restore monarchical absolutism. But the activities of the *émigrés* were singularly unsuccessful, and they in fact alienated the King of Sardinia who ordered them to leave Turin early in 1791.

The *émigrés* failed because they could not secure the assistance from foreign governments essential for success and, in particular, the support of the Austrian Habsburgs, whose attitude in 1789–92 was decisive. Vienna had never been especially sympathetic towards the *émigrés*. Joseph II had peremptorily cut short their stay in the Austrian Netherlands by ordering them out of Brussels. Leopold II, who succeeded on his brother's death in February 1790, was initially little disposed to support the cause of counter-revolution in France. The new Emperor was himself favourable to constitutional, even representative, government, as he had made clear during his rule as Grand Duke of Tuscany (1765–90), the Habsburg dependency in Italy. Leopold had enthusiastically welcomed the first news of the upheavals in France and he was not wholly out of sympathy with the early, moderate reforms. The acute and immediate domestic problems which Leopold faced on his accession were in any case his main concern.

Joseph II's own intransigent attempts at reform had provoked open insurrection in the Austrian Netherlands and near-rebellion in Hungary, as well as arousing a considerable body of opposition throughout the Habsburg lands. There was also the problem of an unsuccessful war against the Turks. Leopold devoted most of his short reign (1790–92) to dealing with this critical situation and generally making the Josephinian reforms more acceptable. Hungarian resentment was skilfully appeased by concessions; the Austrian Netherlands were reoccupied by Habsburg troops; and Austria quickly withdrew from the war in the Balkans (see pp. 240–1). Leopold's preoccupation with purely Habsburg problems made him even more disposed to ignore the pleas of the *émigrés* for assistance.

There were, however, solid reasons why Leopold might be drawn to intervene in French affairs. As emperor, he was constitutionally obliged to defend the territory and uphold the privileges of the German princes against the militant demands which the French were making along the Rhine. As the brother of the Queen of France he was naturally concerned about the safety of the French royal family. As the most obvious source of substantial military support, he was the target of incessant pleas from the *émigrés*. Yet until summer 1791, Leopold revealed little interest in French affairs. In May he had a meeting with Artois at Mantua where he showed his unwillingness to act against the new regime in France. The Emperor's own pacific attitude, together with an understandable anxiety not to do anything that might imperil the position of the French royal family, made him continue to reject all appeals for assistance.

This reluctance to contemplate war against the French Revolution was only slowly undermined by events in France and, in particular, by the increasing personal danger to the royal family. Central to this change in Leopold's outlook was the episode of the flight to Varennes (June 1791). From the very outset there had been a succession of schemes for Louis XVI to flee France and to place himself at the head of an army of reconquest, but these plans had always foundered on the King's sense of duty and his refusal to desert his post. Only in spring 1791 was such a scheme finally sanctioned by Louis XVI, increasingly conscious that his hopes that the Revolution would simply run out of steam were not going to be realised and tormented by the approval he had been forced to give to the religious reforms. The King now recognised that only foreign intervention could save his throne, and he tried to ensure this by leaving France. The attempt was a fiasco. Once outside Paris the flight became a leisurely royal progress and the royal party was ignominiously recaptured at Varennes and brought back to the capital under guard. Shortly afterwards the King was suspended from his functions, with the Constituent Assembly taking over full control of government.

The repercussions of the flight to Varennes were considerable.

There was widespread anxiety within France that foreign intervention was on hand, and military preparations were hastily begun. The apparent existence of an external threat to the Revolution was, henceforth, an increasingly important factor in French domestic politics. The episode, however, was of even greater importance outside France. A wave of sympathy for Louis XVI, indignation at his treatment and anxiety for his fate swept round Europe. It was aided by Marie Antoinette's incessant intrigues and pleas for assistance. In the immediate aftermath of the attempted flight, Leopold was moved to issue a circular (July 1791) to his fellow rulers proposing a joint declaration to secure the release of the royal family. The Emperor assumed that France's new leaders could be intimidated by a display of monarchical solidarity. Leopold was not prepared to go any further than this kind of intimidation and he never sought a war against Revolutionary France.

Leopold's fellow monarchs were no more united in their desire to intervene directly, though they all gave considerable subsidies to the *émigrés*. Gustav III, the Swedish King, fervently preached the doctrine of intervention, but his resources were limited and Sweden was too far away for him to act effectively on his own. He was, in any case, assassinated in March 1792. Catherine II was undoubtedly as ill-disposed to the Revolution, and she took the opportunity to insult the French ambassador. But her attention remained fixed on Poland and the Ottoman Empire and the opportunity for territorial acquisitions there (see Ch. 8). Britain seemed simply indifferent (see p. 282). Only the King of Prussia, Frederick William II, consistently called for military intervention; yet he too wanted to annex Polish territory and he was, moreover, unwilling to act unilaterally against France. There was, in mid-1791, little prospect of any concerted action against the Revolution, despite the increasing hostility of individual governments. The Austro-Prussian *rapprochement* (see p. 240) which had been under way since Leopold II's accession, now produced the declaration of Pillnitz (27 August 1791), a joint statement by the Emperor and the King of Prussia of their concern at the difficult situation of Louis XVI and their hope that united action would be undertaken by the great powers to extricate him. This declaration, however, was much less menacing than it appeared at first sight: it also stated that Austria and Prussia would do nothing unless and until they were joined by the other European states. This never happened and the declaration was in effect a discreet recipe for inaction.

The declaration of Pillnitz, none the less, contributed to the mounting anxiety already visible in France. Its threatening tone could only increase French fears that outside intervention was imminent. In the second half of 1791, moreover, war came to be seen by several political factions within France as the way to achieve their particular objectives. The war party in the Jacobin Club, fervently led by J. P.

Brissot, made marked progress in the winter of 1791–92, while King, court and aristocracy all saw war as a means to restore the traditional order. In this febrile atmosphere it is understandable that the activities of the *émigrés* should arouse particular alarm within France: an alarm far in excess of the threat they actually posed. The fact that Artois and Calonne had been present at Pillnitz was what impressed observers in Paris, although the actual influence of the *émigré* leaders had been minimal. In a similar way, the concentration of *émigré* activity in the Rhineland and in particular at Coblenz (which had become the central point of the movement after its expulsion from Turin) aroused considerable anxiety because it was so close to French territory. The 'court in exile' at Coblenz was known to be in contact with counter-revolutionary forces within France. It was – in view of the declaration of Pillnitz – wrongly believed capable of exerting considerable influence at the other European courts. It was heavily subsidised by the major continental rulers and it was maintaining a considerable army in the Rhineland, financed by these subsidies (though this army began to disintegrate in the winter of 1791–92 as the money ran out). Viewed from Paris, the threat from the Rhineland appeared a very real one. The importance of the *émigrés* lay not in what they had achieved, which was little enough, but in what they symbolised and seemed capable of achieving.

During the winter of 1791–92 there was mounting tension, caused partly by French fears of an attack and partly by Austria's continuing conviction that France could be coerced. These Habsburg threats in turn increased French anxieties and helped to raise the political temperature in Paris. Although Leopold's strategy of intimidation was really intended to strengthen the moderates in French politics, it merely strengthened the radicals.

Vienna's blustering support for the German princes who claimed that their rights in Alsace had been infringed caused particular resentment in the final months of peace. This complex dispute was a product of the ambiguity of the peace of Westphalia (1648) over the status of Alsace. Although this peace had ceded Habsburg possessions in Alsace to France, it had specifically guaranteed the rights of certain German princes to maintain feudal privileges there. This obvious limitation of French sovereignty had been specifically confirmed by several later treaties. The problem was how far, if at all, these Imperial enclaves were affected by the declaration of August 1789, which had abolished the feudal regime throughout France. The French government believed that Alsace was part of France and that territorial sovereignty enabled it to legislate there as it wished. The German princes, on the other hand, believed that their feudal privileges in Alsace were guaranteed by treaty and could not simply be swept away by the French government. The princes refused to listen to offers of possible compensation and appealed to the Emperor.

Leopold II, with problems enough and reluctant to provoke France, was at first happy to exploit the considerable opportunities for delay provided by the cumbersome machinery of the Empire. In July 1791, however, the Imperial Diet pronounced in favour of the princes' claim, and the Emperor was finally obliged to take up the matter with France in December 1791. The high-handed tone of Leopold's resulting dispatch aroused resentment in Paris, as did the apparent protection being given to the *émigrés* by two Rhineland Electors, the Archbishops of Mainz and Trier. France's protest at this was met with a statement by the Emperor that, while he agreed that the *émigrés* should be dispersed, he would protect the territory of the Elector of Trier if it was infringed by French troops seeking out *émigrés*. The inflammatory language and apparently provocative tone of these diplomatic exchanges between December 1791 and March 1792 accurately reflected, and also contributed to, the hardening of attitudes in Paris, where a new willingness for war was visible. At the same time, these negotiations revealed Leopold's continuing conviction that France could be intimidated into making concessions.

The decisive factor leading to war was the death of the Emperor on 1 March 1792. Leopold II had always resisted the arguments of the *émigrés*, of Frederick William II and of the German princes for a war against France. His own desire for peace made him favour the strategy of intimidation which had been the limit of Vienna's policy, and he had been more willing than most to view as satisfactory Louis XVI's restoration in September 1791. Even a defensive alliance with Prussia signed in February 1792 had been intended by Leopold as an insurance against the danger of a war, rather than as a preliminary to fighting with France. His death completely altered the situation: his successor, Francis II, was a ruler of a very different stamp. An immature twenty-four-year-old, he was bellicose and impetuous where Leopold had been pacific and cautious. The new reign saw more belligerent spirits in the ascendancy at the Habsburg court and the final exclusion of the generally cautious influence of the old chancellor, Kaunitz. Intimidation as a substitute for war was now replaced in Vienna by intimidation as a prelude to war.

This firmer line in Habsburg policy crystallised the mounting anxieties of the French government that a war of intervention was on hand. A political change now reflected the growing desire for war in Paris. Dumouriez, one of that band of adventurers who found a career in the French Revolution, was swept to power as foreign minister advocating a policy of aggressive war against the Habsburgs. A determined and long-time enemy of Austria, Dumouriez made war inevitable. The latest in a series of Habsburg ultimatums was rejected out of hand and on 20 April 1792 France declared war on Austria.

The war was not entirely a matter of deliberate political calculation on either side. Attitudes were as important as policies. For Austria and for Prussia, the war was essentially a police action to restore order in France, similar to the Anglo-Prussian intervention against the Dutch Patriots in 1787 and to Austria's restoration of her authority in the Austrian Netherlands by force in 1790. For France, it was the 'war of peoples against kings' which Brissot had been preaching ever since October 1791. The French certainly believed that they would be assisted in their war against Austria by the subject peoples of the Habsburgs. But if the origins of the war were primarily ideological, the speed with which France's enemies laid down their own territorial objectives was firmly in the tradition of eighteenth century limited warfare. And these objectives also reflected the widespread belief that the war would be short and that the Revolutionaries would be no match for the disciplined armies of Austria and Prussia. The threat from Paris to the rest of Europe was also not fully appreciated at this stage. Anxiety at events in France was certainly becoming more wide-spread among other governments and it was fostered by the shrill pleas of the *émigrés*, but French domestic developments were not yet seen as a threat to the rest of Europe. Even the French annexation of the Papal enclave of Avignon in September 1791, though it had aroused some anxiety, had not really alarmed the great powers. It was the victories of the French armies in 1793–95, the annexations which followed and the aggressive attempts to export the Revolution which made the struggle between France and Europe the overriding issue in European politics.

THE WAR OF THE FIRST COALITION 1793–1797

French leaders had originally hoped to isolate Austria, but their vision of a war against the Emperor alone was quickly dispelled. Prussia declared war on 21 May 1792 (as she was bound to do under the terms of the defensive alliance concluded in February). France was soon threatened by separate attacks from the north, north-east and south-east, where the King of Sardinia (another ideological opponent of the Revolution) also prepared for war, though he did not yet take the field. Prussia, still regarded as the foremost military power in Europe, took the lead in the campaign of 1792. Her ruler, Frederick William II, was more intent on reversing the course of events in France, and more anxious for military glory, than the Emperor whose earlier bel-licosity was now somewhat modified as he came to understand the weakness of Austria's position. The Prussian army, accompanied by contingents of *émigres* (whose military value was negligible) and under the command of the Duke of Brunswick, a veteran who had served Frederick the Great, invaded France; but its advance was slowed by a combination of its own lethargy and the late summer rains and was finally halted by defeat in a skirmish at Valmy (September 1792). Encouraged by this success, the French swept into the Rhineland and captured the strategically important town of Mainz, which controlled a passage across the Rhine. Further confidence and encouragement were provided by the significant victory which Dumouriez's invading army achieved over the Austrians at Jemappes (November 1792), a success which gave the French effective control over most of the Austrian Netherlands.

These initial successes, and the further progress made in the Rhineland and in Italy during the winter of 1792–93, both contributed to and were themselves sustained by events in France which were now taking a more radical direction. The constitutional monarchy which had been created in the early years of the Revolution had attracted some favourable attention outside France and it had certainly not aroused widespread hatred or fear; but it was now bloodily destroyed. In the summer of 1792, in an atmosphere of imminent invasion and with a royalist coup expected at any moment, long-held suspicions about the counter-revolutionary intentions of the King had inevitably crystallised, and in August Louis XVI was suspended from his functions as monarch. This was the first real success for the popular, radical movement, based on the Paris sections, which steadily gained ground in the following months. The overthrow of the monarchy was followed a few weeks later by the first large-scale act of revolutionary violence, the 'September Massacres', when many of the prisoners in the Parisian gaols were butchered by the mob. Political leadership was now assumed by the National Convention which declared France a republic and, hesitantly accepting the logic that its own survival was incompatible with that of Louis XVI, tried and executed the King.

The execution of Louis XVI (January 1793) focused the growing international anxiety about the new and, by now, very radical regime in Paris. The truly revolutionary nature of events in France was now apparent, and it was becoming evident that this Revolution might also be exported. The proclamation by the Convention that it would aid all peoples trying to imitate the French and overthrow their oppressors (the 'fraternity and assistance' decree of November 1792) and France's substantial territorial gains in the winter of 1792–93 (in particular the annexation of Nice and Savoy from Sardinia and the temporary incorporation of the former Austrian Netherlands) revealed the aggressive policy of France's new rulers. The opening of the River Scheldt, contrary to the provisions of the peace of Westphalia, as part of an attempt to secure the support of the commercial interests of Antwerp, and the implied threat of a French attack on Holland, also aroused resentment, particularly in Britain. Further alarm was aroused by the enunciation of the principle of 'natural frontiers', the doctrine propounded by the Convention that France had a historic right to all the territory within the area bounded by the Alps, the Rhine and the Pyrenees. The manner in which Belgium (the former Austrian Netherlands) was treated during the French occupation revealed that France's conquests would be exploited and revolutionised. By the beginning of 1793, the aggressive, expansionist, regicide rulers of France stood revealed as a challenge to the political system of Europe, and by March the Convention had declared war on Britain, Holland and Spain. A general war had become inevitable: the French declaration of war on Britain (1 February 1793) merely anticipated a similar declaration by the British government.

Britain's entry into the war represented a reversal of offical policy and a considerable change in public attitudes since 1789. The French Revolution at first had been generally welcomed in Britain, though this enthusiasm rested partly on a misunderstanding. Events in Paris were widely portrayed as the equivalent of 1688 in England, the beginnings of constitutional monarchy on the other side of the Channel. But the growing radicalism in Paris diminished support in Britain for the Revolution, and quickly polarised opinion. Edmund Burke had immediately denounced the Revolution as 'a wild attempt to methodise anarchy'. most notably in his *Reflections on the Revolution in France*, published in November 1790, and his viewpoint found an increasing number of adherents. At the same time, however, the radical supporters of the Revolution in Britain continued to make progress. By 1792, the strength of the popular societies, and their links with the revolutionaries, was beginning to alarm the prime minister, William Pitt. But official policy remained the strict neutrality adopted at the outbreak of the French Revolution.

This neutrality reflected the belief of British ministers that the Revolution would weaken France internationally, a view which long persisted. In February 1792, two months before the French declaration of war on Austria, Pitt had predicted that the weakness of France would give Britain fifteen years of peace, and he had made further cuts in military expenditure; the prime minister knew his attempts at economic and financial reform would be undermined by war. On the outbreak of the continental war in April, Britain had declared herself neutral, and Pitt's neutrality was unshaken by the initial allied defeats in the summer and autumn of 1792. The prime minister became undoubtedly concerned, however, at the more radical course taken by the Revolution in the second half of 1792. There was widespread revulsion in Britain at the trial of Louis XVI, and diplomatic relations were broken off on the execution of the King. For Pitt, however, the King's execution was not the main cause of the war. As in 1787–88, the instability of the Low Countries was seen as a threat to British security. Pitt was particularly alarmed by the French victory at Jemappes and the easy conquest of the Austrian Netherlands which followed, because this menaced the Dutch Republic. The opening of the Scheldt then increased his fears. The French advance into the Low Countries had made war inevitable. But if strategy was more important than ideology for Pitt, the foreign secretary Lord Grenville and King George III were more concerned to combat the ideas of the Revolution. Although Britain's motives for entering the war were mixed, it was characteristic of this conflict that Britain immediately agreed with Russia to prevent the import of grain to France (25 March 1793, reinforced by a British Order in Council of 8 June 1793). This had occasionally been done in the past; but the immediate introduction of a blockade of foodstuffs indicated the novel totality of the struggle between Europe and the French Revolution.

The achievements of the new leaders of France in 1792–93 had been remarkable, yet this success rested on insecure foundations. Austria and Prussia had been disheartened by their initial defeats and the Prussian King was soon distracted by the Polish problem and the territorial gains it offered. He combined with Catherine II of Russia to bring about the second partition, announced in January 1793 and implemented in the course of the same year (see pp. 248–9). This renewed preoccupation with Poland and the slowness with which France's enemies banded together gave the Revolutionaries a necessary breathing-space. The new rulers of France were confronted by dangerous internal problems for much of 1793: the civil war in the Vendée, the federalist revolts in the summer and serious economic difficulties throughout the year. These internal problems and the renewed threat of foreign invasion in turn produced more radical measures within France itself, with the emergence of the war government of the Committee of Public Safety led by Robespierre and the suspension of the republican constitution (October 1793). This new leadership, in the long term, may be said to have saved the Revolution. In the short term, France owed its survival more to the failure of its opponents to deliver a properly co-ordinated attack.

The First Coalition was largely organised by Britain and took shape in the months following the outbreak of general European war (February–March, 1793). Traditional suspicion of a standing army had ensured that the British military establishment was minute, when compared with that of any major continental power, and in the past the emergency of a war had usually been met by hiring continental (principally German) mercenaries. This was done again in 1793. A series of subsidy treaties was signed with minor German states: Baden, Hesse-Cassel, Hesse-Darmstadt, George III's own electorate of Hanover. A subsidy was also paid to the King of Sardinia to enable him to maintain an army in the field against France. The other members of the First Coalition were Prussia, Austria, Holland, Naples, Spain, Portugal and (on paper) Russia. Britain signed a bilateral treaty with each, though there was as yet no question of a British subsidy for the larger states. Britain, inspired by memories of the successes of the Grand Alliance in the wars against Louis XIV, made determined but unsuccessful efforts to transform this series of bilateral treaties into one all-embracing alliance against France. The First Coalition was consequently never more than a heterogeneous political partnership of states who, though they recognised the need to defeat the Revolutionaries, were more concerned with the pursuit of their individual, and usually territorial, objectives at the expense of France or in eastern Europe.

The system of partition which had dominated diplomacy in eastern Europe since the Seven Years War continued during the early stages of the struggle against the Revolution, and it exerted an important if somewhat intermittent influence on this conflict. Prussia, for example, simply could not support two separate armies and was soon forced to choose between Poland and the war against France. But the clearest illustration of this was provided by Russia, whose membership of the First Coalition was never more than nominal. From the beginning, Catherine II was undoubtedly alarmed by events in France and she took measures to keep the Revolution out of Russia. She was horrified by the execution of Louis XVI. She had immediately broken off diplomatic relations with France and thereafter provided limited financial aid, and rather more advice, for the *émigrés*. This anxiety, however, did not divert her from her preoccupation with the Ottoman Empire and, more especially, Poland. The Tsaritsa ignored pleas to provide active support for the war against France. Indeed, Catherine realised that this struggle was potentially very useful for her: Austrian and Prussian involvement in western Europe gave Russia considerably greater freedom in Poland. Precisely the opposite calculation was made in Vienna and Berlin, where the dangers of leaving the fate of Poland entirely in Russian hands were certainly appreciated. The problem of Poland ultimately did much to undermine the First Coalition. Above all, the second partition destroyed the good relations between Austria and Prussia built up between 1790 and 1792, and the resulting tension weakened their military effort against France. Prussia was preoccupied with securing her gains from Poland, as was Russia throughout the final years of Catherine's reign. Austria, at first resentful of her exclusion from the second partition, was quick to join her eastern neighbours in destroying the Kosciuszko rebellion and completing the territorial destruction of Poland by the third partition of 1795. The price for the survival of the French Revolution was, in a very real sense, the destruction of the Polish state.

This continuing preoccupation with Poland reflected a widespread assumption that the defeat of the Revolution would be a relatively easy matter, particularly in view of the internal chaos in France and the apparently overwhelming forces at the disposal of the coalition. This belief in turn led each of the allies to formulate its own territorial

objectives in the war against France, and these came to be more vigorously pursued than the aim of defeating the Revolution. Coalition
warfare was still a novelty and there was little appreciation of the need
for co-ordinated military planning and regular political consultation
between the allies. As a result, there was never an effective strategy.
When the anticipated easy victories did not materialise, the members
of the coalition lost heart and, in the case of Prussia and Austria,
sought compensation in Poland; this concern had a parallel in Britain's
growing desire to plunder colonies from France, which inevitably
diverted British attention from the Continent. The military performance of the allies in 1793–95 reflected the belief of the members of the
First Coalition that they were fighting an old-style war.

France's weakness and preoccupation with her urgent internal
problems initially gave the allies some easy, unco-ordinated successes
in the spring and summer of 1793. These were not properly exploited,
and the opportunity for an early, decisive victory was missed. The
armies of the coalition, all but immobilised by a traditional obsession
with manoeuvre and siege warfare, began to disintegrate at the first
signs of serious French resistance in the autumn. The new Jacobin
leaders, having crushed internal opposition and survived the crisis of
the summer of 1793, now moved on to the offensive with spectacular
success. Their armies carried almost all before them in the closing
months of 1793 and, despite the fall of the Jacobins, in the years that
followed. A series of victories in 1794 firmly established Revolutionary control over Belgium. The Austrian defeat at Fleurus (June 1794)
signalled the effective abandonment by the Habsburgs of their former
possessions in the Southern Netherlands. Thereafter, Vienna aimed
to compensate for this loss either in northern Italy or in Germany.
Other French armies advanced into the Rhineland, into Spain and
against the King of Sardinia. Holland was occupied, with surprising
ease, in the winter of 1794–95, the British expeditionary force having
to be evacuated with heavy losses. The Austrian and Prussian armies
in the Rhineland were forced to retreat in the face of the French
onslaught.

Military defeat thus completed the destruction of the First Coalition, which by 1795 visibly fell apart, as individual states came to terms
with France. The King of Prussia, discouraged by military failure and
with his finances in ruin, concentrated even more on Poland. He
withdrew from the coalition, concluding first an armistice (November
1794) and then a separate peace with France, by which he handed over
all Prussian territory on the left bank of the Rhine (peace of Basle,
April 1795). Prussia's desertion of the coalition was covered by her
creation of a neutralised zone in northern Germany. In the following
year (1796) this was fixed, broadly, along the line of the River Weser
and an army was set up to defend it by the states (principally Prussia)
which lay behind it. Neutrality was by now a necessity for Prussia.

The adventurous policy pursued by Frederick William II since his accession in 1786 had all but bankrupted his state and, at the same time, revealed the fragile nature of Prussian power. The neutrality of northern Germany was seen by its originator, the Prussian minister Haugwitz, as a realistic means of eventually extending Prussia's influence in this region; in particular, it placed Hanover under Prussian dominance. But increasingly neutrality became a policy of weakness, especially after the accession of the indecisive and determinedly pacific Frederick William III in 1797. After 1795, Prussian policy was reduced to that of upholding her own neutrality. It was to be 1806 before Prussia again fought France and 1813 before she joined a coalition against Napoleon. This was a considerable blow to the allies, less because of Prussia's military strength than because of the strategic threat which she might have posed to France. Her neutrality removed any threat of an attack from the east against France's Dutch satellite or the former Austrian Netherlands, and it was for this reason welcomed by the French. Spain followed Prussia's example and deserted the alliance to make peace in July 1795, while most of the minor German states also withdrew from the war. By the middle of 1795, the only important members of the First Coalition still nominally at war with France were Austria, Britain and Sardinia. France, moreover, strengthened her international position considerably by alliances with the new Revolutionary Dutch Republic (now called the Batavian Republic) in 1795 and with Spain the following year, this last a revival of the traditional anti-British alignment in the colonial sphere.

The considerable French successes in 1793–95 were not merely the results of divisions within the First Coalition, serious as these undoubtedly were. They were also the product of the beginnings of a revolutionary transformation in the nature of warfare on land – a transformation brought about by France. These changes were not a matter of new weapons, nor were they, primarily, produced by tactical innovations. The changes in tactics which were introduced had, for the most part, been widely discussed long before the wars of the French Revolution. The really dramatic change was the appearance of the 'nation in arms'. This development did not come about overnight. The initial campaigns were conducted, on both sides, with strict attention to the dogmas of eighteenth century limited warfare. Opposing commanders concerned themselves, in 1792–93, with besieging and capturing key towns and fortresses. The new style of warfare was caused by the desperate internal and external situation faced by France. By the summer of 1793 it had become apparent that the necessary armies could no longer be supplied by volunteers. To meet this crisis, the *levée en masse* was decreed in August 1793, imposing universal conscription on the French people. Although many evaded conscription, the resulting increase in the size of the Revolutionary armies was dramatic. By the following spring France had

750,000 men under arms. A military establishment of this size was wholly novel in modern history. Prussia, for example, though regarded by contemporaries as the foremost military power in Europe, only had an army of around 200,000 men in 1786, while the French army in 1789 had contained some 160,000 regulars.

The size of the new Revolutionary army and the extent of the emergency which France faced meant that lengthy formal training was no longer possible. The resulting lack of discipline, however, was more than compensated for by the enthusiasm of the conscript soldiers for the Revolutionary cause. The campaigns of 1793–95 were the heroic period of the French Revolutionary armies, when their immense numerical superiority and their patriotism carried almost all before them. The new-found ardour was reflected in the more aggressive mobile tactics which could be employed. Total victory was the object, ferocity part of the means to achieve it. The most important tactical innovation was the widespread use, after preliminary skirmishing, of attacks by massed columns, rather than the traditional line formation. The concentration of France's greater numbers in this way proved highly effective against opponents who remained wedded for too long to the conventions of eighteenth century warfare. Moreover, France's enemies were unable to increase their military establishments, which were everywhere a matter of precise financial calculation, to the size made necessary by the appearance of the 'nation in arms'. The wretched performance of Austria and Prussia in the First Coalition, at one level, simply reflected their chronic financial difficulties and the inadequate size of their armies.

The vastly enlarged Revolutionary armies needed to be equipped and supplied, and their triumphs on the battlefield were, to a significant extent, made possible by the work of Carnot, the 'organiser of victories'. In 1793–94 a war economy was established in France and its decrees enforced by the guillotine. For a time the needs of the French army were made the only object of trade and production. Revolutionary France provided the first example of modern 'total war'. The enlarged military establishment, however, proved easier to create than to control, and in this way war came to acquire its own momentum. In the past, the demobilisation of armies at the conclusion of war had often been attended by considerable dislocation, since it was not easy to integrate a substantial number of adult males into civilian society, particularly one experiencing the economic difficulties that often followed a war. This fundamental problem was considerably magnified by the unique proportions of the Revolutionary armies. After the victories of 1793–95 and the peace settlements which these produced, it proved very difficult to demobilise the swollen French army; but, equally, with the ending of the Reign of Terror (July 1794) and the steady undermining of the war economy, it was also proving increasingly difficult to feed and equip the troops still in the army. The attraction of further military adventures (which would enable the armies to live off occupied territory) as a means of postponing the difficulties of demobilisation and of solving the problem of maintaining the remaining troops was considerable. Further territorial expansion was undertaken by successive French governments largely for this reason.

The principal target for these renewed adventures after 1795 came to be Austria, since Britain (the other major remaining belligerent) retained her control of the seas and was thus in practice safe from direct attack or from the invasion of Ireland which France long considered. The Directory, which ruled France after October 1795, directed the Revolutionary armies against Austria, which was menaced by a two-pronged attack in south Germany and in Italy. The Austrians put up surprisingly effective resistance in Germany, but were hopelessly defeated in Italy. A series of victories which first brought the young Napoleon Bonaparte to prominence quickly forced Sardinia to make peace and, within a year, destroyed Habsburg primacy in the peninsula and produced the peace of Campo Formio (October 1797), the political obituary of the First Coalition.

The peace of Campo Formio, and the dramatic changes in Italian political geography which accompanied it, were the work of the personally ambitious victorious commander in the peninsula, Napoleon Bonaparte, not of his superiors in Paris. The Directors were presented with a *fait accompli* which they reluctantly endorsed. They were particularly unhappy at the way Bonaparte's blueprint for Italy involved the destruction of the independent states of Genoa, Modena and Venice, though none of these had actually been at war with France. By the peace of Campo Formio, the Habsburgs recognised the extension of France's eastern frontier to the left bank of the Rhine and the French annexation of Belgium. In the Italian peninsula, Austria was given a substantial portion of Venetian territory, including Venice itself and the lands on the Dalmatian coast, both as compensation for the loss of Lombardy (to France) and as an inducement to accept the creation of French satellite republics in northern Italy. Contrary to the specific instructions of the Directory, Bonaparte used military force (April 1797) to carry out the destruction and partition of the neutral republic of Venice which made this possible. The French share of this partition (the lands west of the Adige) was united with Lombardy, Modena and the former Papal territories of Ferrara, Bologna and the Romagna (seized from the Pope in February 1797) to form the nominally independent Cisalpine Republic. Austria's traditional dominance in Italy had thus been undermined, though the Venetian territories (which gave much better access to the Adriatic) were some compensation. France also took possession of what was left of Venice's former eastern empire, the Ionian Islands, while Bonaparte completed his redrawing of the political map of Italy by creating the Ligurian Republic out of the formerly independent state of Genoa (June 1797). These changes made the northern half of the peninsula predominantly republican and French while southern Italy remained solidly monarchical and nominally independent. This division was clearly unstable.

The political settlement which Bonaparte imposed on Italy in 1797 represented a significant change in relations between the French Revolution and Europe. Until this point, France had made comparatively limited territorial gains by outright annexation. French acquisitions could be justified, to a considerable extent, in terms of the doctrine of 'natural frontiers'. In keeping with this principle, Belgium – occupied briefly in 1792–93 and permanently from June 1794 onwards – had been formally annexed in October 1795. No attempt had been made, however, fully to annex the Dutch Republic (the Batavian Republic) after the success of the French invasion early in 1795. The territorial changes in Italy in 1797 went far beyond these comparatively limited gains. They implied a policy of direct, aggressive expansion, the exporting of the Revolution. Bonaparte showed scant regard for the sovereignty of the Italian states in his remodelling of the political geography of the peninsula, and the Directory soon followed his example.

French expansion did not cease with the conclusion of the peace of Campo Formio. On the contrary, in the months that followed it seemed to gather pace. Military intervention in Switzerland led to the proclamation of the Helvetic Republic (22 March 1798). The enthusiasm of Swiss republicans provided a convenient pretext for an action which the Directors believed necessary to protect France's south-eastern frontier and to secure military communications with northern Italy. The instability of the political settlement in the Italian peninsula was a factor in causing further expansion there. Disturbances in the Papal States led to the intervention of French troops and the proclamation of the Roman Republic (15 February 1798), which remained occupied by the French. These months also saw an increase in the Directory's control over the various satellite republics. The Batavian Republic, for example, suffered further French intervention and the imposition of a new constitution (April 1798). In December 1798 the French seized control of the kingdom of Sardinia, while in the following month (January 1799) the Parthenopean Republic was established at Naples. Everywhere, in 1797–98, the French Revolution again appeared to be on the march and, while the actions of the Directory aroused considerable resentment and anxiety, this renewed French expansion seemed irresistible. For, with the final collapse of the First Coalition, Britain was the only major state still at war with France.

THE WAR OF THE SECOND COALITION, 1798–1802

The War of the First Coalition had revealed the inadequacy of traditional British strategy in the new circumstances of the 1790s. Britain's initial involvement in the war against France had been both belated and reluctant. It had been widely assumed in England, as on the Continent, that this war would be a short one, and at first Pitt had hoped that it would be possible to limit British involvement. In practice, however, Britain's commitment to the struggle had steadily increased throughout the War of the First Coalition. The junior partner of 1793 had become the director of the coalition by 1795–96. British diplomacy had created such unity as the First Coalition had possessed, while subsidies to some of the smaller German states and to Sardinia had indirectly helped the military struggle.

Britain's strategy throughout the War of the First Coalition had remained the traditional formula of 'colonial' warfare, that is, tying France down in Europe while defeating her overseas. Initially, Pitt's strategy had closely resembled that employed by his father during the Seven Years War (see pp. 197ff.). Indeed, the renewed struggle had originally been seen as an opportunity to make good British losses during the War of the American Revolution. Central to this was England's continuing naval supremacy. This was amply demonstrated in 1794 by Howe's victory off Ushant on the Glorious First of June and by Britain's blockade of the French coastline, which slowly strangled French trade. British supremacy was made easier by the upheavals in the French navy produced by the Revolution. By pursuing this strategy Britain managed to make small gains at France's expense in the Caribbean and in India. Sea power, however, was an essentially defensive weapon. It could only slowly be brought to bear and it could do nothing to check the spectacular French military successes of 1793–97. The resulting collapse of opposition to France on the Continent undermined the prospects for the negotiated settlement aimed at by British strategy. Extended Anglo-French peace negotiations in 1795–96, and briefer discussions in 1797, were both unsuccessful, largely because of France's extravagant terms. As France's successes on land multiplied, moreover, British naval strength had become dangerously over-extended in the attempt to counter them. The War of the First Coalition had thus revealed that a naval and colonial conflict of the traditional kind would not be sufficient to defeat France. If the dramatic progress of the Revolution was to be checked, a new strategic initiative was essential. Yet it was by no means clear that Britain, the only major state still undefeated, was herself in any condition to undertake such an initiative.

Britain's situation in 1797, the year of the peace of Campo Formio, was desperate. The threat of a French invasion could not totally be discounted, though British mastery at sea seemed to guarantee that

England would not have to face a direct attack. Ireland remained an inviting target, and Irish dissatisfaction with English rule had almost reached the level of rebellion. There was a severe financial crisis in London and, for a moment, it seemed as if the government's credit might collapse. The war was generally unpopular in the country. In the spring and early summer of 1797 the fleet was paralysed by mutinies at Spithead and the Nore. Naval victories over the two states forced into alliance with France did something to restore British confidence. In February 1797 Jervis defeated the Spanish navy at St Vincent and in October Duncan destroyed the formidable Dutch fleet (which might have been used in an attempted invasion of England) at Camperdown. Britain gradually recovered from her desperate plight, but the initiative lay with France.

The solution sponsored by the British foreign secretary, Lord Grenville, and endorsed by the prime minister, William Pitt, was the formation of a new and all-powerful alliance which would defeat France, dictate a satisfactory peace and then maintain this settlement by means of regular meetings of the great powers. This scheme obviously foreshadowed the alliance of 1814 and the Congress System; its ancestor, and perhaps its inspiration, was the Grand Alliance which had fought against Louis XIV. Grenville's grand design had obvious attractions and it rested on a sound appreciation of the basic weakness of the First Coalition: the absence of any agreement among the allies over political aims and the military strategy necessary to achieve them. These weaknesses, however, proved to be easier to identify than to avoid. The 'strategy of overthrow' pursued in 1798–99 ultimately foundered on many of the same obstacles that had destroyed the First Coalition.

Grenville's plan was for close political and military co-operation between Britain and the three eastern powers, Austria, Prussia and Russia, an anti-French coalition in form as well as in name. The barriers to any such quadruple alliance were considerable. The chief problem was always that of reconciling old antagonisms and internal tensions in order that a united war could be waged against France. Poland no longer remained to distract and divide the continental states, yet the acrimony its destruction had engendered, and the traditional rivalries in eastern Europe (in particular that between Vienna and Berlin) remained serious obstacles to the proposed coalition. Neither Austria nor Prussia was as yet fully convinced of the novel extent and nature of the threat from France. Both believed that French power should be limited by the traditional formula of territorial forfeits after a limited war. Relations between London and Berlin at this time were cool, since British ministers resented Prussia's early desertion of the First Coalition and the equivocal neutralism of her foreign policy since 1795. It proved impossible for Grenville to persuade the new Prussian King, Frederick William III, to join the Second Coalition. Britain's relations with Austria, which was still seen in London as the natural ally against France, were soured by British resentment at Vienna's unilateral peace at Campo Formio and at Austria defaulting on repayments on the Imperial loans. (Austrian loans raised on the London money market in the mid-1790s in order to finance the war had been guaranteed by the British government, but Vienna had suspended repayments in 1797.)

These obstacles to the conclusion of a quadruple alliance gradually became apparent in 1798–99. A new coalition was delayed at critical moments by the difficulty of conducting complex negotiations over vast distances, particularly during a very severe winter. It also reflected the difficulty the diplomats had in keeping up with the fast-changing military situation. The Second Coalition, which finally emerged, was far removed from Grenville's original conception. Its final form owed less to the British foreign secretary's diplomacy than to Bonaparte's Egyptian expedition of 1798–99 (see pp. 297ff.). It proved to be a loose series of alliances, scarcely more of a coalition than its predecessor. Two of its prospective members, Prussia and Austria, were simultaneously discussing the quadruple alliance with Britain while negotiating with the intended enemy, France. Nor was this uncertainty resolved quickly. Prussia finally vacillated into neutrality, while Austria eventually rushed into a war with the Directory and only then sought the further British financial support necessary to fight it. These events revealed Grenville's inability to mould continental politics to his own pattern. This was even more apparent in the case of Russia.

A central element in Grenville's strategy was the active participation of Russia, which until now had played no effective part in the struggle against France. Throughout the War of the First Coalition, Catherine II had remained aloof, indifferent to repeated appeals for aid against the Revolutionaries. A token squadron to reinforce Britain's North Sea fleet after 1795 was as far as Russia's ruler had been prepared to go, for she was fully occupied with the situation in Poland. By 1796, however, the Tsaritsa had completed the destruction of Poland. She was also becoming seriously concerned at the extent of French successes, particularly in Italy. Catherine II's gains at the expense of the Ottoman Empire had given the eastern Mediterranean a new importance in Russian foreign policy. For the Tsaritsa, as for her successors, French expansion in the Italian peninsula was a threat to Russian security and this made her increasingly disposed to join the struggle against France. When Catherine died in November 1796, negotiations were far advanced for a Russian army to fight in western Europe in return for a British subsidy. Her son and successor, the mercurial and idealistic Paul I, immediately reversed this policy and refused to send troops to the Rhine. The new Tsar wished to inaugurate a period of peace and reform and he was anxious to spare his people further war, with the burdens it imposed. He also desired peace to concentrate on the social and administrative reforms which he believed were essential. Paul initially hoped that it would be possible to prevent the spread of the continental war into areas where Russian security was involved. There were obvious echoes of the 'Northern System' of his former tutor and political adviser, Nikita Panin, in the Tsar's idea of defensive alliances to protect Russian interests in eastern Europe and in his abandonment of the aggressive and expansionist policy pursued during the second half of Catherine II's reign. Yet his hostility towards the French Revolution was undoubted. The new Tsar feared the challenge it offered to the traditional order in Europe and he detested the brutal assault it had made on the sacred institution of monarchy. Paul I's view of foreign affairs was in conception, if not in fact, ideological. For a time, he was disposed to believe Bonaparte would tame the Revolution; legitimacy mattered less to Paul than good order.

Paul's gradual realisation that it was impossible to live at peace with the Revolution was not a response to British urgings nor was it caused by the continued expansion of France in western Europe. It was rather the product of French expansion in the Mediterranean. Paul was alarmed by Bonaparte's conquests in Italy and he was affronted by the sweeping French gains by the peace of Campo Formio. In particular, he resented the French annexation of the Ionian Islands and France's seizure of Malta. The crusading Order of the Knights of St John had taken refuge on the island of Malta after the loss of their base on Rhodes to the Turks in the 1520s. By the eighteenth century the Order was manifestly in decline, though it continued to maintain a rather futile hostility towards Islam. The confiscation in 1791–92 of its rich properties in France deprived the Order of three-fifths of its income and was a severe blow. The potential strategic importance of the island to France's enemies, together with the lure of the remaining wealth of the Order (and particularly its plate) led Bonaparte to occupy Malta on his way to Egypt in 1798. The token resistance to the French conquest reflected the weakness of the Knights. The Order, however, now found a new champion in the unlikely figure of the Tsar.

Ever since his youth, Paul had been attracted by the chivalric ideal which the Knights represented. He had recently given more tangible proof of this sympathy. A priory belonging to the Order in Volhynia had been part of Russia's share of the second partition of Poland, but Catherine II had refused to restore its income to the Knights. Paul, however, had not merely restored this income on his accession. He had actually increased it and backdated it to the time of the second partition. In addition, the priory was transferred to St Petersburg, enlarged and henceforth entirely financed by Paul. In gratitude, the Order declared the Tsar its protector in autumn 1797. The cause of the Knights seems slowly to have become merged in Paul's mind with an almost messianic notion of a crusade against liberal and revolutionary movements everywhere, but especially in France. This link was strengthened by the irregular election of the Russian ruler as grand master of the Order (November 1798). Paul intended that the Knights, based in Russia and reinforced by a considerable influx of Russian noblemen, would be the swordbearers in his crusade for order and monarchy against the new infidels of the Revolution; the problem of imposing Orthodox Russians on a Catholic Order did not greatly trouble him. The Tsar now fully assumed the role of champion of the Knights and made unsuccessful demands for the French to evacuate Malta.

Bonaparte's earlier seizure of the Ionian Islands from Venice in the summer of 1797 and their formal incorporation into the French Republic following the peace of Campo Formio was a more wholly political concern for Russia. These islands off the western coast of Greece were of considerable strategic value in any struggle for control of the eastern Mediterranean. The French annexation was seen as a powerful challenge to Russian interests in this area and potentially to Russia's control of the Black Sea, for it was assumed in St Petersburg that France would use the islands to extend her influence in the Balkans. Strategy thus merged with chivalry to make Paul increasingly concerned at French expansion in the Mediterranean. This growing anxiety, together with a general unease about the instability of southern and central Europe after Bonaparte's victories in Italy, finally convinced the Tsar that Russia should declare war on France.

French expansion in the Mediterranean was also responsible for the Ottoman Empire joining the ranks of France's enemies. Here, as in the formation of the Second Coalition generally, Bonaparte's invasion of the Ottoman dependency of Egypt was decisive (see pp. 297–8). The Sultan, Selim III, had remained aloof during the War of the First Coalition, preoccupied with internal problems and content to pursue a neutrality that was openly favourable to France – the Porte's traditional ally and an important source of technical aid to the Ottoman army. The French annexation of the Ionian Islands, which lay immediately off the Sultan's coastline and which brought French influence very close to Ottoman territory, fatally undermined this harmony. Well-founded anxiety about the precarious nature of Constantinople's control over its outlying provinces, together with the assumption that France would soon try to extend her influence in the Balkans, produced a swift reversal of the diplomatic alignments that had existed since 1792. This was facilitated by the desire of the new Tsar for a *rapprochement* with the Sultan. Napoleon's invasion of Egypt in the summer of 1798 (see p. 298) crystallised this mounting concern at the Porte over French expansion. In particular it halted, at least temporarily, the vital food supplies which the densely populated and volatile city of Constantinople obtained from Egypt. The Sultan now declared war on France (September 1798) and, after some delay, concluded alliances with Russia and Britain (January 1799). These new diplomatic alignments brought an immediate military success. Early in 1799 a Russo-Ottoman force evicted the French from the Ionian Islands. The alliance of two such traditional and bitter enemies as Russia and the Ottoman Empire was not the least remarkable of the diplomatic revolutions produced by the need to contain France.

The complex and rather divergent diplomacy of 1798–99 produced a ramshackle coalition. By the spring of 1799, Britain, Austria, Russia and the Ottoman Empire were at war with France (as were Naples and Portugal) and these states were united by a series of separate alliances. But there was no overall coalition; nor was there, as yet, an alliance between London and Vienna, though this was likely to be the linchpin of any war against France. There was no agreement about a unified military strategy, and Grenville's attempts to fill this gap were all unsuccessful.

These obvious failings did not prevent the Second Coalition from initially enjoying considerable military success. Russian forces were sent to fight alongside the Austrians, first in Italy and then in Switzerland. The venerable Suvorov, whose genius had earlier transformed the brave but stolid Russian troops into a mobile and aggressive army with an attacking strategy that anticipated Napoleon, was recalled (at Vienna's request) from retirement. Now almost seventy and a veteran of campaigns in Poland and against the Turks, he was given command of the combined Austro-Russian forces in north Italy, where his triumphant advance effectively cleared the French out of the peninsula. The Austrians pushed forward in Switzerland while, in the south, a counter-revolution assisted by Nelson evicted the French from Naples. By the summer of 1799, the French had been forced back across the Rhine and the allies appeared to be on the point of launching an invasion of France from Switzerland which, it was hoped, would end the war. This eastern front was one dimension of the offensive against France. The other was an ill-fated Anglo-Russian landing in Holland.

After the French conquest of Holland in 1795, Britain had lacked a suitable arena for her troops on the Continent. In the autumn of 1799, however, a determined attempt was made to open up a second front at the Helder in north Holland, which British ministers believed to be the most vulnerable part of French defences in western Europe. It was hoped that the expedition would stimulate a Dutch rising against the French and in favour of the deposed House of Orange. Grenville believed that it might also force Prussia back into the war; a decade before the Prussians had played an important part in an Orangist restoration (see pp. 267–8). Both hopes proved unfounded and the whole affair was to be little short of a fiasco. A British expeditionary force did effect a landing, in itself a considerable feat in the context of eighteenth-century combined operations, and it was later reinforced by Russian and British troops. But the Anglo-Russian army encountered stiffer opposition than had been anticipated, for the French leaders were determined to retain their Belgian gains and defended Holland vigorously. The Anglo-Russian force was confronted with the inevitable problems of supply; disease was soon rife in the camp and the arrival of French reinforcements meant that the allies were quickly outnumbered. These factors and some hesitancy in following up their success in breaking through the French cordon condemned the expedition to failure. Amidst bitter recriminations between the British and Russian commanders, and with the onset of winter, the expedition obtained an armistice from the French and the allied forces were evacuated at the end of October 1799. Paul's resentment over this episode was considerable, and he was further alienated by Britain's refusal to allow Russian troops to share in garrisoning Malta, recaptured by a British fleet in September 1798.

A second severe blow to the coalition was the almost simultaneous collapse of the allied campaign in the east, where the planned invasion of France from Switzerland had to be abandoned. The prospect of victory now proved as divisive to the allies as defeat had previously been. The difficulties arose principally from Vienna. Austria's relations with her two allies were not harmonious. Her foreign minister, Thugut, distrusted British intentions in the Southern Netherlands. He was, moreover, envious and resentful of Russia's successes in Italy; Austro-Russian military co-operation had never been very smooth. Ministers in Vienna did not yet share Britain's view of the war as a struggle to extinguish the Revolution. The notion of total victory was no part of Habsburg thinking. On the contrary, the Habsburgs remained devoted to the limited warfare of the *ancien régime*. They assumed that military successes could be turned to immediate account in the shape of territorial acquisitions, and this doctrine now revealed itself. Austria hoped to use the victories over France to make substantial gains in Italy (perhaps by means of an exchange of Belgium for the kingdom of Sardinia) and in western Germany. Moreover, Vienna was anxious to deny Prussia any substantial territorial gains in Germany. Habsburg ministers had long feared that their traditional rival would demand a share in the territorial readjustments which would follow a French defeat.

The territorial ambitions of the Habsburgs undermined the coalition in the second half of 1799. Paul's view of Russian interests in the eastern Mediterranean also made him hostile to Austrian expansion in Italy, though until now this attitude had been softened by the pressure of events. He expected that the expulsion of the French from the peninsula, achieved by the summer of 1799, would be followed by the restoration of the former rulers. But it became clear that Vienna had designs on France's Italian satellites. The Habsburgs refused to take part in an invasion of France and instead diverted their troops to the pursuit of Austrian territorial aims in Italy. The Russians, abandoned by the Austrians, were defeated by the French at the second battle of Zürich (September 1799). Suvorov's escape from the exposed position in which this left him, by the brilliant passage of the Alps into Germany in the late autumn of 1799, was only accomplished with heavy losses. The conduct of his allies and, to a lesser extent, the defeats suffered by his own armies, disillusioned Russia's ruler. Paul felt himself betrayed by the Habsburgs and he now withdrew from the Second Coalition (November 1799), which, he wrote to the Emperor Francis, had become a war for Austrian aggrandisement. His withdrawal also ended the short-lived Anglo-Russian *entente*. Britain was forced to choose between the two eastern powers and her automatic preference was Austria, who by tradition, geography and recent performance was a more dependable ally against France. This choice, rather than Paul's resentment over Malta or the north Holland expedition, was the real cause of the Anglo-Russian breach which was apparent by the beginning of 1800. The Second Coalition had collapsed.

The disintegration of the allied war effort in the second half of 1799 could not totally disguise the reverses which the Directory had suffered, particularly in Italy. Nor could France derive much consolation from the Egyptian expedition of 1798–99. The command of this had been given to Napoleon Bonaparte, the rising star of French military life. Born in Corsica in the same year as the French annexation (1769), Bonaparte had received his military education in France and had been commissioned into an artillery regiment in the final years of the *ancien régime*. The French army suffered from a shortage of officers during the 1790s: over 60 per cent of the officer corps had emigrated between 1789 and 1792, and the ups and downs of Revolutionary politics inevitably caused further losses. This had ensured rapid advancement for the young Bonaparte who, by 1796, when he was still only twenty-seven, had risen to the command of the army in Italy. His successes in the peninsula, carefully publicised by his own propaganda, established his reputation in France. Bonaparte's military talents had always been accompanied by intense political ambition, and his willingness to play for the highest stakes was already apparent. His decisive part in commanding the troops who had defeated a royalist insurrection in Paris on 5 October 1795 (13 *Vendémiaire* IV: the legendary 'whiff of grapeshot') had further increased his standing in France. By 1797 Bonaparte enjoyed considerable political influence, and he certainly possessed the ambition and ability to exploit this; furthermore, the Directory was by now almost entirely dependent on the army to defeat its many political opponents.

The Egyptian expedition was principally intended to further the struggle against Britain, though the potential threat to the Ottoman

Empire and Egypt's value as a permanent colony and as a base for further French penetration of the Levant were important. Britain, the only major state at war with France after the peace of Campo Formio, was largely safe from direct attack. The invasion of England was seriously considered by the Directory in the winter of 1797–98, but the lack of sea power made it impracticable. It was only when this scheme was shelved early in 1798 that the Directory decided on the Egyptian expedition. French strategists had long considered the acquisition of Egypt (nominally a part of the Ottoman Empire but effectively ruled by the Mamelukes) and such a project was currently being advocated by the foreign minister, Talleyrand. Bonaparte, aware that personal inactivity might be fatal to his own political ambitions, took up this scheme and secured its adoption by the Directors, who were not sorry to see the departure from Paris of such a successful and ambitious general. They believed that the capture of Egypt would be a blow to British trade and therefore to her prosperity, as well as a potential threat to her possession of India; these ideas seem rather grandiose, but they were at the heart of French policy. The romantic streak in Bonaparte and his lifelong fascination with the 'East' led him to see the conquest of Egypt as the prelude to further eastern adventures, with himself cast in the role of a latter-day Alexander the Great.

The French expeditionary force landed in Egypt on 1 July 1798, having easily captured the island of Malta (see pp. 293–4) and then fortuitously avoided a British fleet commanded by Nelson. Bonaparte soon routed the Mameluke army at the decisive battle of the Pyramids (21 July 1798). This victory gave the French control over Lower Egypt, but the promising opening to the expedition was not maintained. Nelson's destruction of the French fleet in Aboukir Bay (battle of the Nile, 1 August 1798) left Bonaparte and his army stranded and, incidentally, deprived them of news of events in Europe. Initial hopes that the expedition would not antagonise the Porte were shattered by the Sultan's declaration of war on France (September 1798). Bonaparte now tried to advance northwards into Syria in order to consolidate his position. This strategy was initially successful, but the failure to capture Acre (March–May 1799) forced him to retreat. The intervention of a British fleet comanded by Sir Sidney Smith proved decisive; above all, it deprived Bonaparte of his heavy siege artillery. The French army fell back to Egypt, suffering heavy losses from plague, but Bonaparte was still able to defeat an Ottoman force sent against him (battle of Aboukir, 25 July 1799). The expedition had now become a military and political cul-de-sac, not least for its commander. News of French defeats at the hands of the Second Coalition and of the volatile state of French domestic politics then reached Bonaparte and sent him hurrying back to France. Abandoning his army, he left Egypt on 22 August 1799 and reached France early in

October. The French occupation of Egypt continued until September 1801, when the army was finally forced to evacuate by an Anglo-Ottoman expeditionary force.

The political situation in Paris was by now critical, though the reverses suffered by the Second Coalition (see pp. 295ff.) made the military situation less acute. Since 1795 France had been ruled by the Directory, but its hold on power had never been secure and was now slipping fast. The Directory had failed to overcome the political chaos in France after the ending of the Terror. Its own political base had always been dangerously narrow and it had had a peculiarly chequered existence. The complex political structure set up in 1795 was, in itself, inherently defective, while the problems which faced the Directory were considerable. Plagued by a permanently critical economic situation and the endless financial problems produced by war, confronted by opposition from all parts of the political spectrum and frequently attacked by its domestic opponents, the Directory had only survived through a series of *coups d'état*. The search for political stability was finally undermined by the financial strain of renewed war in 1798–99 and by the defeats France suffered at the hands of the Second Coalition. By autumn 1799, it was more evident than ever that the Revolution's only hope of survival was the army, and some politicians were searching for a general to carry out another coup. Bonaparte's return to Paris in mid-October was opportune. Within a month he had carried through the coup of 18–19 *Brumaire* (9–10 November 1799) which resulted in the establishment of the Consulate. It had been intended that he should merely be the instrument for a change of government but, to the surprise of his fellow conspirators, the ambitious Bonaparte emerged as the dominant voice in the new regime and his post of first consul gave him immense power.

The internal problems bequeathed by the Directory to France's new ruler were formidable. The economy was in disarray, the country weary of war; there was also the long-standing rebellion in the Vendée. Bonaparte's own hold on power would depend substantially on his success in solving these problems, and this made peace essential, particularly as the French armies were now in a poor condition. The first consul made real attempts to negotiate peace with Vienna and London during winter 1799–1800, but these negotiations were unsuccessful. The Habsburgs, having made substantial territorial gains in Italy in 1799, were unwilling to return to the position created by the peace of Campo Formio, while the British government was, as yet, unwilling to sign a peace that left Holland and Belgium in French hands. Each state had its own view of what was an equitable settlement and these proved incompatible; nor had either side won a decisive victory which enabled it to dictate terms. Peace, Bonaparte concluded, could not be negotiated; it would have to be imposed after further French successes.

Bonaparte's position and his future prospects rested on the outcome of the campaign of 1800. The difficulties of the Second Coalition in the final months of 1799 had given France a welcome respite, but her strategic position remained serious. French security and the first consul's own career both demanded early victory and a speedy peace. Russia had withdrawn from the Second Coalition in the previous year and Britain could not be attacked directly; the campaign of 1800 was therefore directed against Austria. Bonaparte quickly grasped that Switzerland and northern Italy were the key to this campaign, though French armies also pressed forward in Germany. Characteristically, he took the initiative, leading the small and hastily improvised 'Army of the Reserve' in a decisive, if ill-managed, march across the Alps into Italy, outmanoeuvring the Austrians and defeating them at Marengo (June 1800). This victory was due almost entirely to the arrival of Desaix and French reinforcements in mid-battle, though Bonaparte was careful to appropriate all the glory to himself. This Habsburg defeat, together with the French advance in Germany, forced the Austrians to conclude an armistice, but the subsequent peace negotiations proved inconclusive. Peace was only concluded after a renewed French advance in Italy and in Germany, where Moreau's decisive victory at Hohenlinden in Bavaria (December 1800) finally ended Habsburg participation in the Second Coalition. The peace of Lunéville (9 February 1801), which Vienna was now forced to accept, was a severe reverse for Austria. It restored the French gains at Campo Formio four years earlier and, in some measure, extended them. The Habsburgs were forced to accept France's possession of Belgium (the former Austrian Netherlands) and the left bank of the Rhine. The Habsburg dependency in Italy, the grand duchy of Tuscany, was lost. With the re-establishment of the Cisalpine Republic the French possessed effective control over northern and central Italy, though Austria was allowed to keep her gain of Venetia. Habsburg power in the Italian peninsula had been destroyed, while her influence in Germany had been partially undermined. Vienna was also obliged to recognise the sovereignty of the satellite republics.

Bonaparte's efforts were less successful elsewhere in 1800–1. His attempt to create a Franco-Russian *entente* by exploiting Paul's resentment at his treatment by Britain and Austria ultimately failed. Bonaparte and his foreign minister, Talleyrand, sought Russian co-operation and perhaps even an alliance in order to exclude British trade from northern Europe. French conquests had closed many continental ports to English goods, and the putative 'Continental System' at which they aimed needed the support of Russia before it could be completed by the closure of the Baltic. A combination of French diplomacy and the widespread resentment among neutral states at Britain's high-handed enforcement of her own interpretation of maritime law had produced an initial success with the formation of a league of Armed Neutrality in December 1800, in which Russia was joined by Denmark, Sweden and Prussia. This second Armed Neutrality for a time intensified Britain's economic difficulties by cutting her off from the vital Baltic and German markets, and it contributed to her increasing willingness to negotiate with Bonaparte. But the league crumbled swiftly after Nelson's bombardment of the Danish fleet off Copenhagen (2 April 1801). The murder of Paul I (March 1801) put an end, at least for the moment, to Bonaparte's lingering hopes of a Franco-Russian *rapprochement*. These hopes had, in any case, been illusory. Paul I had always been hostile to France. The Tsar's own aim in 1800–1 was a restored equilibrium in Europe by means of armed mediation, though Prussia's refusal to co-operate with him ruined this Russian initiative. His successor, Alexander I (1801–25), was also hostile towards France. On the credit side, both Portugal, which had nominally been at war with France since 1793, and Naples (briefly the Parthenopean Republic) came to terms in 1801.

Only Britain, the architect of the Second Coalition, remained at war. British sea power still prevented the realisation of France's continuing plans for an invasion of England. After a decade of war, however, Britain's financial and economic situation was rapidly worsening and the nation's will to carry on the struggle was waning. Overseas trade, Britain's life-blood, had been severely affected by the fighting. The closure of the French market in 1793 itself had been significant, since France had occupied a wholly new importance in the pattern of British commerce after the conclusion of the commercial treaty in 1786. French territorial expansion in the 1790s, moreover, had closed many of the traditional outlets for British trade, particularly in the Low Countries and the Mediterranean. The war-weariness which these economic difficulties induced was further strengthened by the direct taxation which Pitt had introduced to finance the struggle against France: income tax first made its appearance in 1799. Above all, the peace of Lunéville had left Britain without a major ally on the Continent. There was, by 1801, no direct way Britain could influence events in Europe. The political crisis over Irish emancipation indirectly increased Britain's willingness to negotiate. George III's refusal to countenance any improvement in the position of Roman Catholics in Ireland led to the resignation early in 1801 of the Younger Pitt, who for almost a decade had directed and sustained Britain's war against France. The new ministry, led by Addington, wanted peace and listened eagerly to French offers to negotiate. The Anglo-French negotiations which began in 1801 were protracted, largely because Bonaparte hoped to hang on to Egypt. Peace preliminaries eventually were signed in London in October 1801. The final treaty largely confirmed these preliminaries. The peace of Amiens (27 March 1802) provided for the withdrawal of French garrisons from the Papal States and from Naples. Britain, for her part, returned all her conquests made during the war, except for the islands of Ceylon (which had been captured from the Dutch) and Trinidad (seized from Spain). Egypt was to be restored to the Ottoman Empire, and Malta was to be handed back to the Knights.

The peace settlements of 1801–2 were intrinsically unstable: they were, in reality, mere truces. After a decade of almost continuous fighting, peace was welcomed by all the belligerents, but the settlements of Lunéville and Amiens were the product of exhaustion, not reconciliation. Austria resented the destruction of her dominant position in Italy and the challenge to her traditional authority in the German lands. She would clearly welcome an early opportunity of overturning the peace of Lunéville. Britain, for her part, had sought peace in 1801 partly in the belief that the Revolution had run its course and that it might now be possible to live at peace with the French Republic; but the negotiations with France disappointed them. The discussions which led to the peace of Amiens convinced British ministers of Bonaparte's 'inordinate ambition' (as the foreign secretary Lord Hawkesbury phrased it). There could be little hope of an enduring peace with such a regime and such a ruler, particularly as the settlements of 1801–2 left France's hegemony in Europe substantially intact.

CHAPTER ELEVEN

Napoleon and Europe, 1802–1815

NAPOLEON AND THE EUROPEAN STATES SYSTEM

The 1790s saw a decisive French challenge to what the Younger Pitt called 'the Public Law of Europe'. This continued and, indeed, was intensified after 1802. By 1812 Napoleon personally ruled a vast empire and controlled Europe to an extent unparalleled since Roman times. The creation and ultimate disintegration of Napoleon's supremacy dominated European diplomacy between the peace of Amiens and the congress of Vienna. There was considerable continuity with the first decade of the struggle against France. The achievement of the Revolutionary leaders in advancing the French frontier into the Low Countries, to the Rhine and into northern Italy, inevitably dictated the framework of Napoleon's policy. In a similar way, Napoleon's decisive military victories magnified a tendency already apparent in the 1790s. Territory was now taken from the major states and not, as before 1789, from those in decline. The limited warfare of the *ancien régime* and the balance of power it upheld had been reflected in this territorial stability. Prussia's seizure of Silesia from Austria had been the only significant transfer of territory between great powers. In the decade after 1802, however, substantial amounts of land were taken from major powers and, in particular, from Prussia and Austria. This was made possible by France's total military victories.

Napoleon had a unique impact on the European states system because of his military success. The decisive defeats he inflicted on his enemies left them completely at his mercy. His victories also largely made the activities of the diplomats irrelevant. Negotiation was impossible for Prussia after her shattering defeat in 1806, or for Austria after the disastrous war of 1809. Each power was incapable of further resistance and therefore handed over the territory Napoleon demanded. His view of international relations always remained that of a general rather than a foreign minister. His impatience meant that

303

he had little time for the delay that was part of all diplomatic negotiations and he frequently censured the dilatoriness of the diplomats. Napoleon also ignored the conventions of international law and diplomacy, and this alienated continental opinion. Particular offence was caused by the kidnapping and subsequent execution of the Duke d'Enghien in 1804 (see p. 310). In 1803, after the resumption of the Anglo-French War, a considerable number of British tourists still on the Continent had been arrested, along with three English diplomats. Such flagrant breaches of international law contrasted sharply with the action of the British government in 1806, when it imprisoned a man who offered to assassinate Napoleon and actually informed France of this. This episode highlighted the abyss which separated Old Europe from the regime in Paris; it also helps to explain why Napoleon's France never became an accepted member of the international community. Most European governments were in any case irreconcilably opposed to Napoleon whom they saw as the heir to the hated French Revolution.

Except for his personal aggrandisement, Napoleon's foreign policy lacked a central theme. But the dominant elements in his strategy can be discerned: opposition to England, control of Germany and Italy, supremacy for France in the Mediterranean and in the Balkans and, increasingly, recognition by the other European powers of his own achievements and those of the Bonaparte dynasty. At various times one or more of these aims was uppermost; but Napoleon's capacity to win decisive military victories meant that he was never forced to make a choice over priorities almost to the end. The Napoleonic empire which existed by 1807 arose piecemeal out of this series of victories; the imperialism was not so much planned as unavoidable. The personal element was very important: Napoleon's unique energy and spirit, together with his individual ambition which verged on megalomania, gave a decisive twist to French policy in these years. Napoleon's own ambitions, which increased with each new military triumph, provide the nearest thing to a unified explanation of his foreign policy. He was essentially an opportunist and an improviser. He sought to exploit the existing jealousies and suspicions among his enemies. In so far as Napoleon had any consistent diplomatic strategy it was to retain at least one great power as a partner: Prussia up to 1806, Russia after Tilsit, Austria after her humiliation in 1809. Each was tempted into partnership by the promise of subsequent gains but none achieved these. Napoleon's use of alliances was always tactical; diplomacy in his view was essentially subservient to military strategy. All problems, he believed, were capable of a military solution. In this he was mistaken. Each new victory in the years after 1803 created the same basic problem: how to produce a stable political settlement between Napoleon and Europe. Each time he sought a military solution, and ultimately he over-extended himself.

THE RENEWAL OF THE ANGLO-FRENCH WAR AND THE FORMATION OF THE THIRD COALITION 1802–1805

England's attitude to the peace of Amiens was ambivalent. After a decade of expensive war and increasing economic difficulties it was welcomed as a breathing-space. The prime minister, Addington, quickly abolished the wartime expedient of income tax and sharply reduced naval expenditure in the hope that it might prove a permanent settlement. At the same time there was widespread grudging recognition that the treaty had ignored many of the fundamental points at issue between the two states. The Addington ministry had bought peace through substantial concessions; within a few months the extent of these concessions became apparent. France's continued control of the mouths of the Scheldt and the Rhine was unacceptable as was Napoleon's dominance over the rest of the Continent. The settlement failed to restore the expected prosperity to Great Britain, or to re-open the markets of France and her dependencies to British goods (because of Napoleon's protectionist policies). The continued bad feeling, on both sides of the Channel, was soon visible in Anglo-French disputes over the execution of the peace settlement, and after the late autumn of 1802, relations deteriorated rapidly.

This deterioration was produced principally by Napoleon's continued ambitions and by the resulting British resentment at what were regarded as breaches of the spirit of the peace of Amiens. Britain disliked the threat of future French colonial expansion involved in the sending of troops to the island of Haiti in the Caribbean (to crush a slave revolt) and in the earlier forced cession of Louisiana from Spain to France (1801). Napoleon's energetic and large-scale reconstruction of the French navy similarly alarmed ministers in London, since this struck at the heart of Britain's security. It was, however, Napoleon's continued annexations in Europe and apparent ambitions in the Near East which most alarmed British ministers, especially as there was now little opposition on the Continent to his further expansion. Napoleon's acquisitions in peace were almost as impressive as his gains by war. His ambitious schemes for the reorganisation of Germany (see pp. 319f.), his military intervention in October 1802 to shore up the Swiss Helvetic Republic, his new acquisitions in Italy (Piedmont – the mainland part of the kingdom of Sardinia –, and Elba were formally annexed to France in September and October 1802), and the treating of the Dutch Batavian Republic and Spain as satellites, were all viewed in London as breaches of the Amiens settlement. Even more anxiety was aroused by fear of a new French attack on Egypt and eventually a challenge to British power in India. The appearance of Colonel Sebastiani's report in the *Moniteur* on 30 January 1803 confirmed this view. Sebastiani was a French agent who had been sent to the Near East. His report emphasised the weakness both of the Ottoman Empire and of the remaining British force in Egypt and concluded that an army of 6,000 men would be adequate to conquer the latter. His conclusions, and their appearance in an official news-paper, confirmed British ministers' belief that Napoleon would re-occupy Egypt as soon as Britain followed the terms of the peace of Amiens and withdrew from the Mediterranean.

The Addington ministry decided, in a belated show of strength, to retain Britain's one remaining base in the Mediterranean, Malta. This was legally a breach of the peace settlement, but by the final weeks of 1802 there was little doubt that war would soon be resumed. Britain's new-found firmness was also reflected in demands that France should evacuate Switzerland and Holland. Napoleon, for his part, believed this novel British stubbornness could be overcome by intimidation – a belief encouraged by Britain's weakness during the previous negotiations for the peace of Amiens. Relations became increasingly acrimonious in the early months of 1803 and, on 18 May, Britain declared war.

The renewed Anglo-French War soon resumed the familiar pat-tern. Britain's dominance at sea, and the effective naval blockade of France's Atlantic ports, made possible the seizure of a succession of French and Dutch colonies overseas; but the same strategic stalemate that had persisted since the War of the First Coalition and had been reflected in the peace of Amiens remained. Neither mastery at sea nor supremacy on land was in itself sufficient to bring complete victory. Until the formation of the Third Coalition in 1805, Britain fought alone and only her navy saved her from defeat. Napoleon, free from continental enemies, seriously contemplated the invasion of England long envisaged by French strategists. A vast force – the 'Army of Invasion' – was maintained at Boulogne from late 1803 until autumn 1805, but no descent could be attempted since Britain retained abso-lute control of the seas.

The contribution of British sea power to the defeat of France dur-ing the Revolutionary and Napoleonic Wars was considerable. The scale of the emergency Britain faced was reflected in the unprece-dented expansion of the naval establishment. In 1793, the British navy had contained 135 ships of the line and 133 frigates; by 1802 the respective figures were 202 and 277. Personnel had increased from some 16,000 to around 135,000 men. But France's continued inferi-ority at sea was primarily because of superior British tactics and lead-ership. The traditional 'line-ahead' formation of the eighteenth century was steadily abandoned, as British commanders came to pre-fer the more aggressive tactics of the mêlée, close combat aimed at isolating and destroying individual ships or sectors of the opposing fleet. In this kind of encounter the superior British gunnery was always likely to prove decisive. British leadership was also far better.

The age of Nelson saw the emergence of a number of able and ener-getic commanders – Howe and St Vincent, Cornwallis and Colling-wood, Nelson himself – thoroughly professional in approach and willing to adopt an aggressive strategy. The French fleet, on the other hand, always lacked experience of sea and combat, and its leadership and administration had been all but destroyed during the early years of the Revolution.

Napoleon's planned invasion of England required that the French navy should establish at least temporary control at sea, so that the 'Army of Invasion' could be transported across the Channel. But this was prevented by the British blockade of the principal French naval bases which stopped a major French fleet being assembled at sea. Central to this stranglehold was the 'close' blockade of Brest main-tained with difficulty from May 1803 until November 1805 – in itself a considerable feat of seamanship. In October 1805, at the battle of Trafalgar, Nelson destroyed a combined Franco-Spanish fleet when it came out of Cadiz (Spain had entered the war on the side of France in December 1804). Thereafter Napoleon never revived the planned invasion and effectively conceded naval dominance to Britain. Sea power, however, remained an essentially defensive weapon which in itself could not bring about the defeat of Napoleon. This was certainly appreciated by Pitt, who had become prime minister again in May 1804. Shortly after his return to office, he began a series of diplomatic initiatives which led to the formation of the Third Coalition.

Pitt's realisation that victory could only be achieved on land made him willing to provide subsidies on an unparalleled scale. This rep-resented a significant modification of British policy. Subsidies had, hitherto, been given reluctantly and selectively. They had been paid either in return for troops or, occasionally, to keep a country in the coalition. Henceforth, Britain was prepared to subsidise any ally, and this was to be very important in the final decade of the struggle against Napoleon. Subsidies, however, were still to be the limit of Britain's commitment. Pitt wanted a coalition but not direct British military involvement on the Continent, and this was resented by potential allies who had to face Napoleon's armies directly.

The new attitude to subsidies indicated Pitt's desire to form a coalition quickly in 1804–5. Military assistance on the scale needed to defeat Napoleon could only come from one or more of the major continental powers. But after a decade of expensive and unsuccessful war, France's enemies were reluctant to join a new coalition. They, moreover, were as afraid of the peace terms which a victorious France might impose as of further military defeat. Twice already – in 1797 and in 1801 – Napoleon had redrawn the political map and demolished traditional institutions at the end of a successful war. Old Europe always feared another war might lead to its final destruction.

Austria, Britain's partner during the first two coalitions, was for long unwilling to resume the struggle against France. Her armies had suffered heavy defeats during the final states of the War of the Second Coalition and she had had to shoulder the main burden of the continental war after the withdrawal of Prussia in 1795. Inadequate resources had always been her Achilles' heel and, by 1802, after a decade of war, her finances were in chaos. Austrian territory had been devastated by French forces, the war had become increasingly unpopular and it had proved difficult to recruit enough soldiers. The Emperor Francis was consequently determined to avoid an early renewal of the struggle. Yet there was little cordiality between Vienna and Paris. Austria resented the imposition in 1803 of the Imperial Recess, which destroyed the traditional influence of the Habsburgs in Germany and led to important territorial changes in the Holy Roman Empire (see pp. 319f.). Relations were further soured by Napoleon's assumption of the title of emperor in May 1804, an affront to the principles of rank and of legitimacy which the Imperial family of the Habsburgs found particularly offensive. By autumn 1804, ministers in Vienna were seriously concerned at Napoleon's continued expansion in Germany and Italy, and in November they concluded a secret military convention with Russia, which agreed on how much help they were to provide in any future war with France. But Austro-Russian co-operation was hindered by each state's belief that the other had deserted it in 1799, and Austria's official policy remained pacific.

The second of the eastern powers, Prussia, was even less likely to join a new coalition. Her foreign policy was elusive, a prey to court faction, and sometimes even contradictory. The reputation her army still enjoyed meant she was courted by both sides, and her policy since 1795 had successfully exploited this. Berlin's policy remained that of standing aloof, inclining slightly towards France, while seeking to increase Prussian territory and influence in northern Germany. This approach had served her well since her withdrawal from the First Coalition, and had won her minor gains from successive French territorial reorganisations of Germany. Yet the pro-French neutrality of Frederick William III was already being undermined. His famous meeting with Alexander I at Memel (Klaipeda) in June 1802 had forged a personal alliance which endured for the next two decades. Thereafter, Frederick William III's emotional commitment to the allied cause was undoubted, but it was several years before this was reflected in his foreign policy. In a similar way, the war party at the Prussian court (those who urged the folly of leaving Napoleon a free hand in the political reorganisation of the Continent) was by 1803–4 gaining strength and confidence, but not enough to push Prussia into a war. The attraction of the future acquisition of Hanover remained central to Prussian thinking, and it was carefully cultivated by the French, who occupied the electorate on the resumption of war with England in 1803. There was very little chance, therefore, in 1803–5 that Prussia would abandon her profitable neutrality and join Pitt's projected coalition.

The prospects for a new alliance with Russia did not, initially, seem much brighter. Indeed, for some time after his accession in 1801 the new Tsar, Alexander I, appeared as hostile towards Britain as towards Napoleonic France, largely because of British naval action against neutral shipping in the Baltic and, in particular, Nelson's raid on Copenhagen in 1801. The continuing British refusal to hand over Malta to Russia was another particular source of friction. At the same time, the internal reforms carried out by France's first consul attracted Alexander I, who had broadly similar ideas. In October 1801 a Franco-Russian peace settlement had been worked out and thereafter Alexander had attempted to remain on friendly terms with Napoleon. The Tsar wanted to concentrate on internal reforms and, in the early years of his reign, Russia managed to stay detached from the struggle against France. There was, so far, little reason for any serious tension, especially as Napoleon's territorial ambitions did not yet impinge on Russian interests. Consequently, Alexander's foreign policy had by 1802 become distinctly isolationist.

By 1803 it was proving increasingly difficult for Russia to sustain her neutral policy, because of her anxieties about Napoleon's territorial ambitions in the eastern Mediterranean (see pp. 305–6). Essentially the same fears which induced Britain to resume the war in May 1803 also persuaded Alexander to enter the struggle. The Ottoman Empire, where there had been serious internal disturbances in 1802–3, seemed weak and on the point of collapse. The Tsar and his advisers, who believed Russia alone should control the destinies of the Ottoman Empire, were alarmed that France would seek to exploit this instability in the Balkans. French expansion there would threaten Russia's security and her fast-expanding Black Sea trade. It would undermine the value of the territorial acquisitions made by Catherine II and might even imperil Russia's access to the Mediterranean through the Straits. In a similar way, Napoleon's expansionist policies in central Europe inspired fears in St Petersburg that France could be a threat to Russia's new-found possessions in Poland.

These anxieties produced a significant worsening in Russo-French relations. A series of other disputes soon led to a further deterioration. The summer of 1803 witnessed an ill-fated Russian attempt to mediate in the renewed Anglo-French War. Napoleon considered Alexander's intervention was pro-English and rejected any idea of a Russian mediation. The French leader made matters worse by delivering a public dressing-down to the Russian ambassador, Markov, who was promptly withdrawn. From the autumn of 1803 there was a serious Franco-Russian quarrel over the status of the Ionian Islands (nominally an independent republic since the expulsion of the French by a Russo-Ottoman expeditionary force in 1799). Considerable offence was caused in St Petersburg, as throughout monarchical Europe, by the d'Enghien episode in March 1804. The Duke d'Enghien, a member of the former French royal family, was abducted by Napoleon's agents from neutral Baden, taken back to France, tried before a military court and summarily executed. Alexander was outraged at what he regarded as murder. Even worse, the abduction had been from his wife's homeland. In reprisal, diplomatic relations with France were broken off in April 1804, a month before Napoleon caused more offence by crowning himself emperor.

Relations had clearly deteriorated in the first half of 1804. This development was facilitated by the growing influence in St Petersburg of the Pole, Prince Adam Czartoryski, a personal friend of the young Tsar. Since 1802 Czartoryski had helped formulate Russian foreign policy; after February 1804 he was Alexander's principal diplomatic adviser. Under his influence, Russia again became fully involved in European affairs. Czartoryski encouraged the Tsar's growing concern at French expansion, especially in the Balkans. He also suggested how Napoleon might be restrained. His plan, the famous 'Grand Design' of 1804, blended *Realpolitik* with idealistic theorising about a future political settlement for Europe which anticipated that of 1814–15. Central to this was inevitably the re-establishment of the kingdom of Poland (swept away by the three partitions at the end of the eighteenth century). But Czartoryski knew that such talk would arouse Russian suspicions, and it was only in 1805 that the idea of a reborn Poland under Russia's tutelage could be publicly canvassed.

The Tsar was himself sympathetic to Czartoryski's ideas. Idealistic, even Utopian, Alexander regarded diplomacy not in terms of particular systems or alliances (as many of his contemporaries did) but in vague and theoretical concepts. The 'balance of power' and the 'community of Europe' were always central to the Tsar's thinking, and he also had some sympathy for Polish aspirations. The fact that the 'Grand Design' aimed to make Russia supreme in the Balkans and in central Europe was a further recommendation. Consequently, Czartoryski's plans were the official basis of Russian diplomacy in 1804–5. An alliance of Russia, Austria and Prussia was to be formed. This would aim, initially, to restrain Napoleon's continuing expansion by means of an ultimatum. Only if this was unsuccessful would the eastern powers consider war. In this event, British participation and, more important, British gold would be essential.

This rather Utopian scheme fell far short of the new coalition which Pitt hoped to create. Although Anglo–Russian alliance negotiations were begun by a British approach in 1804, by early the next year the prospective allies were still far apart. In particular, Britain's refusal to hand over Malta caused friction. Alexander had no wish to see another British base in the Mediterranean, since this could become as serious a threat to Russian interests as that currently posed by

France. Russia also resented the fact that Britain would still commit only money, not men, to a war on the Continent. Pitt, though he desired a new coalition, would not make the concessions necessary to bring it about. An Anglo-Russian subsidy agreement was actually signed in St Petersburg in April 1805, but Britain was at first unwilling to ratify the terms which her representative had been forced to accept by Russian ministers.

Napoleon's unbridled ambitions now created the coalition which had eluded Britain and Russia's diplomatic efforts. On 18 May 1805 Napoleon took the throne of the previous Cisalpine Republic, now the kingdom of Italy. The following month (6 June) he annexed Genoa (the Ligurian Republic) to France. These two actions, and the vast ambitions to which they testified, created, in two months, the coalition which two years of diplomacy had failed to produce. In July 1805 Britain ratified the April treaty with Russia, while Austria (whose support was essential, given Prussia's continuing neutrality, if Russian troops were to reach the central European battlefields) also decided on war. Napoleon's actions in Italy were clear breaches of the Austro-French peace of Lunéville (1801) and this finally convinced Habsburg statesmen that peace with France could be as dangerous as war. Vienna formally entered the war in August 1805 by adhering to the Anglo-Russian treaty – having successfully forced an increase in Britain's subsidy to her. Britain similarly paid a hefty subsidy to Sweden, in October, so that Russia could use the remaining strip of Swedish Pomerania as a base for operations in Germany. Naples became the final member of the coalition by her treaty with Russia (September 1805). The extent of Napoleon's dominance in Germany was reflected in the fact that most of the smaller German states, many of whom had joined the two previous coalitions, now stayed neutral. Prussia, for the moment, clung to her neutrality in the face of appeals for assistance from all sides, but Baden, Bavaria and Württemberg, three of the principal beneficiaries from the Imperial Recess of 1803 (see p. 320) actually joined Napoleon.

THE DESTRUCTION OF THE THIRD COALITION 1805–1807

The Third Coalition satisfied neither Britain nor Russia. Alexander's dreams of a crusade to restore peace and Pitt's notion of an all-embracing coalition were both disappointed by the military alliances hurriedly created in the summer and autumn of 1805 in response to Napoleon's ambitions. The coalition's resources were considerable, but the reluctant allies still viewed the war in different, and occasionally contradictory, ways. The war which followed soon demonstrated the fragility of this recent unity.

The campaign of 1805, begun precariously against the background of a severe financial crisis in France, proved a triumph for Napoleon. Austria was not yet ready for the war she had declared. The military reforms introduced by the Archduke Charles had barely begun to take effect. Vienna was still intent on retrieving her position in Italy and mistakenly sent large numbers of troops there. Napoleon, however, advanced rapidly in Germany, surprised and outmanoeuvred General Mack, latest in a long line of inept Austrian commanders, and forced him to a humiliating surrender at Ulm (20 October 1805). The French went on to occupy Vienna in mid-November before Napoleon brilliantly defeated a combined Austro-Russian army at Austerlitz (2 December 1805). Austria now withdrew from the Third Coalition and signed the treaty of Pressburg (Bratislava) on 26 December 1805 by which she acknowledged her exclusion from Italy and the destruction of Habsburg authority in Germany. In return for minor gains from Bavaria, Austria lost Venetia, Istria and Dalmatia (to the kingdom of Italy), the Tyrol and the Vorarlberg (to Bavaria) and the Breisgau (to Württemberg and Baden). Vienna was also forced to recognise Napoleon's German clients (Bavaria, Württemberg and Baden) as independent kingdoms and to pay a substantial indemnity.

Austria had all along hoped that Prussia would join the Third Coalition and had negotiated intensively at Berlin for this. These efforts failed. Frederick William III was pacific by inclination, and preoccupied with largely unsuccessful attempts at internal reform and with paying off his predecessor, Frederick William II's substantial debts. Neutrality had served Prussia well since 1795, while political tradition ensured that Vienna's eclipse in Germany and elsewhere was not wholly unwelcome to Berlin. Napoleon, moreover, could now offer the enticing bait of Hanover as the reward for continued neutrality. The prospect of acquiring Hanover (which would confirm Prussia's dominance in north Germany) and the desire for peace in Berlin, which reflected an awareness of Prussia's military vulnerability, were enough to frustrate all the attempts of the Third Coalition to secure Prussia's support. Instead, Frederick William III sought terms from Napoleon. By the treaty of Schönbrunn (15 December 1805), Prussia gave up some minor fiefs and, in return, secured the coveted cession of Hanover; it would be long before this transaction was forgotten at the Habsburg court – or, indeed, in London.

Prussia, however, had been too clever for her own good: she was now at Napoleon's mercy, as Frederick William III soon discovered. By the treaty of Paris (15 February 1806) Berlin was forced to promise and (if required) to supply troops for the continuing war against Russia. She was also obliged to join the Continental System (Napoleon's economic blockade against Britain – see pp. 322–5) and to close her ports to British shipping, moves which ended a period of Prussian economic prosperity. Britain responded by declaring war on Prussia (11 June 1806) and attacking Prussian shipping. Berlin was also afraid that Hanover might even now be snatched away, for in the summer of 1806 Napoleon was rumoured to be offering the electorate to Britain in return for peace. A sense of national humiliation, coupled with a growing appreciation that Prussia was already a French satellite, whose future would be determined by the whim of Napoleon, finally drove Berlin to war. Frederick William III mobilised (6 August 1806) and sent an ultimatum demanding the return of some Prussian territories and the withdrawal of French troops from Prussia's frontiers. Characteristically, the Prussian King picked the worst possible moment for this display of resolution. Napoleon, having defeated Austria and forced Russia to retreat, simply ignored his demands and launched an attack against the isolated Prussia. In an immensely swift and brilliantly improvised campaign lasting only a week Napoleon smashed the Prussians at the twin battles of Jena–Auerstädt (14 October 1806) and overran the central core of Hohenzollern territories. This catastrophic defeat shattered the myth of Prussian invincibility which the victories of Frederick II had created, and paved the way for some important internal reforms. But Prussia's defeat had a wider significance. In 1806 the strongest army of the *ancien régime* was shattered by the new-style warfare which had emerged during the 1790s and been perfected by Napoleon.

The victories of 1805–6 achieved by short and relentless campaigns, showed clearly the decisive role of warfare in this period. Napoleon's principal achievement in military history was to restore battle to a place of primacy. In the eighteenth century, battle had largely been seen as a last resort. With one or two significant exceptions, commanders had preferred to conduct manoeuvres and sieges, rather than risk the destruction of their expensive mercenary armies in battle. The first real challenge to this limited and defensive approach to warfare had come in the 1790s, when the Revolutionary armies, with their abundant manpower and enthusiasm, had successfully adopted the offensive. Napoleon now refined and perfected the changes first introduced in the 1790s. Central to the Emperor's conception of warfare was the ending of the traditional distinction between strategy (the overall conduct of a campaign) and tactics (the actual fighting of battles). Napoleon fused these two elements: a decisive battle was always his principal aim. The Emperor's ability to move his troops over long distances at high speeds and then to concentrate them against a vulnerable enemy was unsurpassed. Basic to this was Napoleon's subdivision of his army into corps, usually of some 25,000–30,000 men. This made possible the deployment of the army over a wide front, which somewhat reduced the problem of obtaining provisions and, more important, hid from the enemy the ultimate objective until the last moment. The various corps could then be assembled quickly just before a battle. Speed was central to Napoleonic warfare: swift, forced marches gave the Emperor the crucial advantage of surprise, which could usually be turned into victory.

On the battlefield, after initial skirmishing and concentrated artillery fire, massed infantry columns attacked to probe for a weakness in the enemy's position. Further artillery fire and infantry reserves were directed against this weak spot until the enemy's line collapsed, giving the French first a decisive local superiority and then total victory. Finally, cavalry was sent on pursuit to scatter the fleeing troops and demoralise the civilian population. These basic tactics, together with a willingness to improvise and an ability to conceive of a battle as a whole and act accordingly, largely explain Napoleon's remarkable series of victories. Not the least of his qualities as a commander was that Napoleon possessed a remarkable ability to inspire his troops and was rewarded with unquestioned obedience. Morale was aided by the system of promotion through the ranks on merit rather than seniority or social status, the 'career open to all the talents' established in the 1790s.

Napoleon's system of warfare did have weaknesses, however, and these became more evident during his final campaigns. The destruction of the Third Coalition had rested on the reorganisation of the French army in the years of peace on the Continent after 1801. Napoleon's Grand Army was simply too strong and well organised for the Austrians and Prussians. This achievement proved impossible to sustain. The central problem was to produce adequately trained replacements for losses suffered, a difficulty compounded by the almost continuous campaigns after 1805 and by the Napoleonic army's ever-increasing commitments. There were plenty of recruits: the system of conscription introduced during the 1790s, which in theory imposed military service on all Frenchmen (with substantial and clearly defined exemptions) provided more than enough new soldiers. But the demand for replacements was too great, particularly after 1806, to give the recruits any sustained training.

Experience in the field, in short, replaced training and Napoleon was consequently forced to modify his tactics. Attack by massed column proved steadily less successful and came decisively to grief against the Austrians at Aspern–Essling in 1809; thereafter Napoleon compensated for the deficiencies of his infantry by heavier reliance on increased numbers of guns; but the victories gained by extended artillery duels proved costly in casualties. And while the provision of recruits for Napoleon's armies became increasingly difficult, particularly after 1812, his enemies who had responded to the mass armies of France by increasing their own dependence on conscripts, proved able to put larger armies into the field. A further growing problem was to provision the French armies. Napoleon's emphasis on speed meant supply trains could not keep up with the advancing army. His forces therefore had to live off the land like the armies of the Thirty Years War, plundering and raising 'contributions' as they marched. (This in itself was one reason for Napoleon's relentless pursuit of further conquests, since ideally populations supposedly friendly to France should be spared these horrors.) The intended solution to this logistical problem was a rapid victory, after which the enemy's magazines or supply bases could be captured and his population forced to support the French army. However, when Napoleon extended his operations into the less fertile lands on the periphery of Europe, Spain, Poland and, in 1812, Russia, the basic problem of supply became even more pressing. In these areas the vulnerability of a strategy based on rapid victory, on *Blitzkrieg*, would become all too apparent; it was already evident during Napoleon's campaign against Russia in 1807.

Russia's diplomatic activity in 1804–5 had not been transferred to the battlefield. After the Austro-Russian defeat at Austerlitz (December 1805), the Russian forces had retreated out of Napoleon's reach. The impact of this immediate reverse on Alexander's complex personality was considerable. His earlier confidence evaporated and, for much of 1806, he took refuge in inactivity and waiting on events. Czartoryski's influence waned after recent defeats and he was effectively dropped at the beginning of 1806. As he was to do at several critical moments, the Tsar now effectively acted as his own foreign minister. Russia's options in foreign policy remained the same as they had been since the later 1790s: an interventionist war, or peace through non-involvement. Alexander, characteristically, could not decide between these strategies and, for much of 1806, contrived to pursue both simultaneously. Negotiations for a peace settlement were conducted in Paris and, as Napoleon wanted peace, a treaty was concluded (Oubril treaty, July 1806). But this was then rejected by Alexander who disliked its terms: he was not yet prepared to recognise Napoleon's dominance in Germany nor French control of Dalmatia (ceded to Napoleon by Austria in 1805). At the same time, Alexander's personal commitment to the Prussian King, Frederick William III, forged at Memel in 1802, remained strong. When Napoleon attacked Prussia in October 1806, Russian troops were sent to Prussia's assistance, though these contingents were as usual slow in moving westwards.

By this point (November 1806) Russia was also involved in a war against the Ottoman Empire, which had sided with France in the second half of 1806. This ended a period of indecisive Ottoman foreign policy which stretched back to 1802. The French invasion of Egypt in 1798 had destroyed the traditional Franco-Ottoman alignment. In the War of the Second Coalition, the Ottoman Empire had fought on the side of France's enemies. However, an armistice had been concluded with Paris in 1801 and a formal peace treaty in June the following year. Thereafter the Sultan would have liked to pursue a neutral line in foreign affairs, but the growing weakness of his state made this all but impossible. Selim III's internal problems were immense and appeared to suggest that the disintegration of the Ottoman Empire might be finally on hand. Constantinople's control over its outlying provinces was now nominal, and this inevitably weakened Ottoman foreign policy. After 1802 the Sultan had tried to restore the traditional alliance with France, who now wanted to recover her previous economic and political influence throughout the Near East. Russia seemed the greatest danger, since she clearly wanted to consolidate and, if possible, expand her own recent gains from the Turks. These were considerable: access into the Mediterranean through the Straits (under the terms of the alliance concluded with the Porte in 1799), a protectorate over the Ionian Islands and, in more general terms, naval mastery in the eastern Mediterranean as well as in the Black Sea. In 1802, the Sultan was forced to accept Russian control over the appointment of the local rulers (hospodars) of Moldavia and Wallachia; thereafter the Danubian principalities acted as a lever for increasing Russian influence within the Ottoman Empire itself. Such dependence was irksome to the Sultan, who also resented the recent growth of Russian influence in the Caucasus and eastern Anatolia.

Napoleon continually urged a firm anti-Russian policy on the Porte and, specifically, tried to persuade Selim III to close the Straits to Russian warships. But these efforts proved unsuccessful, and by 1805 Napoleon aimed only for Ottoman neutrality and was instead interested in alliance with Persia, directed against Russia and against British power in India. However, Napoleon's military successes against the Third Coalition in the closing months of 1805 (see p. 312) led to the recovery of France's influence in Constantinople. Selim III, on hearing of French triumphs at Ulm and Austerlitz, sought to save his empire by alliance with Napoleon. The prospect of recovering territory previously lost to Russia and, in particular, the Crimea, had been emphasised by French diplomacy, and this now became the Sultan's objective, through a war alongside France and Persia. Matters came to a head in the autumn of 1806. The Sultan replaced the hospodars of Moldavia and Wallachia by men sympathetic to France and then declared the Straits closed to foreign warships, thereby preventing the Russian Black Sea fleet reinforcing the Ionian Islands. These actions outraged St Petersburg, where an influential group had long urged further southward expansion. In early November, Russian troops invaded the Danubian principalities, and the following month Selim III formally declared war on Russia.

By the end of 1806, Alexander was at war on two fronts, as French troops moved eastwards to attack Russia. Napoleon had not been anxious for the war, but his attitude changed on reaching Berlin after defeating the Prussians. Captured Prussian state papers revealed the closeness of Russo-Prussian contacts in the summer of 1806. For Alexander I had clearly been playing a double game by encouraging Prussian resistance while negotiating peace with France. Napoleon now determined on war and, at the same time, decided against a unilateral peace with the defeated Prussia. French forces advanced into Poland in December 1806, winning an expensive technical victory in the snow at Eylau on 8 February 1807. But by this point Napoleon's military situation was precarious: food was short, reinforcements were needed and his lines of communication were dangerously exposed and harried by guerrillas. The diplomatic situation was also insecure. Napoleon was not wholly confident that Austria would remain at peace, while he also feared an increased British commitment to the war in Europe. His complex diplomacy aimed in 1806–7 to combat the menace of a reinvigorated Third Coalition, although he overestimated the threat this posed. He tried to divide his enemies, and at the same time to intimidate Austria into staying neutral. These months provide perhaps the clearest illustration of his conception of the role of diplomacy, that it should always be subservient to military strategy. Consequently, in 1806–7 his 'peace tactics' reflected his difficult military situation: he aimed less at establishing a durable peace on the Continent than at reinforcing and supplying his army which was trapped in a Polish winter.

Austria now had a new, anti-French foreign minister in Stadion, who had taken office in December 1805. But even his hatred of Napoleon could not overcome Vienna's fear of another disastrous war, especially after the collapse of Prussia in October 1806. Britain, for the moment, seemed even more insular than usual. The 'Ministry of All the Talents' which came into office on the death of Pitt (January 1806) was indecisive, slow and parsimonious. It reacted against Pitt's subsidy policy of 1804–6 and generally drew back from continental commitments. Consequently, Britain's relations with potential allies became poor. The shift to a colonial strategy at the same time confirmed Britain's return to an isolationist policy, and this was more so after the death of Charles James Fox in September 1806. Neither the British military diversion nor the Austrian intervention materialised, and when the campaign reopened in the spring of 1807, Russia faced Napoleon's armies alone. Two months later the issue had been decided: on 14 June 1807 the Russian army suffered a major defeat at Friedland.

TILSIT AND THE FRANCO-RUSSIAN *RAPPROCHEMENT*

It was quite clear to Alexander after Friedland that Russia had lost her war with France. Yet this was less evident to Napoleon, who had been impressed by the bravery and tenacity of the Russian army at Eylau and Friedland and knew he had only defeated an army in the field. He was not in a position to dictate terms, and he had no wish for a campaign in Russia, with all the attendant problems of supply. He was anxious to leave eastern Europe in order to complete the reorganisation of Italy and Germany, and, more especially, to concentrate on the struggle with England. Napoleon therefore wanted a speedy political settlement with Russia; he also saw short-term advantages in a political alliance with the Tsar. Alexander, for his part, was similarly anxious for a quick peace. He was disillusioned with his partners in the Third Coalition. In particular, he resented Britain's inactivity in 1806–7 and her meanness over subsidies. The help which Russia expected and needed never came, as British troops were not committed to the Continent but were sent overseas to mop up French colonies. What the *Edinburgh Review* called 'our love of sugar islands' played a considerable part in alienating Russia. Alexander I had also been disappointed by Austria's inactivity and even more by Prussia's supine conduct in 1806–7; there were to be considerable Russo-Prussian recriminations over each other's military performance. The Russian ruler's psychological make-up was also important. Having suffered a decisive military defeat, Alexander was offered the opportunity to repair his own damaged reputation by an apparent diplomatic triumph. This dimension was cleverly exploited by Napoleon in a series of private conversations with the Tsar which began on 25 June 1807, initially on a raft in the middle of the Niemen, and then in the town of Tilsit (Sovietsk).

Alexander quickly accepted the proferred alliance with Napoleon. But the real significance of Tilsit is not the Franco-Russian *rapprochement*, important as this undoubtedly was. It is rather Russia's abandonment of Prussia, which Napoleon achieved through his personal mastery over the Tsar in their private talks. Alexander surrendered more completely than he had intended, and Prussia was the victim of this, though 'out of regard for the Emperor of the Russias' (in the words of the formal treaty) Napoleon did allow Frederick William III to keep his throne and part of his kingdom.

The series of treaties signed at Tilsit (7–9 June 1807) consisted of a general territorial settlement, a Franco-Russian alliance and a Franco-Prussian peace treaty. Though defeated on the battlefield, Russia's losses were comparatively slight: her recent gains in the Adriatic, Cattaro (a military outpost in Dalmatia) and the Ionian Islands, were both ceded to France, while in return Alexander gained a fragment of Prussian Poland, the province of Bialystok. The two emperors had vaguely discussed joint action against the Ottoman Empire, but no formal agreement emerged. Alexander, however, did have to accept French mediation in his war with the Sultan. Finally, as part of

Napoleon's broader strategy of turning the Continent against Britain, Russia promised first to mediate and, if this failed, to declare war on England and to join the Continental System (see pp. 322–5). It was also agreed that Sweden, Denmark and Portugal were to be compelled to do the same thing. Tilsit appeared to divide the Continent into two spheres of influence between two triumphant emperors: France dominated western and, increasingly, central Europe, while Russia was supreme in the Baltic, in the east and in the south-east. But in reality Tilsit created considerable barriers to future Russian expansion. Russia had lost her foothold in the Mediterranean and was threatened by Napoleon's gains in Germany and by the creation of the Grand Duchy of Warsaw (see p. 331f.). The political settlement at Tilsit was thus fundamentally unstable, for Napoleon never intended Alexander to be his equal.

The two principal victims were Prussia and Austria. Prussia's defeat in 1806 had been total. French armies had occupied all her territories except East Prussia. Alexander's intercession enabled Frederick William III to retain his throne, but Prussia lost one-third of her territory and almost half her population. Napoleon intended that a truncated Prussia should become a buttress against Russia, while being no competitor to France in Germany. Frederick William III's Rhineland provinces were therefore given to the newly formed kingdom of Westphalia (see p. 322) while all Prussia's gains from the Polish partitions (except a thin strip of West Prussia) became the new, French-dominated grand duchy of Warsaw. Finally, French troops were to occupy key Prussian fortresses until a war indemnity was paid.

In many ways Austria lost even more by the Tilsit agreement and by the political changes which accompanied Napoleon's defeat of the Third Coalition. Her territorial losses in 1805 (see p. 312), together with the subsequent remodelling of the Continent, undermined traditional Habsburg influence both in the Balkans and in Germany. (Austria had already been expelled from Italy.) Her decline was symbolised by the formal abolition of the Holy Roman Empire in 1806. This was the culmination of a political and territorial revolution in Germany over the past decade in which Napoleon had played the decisive part. The mosaic of territories which made up the Empire had traditionally been dominated by Austria and latterly by Prussia. This was now replaced in the west by the Confederation of the Rhine, established in July 1806, comprising several enlarged secular states and controlled by France. The origins of this transformation lay in the victories of the Revolutionaries in the 1790s and the establishment of France's frontier in the Rhineland, which opened the way for the further growth of French influence in Germany and made the fate of the German Empire dependent on France. Napoleon's defeat of the Second Coalition confirmed France's dominant role, and enabled him to complete the reconstruction of Germany (excluding the north-west, where the kingdom of Westphalia would be formed in 1807 – see p. 322). After protracted and complex negotiations, first at Rastadt (1797–99) and then at Regensburg (1801–3), the Imperial Recess (*Reichsdeputationshauptschluss*) was issued in February 1803 and accepted by Austria in April. This destroyed the old constitution of the Empire, cut the number of ecclesiastical princes dramatically, from 81 to 3, and the Imperial cities from 51 to 6. In the accompanying territorial redivision the principal beneficiaries were Prussia and Nassau, and those states that were the basis of the later Confederation of the Rhine (already taking shape in Napoleon's mind): Bavaria, Württemberg, Baden and Hesse-Darmstadt. The Holy Roman Empire was thus effectively dead in 1803, as Francis acknowledged when he assumed the title Emperor of *Austria* (August 1804). It was not to be buried until 1806.

The defeat of Austria in 1805 prepared the way for the Empire's final eclipse. Napoleon now divided the remaining small states in 1805–6 between the four principal French clients: Bavaria, Baden, Hesse-Darmstadt and Württemberg. This was accompanied by the establishment of the Confederation of the Rhine (July 1806), essentially a political alliance between Napoleon and his four German client states, which placed these firmly under French control. A series of dynastic marriages between the Bonaparte family and the German princely families then followed. Finally, on 6 August 1806 the Habsburg Emperor Francis, at Napoleon's instigation, formally dissolved the Holy Roman Empire. In all this, the aim of defeating Austria was uppermost in Napoleon's mind. The political and territorial transformation of Germany which followed was largely spontaneous, a series of responses to the situation created by each new military victory.

THE GRAND EMPIRE

Napoleon's power was at its height in the years after Tilsit. The territories under his control had doubled since 1802 and his dominance over the Continent, established by his military victories, was unparalleled. A successful challenge to Napoleon's Grand Empire was, for the moment, impossible. The French Emperor, according to Metternich, was 'the only man in Europe who wills and acts'. Napoleon now had complete freedom of action to continue the political reorganisation of Europe and to enforce the Continental System. This in itself had the effect of making diplomacy all but redundant for the next few years. Napoleon, as part of his attempt to turn the Continent against the British, forced Russia, Prussia and Austria to declare war on England in the winter of 1807–8. This formal breach of diplomatic relations cut Britain off from her potential partners. Unable to create a new coalition by diplomacy, she was at last forced to make a more direct military commitment to the war, for by now it was an article of faith among British statesmen that no stable or permanent settlement could be made with Napoleonic France.

Napoleon's policy acquired two new, but clearly connected, characteristics in the years after Tilsit. In the first place, he became increasingly concerned with establishing the monarchical respectability of his family and with securing his own achievement. Stendhal said that 'Napoleon had the defect of all parvenus, that of having too great an opinion of the class into which he had risen'. He never fully secured the moral acceptance by the old dynasties for which he craved, largely because of his successful military imperialism. Napoleonic usurpation was a new phenomenon, the memory of which continued to alarm the other great powers long into the nineteenth century. Secondly, the French Emperor became increasingly ruthless and despotic. Metternich, who as Austrian ambassador in Paris observed the Emperor at first hand, wrote in October 1807 that 'there has recently been a total change in the methods of Napoleon: he seems to think…moderation is a useless obstacle'. An illustration of this was the dismissal of the foreign minister, Talleyrand, in August 1807. Talleyrand was an extremely ambiguous figure whose precise influence on Napoleon's policy is unclear: even after 1807 he continued to be consulted. But his independence and the sometimes critical tone of his advice was no longer welcome to the imperious Napoleon, whose increasing lack of restraint was seen in a further series of annexations: Tuscany, Parma and Piacenza were all formally joined to the French Empire in 1808 and, against a background of steadily worsening relations with the Pope after 1805, the Papal States were also occupied in April 1808. They were formally annexed in May 1809, and when Pius VII replied by excommunicating Napoleon he was arrested and only released at the beginning of 1814. Napoleon's increasing ruthlessness was also evident in the completion of the organisation of the Grand Empire. The unique extent of the Napoleonic Empire posed considerable problems of government. The Emperor disliked the semi-independence which the satellite republics had formerly enjoyed and he now replaced these by vassal kingdoms. The system of subject kingdoms was largely made possible by Napoleon's victories in 1805–7, though some important modifications were made subsequently. The experiment rested on the considerable family loyalty of the Bonapartes who were, in essence, to be royal prefects. Each kingdom was ruled by a member of Napoleon's own family, who was intended to provide the obedience to centralised direction which had hitherto been lacking. In particular, they were expected to implement the Continental System (see pp. 322–5).

The earliest satellite was the kingdom of Italy, created in spring 1805 and ruled, as viceroy for the absent King (Napoleon himself) by Prince Eugene de Beauharnais who was the son of Napoleon's wife Josephine by her first marriage. A second Italian satellite was established a year later: the kingdom of Naples, ruled by the Emperor's brother, Joseph, from 1806 to 1808 and then by Napoleon's brother-in-law, Murat. The kingdom of Holland was also created in 1806 from the Batavian Republic and ruled by Louis Bonaparte. But it was beset by financial problems, and King Louis proved rather too 'Dutch' for his brother's liking. His failure to deal satisfactorily with the Walcheren expedition (see p. 329) finally led Napoleon to force his brother to abdicate (July 1810) and to incorporate Holland into France. In 1807 the kingdom of Westphalia had been set up out of territories seized from some of Napoleon's opponents in 1806–7: in particular Hesse-Cassel, Brunswick, part of Hanover and Prussia west of the Elbe. Ruled by Jerome Bonaparte, it became part of the Confederation of the Rhine (see pp. 319f.) where it was intended to be the dominant voice. Finally, the satellite kingdom of Spain was inaugurated in the summer of 1808 with Joseph as king, but a revolt against French rule was already under way and his authority was never fully established (see pp. 325ff.). Spain was certainly the least successful of the satellites – if indeed it ever was a satellite in the way that the other kingdoms were.

Although Napoleon expected unquestioned obedience from his relatives, they inevitably acquired new, national interests with their crowns and they could never fully disregard these. The resulting tensions, together with the need to intensify the Continental System, led Napoleon by the summer of 1810 to contemplate dissolving the satellite kingdoms and replacing them by a European-wide government resembling the Roman imperial system. But the increasing menace of Russia saved the satellites from extinction. Most struggled on to be destroyed, along with their creator, in 1814–15. The system was not a total failure. All the satellite kingdoms (except Spain) benefited from important domestic reforms and the introduction of the Napoleonic codes. Together, they made a significant military contribution to Napoleonic imperialism. Two-thirds of the Grand Army which invaded Russia in 1812 was non-French; the kingdom of Westphalia was a particularly important source of conscript soldiers. Napoleon had intended that the satellite kingdoms should be financially self-sufficient and even contribute to the French treasury; but in practice these states, and Spain in particular, were a considerable drain on his own exchequer. And, though only Spain contributed substantially to Napoleon's downfall (see pp. 325ff.), significant resentment was aroused in all the kingdoms by conscription, by taxation and by the economic distress produced by the Continental System.

Napoleon's satellite kingdoms were to play a key role in establishing and enforcing the Continental System. This was essentially a determined attempt to defeat Britain economically, pursued from 1806 until its collapse in 1812/13. Economic warfare was always an element in the Revolutionary and Napoleonic Wars: the Anglo-French Wars of the century after 1689 had been commercial as well as political conflicts and this economic rivalry had continued in peacetime. The economic struggle assumed more prominence in the years after 1806, when Napoleon pursued more rigorously the economic policies of previous French regimes. The novelty of the Continental System lay in its scope, made possible by France's remarkable territorial expansion and the resulting control of Europe's coastline, and in its more consistent application.

Successive French Revolutionary regimes had tried, largely unsuccessfully, to keep British goods out of France and, increasingly, out of those areas under French control, while Britain made her usual attempts to stop neutrals trading with France and her satellites. The resentment aroused by Britain's high-handed behaviour towards neutral traders later helped the initial acceptance of the Continental System. These familiar mercantilist ideas were one element in the Continental System. The other component – seen in the very name: 'Continental System' – was the unique combination of European countries involved. Napoleonic conquests made it possible to attempt after 1806 to close *all* continental ports to British trade.

The central idea was that Europe should refuse to import British goods while continuing to export her own manufactures to Britain. Aimed only at Britain's exports, the Continental System was essentially a boycott or self-blockade. Since Britain's credit system depended ultimately on her trade, Napoleon believed a contraction of her exports would make her unable either to finance further campaigns against France or to subsidise continental allies. In time, she would be forced to accept peace on French terms. Economic, or rather financial, strangulation would achieve what Napoleon's army was prevented from accomplishing by British sea power. The Emperor also hoped that eventually France might be able to replace Britain as the leading trading and industrial nation in Europe.

Napoleon had attempted to create an embryonic Continental System in 1800–1 (see pp. 300f.) and the trade war against England was vigorously pursued thereafter. But it was only in 1806–7 that Napoleon was able systematically to pursue economic warfare against Britain. The Berlin decrees (21 November 1806) codified the Continental System. Subsequent edicts, in particular the second Milan decree (December 1807), extended and intensified the boycott. Its geographical scope was similarly extended. Russia joined at Tilsit, while later in the same year (1807) Napoleon forced Portugal to close her ports to British goods. The French Emperor now found himself driven to further territorial expansion in a vain attempt to make the Continental System watertight. As the blockade failed to work, he intensified it.

In 1810–11, France annexed those territories lying on the North Sea coastline as far north as the Baltic. Earlier, the principal state not involved in the blockade, Sweden, had been attacked by Russia and her king, Gustav IV, deposed; he was soon replaced by the French Marshal Bernadotte. In January 1810 Sweden was forced to join the Continental System, but this was very much a paper promise as British trade with her continued largely uninterrupted.

Although the Continental System was a real threat to Britain, it was never applied for long enough periods to be effective. It was only enforced rigorously from July 1807 to July 1808, and from spring 1810 until the Russian campaign of 1812. During these two periods, Britain suffered severe economic difficulties. Her exports to the Continent, particularly of manufactured goods, fell dramatically. But Napoleon did not seek to prevent the export of grain to Britain, which would have intensified her difficulties. In 1811 continental grain actually saved her from starvation. The failure to apply the Continental System rigorously was largely due to Napoleon's political miscalculations, in particular over Spain and, later, over Russia. The Spanish revolt of 1808 (see pp. 325ff.) greatly extended the markets of Spain and Spanish America to British goods. It also diverted French troops in increasing numbers to the Iberian peninsula and this, in turn, made breaches of the blockade easier in the all-important Baltic region, where Britain had already been particularly successful in overcoming the Continental System. The Baltic was important both as the principal source of vital naval stores and as an entry point for British goods to Europe as a whole. Britain's naval activity was successful in keeping the Baltic open to British commerce. Concern that Denmark would abandon her previous neutrality, move into the French orbit and imperil British trade by closing the Sound, led to the pre-emptive bombardment of Copenhagen and seizure of the Danish fleet in the late summer of 1807. This ruthless action made Denmark one of the strongest supporters of the Continental System. Thereafter, a fleet was sent to the Baltic each year until 1813 to protect British trade, particularly against Danish privateers. British squadrons instituted a convoy system for merchantmen and also patrolled the trade routes in the Mediterranean as well as the Baltic. Napoleon's economic warfare was also defeated by the inherent strength and adaptability of the British economy and by its ability to open up new markets, especially in South America. The formal British response – the attempt to impose a system of licences on the neutrals by orders in council – was less important in defeating the Continental System, but it did lead to the insignificant and inconclusive Anglo-American War of 1812–14. But, ultimately, the blockade was undermined by the increasing lack of enthusiasm for its enforcement by the allied and vassal states which made up the Napoleonic Empire. Support had never been very widespread, and it was quickly diminished by the undoubted economic hardship which the blockade caused the participants. The Continental System ultimately did much to undermine the Napoleonic Empire.

THE CHALLENGE TO THE NAPOLEONIC EMPIRE, 1808–1812

Napoleon's dominance after Tilsit was directly challenged on three occasions: by a Spanish rising which began in 1808, by an Austrian attack in 1809 and then by Russia's growing independence which culminated in war in 1812. The first serious military challenge to the Grand Empire came from Spain, and the failure to suppress this rebellion proved immensely significant.

Spain, after initial hostility to the French Revolution, had been forced by her own weakness to leave the First Coalition in 1795 and to ally with France in the following year (treaty of San Ildefonso). Thereafter she had become merely a tool of French policy. Spain had been obliged to fight on France's side from 1796 to 1802 and again after December 1804, although Madrid had been slow to re-enter the renewed Anglo-French War. But her military contribution had been negligible and even her navy had been of little use against Britain. Yet the illusion of Spanish power was hard to dispel, in view of her glorious past and her extensive empire, and Napoleon persisted in regarding Spain as potentially a great power.

Spain had repeatedly disappointed Napoleon: as a naval power at Trafalgar, as a source of wealth (her empire, principally in South America, failed to yield the expected silver) and finally as a member of the Continental System, which she failed to enforce rigorously. Moreover, by 1807, factional strife at the Spanish court was further reducing Spain's value as a political partner. Charles IV had been king since 1788, but the real ruler had long been the Queen's favourite, Godoy, who was a supporter of the French alliance. But Godoy was unpopular and his overthrow by one of the opposing factions appeared increasingly likely. Napoleon now decided to create another satellite kingdom in order to control directly Spanish resources and Madrid's policy. In the final months of 1807, under cover of a joint war to place Portugal under French control, Napoleon's troops were sent to Spain. The following spring saw a full-scale French take-over.

In mid-March 1808, a Madrid mob brought about first the dismissal of Godoy and then the abdication of the complaisant Charles IV in favour of his son who became king as Ferdinand VII. But two months later at Bayonne Napoleon forced both father and son to surrender the throne to him, and the Emperor gave it to his own brother, Joseph Bonaparte, who was transferred to Spain from the kingdom of Naples

(5 May 1808). This latest satellite kingdom was always unstable. A patriotic rising against the occupying French army commanded by Murat had already begun in Madrid (2 May 1808) and it was intensified by news of Ferdinand VII's forced abdication. The insurrection gathered strength and received widespread popular support. With the emergence of juntas throughout Spain, leadership of the revolt passed from the hesitant aristocracy and officials into the hands of minor local notables, and it was they who directed the war effort against the occupying French for the next six years. In July 1808 Spanish irregulars won a striking victory at Bailén. In purely military terms this success was misleading: the French army had consisted of raw recruits and the Spaniards now had an exaggerated view of their prowess in pitched battles. Thereafter, the Spanish regular army (which Napoleon deemed to be the worst in Europe) suffered successive humiliating defeats at the hands of the experienced French troops which were now sent to the peninsula. However, the Spanish turned instead to an increasingly ferocious guerrilla war, which the French were unable to defeat.

By 1807, Britain had been effectively shut out from Europe by the rout of the Third Coalition. The Spanish revolt gave an immediate, and ultimately decisive, way back, providing an arena for direct military intervention. The Spanish juntas had appealed to Britain for aid and in early August 1808 Sir Arthur Wellesley (later Duke of Wellington) landed in Portugal with 15,000 men. This expedition, and the resulting successes in the peninsula, were the product of a decisive change in British policy, which was now controlled by more forceful and imaginative figures. Canning, foreign secretary from 1807 to 1809, together with his political rival Castlereagh, the secretary of war, gave a new initiative to Britain's strategy. London now announced that, in effect, Britain would underwrite any European revolt against Napoleonic hegemony. Napoleon's great victories in 1805–7 had finally convinced British statesmen that the previous, and essentially traditional, strategy of attacking France's commerce and colonies while subsidising allies in Europe would not bring victory. Britain would have to increase her commitment and her troops would have to fight on the Continent. Hitherto, Britain's military effort had been limited to clearly defined British areas of interest in north-western Europe; but now British troops were to be sent in increasing numbers elsewhere on the Continent and contributed significantly to the final defeat of Napoleon. Canning also supervised a fundamental, though gradual, change in the nature of British aid. Previous ministries had concluded what were essentially troop-hiring treaties in which payment was carefully supervised and weighed against the number of soldiers actually provided. These treaties had aroused resentment, with widespread accusations of penny-pinching, among her hard-pressed continental allies. Canning now sought to aid

Napoleon's enemies to the full extent of Britain's ability. At the same time, British aid ceased to be a matter of simple cash payments. The length and cost of the struggle and, more recently, the operation of the Continental System had, by this time, left Britain short of bullion. Canning therefore inaugurated what became the pattern for British policy in the final years of the war: he reduced the amount of money and instead sent arms and equipment, especially clothing, which industrial Britain could provide and which continental allies needed almost as much as cash.

Wellesley's army quickly achieved his initial aim to secure a base in Portugal. An immediate victory at Vimiero (August 1808) provided a boost to morale, but the first invasion of Spain (in 1808–9) was a failure. Portugal, however, remained secure, and the importance of this base which could be supplied by the fleet was increased by the events of 1809. The defeat of Austria by Napoleon (see pp. 328–9) and the failure of Britain's Walcheren expedition (see p. 329) left the peninsula as the only arena in which Britain could continue the struggle. In 1809, Wellesley invaded Spain and in July won a victory at Talavera (and the title of Viscount Wellington for himself) before being forced to retreat again. In 1810 the French made a determined attack on Portugal which Wellington halted in the winter of 1810–11 at the lines of Torres Vedras, near Lisbon. Only in 1812 could Wellington abandon his necessarily defensive strategy and go over to the attack. An increased British commitment to the Peninsular War – in spite of its failure to bring any decisive results, as the opposition in parliament emphasised – enlarged Wellington's army to around 100,000 men, and with this in 1812–13 he won a series of decisive victories, particularly at Salamanca (July 1812), and effective control of southern Spain. The conquest was completed by a triumph of Vittoria in June 1813. Early the following year Wellington could advance into France itself.

British victories in the peninsula were achieved with the assistance of Portuguese auxiliaries and the Spanish insurgents. Wellington's campaigns and the Spanish guerrilla war were a considerable, and ever increasing, drain on French manpower and resources. By 1812 France was maintaining no less than 300,000 troops south of the Pyrenees. The majority of these were in garrisons or involved in pursuing guerrillas, so that the French could never concentrate more than 70,000 men against Wellington. The 'Spanish ulcer' eventually cost Napoleon 300,000 casualties and perhaps 4 billion francs, and it seriously damaged France's military reputation. These were the first serious defeats inflicted on Napoleonic armies, and they encouraged other European nations to resist French hegemony. The Peninsular War was also part of a larger change in Britain's relations with the continental states: it gradually destroyed the widespread belief that Britain was only interested in colonial gains and indifferent to the Continent. Moreover, it raised the previously low prestige of the British army.

Britain initially saw the Peninsular War as essentially diversionary. Her statesmen hoped that, by increasing Napoleon's difficulties they would encourage Alexander I to abandon the alliance concluded at Tilsit, since they believed he had only accepted it out of necessity and wanted to abandon it as soon as practicable. It was also assumed that the rest of northern Europe (Sweden, Denmark and Prussia) would follow the Tsar into war with France. The first challenge to Napoleon, however, came not from Russia but from Austria, though France's difficulties in Spain were certainly an important factor in the Habsburg decision to declare war in April 1809.

Austria's eclipse in 1805 had been complete. Her army was defeated and demoralised, her treasury was empty, her ministers were discredited. Vienna had been powerless to resist Napoleon's damaging territorial reorganisation in 1806–7. Her influence in Germany had been finally destroyed while the Franco-Russian agreement at Tilsit deprived Vienna of any influence in the Balkans. However, after the humiliation at Austerlitz, younger and more vigorous spirits came to the fore in Vienna, above all the Archduke Charles and Stadion, who became foreign minister in December 1805. The new foreign minister was a Rhinelander and a career diplomat, whose undoubted hatred of Napoleon was intensified by the fact that the French had confiscated his family estates. Stadion advocated a war of revenge against France, a people's war in Germany and Austria which would defeat Napoleon. To achieve this, Stadion believe that social and political reforms were first essential to arouse enthusiasm and encourage the people in Germany to rise. However, only in the military sphere were any significant reforms actually accomplished. Archduke Charles began a major reform and reorganisation of the Habsburg regular army, and in 1808 a provincial militia (*Landwehr*) was set up. But the Austrian finances were still in disarray. The war of 1805, like its predecessors, had largely been financed by printing money and inflation was rampant. The international situation also seemed unfavourable for a new war against Napoleon.

Throughout 1808, however, the war party at the Austrian court steadily gained ground. It was aided by the Emperor Francis's third marriage early in 1808 to Maria Ludovica of Este. The new Empress enthusiastically adopted Stadion's ideas of a German national rising against Napoleon and became a forceful advocate of war, as did the Emperor's mother-in-law, who resented the loss of her duchy of Modena. Napoleon's difficulties in Spain in the summer of 1808 and the news of Bailén made a particular impression in Vienna. Further support came from Austria's ambassador in Paris, Metternich, who was becoming increasingly hostile towards Napoleon, as he realised the scope of the French Emperor's pretensions. But the ambassador also recognised that Austria could not fight another war until the

Habsburg state was stronger and there was some realistic hope of foreign assistance. However, his over-optimistic reports of mounting
domestic opposition to Napoleon and his assessment of France's vulnerability because of her immense military commitments, arrived in
Vienna at a critical time and may have tipped the balance in favour
of war. The Archduke Charles, aware that his military reorganisation
was incomplete, pleaded in vain for a delay. But nothing could stop
the war party and, on 9 April 1809, war was declared on France.

The war of 1809 lasted barely three months and added yet another
entry in the catalogue of Habsburg military disasters. The army was,
as the Archduke Charles had feared, unequal to the task and the
international support on which Vienna had counted simply did not
materialise. There was no German national rising, and neither Russia,
Prussia nor the German princes helped. Only Britain gave any support: a subsidy and a diversionary attack in the northern Netherlands,
but these were of little real help to the Habsburgs. Britain's attempt
in the late summer of 1809 to seize the island of Walcheren at the
mouth of the Scheldt and to destroy the French naval base there was
a fiasco. A large-scale combined operation involving 70,000 men was
wrecked by divided and hesitant command and by the fever which
was soon rife among the soldiers, and it withdrew with heavy losses.
By this time, the war was over, for Austria alone was no match for
the might of Napoleon's armies. By the middle of May (a month after
war was declared) the French Emperor had occupied Vienna and
though the Archduke Charles won a brave, and costly, victory at
Aspern–Essling (May 1809) he could not press his advantage. The
campaign was decided by another impressive Napoleonic victory at
Wagram (6 July 1809) and an armistice was signed a week later.

The peace settlement of Schönbrunn which followed was effectively dictated by Napoleon (14 October 1809) and brought further humiliations for the Habsburgs. Austria was forced to make substantial territorial cessions: in particular she had to cede her share of the Polish
partitions (to the Grand Duchy of Warsaw), the strip of the Dalmatian
coast she had retained on the Adriatic (to the kingdom of Italy), and
areas round Salzburg and Berchtesgaden and some of Upper Austria
(to Bavaria). They were forced to join the Continental System
(though they now had no ports to close to British trade!), the Austrian
army was limited to 150,000 and, though Habsburg finances were in
ruins, an indemnity of 85 million francs was exacted. The only consolation was that the Austrian Emperor was not actually forced to
abdicate.

The disasters of 1809 inevitably ended the influence of Stadion, and
of Archduke Charles, who was coldly dismissed by his brother (the
Emperor Francis) in July. The new foreign minister, or chancellor,
who took office early in October, was Metternich, who remained in
power until 1848. Fundamentally, Metternich was almost as hostile

towards Napoleon as Stadion had been, but in the aftermath of the disastrous war of 1809 his policy was necessarily that of co-existence. In August 1809, Metternich defined Austria's future policy as being 'tacking, wiping away the past and collaboration' and he argued to the Emperor in the same month that 'we can seek our security only in adapting ourselves to the triumphant French system'. Metternich, however, ultimately aimed to supplant Russia as Napoleon's major continental ally. Diplomacy might revive Austria's fortunes in a way that her armies manifestly could not. Metternich put great store on recovering Austrian influence through marriage-diplomacy, a traditional Habsburg tactic. Napoleon was known, because of his dynasticism, to want to divorce his first wife, Josephine (who had not provided him with a son) and remarry to perpetuate his achievement. Metternich intended that Napoleon's new wife should be the Archduchess Marie Louise, the eldest and favourite daughter of the Emperor Francis. The attractions of such a match were considerable and in spring 1810 Napoleon, after divorcing Josephine, married his Habsburg archduchess. But Metternich's hoped-for diplomatic recovery failed to materialise. Austria remained a Napoleonic satellite, as became very clear during the war with Russia in 1812.

The Franco-Russian *rapprochement* at Tilsit had been, on both sides, a matter of temporary convenience (see p. 317ff.). Yet this alignment endured, at least superficially, until Napoleon's invasion of Russia in 1812. Napoleon's desire in 1807 to concentrate on the political reorganisation of his conquests, on the Continental System and on the struggle with England made him favour a period of co-operation with Russia, and this was intensified by the Spanish revolt in 1808 and the Austrian war in 1809. Alexander's public support for France after 1807 was reflected in his choice of foreign minister, N. P. Rumiantsev, who was a partisan of the French alliance. The new foreign minister believed that Russian involvement in western Europe distracted attention from what should be Russia's primary aim, that of renewed expansion to the south. Rumiantsev supported the French alliance because he believed (wrongly) it showed Napoleon would leave Russia a free hand in the Balkans against the Ottoman Empire. But in reality the French Emperor was always determined to prevent Russia's seizing Constantinople, and his refusal to sanction Russian expansion in the Balkans effectively wrecked any chance of a permanent alliance with Russia.

In any case, Rumiantsev was a cover for Alexander's real objectives at this time. The foreign minister's well-known support for the French alliance would reassure Napoleon and he would be a convenient scapegoat within Russia, where the alignment was widely unpopular, both at court and among the nobility. In any case, the Tsar was himself actively involved in foreign affairs, often corresponding directly with Russian diplomats abroad. This was essential, because Alexander's real intention was to prepare for a future war with France. The spell cast by Napoleon at Tilsit soon lifted, as the Tsar came to realise the alignment's unpopularity in Russia and the French Emperor's opposition to further Russian gains. Alexander defined his policy after Tilsit as being 'to gain a breathing-space and, during this precious interval, build up our resources'. Consequently, he sought to strengthen the Russian army, overhaul the administration and improve Russia's international position. The Tsar was largely successful in disguising his real intentions. It was only in 1811 that Napoleon fully admitted that a war against Russia would be necessary, and he always underestimated the Russian Emperor's astuteness and determination. France's increasing difficulties in Spain and, in 1809, with Austria, were exploited by Alexander to reassert his own political independence. Napoleon was forced to withdraw French troops from Germany to deal with these emergencies, and this inevitably increased both his need of Russian support and Alexander's freedom of action. In 1808 Russia attacked Sweden and seized Swedish Finland, which was formally united to Russia the next year, with Alexander ruling as grand duke. This gain did much to eradicate traditional Russian fears about their vulnerable north-western frontier, though the war with Sweden (undertaken on French urging to compel her to enter the Continental System) was unpopular since it also revealed Russia's continuing subservience to France.

The meeting of the two emperors at Erfurt in late autumn 1808 showed the cracks that had appeared in the alliance since Tilsit, and these became more apparent on the outbreak of the Austro-French War in 1809. Napoleon immediately requested the military assistance Russia was required to provide under an agreement concluded at Erfurt. Though he formally declared war, Alexander secretly informed Vienna that Russia would remain neutral. He delayed so long in dispatching aid that Russian soldiers played no part in the defeat of Austria. Napoleon was outraged; but he now had problems enough without provoking Russia. In order to retain Russia's friendship he allowed Alexander to make minor territorial gains in eastern Galicia from the peace settlement with Austria in October 1809. The Franco-Russian alliance was henceforth to be increasingly shaky, and for his part, Napoleon only upheld it after 1809 because of his mounting problems elsewhere.

A major source of Franco-Russian friction was the Grand Duchy of Warsaw, created by Napoleon in 1807 from Prussia's Polish lands. Ruled *in absentia* by a client of Napoleon, the King of Saxony, the duchy was governed by a French-dominated regency and was an outpost of Napoleonic influence in eastern Europe. Alexander feared that it might become the nucleus of a reborn, independent and pro-French Polish state which would imperil Russia's own recent gains from the partitions of Poland. Alexander's fears were intensified in 1809 after the defeat of the Habsburgs, when the addition of parts of Galicia considerably increased the size of the duchy. Although he wanted to see a revived Polish state, it should be within the Russian empire and firmly under his own control. The Tsar's suspicions over Poland accurately mirrored the lack of mutual trust in the Franco-Russian alignment. The Polish nobility themselves believed, or at least hoped, that Napoleon intended to re-establish their homeland; in 1812 they were to contribute 100,000 men to the Grand Army that invaded Russia. But they were mistaken, for Napoleon was entirely opportunistic in his dealings with the Poles.

The *rapprochement* with France had always been unpopular in Russia, especially because it entailed Russia's entry into the Continental System, which took effect in November 1807. Trade with England, which was now officially ended, had been long established and proved very profitable for Russian merchants and for many of the nobility. The Continental System, though its economic impact on Russia has often been exaggerated, did produce severe commercial difficulties in 1808. The situation improved thereafter, but these problems increased the unpopularity of the French alliance. On 31 December 1810 Alexander in effect withdrew from the Continental System by introducing a new tariff which discriminated against French and in favour of English commerce. In part this was a response to Napoleon's annexations of territories along the North Sea coastline in the closing months of 1810 and to the implied threat to the duchy of Oldenburg, which was formally annexed on 22 January 1811. Oldenburg was ruled by relatives of the Tsar and its independence had been guaranteed at Tilsit. Its annexation worsened relations, as did the seizure of Lübeck at the same time, for this seemed to foreshadow a French challenge to Russia's dominance of the Baltic. Alexander also resented the continued French occupation of Prussian fortresses on the Oder. Further friction was produced by Napoleon's search for a new wife (see p. 330). Alexander in effect refused to give the French Emperor one of his sisters as a bride, and this was resented in Paris, while the Austrian marriage similarly aroused resentment at the Russian court, principally because of its anti-Russian implications.

There was thus no shortage of sources of friction, particularly by 1810–11. By early 1811, it was clear to Alexander that he would soon be at war with France. For his part, Napoleon determined on a war to re-establish the control he seemed to have achieved at Tilsit and thereby shore up the Continental System. The French Emperor also hoped that a decisive victory over Russia might bring Britain to her knees, for Alexander was now the main hope of British statesmen. Napoleon was therefore planning for an invasion of Russia from autumn 1811 onwards. Both sides tried simultaneously to strengthen their diplomatic positions. Alexander sought support from Austria and Prussia, but Napoleon successfully intimidated both states into supporting him, or at least not actively opposing him. However, early in 1812 the French Emperor failed to secure an alliance with the Ottoman Empire, which had been involved in war with Russia since 1806 (see pp. 315f.). The Sultan, in fact, soon made peace with Russia.

The imminence of war with Napoleon made Russia equally determined to end the fighting with the Ottoman Empire, especially as the intermittent military campaigning had been indecisive. The Tilsit agreement had anticipated a Russo-Turkish armistice and this had duly been concluded in August 1807; but it had foundered on Russia's desire to retain the Danubian principalities (substantially occupied by Russian troops), and at Erfurt in 1808 Napoleon had been forced to consent to this eventual gain. But the Ottoman Empire was as stubborn as ever about actually ceding territory. As war with France loomed, however, Alexander became increasingly determined to extricate himself from the indecisive war in the Balkans. Serious peace negotiations began in October 1811, but they were prolonged and St Petersburg's bargaining position grew steadily weaker as Napoleon's preparations for an invasion of Russia became apparent. Initially, the Russians had been prepared to buy peace by the return of Wallachia to nominal Turkish control, but they were eventually forced to evacuate Moldavia as well. The Russo-Turkish War was ended by the peace of Bucharest (17 May 1812) by which Russia acquired most of Bessarabia, a significant gain which brought her as far south as the Danube, but far less than she had once seemed likely to achieve.

THE DEFEAT OF NAPOLEON 1812–1815

Napoleon crossed the Niemen in the final week of June 1812 without any formal declaration of war. He had assembled 600,000 men in Poland, of whom only 250,000 were French, and some 500,000 of these began the invasion of Russia. This massive force far outnumbered the Russian armies which had to retreat ever deeper, fighting courageous small-scale rearguard actions but avoiding a major battle. Napoleon was certainly aware of the unique logistical problems involved in fighting in Russia and he made more extensive preparations for the 1812 invasion than for any other campaign. But his strategy was undermined by his failure to bring the Russians to a pitched battle. Unlike in earlier campaigns the army of 1812 was large and unwieldy. It proved unable to move rapidly enough to catch and then defeat the retreating Russians. Moreover, many of Napoleon's most experienced troops were fighting in Spain; war on two widely separated fronts ultimately led to failure in both. The French units in the invading force contained many new conscripts, while the foreign contingents were very uneven in quality. There was widespread desertion and indiscriminate plundering, instead of the systematic requisitioning the army needed for its food. These supply problems were intensified by the very extended lines of communication and by the Russians' scorched earth policy.

On 7 September 1812 Napoleon won a technical and costly victory in an artillery duel at Borodino. But this was not the decisive victory demanded by his strategy, for though the French could occupy Moscow in mid-September, the Russian army withdrew from the battle-field in good order and remained a threat. Even the occupation of Moscow did not, as Napoleon expected, bring Alexander to make peace. The Tsar would not – and indeed could not – negotiate. Napoleon never appreciated that a second Tilsit, a second surrender to France, might imperil Alexander's throne. The patriotic enthusiasm produced by the French invasion made any concession impossible. Ignoring warnings about the severity of a Russian winter – the autumn of 1812 was in fact unusually mild – Napoleon lingered in Moscow until 19 October. Only then did the retreat begin: a retreat slowed by the army's loot, its casualties and its 600 guns. There was also continual harassing by Cossacks, partisans and some Russian regular units; this in turn made foraging all but impossible and the army was soon disintegrating through hunger. Its sufferings were increased by snow early in November and severe frosts in December. By the end of 1812 only 40,000 men – of the original 500,000 – crossed back into Poland.

The costs of Napoleon's Russian campaign were immense: 270,000 dead and 200,000 prisoners. The further loss of around 200,000 horses and 1,000 guns seriously weakened the French cavalry and artillery in subsequent campaigns. Material losses, however, were only a small part of the story. The disaster of 1812, together with French reverses in the Peninsular War, finally shattered the myth of Napoleonic invincibility and, in only six months, transformed the European situation. By the end of 1812 Napoleon was fighting for his own survival, not – as previously – for new conquests. The collapse of the Grand Empire was to occur with surprising speed.

Napoleon's disaster in Russia produced a general reversal of diplomatic alignments. It was begun by the convention of Tauroggen (30 December 1812), an armistice between Prussia – or, rather, General Yorck, commanding Prussian units covering Napoleon's left flank in 1812 – and the advancing Russian army. This convention allowed the Russians to occupy East Prussia and forced the French to pull further back. Alexander now offered an alliance to Frederick William III, who was still hesitant but was forced into war principally by popular pressure. Since the collapse of 1806, Prussian patriotism had been fostered by an impressive, though short-lived, series of administrative, social and military reforms and there was considerable popular support for the war of 1813, not only in Prussia but throughout Germany. On 28 February 1813 Russia and Prussia signed the treaty of Kalisch (Kalisz), a military alliance against France, and in March Prussia formally entered the war.

Alexander now saw himself as the Liberator of Europe. The dark days of 1812 had imbued him with a sense of his Christian mission to defeat Napoleon and to free Europe from French dominance. The Tsar's mystical fervour, and the parallel desire to extend Russian power, provided a major impetus behind the allied coalition in 1813–14. By the middle of 1813 the Fourth Coalition, consisting of Russia, Prussia, Britain, Sweden, Spain and Portugal, had come into existence, though Austria still remained aloof. Its principal foundations were the bilateral Anglo-Russian and Anglo-Prussian alliances signed at Reichenbach (June 1813). Britain provided the allies with much-needed munitions and her armies continued to drive back the French in Spain, but her principal contribution to the Fourth Coalition was financial. In 1813 British subsidies (notably to Russia, Prussia and Sweden) amounted to £11 million, almost equal to the *total* paid out during the first two coalitions of 1793–1802.

The early months of 1813 saw a triumphant allied advance across central Europe, as Napoleon hastily scraped together another army in France. The quality of recruits was very poor and the French infantry contained too many youths, veterans and invalids, while the immense loss of horses in Russia meant France was now critically short of cavalry. At the end of April 1813 the French counter-attacked, and in May Napoleon won two indecisive victories at Lützen and Bautzen in Saxony. But France was still engaged in a war on two fronts and needed to provide soldiers for Spain, where Wellington's decisive advance had begun (see p. 327). This weakened the French effort in central Europe, and in June Napoleon eagerly accepted an Austrian-inspired armistice and the summoning of a peace congress at Prague. He had no intention of accepting a negotiated settlement, but he hoped – as did the allies – to strengthen his military position during the lull in the fighting.

Austrian foreign policy had only slowly adjusted to the changing situation after Napoleon's disaster in Russia. Metternich's progress towards armed intervention and membership of the Fourth Coalition was slow and reluctant. The Austrian chancellor was uncertain how the struggle might end, and he saw real dangers for Austria in the destruction of Napoleon's Grand Empire. He was alarmed by the patriotic and popular tone of the Russo-Prussian campaign: the appeal for a German national crusade against the French could have anti-Habsburg implications. Moreover, Napoleon's marriage to the Habsburg archduchess, Marie Louise, made Vienna, still nominally the ally of France, more willing for a settlement which kept either Napoleon or his son, the King of Rome (born in March 1811), on the French throne. But the real focus of Habsburg foreign policy in 1813–14 was concern about the shape of the future settlement, particularly in Germany.

Metternich and the Emperor Francis were both deeply suspicious of Alexander's ambitions. In one sense, Metternich feared the growing ascendancy of Russia more than he had the dominance of Napoleon, and it is clear that he wished to maintain France as a strong state to balance Russian strength. Austria had no wish to see Russian dominance of Germany replace that of France, while Alexander's ambitions towards Poland and in the Balkans also seemed a threat to Habsburg interests. From late in 1812 Metternich principally aimed to defend Austrian interests at any subsequent peace, first by armed neutrality, then by mediation and finally by joining the Fourth Coalition. His essential moderation was reflected in a series of Austrian-inspired attempts at a negotiated peace. Only Napoleon's continuing refusal to negotiate, together with the news of Wellington's victory at Vittoria (marking the effective end of French power in Spain), finally drove Austria to declare war on France on 12 August 1813. Significantly, this was the first occasion on which *all* the other great powers – Britain, Austria, Prussia and Russia – had fought Napoleon; it was also the first time since 1795 that Austrian and Prussian troops co-operated against France. But even now there was no formal alliance, only a military convention, between Austria and the Fourth Coalition. The treaty of Teplitz (9 September 1813) bound Austria, Russia and Prussia to maintain 150,000 men each in the field. Metternich would not commit Austria to the emerging Russo-Prussian plans for a future settlement, nor would he accept a treaty which would prevent a negotiated agreement with France, however unlikely this had become.

Napoleon could have obtained peace on reasonable terms in the summer of 1813 and – though this is less certain – may even have been able to remain ruler of France. The negotiations might also have sown dissent among the allies, not least because of the potential ambivalence of Habsburg policy. Europe was exhausted and war-weary and might have made peace. But Napoleon resolutely refused to make the necessary concessions and, characteristically, sought military salvation. Aiming for total victory he risked complete defeat. In part, this reflected his predictable preference for warfare rather than diplomacy. Napoleon also believed that a negotiated settlement would mean the end of his own power, for he was not a hereditary sovereign. He was now well aware of the unpopularity of his regime in France, where opposition had reached dangerous proportions. An unsuccessful conclusion to the long and burdensome years of war would spell the end of the Bonaparte dynasty – whatever the allies might do. But, equally, his generalship in the autumn of 1813, on which he staked everything, was strangely indecisive and hesitant, reflecting his own personal exhaustion.

The end of the armistice in mid-August led to the resumption of the fighting. The numerical superiority of the Fourth Coalition armies was considerable and by mid-October this produced a decisive if costly victory at Leipzig (the 'Battle of the Nations', 16–19 October). This defeat destroyed Napoleon's influence in Germany, and as he retreated across the Rhine at the close of 1813, his Grand Empire collapsed and his satellites deserted him. The extent to which Napoleonic hegemony had always depended on military supremacy now became fully apparent. Napoleon had received little real support from the peoples he conquered, except perhaps from the middle classes in parts of western Germany and northern Italy, and there had been increasing revulsion against the burdens his regime imposed. His victories and conquests aroused nationalist feelings everywhere, especially in Spain and Russia. But, though there were nationalist risings against him, these played a small part in his final defeat. That was accomplished by the professional armies of the great powers, whose numerical superiority was now overwhelming.

The allies, remembering the defeats of the First Coalition when it had invaded France two decades before, hesitated and their armies made only slow progress in the winter of 1813–14. But the Fourth Coalition was given a new sense of purpose early in 1814 by the arrival at the allied headquarters of Castlereagh, British foreign secretary since March 1812. Castlereagh was determined to bring down Napoleon and to restore France to her pre-Revolutionary position. He imposed the alliance of Chaumont (9 March 1814) on the coalition powers, which committed them not to conclude a separate peace and outlined a future settlement for western Europe.

Napoleon enjoyed a successful final fling in the early months of 1814, winning some impressive if small-scale victories as the allies invaded France. He was by now critically short of men and munitions, for his attempt to rebuild yet again a shattered army had met with considerable resistance within France. A renewed allied advance captured Paris at the very end of March 1814 and on 6 April Napoleon formally abdicated. Alexander, alone of the allied leaders, was now in Paris and could decide the fate of France and her Emperor. But the Tsar determined to play the magnanimous victor, and he ensured that Napoleon received surprisingly lenient treatment. The treaty of Fontainebleau (11 April 1814) gave him a revenue of 2 million francs from French funds, the title of emperor and sovereignty over the Mediterranean island of Elba, of which he took possession early in May 1814. The Empress Marie Louise was given Parma and the reversion of the duchy to her son.

In the months that followed, Napoleon kept a close watch on the negotiations between the victorious allies, who were soon seriously divided over the terms of a general peace settlement (see pp. 339ff.). He was equally interested in the new government in France, where

Louis XVIII had been restored on British insistence. The King and his advisers behaved ineptly and it was soon apparent that the French, particularly the army, were unreconciled. Napoleon was aware of this and made a final bid for power (the 'Hundred Days'). Landing on the mainland on 1 March 1815, he quickly acquired support and by the 20th he was in Paris and again ruler of France. But allied armies were immediately sent against him and, after a rapid campaign in the Southern Netherlands, he was narrowly defeated at the battle of Waterloo (18 June 1815). Napoleon abdicated for the second time four days later and, at Castlereagh's insistence, lived out the rest of his life as a British prisoner on the South Atlantic island of St Helena.

CHAPTER TWELVE
The great powers in 1815

The European settlement was accomplished in two stages. That for western Europe, largely shaped by Castlereagh, was embodied in the first peace of Paris (30 May 1814); this was subsequently modified after the 'Hundred Days' by a second and more severe treaty in November 1815. The more complex reconstruction of central and eastern Europe, where Alexander I's views largely predominated, was the work of the congress of Vienna (October 1814–June 1815). The rapid collapse of Napoleon's Grand Empire in 1813–14 left numerous problems to be solved, particularly of frontiers. The map of Europe, several times redrawn in the last quarter-century, now had to be revised yet again. The stabilisation of Europe after more than two decades of near-continuous war was a complex business. The allied negotiators were also always constrained by previous obligations, by certain *faits accomplis* and by military realities, especially in eastern Europe. In the final stages of the war, several minor states had deserted Napoleon in return for allied promises to respect their sovereignty, and these obligations significantly pre-empted the peace settlement, particularly in Germany. Such practical considerations were always more important than ideology. In the event the Vienna settlement emerged piecemeal out of the negotiations, treaties and military campaigns of 1813–15.

The dominant motive among the allies was the desire to avoid another generation of political and social upheaval on the scale of 1789–1815. The Vienna settlement was designed to prevent not only revolution and constant warfare in the future but also the domination of one state, to create a lasting balance of power, which it was believed would be the best guarantee of future peace. But since each state perceived the balance of power in different terms, the details of the settlement proved a fertile source of disagreements, especially as the peacemakers were suspicious of each other. Apart from a very general desire to establish a balance of power and to safeguard against future challenges to the political status quo, the allies were little influenced

339

by ideology. Although the ubiquitous Talleyrand, now the servant of the restored Bourbons in France, preached the doctrine of legitimacy, this was not consistently applied. It was invoked to justify the return of the exiled Bourbons to France, Spain and, after the 'Hundred Days', to Naples, but it was frequently ignored elsewhere. Indeed, some of Napoleon's work was tacitly accepted, particularly the suppression of a number of smaller states. In Germany, his destruction of the ecclesiastical principalities was confirmed and the number of sovereign units brought together under a new confederation reduced from over 300 to 38.

The ideas for a general settlement had first been expressed by Pitt during the Anglo-Russian alliance negotiations of 1805. These notions were rather similar to the thinking behind the 1713/14 settlement: France was to be contained by a ring of states around her frontiers. But instead of the feeble neighbours which had collapsed so completely in 1792–93, strong buffer states were to guard against French aggression in the future. It was above all Britain which argued for this kind of settlement. Her financial and military contribution to the final coalition, and the presence of her foreign secretary, Castlereagh, on the Continent in 1814–15, together ensured that British diplomacy played a key role. Castlereagh secured his barrier of strengthened states and, at the same time, ensured that the Low Countries (and the Scheldt in particular) should be in friendly hands, a time-honoured British concern because of the strategic importance of the region. The new kingdom of the Netherlands (made up of Holland and Belgium, to be ruled by the House of Orange) together with Prussia, which was given extensive new Rhineland territories, stood guard on France's northern and north-eastern borders. In the south the chief sentries were the strengthened kingdom of Sardinia (comprising the island of Sardinia, Savoy, Nice, Genoa and Piedmont) and Austria, with her new-found dominance in Italy. In this way the areas which France had most frequently threatened in the seventeenth and eighteenth centuries were strengthened against any future aggression. The 1815 settlement in western Europe was dominated by the idea of containment and, as such, coincided with British interests.

Britain was primarily concerned in 1814–15 with the political and territorial reorganisation of Europe, but Castlereagh was careful also to defend Britain's naval supremacy. The Vienna settlement confirmed and extended Britain's dominance overseas. During the war against France, Britain had mopped up her colonies and those of her satellites, especially Holland. Castlereagh's preoccupation with the Continent led to most of these conquests being returned at the peace. But Britain did retain some of these gains to protect her trade and communications. The addition of Tobago, St Lucia and part of Guyana (Trinidad had been secured in 1802) significantly strengthened her in the West Indies. The acquisition of Mauritius and Cape Colony to add to Ceylon (also acquired in 1802) gave the British a firmer foothold in the East and protected communications with India, increasingly seen as the jewel of her empire. In Europe, Britain obtained Heligoland off the coast of Hanover, which was returned to George III, and a protectorate over the 'Septinsular Republic' of the Ionian Islands, which together with Malta (which she retained) and Gibraltar secured her naval position in the Mediterranean. The Vienna settlement enhanced Britain's economic, colonial and maritime supremacy, the foundations of her position as a great power. The wars of 1792–1815 had weakened her Dutch, Spanish and particularly her French rivals overseas, and her dominance was now greater even than in 1763. From the later eighteenth century, moreover, the Industrial Revolution was simultaneously adding a formidable new dimension to British power, which had always depended heavily on her economic strength.

Britain's emergence since the end of the seventeenth century had been truly spectacular, but it had not been accompanied by a permanent British commitment to continental politics. Despite the links with Hanover, Britain's situation as an island often enabled her – unlike the other great powers – to abstain from European alliances and diplomacy, and this was a source both of strength and of suspicion. Periodically Britain had played the role of a great land power, especially when the Low Countries or Hanover were in danger. She sent troops to the Continent while at the same time pursuing her own maritime and colonial interests overseas. But such involvement had been interspersed with long periods of insularity, if not outright isolation, and there was no reason in 1815 to believe that her ambivalent membership of the European states system had been altered. Continental states could not ignore Britain, but British statesman could relegate continental issues to a subsidiary position: this was part of the explanation for Britain's greatness.

Britain's traditional rival, France, was the principal loser by the wars of 1792–1815, and the Vienna settlement was specifically directed against any resurgence of French power. But after two decades of war which France herself had largely provoked, her losses were less than might have been expected and were largely limited to her own territorial conquests. The great powers treated the defeated France comparatively leniently. The Second peace of Paris (20 November 1815) was certainly more severe than the earlier treaty of May 1814. France was punished for her support of Napoleon during the 'Hundred Days' in 1815, by a reduction of her frontiers to those of 1790 (instead of 1792 which the allies had previously been prepared to allow; her most significant losses were the Saar to Prussia and part of Savoy to the kingdom of Sardinia), by a five-year occupation by allied troops (this could be, and was, reduced to three) and by a massive indemnity of 700 million francs. But France's former territorial integrity was confirmed and she remained a great power, if no longer the dominant state in Europe.

Although Prussia in particular wanted a partition of France, the other allies resisted this in case it made the position of the restored Bourbon Louis XVIII more difficult than it would be anyway: monarchy was seen as the best defence against revolution. The allies also believed France had a role to play in the European states system. Metternich in Austria, menaced by Russian expansion westwards and a Russo-Prussian alignment, was already anxious to encourage France's re-emergence as a major state able to help counteract Russia. The 1815 settlement enabled France to recover her international position, and she remained potentially a very strong state in terms of her abundant resources, probably second only to Russia on the Continent in 1815. But her international position was undermined less by the wars of 1792–1815 than by the transformation which had occurred since the reign of Louis XIV. In the later seventeenth century France had been clearly the leading state, the only truly great power in Europe. The emergence of Britain, Russia and Prussia in the course of the eighteenth century eroded this dominance. Moreover, France always remained trapped between the demands of the continental struggle and her world-wide conflict with Britain, and there was no indication that this problem had been resolved in 1815.

Russia gained most from the Revolutionary and Napoleonic Wars. Her central role in the final defeat of France was reflected in her gains at Vienna. In 1814–15 the Tsar, closely advised once again by the Pole, Czartoryski, was intent on realising his pet scheme for a reborn Poland under Russian control, one which should include as much as possible of Austria's and Prussia's Polish lands. Since Russian troops occupied Poland it was not easy to resist Alexander's demands. But early in 1815, under the threat of an alliance between Austria, Britain and France, the Tsar made some concessions and a settlement was concluded. Prussia received the western fringe of the Napoleonic Grand Duchy of Warsaw (including Posen and Thorn) and Austria retained Galicia, while Cracow became a free city. The rest of the Grand Duchy was given as a kingdom ('Congress Poland') to the Tsar and was promised a constitution. Poland's destiny was now permanently linked to that of Russia. The Vienna settlement amounted to a fourth partition. This immense Russian gain, when added to the earlier gains of Finland (from Sweden in 1809) and Bessarabia (from the Ottoman Empire in 1812), marked the greatest westward expansion of Russia so far.

The emergence of Russia as a major continental state had been the central political development of the eighteenth century and the wars of 1792–1815 made her the dominant European power. The appearance of Alexander's armies in western Europe made Russia's vast manpower and military might feared for a generation. Her challenge to the declining Ottoman Empire was more apparent than ever. Nor were Austria or Prussia alone able to resist further Russian encroachments: fear of Russia was already central to Metternich's foreign policy. The only restraints on Russia's dominance were her own extensive commitments, in Asia as well as in Europe, her limited economic resources and the extent to which her foreign policy could depend on the whim of her ruler. Throughout the wars of 1792–1815, Russia had alternated – as indeed throughout the eighteenth century – between absorption in her own affairs and involvement in the European power struggle. Alexander's mystical devotion to the 'Liberation of Europe', and the successes of Russian armies in 1812–14, had given Russia a dominant voice among the peacemakers, particularly in the settlement of eastern and central Europe. But there was no certainty that Russia would continue this European role after 1815.

Prussia's part in the final defeat of Napoleon allowed the allies conveniently to forget her earlier neutralism and she was permitted substantial gains. She received considerable territory in Westphalia (as part of the Rhenish 'barrier' against France), Swedish Pomerania, Posen and two-fifths of Saxony, which was punished severely for its loyalty to Napoleon. The Saxon lands in particular were compensation for Prussian gains by the second and third partitions of Poland which now largely passed into Russian hands as part of 'Congress Poland'. Prussia's acquisitions in 1815 made her once again a comparatively strong state. She was now clearly dominant in northern Germany and at least the equal of Austria within the new German Confederation. But the shattering defeat of 1806 had revealed the fundamental weaknesses of the Prussian state and the reform era afterwards had only partly remedied them. For a generation to come, Prussia remained – with Austria – the weakest of the great powers: both were menaced by Russia's growing dominance, a threat which Prussia tried to solve by a close association with St Petersburg.

Austria's relative position among the great powers had also been weakened by the wars of 1792–1815. Superficially, the Habsburg recovery was complete. Despite successive defeats at the hands of France, Austria recovered and, in some measure, expanded her territories. She retained Galicia, and Bavaria ceded to her those territories acquired in 1805 and 1809 (Bavaria received Würzburg, Frankfurt and part of the Lower Palatinate as compensation). Austria also made very significant acquisitions in Italy, principally to compensate for Russian and Prussian gains elsewhere and to replace Belgium. She received Venetia and regained Lombardy as well as having influence over the other restored Italian rulers. This gave Metternich virtual control over the whole of Italy after 1815, the final realisation of Austria's eighteenth century ambitions in the peninsula.

Austria retained the status of a great power right up to the First World War, more because of her extensive commitments than for her own intrinsic strength. Up to the Crimean War she was also seen by the western powers as a barrier against Russia, and by the latter as a barrier against France. The central problem was, as ever, that Austria's commitments outran her resources, and the 1815 settlement increased these commitments, particularly in Italy. Elsewhere Habsburg interests were also adversely affected. In Germany, Austria was now at best the equal of Prussia; together they dominated the new German confederation established in June 1815 with Austria as permanent chairman. But Prussia's gains in western Germany finally signalled the end of Austria's traditional role as defender of the Rhine against France and they were to help the growth in Prussian power which ultimately led to Austria's expulsion from Germany. The Habsburgs had increasingly to concern themselves with Italy but also with eastern Europe, where Russia's advance in 1815 threatened their interests and security. Metternich's primary task was to resist the Russian challenge, though he still feared French power. Russia's dominance of Poland, her close links with Prussia, her new position on the Danube (by the acquisition of Bessarabia in 1812) and the threat she posed to the Ottoman Empire were all against Vienna's interests, but it was not clear how Russia might be resisted, given Austria's problems. Austria thus remained, as she had been since the seventeenth century, a state with the responsibilities of a great power but without the means to be one.

At the congress of Vienna decisions were effectively taken by the four allies together with France (quickly readmitted on a limited basis to the ranks of the major powers) and then simply imposed on the other states. This dominance was confirmed by the Quadruple Alliance of 20 November 1815, a treaty between Britain, Russia, Prussia and Austria which provided for regular meetings of allied rulers or their ministers and led to the foundation of the so-called 'Congress System' of 1815–23. In this way the major powers claimed and exercised the right to supervise developments throughout the Continent, even to intervene militarily in a state's internal affairs. The European states system restored in 1815 was in intention a collection of great powers, approximately equal in strength and together completely dominant within Europe. Such a system had emerged in the eighteenth century, but had then been overturned by Napoleon's bid for hegemony. The defeat of Napoleonic imperialism marked the consummation of the rise of the great powers which had taken place since 1648.

Bibliography

This bibliography is intended as a guide to further reading. It concentrates on books in English and generally excludes articles in scholarly periodicals. The majority of the works listed includes extensive bibliographies. Books in English are published in London and those in French in Paris unless indicated otherwise.

GENERAL

The best surveys for these years are M. Immich, *Geschichte des europäischen Staatensystems von 1660 bis 1789* (Munich, 1967, reprint of 1905 edn) and A. Wahl, *Geschichte des europäischen Staatensystems im Zeitalter der französischen Revolution und der Freiheitskriege, 1789–1815* (Munich, 1967, reprint of 1912 edn). A less full French series (Histoire des relations internationales, ed. P. Renouvin) also contains two useful volumes: G. Zeller, *Les Temps modernes, ii: De Louis XIV à 1789* (1955) and A. Fugier, *La Révolution française et l'empire napoléonien* (1954). An imaginative analytical survey of the whole period and beyond is J. Droz, *Histoire diplomatique de 1648 à 1919* (2nd edn, 1959). Two splendid wide-ranging works are A. de St Léger and P. Sagnac, *La Prépondérance française, Louis XIV. 1661–1715* (1935) and P. Muret, *La Prépondérance anglaise, 1715–1763* (1937). There are no comparable surveys in English, although a convenient narrative of events is provided by the relevant chapters of volumes iv–ix of the *New Cambridge Modern History* (13 vols, Cambridge, 1957–79); these volumes are also useful for general reference, as are D. H. Pennington, *Seventeenth-Century Europe* (1970), M. S. Anderson, *Europe in the Eighteenth Century, 1713–83* (2nd edn, 1976) and F. L. Ford, *Europe, 1780–1830* (1970).

For the foreign policies of individual states, Britain is best served

345

for surveys of long periods. D. B. Horn, *Great Britain and Europe in the Eighteenth Century* (Oxford, 1967) is authoritative, although the arrangement of chapters makes it difficult to use. P. Langford, *The Eighteenth Century, 1688–1815* (1976) is a sound guide; and there are two valuable books by J. R. Jones, *Britain and Europe in the Seventeenth Century* (1966) and *Britain and the World, 1649–1815* (1980). For the latter part of the period *The Cambridge History of British Foreign Policy, i: 1783–1815*, ed. A. W. Ward and G. P. Gooch (Cambridge, 1922) is valuable for information. For French policy, a helpful guide is P. Rain, *La Diplomatie française, i: D'Henri IV à Vergennes, ii: De Mirabeau à Bonaparte* (1945–50). For Dutch policy, there is A. C. Carter, *Neutrality or Commitment: the Evolution of Dutch Foreign Policy, 1667–1795* (1975), which should be read with J. W. Smit, 'The Netherlands and Europe in the seventeenth and eighteenth centuries', in *Britain and the Netherlands in Europe and Asia*, ed. J. S. Bromley and E. H. Kossmann (1968). There is nothing comparable for other European states, although R. A. Stradling, *Europe and the Decline of Spain: a Study of the Spanish System, 1580–1720* (London, 1981) was published too late for use.

Colonial rivalries are outlined by J. H. Parry, *Trade and Dominion: the European Overseas Empire in the Eighteenth Century* (1971) and G. Williams, *The Expansion of Europe in the Eighteenth Century* (1966), and their diplomatic repercussions for one area by M. Savelle, *The Origins of American Diplomacy: the International History of Anglo-America, 1492–1763* (New York, 1967) and G. S. Graham, *Empire of the North Atlantic: the Maritime Struggle for North America* (1958). The naval side can be followed in P. M. Kennedy, *The Rise and Fall of British Naval Mastery* (1976) and E. H. Jenkins, *A History of the French Navy* (1973). General histories of warfare are listed below, but an excellent treatment of the role of armies in our period is A. Vagts, *A History of Militarism* (1938).

The working of the European states system is described best in the first volume of A. Sorel's classic, *L'Europe et la Révolution française*, translated as *Europe and the French Revolution: the Political Traditions of the Old Régime* (1969). An interesting, if rather nebulous, survey is G. Livet, *L'Equilibre européen de la fin du xve à la fin du xviiie siècle* (1976). The best brief introduction to eighteenth-century diplomacy is Chapter 8 of M. S. Anderson, *Europe in the Eighteenth Century, 1713–83* (2nd edn, 1976). Important theoretical discussions are J. Viner, 'Power versus plenty as objectives of foreign policy in the seventeenth and eighteenth centuries', *World Politics* **1** (1948); M. S. Anderson, 'Eighteenth century theories of the balance of power' in R. M. Hatton and M. S. Anderson (eds), *Studies in Diplomatic History* (1970); F. Gilbert, 'The "new diplomacy" of the eighteenth century', *World Politics* **4** (1951); R. M. Hatton, *War and Peace, 1680–1720* (1969); and F. Hinsley, *Power and the Pursuit of Peace* (Cambridge,

1963). Useful collections of documents are M. Wright (ed.), *Theory and Practice of the Balance of Power, 1486–1914* (1975) and G. Symcox (ed.), *War, Diplomacy and Imperialism, 1618–1763* (New York, 1973).

Only the diplomatic services of Britain and France have, as yet, been treated adequately. For Britain see D. B. Horn's masterly introduction, *The British Diplomatic Service, 1689–1789* (Oxford, 1961) and P. Lachs, *The Diplomatic Corps under Charles II and James II* (New Brunswick, N. J., 1965). For France see C. G. Picavet, *La Diplomatie française au temps de Louis XIV* (1930), F. Masson, *Le Département des affaires étrangères pendant la Révolution, 1787–1804* (1897) and E. A. Whitcomb, *Napoleon's Diplomatic Service* (Durham, N. C., 1979). A good general study of Torcy's 'School for Ambassadors' is by H. M. A. Keens-Soper, 'The French Political Academy', *Europ. Stud. R.*, **2** (1972), and for its origins see the admirable account by J. Klaits, 'Men of letters and political reform in France at the end of the reign of Louis XIV', *J. of Mod. Hist.* **43** (1971). The latest discussion of the foundation of the Russian diplomatic service is D. Altbauer, 'The diplomats of Peter the Great', *Jahrbücher f. Geschichte Osteuropas* **28** (1980), while the Turkish entrance into the states system is outlined by T. Naff, 'Reform and the conduct of Ottoman diplomacy, 1789–1807', *J. of the American Oriental Soc.* **83** (1963). O. T. Murphy, 'Charles Gravier de Vergennes; profile of an old regime diplomat', *Pol. Science Qu.* **83** (1968) examines how this late-eighteenth-century statesman, although perhaps an untypical one, viewed the European system. Finally, J. W. Thompson and S. K. Padover, *Secret Diplomacy: Espionage and Cryptography, 1500–1815* (1937), a lurid and unconvincing book, is the only general treatment of an important subject.

CHAPTERS ONE AND TWO

Probably the best introductions in English to the period are the chapters in the *New Cambridge Modern History*, vols iv–vi, together with F. L. Nussbaum, *The Triumph of Science and Reason, 1660–1685* (New York, 1953) and J. B. Wolf, *The Emergence of the Great Powers, 1685–1715* (New York, 1951). For useful insights and the flavour of the period, as well as excellent bibliographies, there is R. M. Hatton, *Europe in the Age of Louis XIV* (1969). Valuable for the early years is J. W. Stoye, *Europe Unfolding, 1648–1688* (1969). A convenient outline of Louis XIV's foreign policy, although with some drawbacks, is G. R. R. Treasure, *Seventeenth century France* (2nd edn, 1981). The best accounts are still L. André, *Louis XIV et l'Europe* (1950) and the rather stolid *Louis XIV* by J. B. Wolf (1968). More recent perspectives can be found in *Louis XIV and Europe* (1976), ed. R. M. Hatton: see especially Hatton's own wide-ranging 'Louis XIV and his fellow monarchs', P. Sonnino, 'Louis XIV and the Dutch War', G. Symcox, 'Louis XIV and the outbreak of the Nine Years War', C. Nordmann, 'Louis XIV and the Jacobites' and the discussion of the partition treaty of 1668 by J. Bérenger. Another useful collection is *William III and Louis XIV* (Liverpool, 1967), ed. R. M. Hatton and J. S. Bromley: particularly valuable are A. Lossky, '"Maxims of state" in Louis XIV's foreign policy' and M. A. Thomson, 'Louis XIV and the origins of the War of the Spanish Succession'. For the economic and social background to Louis's wars, see P. Goubert, *Louis XIV and Twenty Million Frenchmen* (1970). Studies of aspects of French policy are H. H. Rowen, *The Ambassador Prepares for War: the Dutch Embassy of Arnauld de Pomponne, 1669–1671* (The Hague, 1957); J. T. O'Connor, *Negotiator out of Season: the Career of W. E. v. Fürstenberg, 1629–1704* (Athens, Georgia, 1978); C. J. Ekberg, *The Failure of Louis XIV's Dutch War* (Chapel Hill, N.C. 1979); G. Symcox, *The Crisis of French Naval Power, 1688–97* (The Hague, 1974).

The policies of the other powers have been less well served than those of France. For works on the Baltic see the next section. There is a good outline of English foreign policy in J. R. Jones, *Court and Country, 1658–1714* (1978); and see G. C. Gibbs, 'The Revolution in foreign policy', in *Britain after the Glorious Revolution, 1688–1714* (1969), ed. G. Holmes, and J. L. Price, 'Restoration England and Europe' in *The Restored Monarchy* (1979), ed. J. R. Jones. Important are the articles by M. A. Thomson in *William III and Louis XIV* (above) and S. B. Baxter's fine biography, *William III* (London, 1966). This work is also essential for Dutch policy. The first two Anglo-Dutch wars are discussed in C. Wilson, *Profit and Power* (1957), and C. Boxer has written 'Some second thoughts on the third Anglo-Dutch War', *Trans. R. Hist. Soc.*, 5th series, **19** (1969). A massive blow-by-blow account of *John de Witt, Grand Pensionary of Holland, 1625–1672* (Princeton, 1978) is by H. H. Rowen. More digestible for Dutch policy are P. Geyl's *Orange and Stuart, 1647–72* (1969) and *The Netherlands in the Seventeenth Century, ii: 1648–1715* (1964). Valuable articles are by M. A. M. Franken, 'The general tendencies and structural aspects of the foreign policy and diplomacy of the Dutch Republic in the latter half of the seventeenth century', *Acta Historiae Neerlandica* 3 (1968), and J. G. Stork-Penning, 'The ordeal of the States – some remarks on Dutch politics during the War of the Spanish Succession', ibid. **2** (1967).

Spanish foreign policy remains largely unexplored, although there is the illuminating 'A Spanish statesman of appeasement: Medina de las Torres and Spanish policy, 1639–1670', by R. A. Stradling in *Hist. J.* **19** (1976); and see the same author's book referred to in the General Section above. Austrian policy by contrast has been very fully covered by J. P. Spielman, *Leopold I* (1976); D. McKay, *Prince Eugene of Savoy* (1977); and C. W. Ingrao, *In Quest and Crisis: Emperor Joseph I and the Habsburg Monarchy* (West Lafayette, Indiana, 1979). An excellent discussion of the very relevant subject of the nature of warfare during the period is D. Chandler, *The Art of Warfare in the Age of Marlborough* (1976). See also the articles by G. N. Clark, 'The character of the Nine Years War', *Camb. Hist. J.* **11** (1954); and J. S. Bromley, 'The French privateering war, 1702–13', in *Historical Essays Presented to D. Ogg* (1963), ed. by H. E. Bell and R. C. Ollard.

CHAPTER THREE

Useful introductions to the expansion of Austria and the retreat of the Turks are J. W. Stoye, *Europe Unfolding, 1648–1688* (1969) and chapters in the *New Cambridge Modern History*, vols. v and vi. There are two impressive books on the siege of Vienna and its background: T. M. Barker, *Double Eagle and Crescent* (Albany, 1967) and J. W. Stoye, *The Siege of Vienna* (1964). E. Eickhoff, *Venedig, Wien und die Osmanen. Umbruch in Südosteuropa, 1645–1700* (Munich, 1970) puts the Turks in a wider European context and has excellent bibliographies. J. P. Spielman, *Leopold I* (1976) and D. McKay, *Prince Eugene of Savoy* (1977) cover the Austro-Turkish conflicts of Leopold's reign, and the latter has a chapter on that of 1716–18. There is still much of value in O. Redlich, *Weltmacht des Barock. Osterreich in der Zeit Kaiser Leopolds I* (Vienna, 4th edn, 1961). A perceptive and stimulating work is W. H. McNeill, *Europe's Steppe Frontier, 1500–1800* (Chicago, 1964), which is useful for the Turkish problem in the Ukraine as well as the Balkans.

Good introductions to Swedish history are S. P. Oakley, *The Story of Sweden* (1966); F. D. Scott, *Sweden, the Nation's History* (Minneapolis, 1977); and the excellent *Grandeur et liberté de la Suède, 1660–1792* (1971) by C. Nordmann. An essential and splendid work is *The Swedish Imperial Experience, 1560–1718* (Cambridge, 1979) by M. Roberts, who has also edited a useful collection of articles, *Sweden's Age of Greatness, 1632–1718* (1973). A short introduction to R. M. Hatton's impressive *Charles XII of Sweden* (1968) is her Historical Association pamphlet, *Charles XII* (1974). Other useful works on the Great Northern War, besides chapters in the *New Cambridge Modern History*, vol. vi, are C. Nordmann, *La Crise du nord au début du xviiie siècle* (1962); J. Kalisch and J. Gierowski (eds), *Um die Polnische Krone. Sachsen und Polen während des Nordischen Krieges, 1700–21* (Berlin, 1962); J. J. Murray, *George I, the Baltic and the Whig Split of 1717* (1969); D. McKay, 'The struggle for control of George I's northern policy, 1718–19', *J. of Mod. Hist.* **45** (1973); and W. Mediger, *Mecklenburg, Russland und England–Hannover, 1706–21*, 2 vols (Hildesheim, 1967), a work of breath-taking scholarship.

Russia's role in the seventeenth century is discussed by G. v. Rauch, 'Moskau und die europäische Mächte des 17. Jahrhunderts', *Historische Zeitschrift* **178** (1954). For her foreign policy under Peter the Great, the best account is M. S. Anderson, *Peter the Great* (1978). A more extensive biography is R. Wittram, *Peter I, Czar und Kaiser*, 2 vols (Göttingen, 1964). Brief and interesting is B. Sumner, *Peter the Great and the Ottoman Empire* (Oxford, 1950). There are two useful articles by L. R. Lewitter, 'Poland, the Ukraine and Russia in the seventeenth century', *Slav. and E. Europ. R.* **27** (1948–49) and 'Russia, Poland and the Baltic, 1697–1721', *Hist. J.* **2** (1968).

CHAPTERS FOUR AND FIVE

There is no adequate account of the years 1714–39 in English, although *La Prépondérance anglaise, 1715–1763* (1937) by P. Muret is excellent. The clearest account of British policy is P. Langford, *The Eighteenth Century, 1688–1815* (1976). The latest research can be followed in R. M. Hatton, *George I, Elector and King* (1978); the studies by B. Williams on *Stanhope, a Study in Eighteenth century Diplomacy* (Oxford, 1932) and *Carteret and Newcastle* (Cambridge, 1943) and by P. Vaucher, *Robert Walpole et la politique de Fleury* (1924) are now rather showing their age. They should be read with G. C. Gibbs's articles, 'Parliament and the treaty of Quadruple Alliance', *William III and Louis XIV*, ed. R. M. Hatton and J. S. Bromley (Liverpool, 1967), 'Parliament and foreign policy in the age of Stanhope and Walpole', *English Hist. R.* **77** (1962) and 'Britain and the alliance of Hanover', ibid. **73** (1958). Of value are S. Conn, *Gibraltar in British Diplomacy in the Eighteenth Century* (New Haven, 1942); J. O. McLachlan, *Trade and Peace with Old Spain, 1667–1750* (Cambridge, 1940); and G. H. Jones, *The Mainstream of Jacobitism* (1954).

The massive nineteenth-century works on French diplomatic history should be approached through two good studies: J. H. Shennan, *Philippe Duke of Orleans: Regent of France, 1715–23* (1979) and A. M. Wilson, *French Foreign Policy during the Administration of Cardinal Fleury* (Cambridge, Mass., 1936). J. L. Sutton, *The King's Honor and the King's Cardinal: the War of the Polish Succession* (Lexington, 1980) adds little to the existing diplomatic picture. For Austrian policy the best short introduction is still O. Redlich, *Das Werden einer Grossmacht: Österreich von 1700 bis 1740* (Vienna, 4th edn, 1962). D. McKay, *Prince Eugene of Savoy* (1977) should be used as a guide to the period before

1736 and to the extensive literature in German. K. A. Roider, *The Reluctant Ally: Austria's Policy in the Austro-Turkish War, 1737–1739* (Baton Rouge, 1972) is short and valuable. *The Struggle for the Ottoman Empire, 1717–1740* (1966) by L. Cassels is stronger on information than interpretation. There are perceptive articles by L. Auer, 'Das Reich und der Vertrag von Sevilla, 1729–1731', *Mitteilungen des Österreichischen Staatsarchivs* **22** (1969); V. L. Tapié, 'Contribution à l'étude des relations entre la France et l'Autriche avant la Guerre de Succession d'Autriche', *Österreich und Europa, Festgabe für H. Hantsch*, no editor, publ. by Verlag Styria (Graz, 1965); and C. W. Ingrao, 'The Pragmatic Sanction and the Theresian succession', *Theresian Austria* (Washington, Pennsylvania, 1981), ed. by W. J. McGill.

There is very little in English on Russia and the Baltic in this period, although D. Reading, *The Anglo-Russian Commercial Treaty of 1734* (New Haven, 1938) is more wide-ranging than the title implies. One of the more useful works on the period 1721–32 is unfortunately in Danish, although it has a very brief English summary: H. Bagger, *Ruslands Alliancepolitik efter Freden i Nystad* (Copenhagen, 1974). In German W. Mediger, *Moskaus Weg nach Europa* (Brunswick, 1952) is rather difficult to use, but his article 'Russland und die Ostsee im 18. Jahrhundert', *Jahrbücher f. Geschichte Osteuropas* **16** (1968) is more approachable. Useful is G. v. Rauch, 'Zur baltischen Frage im 18. Jahrhundert', ibid. **5** (1957). Given the importance of Spain in this period, the existing literature is surprisingly sparse, although see Conn and McLachlan above. There is no modern biography of Alberoni or Elizabeth Farnese. W. N. Hargreaves-Mawdsley, *Eighteenth-century Spain, 1700–1788* (1979) is brief and has some drawbacks. M. Martin, 'The secret clause: Britain and Spanish ambitions in Italy, 1712–31', *Europ. Stud. R.* **6** (1976) is useful, if occasionally confusing. There is no modern biography of Victor Amadeus of Savoy, although the importance of Italy can be appreciated through G. Quazza, 'Italy's role in the European problems of the first half of the eighteenth century', *Studies in Diplomatic History* (1970), ed. by R. M. Hatton and M. S. Anderson. The only extensive work on Italy and international relations is by G. Quazza, *Il Problema Italiano e L'Equilibrio Europeo, 1720–1738* (Turin, 1965).

CHAPTER SIX

The best introductions to these decades are W. L. Dorn, *Competition for Empire 1740–1763* (New York, 1940) and Part 4 of P. Muret, *La Prépondérance anglaise 1715–1763* (1937). Prussia's impact on Europe is outlined by D. B. Horn, *Frederick the Great and the Rise of Prussia* (1964) and its diplomatic repercussions are examined in R. Lodge, *Studies in Eighteenth-century Diplomacy 1740–1748* (1930). For the Anglo-Spanish War, see H. W. V. Temperley, 'The causes of the War of Jenkins' Ear (1739)', *Trans. Royal Hist. S.*, 3rd series, **3** (1909) and J. O. McLachlan, *Trade and Peace with Old Spain 1667–1750* (Cambridge, 1940). R. Pares, 'American versus continental warfare, 1739–1763', *English Hist. R.* **51** (1936) is fundamental. The best account of the Anglo-Bourbon conflict is by Pares: *War and Trade in the West Indies 1739–1763*; (Oxford, 1936); see also M. Savelle, *The Origins of American Diplomacy: the International History of Anglo-America 1492–1763* (New York, 1967) and L. H. Gipson, 'British diplomacy in the light of Anglo-Spanish New World issues 1750–1757', *Am. Hist. R.* **51** (1946). A masterly introduction to the mid-century 'reversal of alliances' is D. B. Horn, 'The Diplomatic Revolution', *New Cambridge Modern History* vii, ed. J. O. Lindsay (Cambridge, 1957); the standard full-scale study remains R. Waddington, *Louis XV et le renversement des alliances* (1896). M. Braubach, *Versailles und Wien von Ludwig XIV. bis Kaunitz* (Bonn, 1952) has been widely praised as a study of the origins of the Diplomatic Revolution, but it is rather deterministic and selective in its use of evidence. There are also some helpful recent articles on the years 1749–56: W. Mediger, 'Great Britain, Hanover and the rise of Prussia', in *Studies in Diplomatic History*, ed. R. M. Hatton and M. S. Anderson (1970); W. J. McGill, 'The Roots of policy: Kaunitz in Italy and the Netherlands 1742–46', *Central European Hist.* **1** (1968) and 'The roots of policy: Kaunitz in Vienna and Versailles 1749–1753', *J. Mod. Hist.* **43** (1971); R. Browning, 'The British orientation of Austrian foreign policy 1749–54', *Central European Hist.* **1** (1968); and D. B. Horn, 'The Duke of Newcastle and the origins of the Diplomatic Revolution', in *The Diversity of History*, ed. J. H. Elliott and H. G. Koenigsberger (1970). D. B. Horn, *Sir Charles Hanbury Williams and European Diplomacy 1747–58* (1930) is a distinguished study of continental diplomacy in the mid-1750s. The debate on the responsibility for the Seven Years War is examined by H. Butterfield, *The Reconstruction of an Historical Episode* (Glasgow, 1951), reprinted in the same author's *Man on his Past* (Cambridge, 1955). The role of Russia is examined, and exaggerated, by H. H. Kaplan, *Russia and the Outbreak of the Seven Years' War* (Berkeley, 1968). For the Seven Years War itself, L. J. Oliva, *Misalliance: a Study of French Policy in Russia during the Seven Years' War* (New York, 1964) examines one troubled alliance, while the relations of two other temporary partners are dealt with in R. Lodge, *Great Britain and Prussia in the Eighteenth Century* (Oxford, 1923) and their celebrated break-up in F. Spencer, 'The Anglo-Prussian breach of 1762', *History* **41** (1956). The best study of the war from a British viewpoint is W. C. B. Tunstall, *William Pitt, Earl of Chatham* (London, 1938); R. Middleton, 'Pitt, Anson and the Admiralty 1756–1761', *History* **55** (1970), is a significant article; while for the Anglo-French peace negotiations see Z. E. Rashed, *The Peace of Paris 1763* (Liverpool, 1951).

For the Bibliography for Chapter 7 see the General Section at the beginning.

CHAPTER EIGHT

The best outline is M. S. Anderson, 'European Diplomatic Relations 1763–90', *New Cambridge Modern History* viii, ed. A. Goodwin (Cambridge, 1965). The introduction to *The Fourth Earl of Sandwich: Diplomatic Correspondence 1763–1765*, ed. F. Spencer (Manchester, 1961) is useful on the early years of peace. The genesis of the most important alliance of the post-war period is examined in H. M. Scott, 'Frederick II, the Ottoman Empire and the origins of the Russo-Prussian alliance of April 1764', *Europ. Stud. R.* **7** (1977). The best study of the Russo-Turkish War of 1768–74 and of the first partition of Poland remains A. Sorel, *The Eastern Question in the Eighteenth Century* (1898); the most recent account is H. H. Kaplan, *The First Partition of Poland* (New York, 1962), but it is unconvincing in its general arguments and inaccurate over details, and it should be read with the devastating review by J. Topolski, 'Reflections on the first partition of Poland (1772)', *Acta Poloniae Historica* **27** (1973). Habsburg attempts to acquire Bavaria are studied by P. P. Bernard, *Joseph II and Bavaria* (The Hague, 1965). The best account of Russian foreign policy is that contained in the magisterial survey by I. de Madariaga, *Russia in the Age of Catherine the Great* (1981); D. M. Griffiths provides a useful outline of 'The rise and fall of the Northern System', *Canadian–American Slavic Studies* **4** (1970), while M. Raeff, 'In the imperial manner', in M. Raeff, ed., *Catherine the Great: a Profile* (1972) is important for Potemkin and southward expansion in the second half of the reign. I. de Madariaga, 'The secret Austro-Russian Treaty of 1781', *Slav. and E. Europ. R.* **38** (1959–60) examines the conclusion of this treaty and Catherine's use of it in 1783 when Russia annexed the Crimea. A W. Fisher, *The Russian Annexation of the Crimea 1772–1783* (Cambridge, 1970) is invaluable for the complex internal struggle within the khanate, but the international dimension is covered best by M. S. Anderson, 'The Great powers and the Russian annexation of the Crimea, 1783–4', *Slav. and E. Europ. R.* **37** (1958–59). For the Russo-Turkish War of 1787–92 see: K. A. Roider, Jr, 'Kaunitz, Joseph II and the Turkish War', ibid. **54** (1976); M. S. Anderson, *The Eastern Question 1774–1923* (1966), Chapter I; and M. S. Anderson, *Britain's Discovery of Russia 1553–1815* (1958), Chapter 6 of which provides the best short account of the confrontation over Ochakov in 1791. The ambitions of Gustav III and international relations in the Baltic region are explored in the following articles: R. J. Misiunas, 'The Baltic question after Nystad', *Baltic Hist.* I (1974), a stimulating survey which covers the whole eighteenth century; H. A. Barton, 'Gustav III of Sweden and the East Baltic, 1771–1792', *J. Baltic Studies* 7 (1976); S. P. Oakley, 'Gustavus III's plans for war with Denmark in 1783–84', in *Studies in Diplomatic History*, ed. R. M. Hatton and M. S. Anderson (1970); and H. A. Barton, 'Russia and the problem of Sweden–Finland, 1721–1809', *E. European Quarterly* 5 (1972). Internal developments in Poland during the era of partitions are most convincingly treated in *History of Poland*, ed. S. Kieniewicz (Warsaw, 1968), though *The Cambridge History of Poland, ii: 1697–1935*, ed. W. F. Reddaway et al. (Cambridge, 1941) remains a valuable source of detailed information on political history. R. H. Lord, *The Second Partition of Poland* (Cambridge, Mass., 1915) is a detailed study, while the same author's 'The Third Partition of Poland', *Slav. and E. Europ. R.* 3 (1924–25) is a valuable sketch. There are also two informative articles by J. Lojek, 'The international crisis of 1791: Poland between the Triple Alliance and Russia', *East-Central Europe* 2 (1975), and 'Catherine II's armed intervention in Poland...1791–92', *Canadian–American Slavic Studies* 4 (1970).

CHAPTER NINE

The absence of an adequate study of Choiseul's ministry is a considerable barrier to the full understanding of Anglo-French relations after the Seven Years War. J. F. Ramsey, *Anglo-French Relations 1763–70: a Study of Choiseul's Foreign Policy* (Berkeley, 1939) is a sketchy outline which relies too heavily on British material; L. Blart, *Les Rapports de la France et de l'Espagne après le pacte de famille, jusqu' à la fin du ministère du duc de Choiseul* (1915) is a better guide. For the origins of the Franco-Spanish alliance, see D. Ozanam, 'Les origines du troisième pacte de Famille (1761)', *Revue d'histoire diplomatique* 75 (1961). M. Roberts, *Splendid Isolation 1763–1780* (Reading, 1970) is a magisterial survey of British foreign policy. Anglo-French relations in the first decade of peace are illuminated by articles by N. Tracy: 'British assessments of French and Spanish naval reconstruction, 1763–1768', *Mariner's Mirror* 61 (1975); 'The gunboat diplomacy of the government of George Grenville, 1764–65', *Hist. J.* 17 (1974); and 'The Falkland Islands crisis of 1770: use of naval force', *English Hist. R.* 90 (1975): these scholarly studies tend to lean too heavily on British sources and to see only the naval dimension of British foreign policy. 'The importance of Bourbon naval reconstruction to the strategy of Choiseul after the Seven Years War' is examined by H. M. Scott in *International Hist. R.* 1 (1979). The attempt at a Franco-British *rap-*

prochement in the early 1770s is outlined in B. du Fraguier, 'Le duc d'Aiguillon et l'Angleterre', *Revue d'histoire diplomatique* **26** (1912) and placed in context by M. Roberts, 'Great Britain and the Swedish Revolution, 1772–73', *His. J.* **7** (1964). The War of American Independence is seen from a British standpoint in the superb study of P. Mackesy, *The War for America 1775–1783* (1964); on France's role there is E. S. Corwin, 'The French objective in the American Revolution', *Am. Hist. R.* **21** (1915–16), and a valuable book by J. R. Dull, *The French Navy and American Independence* (Princeton, 1975), though this does not wholly supersede S. F. Bemis, *The Diplomacy of the American Revolution* (New York, 1935). R. W. Van Alstyne, *Empire and Independence: the International History of the American Revolution* (New York, 1965) provides an American view, but is not always reliable on the European dimension; the best account of continental diplomacy is I. de Madariaga, *Britain, Russia and the Armed Neutrality of 1780* (1962). A modern study of the Anglo-Dutch War of 1780 is badly needed; the best available is probably P. J. Blok, *History of the People of the Netherlands*, vol. v (New York, 1912), Chapters 9 and 10. V. T. Harlow, *The Founding of the Second British Empire 1763–1793, i: Discovery and Revolution* (1952) discusses the negotiations which led to the peace of Versailles, though Harlow claims too much for Shelburne and takes a rather insular view of the discussions. R. B. Morris, *The Peacemakers: the Great Powers and American Independence* (New York, 1965) is rambling and discursive, but provides much important detail. The best general account of Pitt's foreign policy before 1790 is J. Ehrman, *The Younger Pitt: the Years of Acclaim* (1969), Chapters 16 and 17; Ehrman has also written a dense monograph on *The British Government and Commercial Negotiations with Europe, 1783–93* (Cambridge, 1962) and there is a useful study of 'The Anglo-French Commercial Treaty of 1786' by W. O. Henderson in *Ec. Hist. R.*, 2nd series, **10** (1957–58). Events in the Dutch Republic are admirably described by S. Schama, *Patriots and Liberators: Revolution in the Netherlands 1780–1813* (1977), while a lively study of Sir James Harris's activities is provided by A. Cobban, *Ambassadors and Secret Agents* (1954). For Anglo-Prussian relations in the later 1780s there is R. Lodge, *Great Britain and Prussia in the Eighteenth Century* (Oxford, 1923). The best account of the Nootka Sound crisis is C. de Parrel, 'Pitt et l'Espagne', *Revue d'histoire diplomatique* **64** (1950), but see also H. V. Evans, 'The Nootka Sound controversy in Anglo-French diplomacy – 1790', *J. Mod. Hist.* **46** (1974).

CHAPTERS TEN, ELEVEN AND TWELVE

The recent proliferation of research and publications on the Revolutionary and Napoleonic periods has often ignored international relations and there are still some considerable gaps. Older studies often remain the best guides. Chief among these is the great work of Albert Sorel, *L'Europe et al Révolution française*, 8 vols (1885–1905), which is unsurpassed for factual information, though its thesis is controversial. The best introduction is Steven T. Ross, *European Diplomatic History 1789–1815: France against Europe* (New York, 1969), which is unfortunately difficult to obtain. A. Fugier, *La Révolution française et l'empire napoléonien* (1954) provides a reliable, if Francocentric, survey; the two studies by G. Lefèbvre, *The French Revolution*, 2 vols (1964) and *Napoleon*, 2 vols (1969) contain a judicious account of international relations. The impact of Revolutionary France on Europe is examined by J. Godechot, *La Grande Nation*, 2 vols (1956) and by R. R. Palmer, *The Age of the Democratic Revolution*, ii: *the Struggle* (Princeton, 1964), while the activities of the *émigrés* are outlined in Part Two of J. Godechot, *The Counter-Revolution: Doctrine and Action 1789–1804* (1972). An up-to-date account of the origins of the Revolutionary Wars is badly needed; until it appears, the best is J. H. Clapham, *The Causes of the War of 1792* (Cambridge, 1899). The first decade of the war is viewed from a British perspective in J. H. Rose, *The Life of William Pitt*, vol. ii (1911), while for Britain's support of the Counter-Revolution there are two fine monographs: W. R. Fryer, *Republic or Restoration in France, 1794–1797* (Manchester, 1965) and H. Mitchell, *The Underground War against Revolutionary France* (Oxford, 1965). Britain's financial contribution to the struggle is covered by a ponderous but informative study by J. M. Sherwig, *Guineas and Gunpowder: British Foreign Aid in the Wars with France, 1793–1815* (Cambridge, Mass., 1969), while the tangled skein of Anglo-Austrian financial relations in the 1790s is unravelled by K. F. Helleiner, *The Imperial Loans* (Oxford, 1965). M. J. Sydenham, *The First French Republic 1792–1804* (1974) is generally reliable on the war, while the vacillations of Berlin's policy are analysed by G. S. Ford, *Hanover and Prussia 1795–1803* (New York, 1903). J. M. Sherwig, 'Lord Grenville's plan for a concert of Europe, 1797–99', *J. Mod. Hist.* **34** (1962) is a useful exploration of the thinking behind British policy. The War of the Second Coalition is seen from Britain's viewpoint in two recent studies: A. B. Rodger, *The War of the Second Coalition, 1798–1801* (Oxford, 1964), idiosyncratic but with some penetrating comments, and P. Mackesy, *Statesmen at War: the Strategy of Overthrow 1798–99* (1974), an admirable study, particularly strong on the interplay between strategy and politics. The Mediterranean dimension is provided by N. E. Saul, *Russia and the Mediterranean 1797–1807* (Chicago, 1970) and another fine study by P. Mackesy, *The War in the Mediterranean 1803–10* (1957). An important theme is inadequately treated by A. A. Lobanov-Rostovsky, *Russia and Europe 1789–1825* (Durham, N. C., 1947). Significant new material on Paul I's foreign policy is contained in *Paul I*, ed. H. Ragsdale (Pittsburg, Penn., 1979) and in

H. Ragsdale, *Détente in the Napoleonic Era* (Lawrence, Kansas, 1980), which details Bonaparte's attempted *rapprochement* with Russia in 1800–1. M. S. Anderson, *The Eastern Question 1774–1923* (1966), Chapters 1 and 2, is the best introduction to the complexities of Balkan politics. The revolutionary changes in land warfare are outlined by M. Howard, *War in European History* (Oxford, 1976), Chapter 5, and by G. E. Rothenberg, *The Art of Warfare in the Age of Napoleon* (1977); for Bonaparte as a military commander see the comprehensive study by D. G. Chandler, *The Campaigns of Napoleon* (1967). Biographies of Bonaparte abound: the most balanced is F. Markham, *Napoleon* (1963). The old volume by C. L. Mowat, *The Diplomacy of Napoleon* (1924) remains a valuable comprehensive study, while the remarkable article by P. Muret, 'Une conception nouvelle de la politique étrangère de Napoléon Ier', *Revue d'histoire moderne et contemporaine* **18** (1913) discusses interpretations of his foreign policy. There are important specialised works on aspects of Napoleonic ascendancy: H. C. Deutsch, *The Genesis of Napoleonic Imperialism* (Cambridge, Mass., 1938), for the years 1800–5; H. Butterfield, *The Peace Tactics of Napoleon 1806–1808* (Cambridge, 1929); O. Connelly, *Napoleon's Satellite Kingdoms* (New York, 1965); H. A. L. Fisher, *Napoleonic Statesmanship: Germany* (Oxford, 1903); and E. E. Y. Hales, *Napoleon and the Pope* (1962). Two of Napoleon's opponents are the subject of readable political biographies by A. Palmer: *Alexander I* (1974) and *Metternich* (1972), and a third is covered by C. J. Bartlett, *Castlereagh* (1966). P. K. Grimsted, *The Foreign Ministers of Alexander I* (Berkeley, 1969) is important for the thinking behind Russian policy. There are some useful studies of Habsburg foreign policy during the Napoleonic period: E. E. Kraehe, *Metternich's German Policy*, i: *the Contest with Napoleon, 1799–1814* (Princeton, 1963), which contains important information, though the interpretation is controversial; M. R. Falk, 'Stadion: adversaire de Napoléon (1806–1809)', *Annales Historiques de la Révolution française* **169** (1962); C. S. B. Buckland, *Metternich and the British Government from 1809–1813* (1932); and J. B. Stearns, *The Role of Metternich in Undermining Napoleon* (Urbana, Illinois, 1948). The Baltic side is discussed by R. Carr, 'Gustavus IV and the British Government, 1804–1809', *English Hist. R.* **60** (1945) and by two articles by A. N. Ryan: 'The causes of the British attack upon Copenhagen in 1807', ibid. **68** (1953), and 'The defence of British trade with the Baltic, 1808–1813', ibid. **74** (1959). Economic warfare is examined in E. F. Heckscher's classic *The Continental System* (1922) and in a large-scale and rather technical study by F. Crouzet, *L'Economie britannique et le blocus continental* 2 vols (1958); perhaps more accessible is the article by Crouzet, 'Wars, blockade and economic change in Europe 1792–1815', *J. Econ. Hist.* **24** (1964). On the final struggle with Napoleon, G. A. Craig, 'Problems of coalition warfare: the military alliance against Napoleon, 1813–14', in his *War, Politics and*

Diplomacy (1966) is an important article, while E. V. Gulick, 'The Final Coalition and the Congress of Vienna 1813–1815', in *New Cambridge Modern History* ix, ed. C. W. Crawley (Cambridge, 1965) is a good political outline. The most satisfactory introduction to the peace conference is D. Dakin, 'The Congress of Vienna, 1814–15, and its antecedents', in *Europe's Balance of Power 1815–1848* ed. A. Sked (1979); a full-scale modern study, dealing adequately with the settlement in central and eastern Europe, is badly needed. Until it appears, the following older studies are all useful within their limits: C. K. Webster, *The Congress of Vienna 1814–15* (1919); H. Nicolson, *The Congress of Vienna* (1946); G. Ferrero, *The Reconstruction of Europe: Talleyrand and the Congress of Vienna* (New York, 1941); and E. V. Gulick, *Europe's Classical Balance of Power* (Ithaca, 1955).

ADDENDUM

Several books published recently are of importance. The need for a study of the important ruler of Savoy (noted p. 351) will be met by G. Symcox, *Victor Amadeus II of Savoy* (in the press). The vast first volume of R. Butler, *Choiseul: Father and Son, 1719–1754* (Oxford, 1980) covers in immense detail the diplomacy of the second quarter of the eighteenth century and has new material on Fleury's policy towards Lorraine. K. A. Roider, *Austria's Eastern Question, 1700–1790* (Princeton, 1982) fills a notable gap. M. Roberts, *British Diplomacy and Swedish Politics, 1758–1773* (1980) illuminates the interplay between Swedish party politics and the rivalry of the great powers. Internal developments in Poland are now best studied in N. Davies, *God's Playground, a History of Poland*, vol. i (Oxford, 1981). A stimulating account of the impact of warfare at the end of the period is provided by G. Best, *War and Society in Revolutionary Europe, 1770–1870* (1982). Finally, E. Ingram, *Commitment to Empire: Prophecies of the Great Game in Asia, 1797–1800* (Oxford, 1981) places Britain's role in the Second Coalition War in its imperial context.

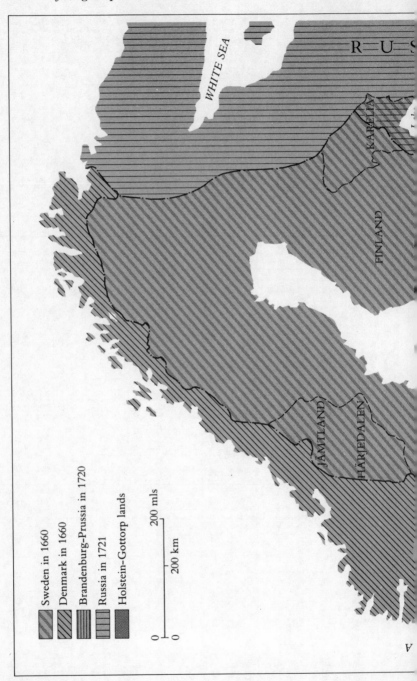

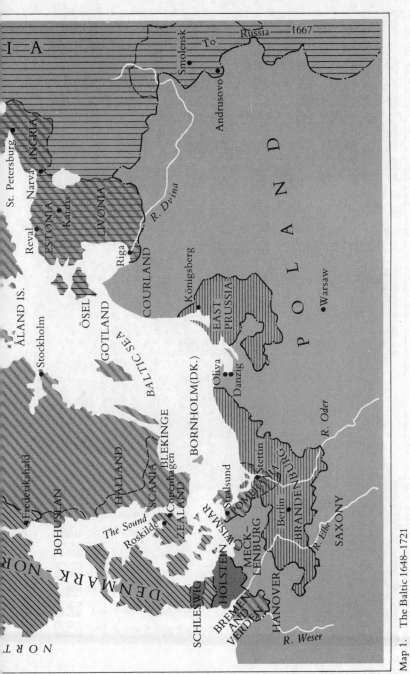

Map 1.   The Baltic 1648–1721

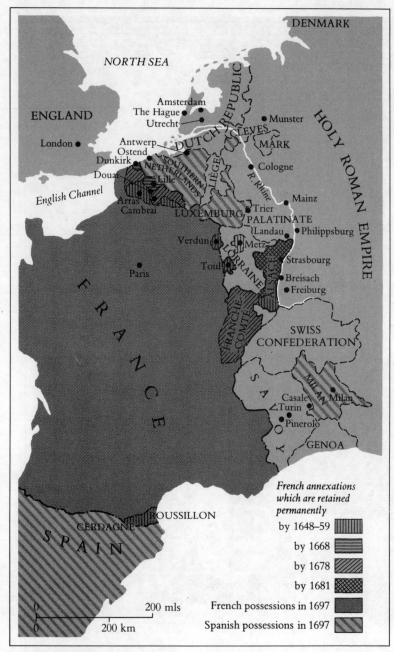

Map 2.   Western Europe 1648–97

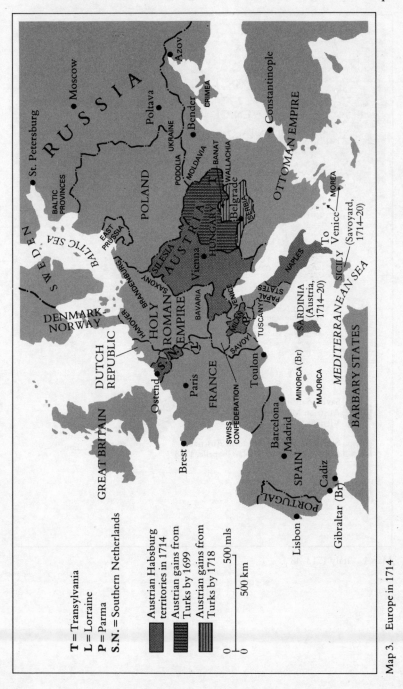

T = Transylvania
L = Lorraine
P = Parma
S.N. = Southern Netherlands

Austrian Habsburg territories in 1714

Austrian gains from Turks by 1699

Austrian gains from Turks by 1718

500 mls

500 km

Map 3.   Europe in 1714

The following labels appear on the map:

SWISS CONFEDERATION

AUSTRIA

FRANCE

SAVOY (from 1720 to Kingdom of Sardinia)

TYROL (from 1714 to Austria)

Milan

MILAN

VENICE

Venice • Trieste • Fiume

ISTRIA (to Venice)

Turin

Casale

Pinerolo

PARMA

MODENA

PAPAL STATES

GENOA

LUCCA

(1735–48 to Austria; from 1748 to Don Philip)

Pisa

TUSCANY

Florence

(from 1737 to Habsburg family)

DALMATIA (to Venice)

ADRIATIC SEA

Leghorn

Siena

CORSICA (to Genoa)

ELBA (1714–35 to Austria)

TUSCAN PORTS (1714–35 to Austria)

Rome

NAPLES (1714–35 to Austria; from 1735 to Don Charles)

SARDINIA (1714–20 to Austria; from 1720 to Savoy as Kingdom of Sardinia)

Naples

MEDITERRANEAN SEA

▤ Savoy-Sardinian gains from Austrian Milan by Peace of Vienna, 1735–38

▥ Savoy-Sardinian gains from Austrian Milan by Peace of Aix-la-Chapelle, 1748

SICILY (1713–20 to Savoy. 1720–35 to Austria. From 1735 to Don Charles)

Cape Passaro

0   200 mls
0   200 km

Map 4.   Italy 1713–48

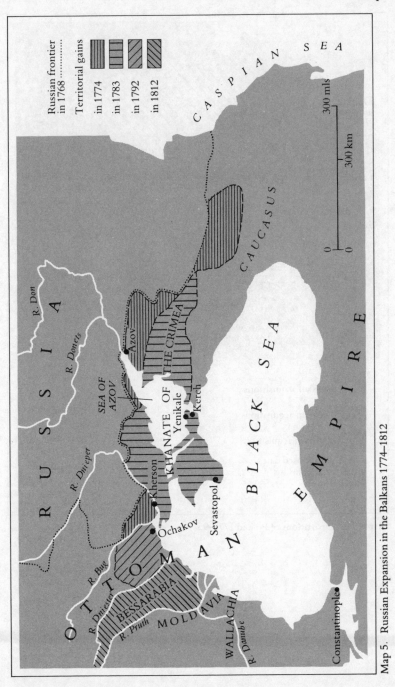

Map 5. Russian Expansion in the Balkans 1774–1812

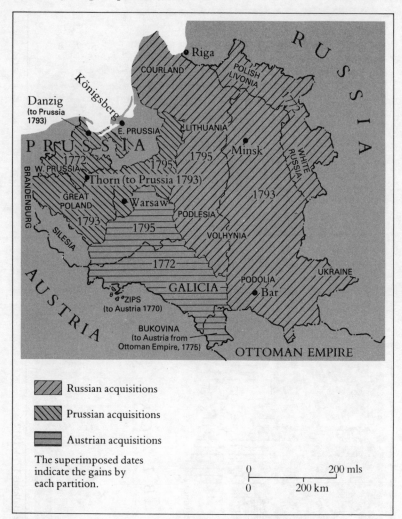

Map 6.   The partitions of Poland 1772–95

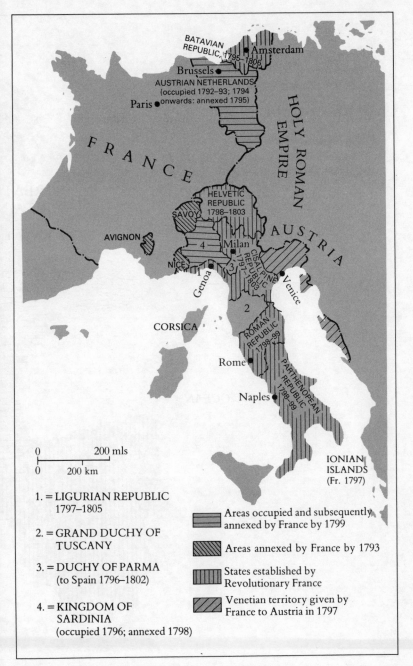

BATAVIAN
REPUBLIC, 1795–1806
● Amsterdam

Brussels ●
AUSTRIAN NETHERLANDS
(occupied 1792–93; 1794
Paris ● onwards: annexed 1795)

F R A N C E

HOLY ROMAN
EMPIRE

HELVETIC
REPUBLIC
1798–1803

SAVOY

AVIGNON

AUSTRIA

4 ● Milan

NICE

1

Genoa

CISALPINE
REPUBLIC
1797–1803

3

● Venice

2

CORSICA

ROMAN
REPUBLIC
1798–99

Rome ●

PARTHENOPEAN
REPUBLIC
1798–99

Naples ●

IONIAN
ISLANDS
(Fr. 1797)

0   200 mls
0   200 km

1. = LIGURIAN REPUBLIC
   1797–1805

2. = GRAND DUCHY OF
   TUSCANY

3. = DUCHY OF PARMA
   (to Spain 1796–1802)

4. = KINGDOM OF
   SARDINIA
   (occupied 1796; annexed 1798)

Areas occupied and subsequently
annexed by France by 1799

Areas annexed by France by 1793

States established by
Revolutionary France

Venetian territory given by
France to Austria in 1797

Map 7.   The expansion of revolutionary France 1789–99

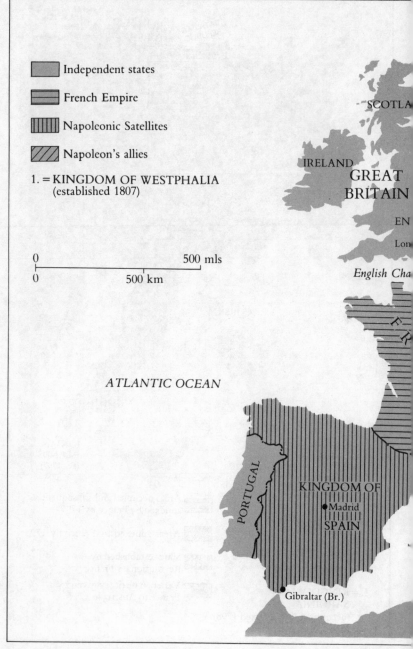

Map 8. Europe under Napoleon 1810

SWEDEN

DENMARK

BALTIC SEA

RUSSIA
(nominally an ally
of Napoleon)

NORTH SEA

HELIGOLAND
(Br. 1807)

PRUSSIA

Berlin

GRAND DUCHY
OF WARSAW

KINGDOM OF
HOLLAND
(1806–10)

CONFEDERATION
OF THE
RHINE

AUSTRIAN EMPIRE

Vienna

SWITZERLAND

KINGDOM
OF
ITALY

ILLYRIAN PROVINCES

HUNGARY

EMPIRE

ADRIATIC SEA

OTTOMAN
EMPIRE

CORSICA

Rome

KINGDOM OF
SARDINIA

KINGDOM
OF NAPLES

IONIAN
ISLANDS

MEDITERRANEAN SEA

KINGDOM
OF SICILY

MALTA

Index

Académie politique 206, 207
Addington (1757–1844) British prime
  minister 1801–4 301, 305–6
Alberoni (1664–1752) Cardinal G.
  leading Spanish minister 102, 107,
  113ff, 130
Alexander I Russian tsar 1801–25 301,
  308ff, 315ff, 318ff, 328, 330–8
  passim, 342ff
Alliances
  Anglo-Dutch (1716) 107
  Anglo-French (1716) 110
  anti-Prussian coalition (1756–63)
    192ff, 196, 218–19
  Austro-Prussian (Wusterhausen:
    1726/1728) 131
  Austro-Russian (1726) 130, 213
  Austro-Russian (1746) 176–7
  Austro-Russian (1781) 232, 236ff
  Austro-Spanish (1725) 128ff
  Charlottenburg (1723) 124, 125
  Chaumont (1814) 337
  First Coalition (1793) 283ff
  First Family Compact (1733) 146ff,
    154
  Fourth Coalition (1813) 335ff
  Franco-American (1778) 230, 259
  Franco-Austrian (1756) 189ff, 216,
    225ff
  Franco-Dutch (1795) 286
  Franco-Spanish (1721) 119ff
  Franco-Spanish (1796) 286, 325
  Fürstenbund (1785) 233, 238
  Grand Alliance (1689) 45, 49
  Grand Alliance (1701) 57ff, 61ff, 106,
    112, 120, 126, 137, 145, 148,
    167, 291
  Hanover (1725) 129ff
  Holy League (1684) 74ff, 81

  League of Augsburg (1686) 40–1
  League of Nymphenburg (1741) 165ff
  League of the Rhine 9–10, 18, 20, 27
  'Northern System' 220ff, 225, 228,
    235, 293
  'Old System' 105, 184, 190, 213
  Prusso-Austrian (1792) 279, 280
  Quadruple Alliance (1718) 115ff,
    118ff, 123, 126
  Quadruple Alliance (1815) 344
  Russo-Prussian (1764) 218, 219–20,
    225
  Second Family Compact (1743) 168,
    181
  Second Coalition (1798–99) 290ff,
    319
  Secret treaty of Dover (1670) 26
  Seville (1729) 135–6
  Third Coalition (1805) 305, 307ff, 318
  Third Family Compact (1761) 213,
    219, 253ff
  Triple Alliance (1668) 21, 22, 23, 24ff
  Triple Alliance (1717) 110, 115
  Triple Alliance (1788) 241, 245, 269,
    271
  Vienna (1719) 89
  Vienna Second Treaty of (1731)
    136–7, 138ff
  Westminster (1716) 107
  Westminster Convention of (1756)
    189ff, 196
Alsace 2, 4, 17, 18, 30, 33, 35, 37, 47, 52,
  62, 65, 99, 278ff
Anglo-French *entente* (1716–31) 110–39,
  212–13, 256
Anna Russian tsaritsa 1730–40 142ff,
  154ff, 162, 170
Anne British queen 1702–14 58, 61, 101
Antwerp 4, 19, 122

Armed Neutrality (1780) 262, 265
Armed Neutrality (1800) 300–1
Asiento 57, 65, 160
Augustus II King of Poland 1697–1733
   and Elector of Saxony 1694–1733
   ('Augustus the Strong') 52, 79ff,
   84, 88, 92, 125, 141, 143ff, 168
Augustus III King of Poland and Elector
   of Saxony 1733–63 144, 151, 164,
   165, 176, 192, 219
Austria
   emergence of, under Leopold I
      (1657–1705) 1, 2, 4ff, 10, 12,
      18, 22, 23, 27, 28, 30ff, 40, 43,
      47ff, 50, 52, 63ff, chapter 3
      passim
   under Charles VI (1711–40) chapters
      4 and 5 *passim*
   under Maria Theresa and Joseph II
      (1740–90) chapters 6 and 8
      passim
   in wars against French Revolution
      and Napoleon chapters 10 and
      11 *passim*
Austrian Netherlands *see* Southern
   Netherlands
Austrian Succession 123ff
Azov 81, 85, 157, 235

Balance of power 96, 211–12, 228, 303,
   339
'Barrier' in Southern Netherlands 35, 53,
   54, 57, 59, 64, 98, 105, 107, 122,
   173
Bartenstein J.C. von (1690–1767)
   Austrian minister 147, 150ff, 155
Batavian Republic *see* Dutch Republic
Bavaria 5, 27, 31, 40–1, 43, 58, 60ff, 65,
   140, 143, 145–6, 148, 149, 152,
   162ff, 165ff, 169, 170, 181, 218,
   229–34, 238, 244, 247, 320, 329
Belgium *see* Southern Netherlands
Belle-Isle Duke of (1684–1761) French
   marshal 165, 168
Bender 85, 223, 240
Bernstorff A. G. von (1649–1726)
   Hanoverian minister of George I
   90, 109
Bestuzhev A. P. (1693–1768) Russian
   chancellor 176, 186ff, 191
Bessarabia 333, 342, 344
Bonaparte *see* Napoleon
Bourbon Duke of (1692–1740) French
   minister 126ff, 132
Brandenburg-Prussia *see* Prussia

Britain
   under Charles II and James II
      (1660–1688) chapter 1 *passim*
   emergence as a major power after
      1688 chapter 2 *passim*
   under George I and George II
      (1714–1760) chapters 4, 5 and
      6 *passim*
   after Seven Years War 215ff, 221,
      227, 241, 245, 252, chapter 9
      passim
   and wars of 1793–1815 chapters 10,
      11, and 12 *passim*
Broglie C. F. de (1719–1781) director of
   Louis XV's *secret du roi* 182, 186

Cambrai Congress of (1724) 116, 119,
   121ff, 126ff, 134
Canning George (1770–1827) British
   statesman 326–7
Carteret J. (1690–1763) British statesman
   119, 126, 166ff
Castlereagh Viscount (1769–1822)
   British foreign secretary 1812–22
   326, 337, 338, 340ff
Catherine II Russian tsaritsa 1762–1796
   195, 211, 218, 219, chapter 8
   passim, 258, 261–2, 269–70, 274,
   277, 283, 284, 292, 293, 309
Charles Archduke (1771–1847) Austrian
   military reformer 312, 328–9
Charles Frederick of Holstein-Gottorp
   124ff, 129, 134, 143
Charles II King of England 1660–1685
   18, 19ff, 25–6, 29, 32
Charles II King of Spain 1665–1700 18,
   22ff, 45, 51, 54ff, 57, 70
Charles III ('Don Charles') King of Spain
   1759–1788 and previously ruler of
   Parma (1732–4) and of the
   Kingdom of the Two Sicilies
   (1734–59) 113ff, 127ff, 135, 136,
   146, 150ff, 168, 199–200, chapter
   9 *passim*
Charles VI Emperor 1711–1740 and
   previously King 'Charles III' of
   Spain 1703–1713 55ff, 59, 61ff,
   64, 88, 101ff, 112ff, 117ff, 121ff,
   127ff, 133ff, chapter 5 *passim*,
   162ff
Charles X King of Sweden 1654–1660
   12–13, 77
Charles XI King of Sweden 1660–1697
   (Regency 1660–1672) 13, 78ff, 84
Charles XII King of Sweden 1697–1718

78–93, 221 his responsibility for
the loss of the Swedish empire 83,
86ff
Chauvelin G. L. de (1685–1772) French
secretary of state 139, 141, 143ff,
151ff, 156
Choiseul Duke of (1719–1785) French
first minister 1758–1770 193, 199,
216, 254–6, 258–9
Colbert J.-B. (1619–1683) financial
minister of Louis XIV 15, 29, 32,
41, 48
his hostility towards the Dutch
Republic 24–5
Confederation of the Rhine 319–20
Congress System 272, 291, 344
Continental System 300, 312, 319ff,
322ff, 327, 329, 332
Corsica 222
Crimea Khanate of 223, 224, 235, 236–8
Czartoryski Prince Adam (1770–1861)
Polish nobleman and adviser to
Alexander I 310, 342

D' Aiguillon Duke (1720–1788) French
foreign minister 1771–74 216,
256–7, 258
Danubian principalities *see* Moldavia and
Wallachia
Danzig 82, 243ff
D'Enghien Duke 304, 310
Denmark 3, 10–11, 12ff, 78ff, 88ff, 100,
125, 143, 195, 221–2, 239, 262,
301, 309, 319, 324, 328
diplomatic immunity 202–3
Diplomatic Revolution (1756) 152,
181–92, 194, 213, 219
diplomats
duties of 207
hierarchy of 203
training of 206–7
Dubois Cardinal G. (1656–1723) French
minister 108ff, 114ff, 118, 125–6
Dunkirk 18, 65, 139, 173, 255
Dutch Republic (Batavian Republic
1795–1813; Holland after 1815)
2ff, 13, 18–19, 20ff, 23, 24ff, 28ff,
37, 40, 44ff, 51, 53, 57, 95, 100,
106ff, 123, 167, 172ff, 177, 184,
190, 203, 205, 241, 245, 262–3,
265, 267ff, 274, 281, 282, 285ff,
289, 295ff, 299, 305, 306, 322, 340

Egypt Napoleon's expedition to 292,
294, 297ff, 305–6
Elba 305, 337

Elizabeth Russian tsaritsa 1741–1762 158,
170, 176, 182ff, 186ff, 191, 193,
195
émigrés 275ff, 278ff, 284
Empire *see* Holy Roman Empire
England *see* Britain
Enlightenment irrelevance of for
relations of great powers 213–14
Eugene of Savoy Prince (1663–1736)
Austrian general and statesman
60, 65, 75, 98, 103, 115, 117,
130ff, 136, 149, 156

Falkland Islands 255, 259
Farnese Elizabeth (1692–1766) wife of
Philip V of Spain 102ff, 116,
119ff, 127ff, 132, 135, 137, 141,
146, 151, 159, 161, 172, 174
Ferdinand III Holy Roman Emperor
1637–1657 3, 5, 13
Ferdinand VI King of Spain 1746–1759
172, 177, 199
Finland 92, 176, 221, 239, 331, 342
Fleury Cardinal A.-H. (1653–1743)
French leading minister
1726–1743 132ff, 138–54, 156,
159, 161ff, 165, 166, 169, 258
aims of his policy 140–1
restores French ascendancy 157–8
Floridablanca Count of (1728–1808)
Spanish foreign minister
1777–1792 260, 271
foreign offices, emergence of 209–10
France
emergence of, as a great power in the
second half of the seventeenth
century chapters 1, 2, and 3
passim
less dominant after 1713 chapter 4
passim
recovery under Fleury 132ff, chapter
5 *passim*
in wars of 1739–1763 chapter 6 *passim*
decline of, after 1763 215ff, 223,
228, 230, 242, 247, 248, 252,
chapter 9 *passim*
in Revolutionary and Napoleonic
Wars chapters 10 and 11 *passim*
in 1815 340, 341
Franche-Comté 2, 4, 7, 18ff, 21, 24, 27,
35, 54
Francis Stephen Duke of Lorraine,
husband of Maria Theresa
(1708–1765) and Emperor Francis
I 140, 145, 150, 152, 162, 170
Francis II Holy Roman Emperor

1792–1804 and Austrian Emperor (after the dissolution of the Empire) 1804–1835 246, 249, 279, 320, 328, 329, 330, 336

Frederick II the Great King of Prussia 1740–1786 16, chapters 6 and 8 *passim*, 267, 280, 313

Frederick William I King of Prussia 1713–1740 86, 88, 130, 152, 163, 175

Frederick William II King of Prussia 1786–1797 238, 243–51, 267ff, 277ff, 280ff, 286

Frederick William III King of Prussia 1797–1840 286, 291ff, 308, 312ff, 315, 318ff, 334ff

French becomes language of diplomacy 202

French Revolution 244, 245, 246, 247, 248, 271, chapter 10 *passim*, 304, 340, 341

Genoa 222, 288–9, 311, 340

George I King of Great Britain 1714–1727 and Elector of Hanover 1698–1727 79, 86, 87ff, 104ff, 108ff, 119ff, 124ff, 134

George II King of Great Britain and Elector of Hanover 1727–1760 134, 148, 152, 166, 167, 169, 177, 178, 180, 187

George III King of Great Britain and Elector of Hanover 1760–1820 199, 256, 283

Gibraltar 62, 95, 116, 119ff, 128, 129, 132ff, 135, 136, 160, 168, 177, 259ff, 264, 341

'Glorious Revolution' *see* Revolution of 1688

Godolphin Earl S. (1645–1712) 58, 60

Grand Duchy of Warsaw *see* Poland

Grenville Lord (1759–1834) British foreign secretary 1791–1801 291ff

Gustav III King of Sweden 1771–1792 222, 228, 234, 239ff, 245, 256–7, 277

Habsburg House of 1, 2, 4, 9, 22, 67, 68, *see also* Spain, Austria

Harris Sir James (1746–1820) British diplomat 267–9

Hanover 58, 86, 88ff, 96, 99, 104, 110, 121ff, 166, 167, 169, 177, 178, 181, 184ff, 196, 283, 286, 308, 312, 322, 341

Heinsius A. (1641–1720) Dutch grand

pensionary 45, 58ff

Holland *see* Dutch Republic

Holstein 79, 81, 82, 86

Holy Roman Empire 2, 4, 5, 40–1, 47, 61, 121, 152, 193, 218, 279, 319–20

Hungary 61, 67ff, 71ff, 99, 103, 166, 240, 274, 276

Ionian Islands 288, 293, 294, 295, 309, 316, 318, 341

Italy great power rivalry and, 1648–1752 49, 55, 96–7, 99, 101, 103ff, 146ff, 150ff, 171
treaty of Aranjuez (1752) ends great power rivalry over 174, 177
during wars of 1792–1815 288–9, 300, 311ff, 343–4

Jacobites 48, 53, 87, 96, 104–5, 106ff, 112, 114, 116, 120, 170, 172, 183–4

James II King of England 1685–1688 39, 44, 46, 48, 52–3

Joseph I Holy Roman Emperor 1705–1711 55, 56, 60ff, 64, 124, 162

Joseph II Holy Roman Emperor 1765–1790 (Co-Regent with Maria Theresa 1765–1780; sole ruler 1780–1790) 220, 224ff, 229ff, 236, 237ff, 240, 268, 275, 276

Jülich-Berg Succession of 131, 163

Kaunitz Prince W. A. (1711–1794) Austrian chancellor 1753–1794 182ff, 218, 222, 226ff, 232ff, 238ff, 279

Knights of St John 293ff, 302

Koprulu dynasty grand viziers in Ottoman Empire 72ff

Leopold I Holy Roman Emperor 1657/58–1705 9, 18, 20, 52, 67–77

Leopold II Grand Duke of Tuscany 1765–1790 and Holy Roman Emperor 1790–1792 240, 246, 247, 275–9

Leszczyński Stanislas (1677–1766) King of Poland 1704–1709 and Duke of Lorraine 1735–1766 82, 83, 127, 143ff, 150, 222

Le Tellier Michel (1603–1685) French war minister 15, 17, 22, 25

Lionne Hugues de (1611–1671) French
    foreign minister 16ff, 21, 27
Lombardy *see* Milan
Lorraine 4, 17–18, 27, 30, 33, 35, 37, 47,
    52, 55, 62, 70, 99, 140, 145, 147,
    150ff, 183, 188, 222
Louis XIV King of France 1643–1715
    (personal rule after 1661) 3, 5, 8,
    9, 72ff, 82, 101, 105, 110, 145, 148
  contribution to French ascendancy
    14ff
  aims of his foreign policy 16ff
  attack on the Dutch Republic as a
    turning point in his foreign
    policy 23, 30–1
  overbearing policies in the 1680s 36ff
  personally directs wars of
    1689–1713/4 49ff
  his responsibility for the Nine Years
    War 42–3
  attempts to solve the Spanish
    Succession by negotiation 54ff
  but his actions make war inevitable
    57ff
  policy in Spanish Succession War 58,
    62–3
  his impact on France's position in
    Europe 97–8
  importance of his reign for the
    development of diplomacy
    201–2
Louis XV King of France 1715–1774
    (Regency 1715–1723) 106, 119,
    127, 132, 143ff, 165, 168, 171ff,
    178ff, 181ff, 189ff, 197, 256
  his *secret du roi* 181–2, 186, 216
Louis XVI King of France 1774–1793
    258, 271, 276ff, 281, 284
Louis XVIII King of France 1814/5–1824
    338, 342
Louvois François Le Tellier (1641–1691)
    minister of Louis XIV 15, 24, 25,
    28, 29, 31, 33, 36, 42, 49
Luxemburg 2, 7, 20, 37, 39, 52, 54, 65,
    185

Malta 293ff, 296, 297, 298, 302, 306, 309,
    310, 341
Maria Theresa Ruler of the Austrian
    Habsburg territories 1740–1780
    140, chapter 6 *passim*, 220, 226,
    228, 231
Marie Antoinette (1755–1793) wife of
    Louis XVI 276ff
Marlborough Duke of (1650–1722)

English commander-in-chief 48,
    58ff, 63, 106
Mazarin Cardinal G. (1601–1661) French
    first minister 1643–1661 3, 6ff,
    14, 17, 21
Mecklenburg Duchy of 87ff, 109ff, 124ff,
    182
Metternich prince C. (1773–1859)
    Austrian chancellor 1809–1848
    320, 321, 328ff, 335ff, 342ff
Milan 2, 49, 51, 55, 56, 61, 99, 102ff,
    141, 146, 168, 174, 288, 343
Minorca 62, 95, 128, 135, 136, 160, 168,
    177, 190, 259ff
Moldavia 73, 154, 156, 223, 224, 239,
    316, 336

Naples 2, 102ff, 113, 117, 146, 147,
    150ff, 190, 253, 283, 289, 295,
    301, 340
Napoleon Bonaparte (1769–1821) French
    Emperor 1804–1815 16, 286,
    288ff, 292, 293ff, 297ff, chapter 11
    passim, 340ff, 344
Nelson H. (1758–1805) British naval
    commander 307, 309
Newcastle Duke of (1693–1768) British
    statesman 148, 169, 172, 178,
    180ff, 187ff, 197
nobility their dominance of higher
    diplomatic posts 205
Nootka Sound Anglo-Spanish
    confrontation over (1790) 241,
    270–1
North Lord (1732–1792) British prime
    minister 1770–1782 256–7, 263
Norway 222

Ochakov Anglo-Russian confrontation
    over (1791) 239, 241–2, 245, 269ff
'Old Pretender': James Stuart
    (1688–1766) son of James II 57,
    66, 103–4, 106, 109–10
Orleans Duke of (1674–1723) Regent of
    France 1715–1723 66, 89, 106ff,
    118ff, 181
Ostend Company 122ff, 126ff, 128, 133,
    135, 136
Ostermann A. I. (1686–1747) leading
    minister of Tsaritsa Anna 134,
    142ff, 149, 154
Ottoman Empire 2, 5, 12, 41ff, 48, 52,
    67ff, 70ff, 76, 79, 100, 101, 103,
    115, 118, 149, 154ff, 182, 202ff,
    219, 223ff, 232, 234, 235ff, 243,

244, 274, 284, 294ff, 297ff, 302,
315ff, 318ff, 330, 333, 344

Panin N. I. (1718–1783) Russian foreign
minister 1763–c. 1780 220ff,
225–6, 235, 236, 293
Parma Duchy of 102ff, 113ff, 119ff,
127ff, 135, 141, 150ff, 168, 174,
185, 190, 253, 264
Patiño J. (1666–1736) leading minister of
Philip V 146, 160
Paul I Russian tsar 1796–1801 238, 292ff,
297, 300ff
peace treaties
Åbo (1743) 176
Aix-la-Chapelle (1668) 21, 23, 24
Aix-la-Chapelle (1748) 171ff
Altranstädt (1706) 82
Amiens (1802) 301–2, 303, 305
Andrusovo (1667) 14, 83
Basle (1795) 251, 285
Belgrade (1739) 152, 156ff, 161
Breda (1667) 19
Breslau (1742) 166
Bucharest (1812) 333
Campo Formio (1797) 288, 290, 292,
293, 298ff
Copenhagen (1660) 13
Dresden (1745) 170, 175
Fontainebleau (1814) 337
Frederiksborg (1720) 91
Hubertusburg (1763) 196, 215, 217
Jassy (1792) 242, 246
Kardis (1661) 14
Karlowitz (1699) 53, 56, 76ff, 99, 157
Kutchuk-Kainardji (1774) 228, 235,
242
Lunéville (1801) 300ff, 311
Nymegen (1678/9) 34ff, 70
Nystad (1721) 92, 119, 124ff
Oliva (1660) 13–14
Paris (1763) 199–200, 215, 253, 264
Passarowitz (1718) 99, 115, 117ff,
122, 155
Pressburg (1805) 312
Pruth (1711) 85, 103, 117
Pyrenees (1659) 7–8
Rastadt (1714) 66
Regensburg (truce: 1684) 39, 41, 43,
74
Roskilde (1658) 13
Ryswick (1697) 50ff
Schönbrunn (1809) 329
Sistova (1791) 240–1
Teschen (1779) 231

Tilsit (1807) 304, 317ff, 328, 330ff
Travendal (1700) 82
Utrecht (1713) 64ff, 95ff, 106, 111,
115, 117, 119, 159, 199, 211
Vasvar (1664) 72
Verela (1790) 240
Versailles (1783) 264
Vienna Third Treaty of (1735/8)
151ff, 161, 222
Vienna (1815) 251, 303, 339ff
Westminster (1674) 31
Westphalia (1648) 1, 3ff, 9ff, 33, 35,
61, 70, 278, 281
Pelham Henry (c. 1696–1754) British
statesman 169, 172, 178, 180, 184
Peter III Russian tsar 1762, 193, 195
Peter the Great Russian tsar 1682–1725
76, 80–93, 96, 109, 117, 125–6,
128, 142
Philip V Duke of Anjou and King of
Spain 1700–1746 56ff, 62ff, 66,
100ff, 106ff, 112, 119ff, 127ff,
132ff, 137, 159, 161, 165, 168,
171, 180
Philip IV King of Spain 1621–1665 3, 8,
18, 20
Pillnitz Declaration of (1791) 277, 278
Pitt the Elder William (1708–1778)
British statesman 168, 169, 180,
196, 197ff, 290
Pitt the Younger William (1759–1806)
British prime minister
1783/4–1801 and 1804–1806
241–2, 266–71, 273, 282ff, 290ff,
301, 303, 307ff, 311ff, 317, 340
Poland 10ff, 38, 48, 68, 70, 72ff, 77, 79,
80ff, 100, 182, 185, 216, 236, 241,
252, 272, 274, 277ff, 283ff, 317,
318
election of 1697 52, 80
Russian satellite after 1709 84–5, 92,
125
election of 1733 141ff
election of 1764 219, 221, 223
first partition (1772) 216, 222–8, 258
second partition (1793) 242–9, 293
third partition (1795) 250–1, 284
Grand Duchy of Warsaw 319, 329,
331ff
'Congress Poland' 342, 344
Pompadour Madame de (1721–1764)
mistress of Louis XV 181ff
Poniatowski Stanislas King of Poland
1764–1795 219, 223, 243ff, 247,
252

Portugal 2, 59, 61, 100, 259, 260, 262, 283, 319, 323, 326ff, 335

Porte the *see* Ottoman Empire

Potemkin G. A. (1739–1791) Russian statesman 235ff

Pragmatic Sanction 124, 127ff, 136ff, 143, 146, 150, 162, 164, 166

Prussia
 her emergence 1640–1740 1, 5, 9, 11, 14, 27, 30, 31, 35, 38, 43, 47, 58–9, 65, 78, 88ff, 99, 121ff, 130
 becomes a great power under Frederick II chapter 6 *passim*, 240ff, 243ff, 267ff,
 and wars of 1792–1815 274ff, 280ff, 285ff, 291ff, 295, 301, 303, 304, 308–9, 312ff, 317ff, 322, 328, 329, 331ff, 334–8, 341ff, 343, 344

Pufendorf Samuel von (1632–1694) German jurist 1

religion decline of as a factor in international relations in the seventeenth century 6, 210

Reichenbach Convention of (1790) 240

Revocation of the Edict of Nantes (1685) 39, 40

Revolution of 1688 in Britain 43ff, 52

Ripperda J. W. (1680–1737) Spanish minister 127ff

Russia
 in seventeenth century 1, 10ff, 48, 68
 emergence of after 1700 77–93
 becomes part of European diplomatic network in early eighteenth century 204
 her advance not continued after Peter the Great's death in 1725 128–9, 130ff, 142, 143
 and Diplomatic Revolution 181–92
 and anti-Prussian coalition (1756–1762) 192ff
 her advance under Catherine II chapter 8 *passim*, 261–2, 283, 292ff, 295ff
 and wars of 1792–1815 chapters 10, 11 and 12 *passim*

Sardinia, Island of 2, 99, 102ff, 113ff, 117

satellite republics, French Revolutionary 288–9, 296, 300

satellite kingdoms, Napoleonic 321ff, 325, 337

Savoy Duchy of (also referred to as the Kingdom of Sardinia) 8, 17, 18, 37, 49, 50, 55, 58ff, 65, 96, 107, 141, 146ff, 150ff, 168, 171, 174, 280, 285, 289, 290, 296, 305, 340, 341

Saxe Marshal M.de (1696–1750) French commander 168, 169, 170, 171, 172, 175, 178

Saxony 5, 27, 79ff, 91, 131, 140, 141, 169, 170, 176, 182, 191, 192, 194, 221, 343

Scheldt River 4, 26, 122, 233, 267, 281, 283, 305, 340

Schleswig 79, 86, 124ff, 129, 130, 131, 143, 195

secret diplomacy its importance exaggerated 208–9

secret du roi see Louis XV

Selim III Ottoman sultan 1789–1807 205, 240, 294, 316

Sicily 2, 107, 113ff, 117, 121, 146ff, 150

Silesia 164, 166, 170, 175, 183, 185, 187, 190, 192ff, 217, 226, 229, 243, 303

Sobieski John King of Poland 1674–1696 38, 52, 72ff

Southern Netherlands (Spanish Netherlands until 1713; Austrian Netherlands 1713–1792; occupied by the French 1792–1814: also referred to as Belgium) 3, 7, 18ff, 24, 27, 30, 33, 35, 37, 46, 49, 51, 51, 52, 54, 56, 59, 99, 100, 103, 106, 108, 122ff, 148, 168ff, 173ff, 178, 181, 184, 185, 229, 232ff, 240, 247, 248, 274, 276, 280, 281ff, 285ff, 288–9, 296, 299, 300, 338, 340, 343

Soissons Congress of (1728–1729) 134

Spanish Netherlands *see* Southern Netherlands

Spanish Succession 8, 18, 20, 22–3, 45, 51, 53, 54ff, 65ff, 70, 76, 96

Spain 2, 4, 7, 17ff, 20ff, 24, 28, 30ff, 38–9, 40–1, 49, 51ff, 54ff, 95ff, 100–1, 132, chapters 4, 5, 6, and 9 *passim*, 273, 282, 285–6, 305, 315, 322, 324, 325ff, 335, 340

Stadion J. P. (1763–1824) Austrian foreign minister 1806–1809 317, 328ff

Stanhope Earl J. of (1673–1721) English general and minister 91, 104, 109ff, 114ff, 118, 119, 125

Strasbourg 4, 37–8, 47, 52, 53, 65

Suvorov A. (1729–1800) Russian commander 242, 250, 295, 297

Sweden
   in seventeenth century 5, 9, 10–14,
      21, 26, 27, 40, 45, 52
   strengths and weaknesses of her
      empire 14, 77ff
   disastrous intervention in Dutch War
      31, 78
   in Great Northern War 81ff
   loss of her empire 90–3
   during 'Age of Liberty' 114, 143, 176,
      193, 195, 216, 221, 228,
      234–5, 239–40, 244, 262, 277
   and wars of 1792–1815 301, 311, 319,
      324, 328, 331, 335

Talleyrand C. M. de (1754–1838) French
   foreign minister 1799–1807 298,
   300, 321, 340
Targowica Confederation of (1792)
   246–7, 248
Torcy Marquis J.-B. C. (1665–1746)
   French foreign minister
   1698–1715 64, 105, 206, 209
Townshend Viscount C. (1674–1738)
   English minister 89, 104, 110ff,
   119ff, 124ff, 126, 128ff, 132ff,
   135ff
Transylvania 67, 71, 72, 75, 76
Turks *see* Ottoman Empire
Tuscany 102ff, 113ff, 119ff, 127, 135,
   141, 150ff, 165, 174, 300

Vauban Marquis S. Le P. de (1633–1707)
   French marshal and fortifications
   expert 15, 33, 37, 39
   his 'iron barrier' 36–7, 42, 49, 60, 63
Venice 48, 74ff, 86, 101, 103, 118, 288
Vergennes Count C. G. de (1717–1787)
   French foreign minister
   1774–1787 213, 216, 230, 233,
   237, 258–68
Victor Amadeus II Ruler of Savoy
   1675–1730 49, 50, 100, 113
Vienna siege of (1683) 38, 39, 73–4

Walcheren Expedition (1809) 322, 327,
   329
Wallachia 72, 154, 224, 316, 333
Walpole Sir Robert (1676–1745) British
   prime minister 1721–1742 89,
   110ff, 119ff, 126, 132, 136–7, 138,
   141, 143, 148ff, 153–4, 161, 166
warfare transformation of 1792–1815
   286–8, 313–15
wars
   American Independence (1775–1783)

   216, 237, 255, 257–65, 290
Anglo-Dutch, First (1652–1654) 19
Anglo-Dutch, Second (1665–1667) 19
Anglo-Dutch, Third (1672–1674)
   25ff
Anglo-Dutch, Fourth (1780–1784)
   262–3, 267
Anglo-French, renewed in 1803 306ff,
   325
Anglo-Spanish (1727) 131ff
Austro-Turkish (1683–1699) 45, 47,
   48, 50, 63–4, 70, 71ff
Austro-Turkish (1716–1718) 77, 109,
   121
Austro-Russian, against Turks
   (1736–1739) 155ff
Austrian Succession (1740–1748)
   162ff, 172, 197, 253, 261
Bavarian Succession (1778–1779) 231
Devolution (1667–1668) 20ff
Dutch (1672–1679) 28ff, 78
First Coalition (1793–1797) 272,
   280–9, 290, 306
Fourth Coalition (1813–1815) 335ff
Franco-Russian (1812) 333ff
Franco-Spanish (1635–1659) 6ff
Great Northern (1700–1721) 81ff, 101
Jenkins' Ear (1739–1748) 159ff, 270
Nine Years War (1688–1697) 43ff, 78
North (1655–1660) 12–14
Polish Succession (1733–35) 138,
   145ff
Russo-Swedish (1741–1743) 176
Russo-Swedish (1788–1790) 239–40
Russo-Turkish (1710–1711) 85
Russo-Turkish (1768–1774) 204,
   224ff, 242, 258
Russo-Turkish (1787–1792) 204,
   238ff, 244ff, 268ff
Russo-Turkish (1806–1812) 316ff,
   333
Second Coalition (1798–1802)
   295–302, 308
Seven Years War (1756–1763) 177,
   178, 192–200, 215, 216, 217,
   219ff, 231, 242, 253, 257, 261,
   262, 290
Spanish Succession (1702–1713/4)
   58ff, 82, 87
Third Coalition (1805—1807)
   311–17, 326
Thirty Years War (1618–1648) 2, 3,
   6, 7, 68, 77
Wellington Duke of (1769–1852) British
   commander 326ff
Westphalia Kingdom of 319, 322

William III Dutch stadtholder 1672–1702
    and English king 1688–1702 19,
    28ff, 37ff, 40ff, 44ff, 50, 94
Witt John de (1625–1672) Dutch grand
    pensionary 1653–1672 18, 19, 21,
    28, 29, 207
Wratislaw Count J. W. (1669–1712)
    Austrian minister 61, 65